CIRCLE TO CIRCLE

STEPHEN YENSER

Circle to Circle

THE POETRY OF ROBERT LOWELL

UNIVERSITY OF CALIFORNIA PRESS
BERKELEY LOS ANGELES LONDON 1975

University of California Press
Berkeley and Los Angeles, California
University of California Press, Ltd.
London, England
Copyright © 1975 by The Regents of the University of California
ISBN: 0-520-02790-6
Library of Congress Catalog Card Number: 74-79778
Printed in the United States of America

FOR MARY

CONTENTS

PREFACE

Although only thirty years have passed since Robert Lowell published his first volume of poems, his work has been the subject of a considerable amount of criticism. Much of that criticism has either informed or inspired me. For that reason, and partly because his impact on the poets and critics of his time is an element in the story of any major poet, and partly too because this book is intended not only for the specialist in contemporary American poetry (if indeed there can be such a type) but also for the student becoming acquainted with Lowell and wanting guidance to other discussions of his work, the reader will find in the following chapters more than a few references to secondary sources.

Many of the most valuable of these are essays, a good number of which have been collected in either *Robert Lowell: A Collection of Critical Essays,* edited by Thomas Parkinson; or *Robert Lowell: A Portrait of the Artist in His Time,* edited by Michael London and Robert Boyers; or both. Of the books on Lowell, perhaps the one to which mine is most closely related is Richard J. Fein's *Robert Lowell,* a compact and sensitive examination of *The Old Glory* and of the poetry through *Near the Ocean.* Although Fein usually focuses on individual poems that seem to him exemplary, in two senses of the word, he sometimes discusses briefly the structures of the volumes, and consequently he and I have some of the same interests. So do Phillip Cooper and I; indeed, when I had seen advertisements for his book, *The Autobiographical Myth of*

Robert Lowell, but before I had read it, I thought that this one might be superfluous. For good or ill, however, that is not the case; we both look at Lowell's poetry as a unified whole, but while Cooper emphasizes the recurrence throughout the poetry of a number of motifs, I am concerned with the ways in which motifs shape, and are shaped within, the individual volumes.

That concern also distinguishes this book from two other and more polemical studies: Patrick Cosgrave's *The Public Poetry of Robert Lowell,* a rigorous analysis from a qualified Wintersian point of view of the moral aspects of Lowell's formal arguments and a definition of his relationship to what Cosgrave calls the line of "gravity" in English literature; and R. K. Meiners's *Everything To Be Endured: An Essay on Robert Lowell and Modern Poetry,* a brief study of what seems to its author the decreasing spiritual and formal vitality in Lowell's work. Marjorie Perloff's recent and detailed investigation, *The Poetic Art of Robert Lowell,* partly because it concerns itself with techniques and genres rather than with the relationships among the poems or the organization of the volumes and partly because it was published well after these wheels had been set in motion, has been of less help to me than Jerome Mazzaro's study, *The Poetic Themes of Robert Lowell,* which follows several of Lowell's major concerns up to and through *For the Union Dead.* But whereas Mazzaro often focuses on the relationships between Lowell's structures and such frameworks as those provided by St. Ignatius's meditations and Nietzsche's discussion of the Apollonian and the Dionysian elements in art, I concentrate on the schemes built within and among the poems themselves. At the same time, and my occasional disagreements with him notwithstanding, I am as indebted to Mazzaro as to any of the other writers mentioned, with all of whom I must join in acknowledging an obligation to Hugh Staples, whose *Robert Lowell: The First Twenty Years* set high critical and scholarly standards.

If in spite of all of this help this book is not unflawed, that is not the fault of any of several sensitive readers of it in manuscript form. Lawrence Dembo, Walter Rideout, and John Sullivan, who read the manuscript in its early stages, showed me

many ways in which it might be improved; and Charles Gullans, Richard Lehan, Thomas Parkinson, and Hugh Staples,
who read it in its later stages, made many profitable suggestions and did their best to save me from flagrant error. Ivan
Soll will, I hope, recognize the passages inspired by his clas-
ses and conversation; and Standish Henning will know that
the book might never have got beyond an early draft if it had
not been for his kindness and understanding. Without the
patience and tact of Susan Crow and Robert Zachary, of the
University of California Press, the last phases of this project
would have been less enjoyable. I am especially grateful to
my brother, Jon Kelly Yenser, for encouraging my work on
Lowell's poetry at a very early stage and for subsequently
offering much valuable advice, to James Merrill, for providing
me with a copy of *Land of Unlikeness*, for finding me a place to
live and work during a crucial period of revision, and for
talking with me about matters related to but more important
than this book; and to my wife, Mary Bomba Yenser, for her
scrupulous reading of my readings and her unflagging
generosity and moral support.

To Lorna Roberts and to Jeanette Gilkison, who not only
typed and retyped the manuscript but also frequently saved
me from time-consuming mistakes, I am deeply indebted.

I am also grateful to three institutions for their financial
support: the University of Wisconsin, whose University Fellowship helped to get the project under way; the International Institute of Education, whose Fulbright Fellowship allowed me to pursue my work in France; and the University of
California, whose Summer Faculty Fellowship permitted my
revision of the manuscript in Greece and whose Faculty Re-
search Grant facilitated its preparation for the press.

A part of chapter nine appeared as a review entitled "Half
Legible Bronze?" in *Poetry*, 123 (February, 1974), and I am
grateful to the Modern Poetry Association for permission to
reprint it with changes here.

Quotations from *Land of Unlikeness*, published by the
Cummington Press, are reprinted with the permission of
Robert Lowell.

Excerpts from *Lord Weary's Castle* and *The Mills of the*

Santa Monica, California
October 1974

S.Y.

INTRODUCTION:

Prospects

Sometime in 1935, or perhaps 1936, New England's best-known living poet received a call from an unpublished young writer who had brought with him "a huge epic on the First Crusade, all written out in clumsy longhand on lined paper." Having read through the first page, the author of "Fire and Ice" observed that the young man had "no compression" and proceeded to read to him William Collins's "Ode Written in the Beginning of the Year 1746" ("How sleep the brave"). "That's not a great poem," Frost allowed, "but it's not too long." Over thirty-five years later, that day's visitor, himself become by then New England's best-known living poet, published a work so long and comprehensive, extending as it does from Genesis to the present, that the Crusades are no more than a detail in it. We have not been told explicitly the mode of that first "huge epic," but it seems that it might have been Miltonic blank verse.[1] *History*, on the other hand, if not precisely a nosegay of lyrics itself, comprises 368 poems, all but a few of which are of standard sonnet length.

The chapters that follow are about what has happened in Robert Lowell's poetry between these two events in his life.

1

They are about a poet who has learned as few have the virtues and the means of lyric and meditative compression and
yet has never ceased courting epic aspirations; and they are
especially about the several kinds of configurations that have
issued from the union of those means and those aspirations.

Proceeding chronologically, and reflecting Lowell's changing concerns, this book moves from a discussion of his
methods of organization at the level of the individual poem,
through an examination of his structures at the levels of the
sequence and the volume, toward a consideration of the
unity of his work as a whole. Perhaps the heart of the book,
as it was the matrix and is the center, is the section from
chapter four through chapter seven, for it is in the volumes
examined there, it seems to me, that Lowell has so far most
successfully reconciled the aesthetic demands of the individual poem with those of its encompassing forms. But just
as an appreciation of the structures of these four volumes
permits an understanding of the most recent and rather startling ramifications of his poetics (the subject of the last two
chapters), so such an appreciation itself must derive from an
understanding of the roots of his poetics (the subject of the
first three chapters). For Lowell's poetry, the several changes
in his style and content notwithstanding, is of a piece.

He must have had an aim of his own in mind when, during
an interview in 1961, he remarked admiringly that T. S. Eliot
"has done what he said Shakespeare had done: all his poems
are one poem, a form of continuity that has grown and snow-
balled."[2] As Lowell's own oeuvre has grown, it has become
more and more apparent that he is emulating the examples of
Eliot and Shakespeare, that his poetry is developing in a
steady, organic manner, so that it has not only that unity
which is bestowed by a distinctive sensibility, but also something of that quality of aesthetic necessity which we expect to
find in individual works of art. Although his successive volumes have hardly been predictable, they do seem in retrospect indispensable parts of an evolving pattern; and if that
pattern is not without its irregularities, the poetry is not the
less an organic whole for that. To study Lowell's career to
date, in other words, is to discover the precision of the
paradox in his phrase "a form of continuity."

When Lowell's first volume, *Land of Unlikeness*, appeared in 1944, it was immediately noted for its prosodic intricacies, its "wit," and above all its energetic, not to say zealous, Roman Catholic tone and imagery. In light of its author's subsequent work, however, this volume now seems most remarkable for the attitude toward language that it reveals, for this attitude not only encourages specific poetic forms, particular sorts of ingenuity, and a peculiar perspective on the religious subject matter, but also gives rise to the basic method of the early poetry. That method, which is not fully developed until Lowell's second volume, consists in the exploitation, frequently at the expense of referential function, of the symbolic dimension of the language, and the cultivation, frequently at the expense of orthodox religion, of a dialectical structure in the poems.

Lowell's early work, that is to say, is closely associated with one of the strongest of our modern traditions, which is rede-fined and referred to in the second chapter as neo-symbolism. With other poets in this tradition, several of whom were his friends and mentors, Lowell shares a modus operandi that is rooted in the assumption that a verbal symbol has an ontological status, that—as Coleridge had it—words are "living things."[3] Among the ramifications of this assumption in its modern form are the implicit principles, explained in detail in the second chapter, that a symbol in a poem contains *ab ovo* the whole poem; that any particular symbol *is* its interactions with other symbols; and that a poem is thus a dynamic structure whose action constitutes its meaning. Lowell has done little public criticism and less aesthetics, but in view of the influences adduced and the structures disclosed in the second chapter, one seems warranted in thinking that these fairly common, although rarely explicit, principles of neo-symbolism underlie his poetry. Certainly these principles help to explain the organizations of individual poems in *Lord Weary's Castle* (1946), as well as the structures of later volumes and the development of the work as a whole.

In fact, it is in his second volume that Lowell, forecasting a development in *Life Studies*, begins to extend his structural principles beyond the boundaries of the poem. Some readers have noticed that beneath the panoply of religious symbolism, several of the poems in *Lord Weary's Castle* are very personal,[4] while at least one critic has pointed out that the volume has a discernible organization.[5] What remains to be said is that more of the poems than have been considered so are concerned with the poet; that some allude specifically to his own work; and that this latent autobiography, in which the poet's experience is figured as a circle whose end is in its beginning, is the major unifying element in the book. At this juncture early in his career, even as Lowell is developing a poetry in which the symbols are organically interrelated, two other changes are taking place: he is beginning to see his poems in the same way that he sees his symbols, and he is starting to organize those poems into a narrative sequence that is itself symbolic.

The latter strategies are suspended in *The Mills of the Kavanaughs* (1951), where Lowell attempts to find a means of plotting individual longer poems. His means—a combination of dream-vision and mythological parallelism—is only partially successful as a method of organization because he treats its elements virtually as though they were more metaphors to be organized; that is, he modifies dream with vision and myth with myth, just as in the shorter poems he modifies image with image, and the result is complexity without a framework. R. P. Blackmur has commented, in another connection, on this weakness in most younger poets:

> What happens in young poets, in poets short of mastery of plot, is that they use the plots of elder poets as if they were, what they appeared to be when seen, actually integral to the poems instead of the mere integrating agent. In short, your young poet treats plot like a detail, as if it were one more tension in his substance.[6]

Perhaps the motivation for Lowell's treatment of plot as a detail in *The Mills of the Kavanaughs* is that he cannot accept the eschatological resolution that accompanies any one of his appropriated parallels, for such acceptance would keep his poems from doing what he says elsewhere they should do: "include a man's contradictions."[7] In any case, the form that his dialectic takes in the longer poems of this third volume is that of careful self-contradiction, the repeated assertion in various ways of contrary analogies until the variants have overlapped often enough that the originally opposed terms are hardly separable.

The development of a poem by means of mutually qualifying analogies is a direct outgrowth of the poetics of *Lord Weary's Castle,* for that poetics emphasized the process of the poem and the dependence of any symbol for its meaning upon its interaction with other symbols. Lowell has never abandoned these operational principles, but with *Life Studies* (1959) he does surrender the attempt to construct a single long poem on the basis of them, and at the same time he relinquishes his religious and mythological symbolism. He does not, however, give up the effort to escape the confines of the lyric. On the contrary, even as he returns to short poems, he seeks to unify an entire book.

That the unity of *Life Studies,* like that of most of Lowell's volumes, has provoked comparatively little discussion can probably be attributed to the beguiling insouciance of many of the individual poems. As the poetry expands beyond the limits of the lyric, the poems sometimes seem incomplete and less self-contained than before; and since Lowell does deal more directly with the world about him as he moves away from religion, it is not unreasonable to suppose that this seeming incompleteness reflects the immediacy and fragmentary quality of raw experience. It is as though the struggle between contraries or within the flux of experience that heretofore has been the substance of Lowell's method were now a single term in his dialectic, with form its opposite member. To put this another way, until *Life Studies* Lowell had taken it for granted that form was a necessary part of the individual poem, a vehicle for the wars that the Powers waged; but now form itself seems almost to be viewed as a deity (of an ambivalent nature) that needs to be challenged. With the formal integrity of separate poems thus a debatable matter, it is easy to forget to look beyond these poems to the new larger structures—the sequence and the book—that Lowell has created. Nevertheless, the term "studies," in the sense of unfinished sketches or preliminary drafts, only describes the appearance of these poems to the casual eye; and that this careless, frequently "confessional" surface is part and parcel of the meticulous, dispassionate organizations of some individual poems is one of the points of the fourth chapter.

A more salient point is that this whole volume is carefully laid out, so that the sequences designated by Lowell not only cohere in themselves but also constitute a single long sequence. Developing a technique employed to some extent in his second volume, Lowell creates by use of motifs a situation in which poems act at a distance on one another. Collectively the poems form a context that helps to shape them individually. Moreover, this context, the book, has a definite organization, for—to appropriate one of C. Day-Lewis's felicitous images—there is one main theme that winds through the book and is reflected as it goes from different angles by each of the sequences.[8] Since this theme is the "breaking up" of the culture, the structure of the volume contributes significantly to the complex counterpoint of order and disorder, for the view of a disintegrating world is itself highly integrated.

The motif is also an important unifying device in *Imitations* (1961), the work that has caused more critical controversy than any other single volume by Lowell. One of the sources of the controversy is the failure on both sides to recognize the nature of the volume and its unity. *Imitations* is primarily neither a collection of translations nor a collection of original poems based on others, but rather a carefully organized *book*, the thematic center of which is the continuity of life and art for the poet. In effect, Lowell exploits the analogy drawn by Renato Poggioli when he says that "like the original poet, the translator is a Narcissus who in this case chooses to contemplate his own likeness not in the spring of nature but in the pool of art."[9] The adjustment that might be made is that in this case the translator is also and primarily an original poet, so that instead of simply seeing himself in the works of others (and thereby making himself an artist), he could also view himself *qua* artist in those works (and thereby remake himself as artist). This is exactly what Lowell does, as he selects poets who not only possess sensibilities akin to his—as any translator would be likely to do—but who also comment, or can be made to comment, on the sort of poetry that he writes. *Imitations* is thus a reflection of the poet's life at the same time that it is an extension of that life.

This book is more than that, however, because it incorporates as both a thematic and a structural element the rationale behind the artist's life. The idea that one creates his life and gives it form in persistently returning to his calling in spite of the knowledge that lasting success is impossible is a recurrent theme in the poems that Lowell has selected. The very organization of the poems embodies this theme, for they constitute a narrative of the archetypal experience of the artist, the progression from commitment through frustration (paradoxically a revitalizing force) to renewed commitment. The structure of this book, like that of *Lord Weary's Castle* and like that of *For the Union Dead*, is thus essentially circular.

The structure of Lowell's fifth volume encourages another spatial metaphor, that of an inverted triangle, since its physical center is its psychological nadir; and this feature, as well as the others just touched upon, is also true of his sixth, *For the Union Dead* (1964). This volume turns on a dark night of the soul, occasioned chiefly by the persona's loss of contact with objective reality and eventuating in his rediscovery of self and thereby of the world about him. Just after the pivotal point, a poem significantly entitled "Myopia: a Night," Lowell seems to allude to a passage in the work of Henri Bergson, which has been glossed by Wylie Sypher in these pertinent terms:

In his effort to "touch bottom," Bergson turns inward to contemplate how the self exists within the flow of time, how it endures behind or within change. . . . If the self is to be known, it must be intuited in the dim and quiet eddies streaming like quicksands far below the mechanism of the rational mind. . . .[10]

After just such an intuition in the middle of *For the Union Dead*, the poems take on a more affirmative tone and the way up in the second half of the volume balances the way down in the first half. Again a collection of poems has been arranged to embody an archetypal experience, and again the volume itself is a symbol that attempts to convert the experience of seeking form into form itself. At the same time that the poems constitute a search for self, the self is being constituted by the search. It is not just the word, as it was in Lowell's beginning, but also the volume that is a "living thing," with a movement that is its meaning.

From such a conjunction of process and product as the last two books mentioned exemplify, it is but a short step to the idea that the proper locus of form is not art but life, or even that aesthetic organization is a spurious reproduction of vital form. The gradual, devious, but undeniable movement that we have been summarizing—from the short, highly compressed lyric dealing ostensibly with religious absolutes, through the sequence of subtly organized poems surveying the poet's past, to the book comprising poems dependent to some degree upon one another for their form and embodying the experience of writing—can be viewed as a tracking of art back to its lair of life, where it might be found to have shed its disguise. To the extent that this aim is accomplished, of course, art loses its identity. If in his beginning the neo-symbolist threatens his own existence as artist by removing himself from the objective world, at this extreme he imperils it by integrating himself with that world. If from the last stage noted above the poet proceeds to the next, so that his books depend upon the actual world for their "form," he has partly undermined his own raison d'être.

One can only speculate whether thoughts such as these were in Lowell's mind after the publication of *For the Union Dead*, but they might have been one motivation for the return to formal verse in *Near the Ocean* (1967). If the ocean is the welter of circumstance that threatens to overwhelm the aesthetic form, Lowell was indeed near it, and the return to a strict prosody in this volume might be a means of reasserting the integrity of the poetry. Rhyme and metre are not, however, the only means by which Lowell establishes objective form in *Near the Ocean*. When first encountered, the vignettes and even the poems in the title sequence might seem to occupy arbitrarily assigned positions, and Hayden Carruth's summary of a trend in modern literature, inspired by a consideration of this book, might seem applicable:

Hence in literature any particular "work" is linear rather than circular in structure, extensible rather than terminal in intent, and at any given point inclusive rather than associative in substance; at least these are its tendencies. And it is autobiographical, that goes without saying. It is an act of self-creation by an artist within the tumult of experience.[11]

After some reflection, however, at least a few of Carruth's comments can serve as foils for, rather than descriptions of, this volume. While it is true that the individual poems in the title sequence and that sequence itself are "extensible" in the sense that they are not informed by a symmetry that imposes a beginning, middle, and end, it is also true that each of these poems and the group as a whole have a chronological progression and therefore acquire some of the irrevocability of position that hours of the day and days of the week have. Moreover, the volume as a whole describes a circular movement, for the chronological sequence in the present at the beginning of the book is balanced by a chronological sequence in the past at its conclusion, the inevitable implication being that the future is a repetition of the past, or that the future is to be found in the past. Borrowing a phrase used by Murray Krieger in another context, one might say that from this point of view the book's structure consists in "the circularizing of its linear movement."[12]

Carruth's comments on the autobiographical and self-creative aspects of this book seem entirely appropriate, on the other hand, not only to *Near the Ocean,* but also to the subsequent volumes, *Notebook 1967–68* (1969) and its revised and enlarged edition, *Notebook* (1970). These volumes undoubtedly make more concessions to the randomness and fragmentation of diaristic autobiography than any preceding book, and from the very title of each to its author's "Afterthought," they exist in the penumbra between flux and form. A notebook is perhaps the closest written analogue to raw experience, a largely unpredictable record of events and thoughts that might otherwise be lost in the shuffle of things, a repository for ephemera and inklings that might later be given more consideration, a higher polish. The dates in the title of the first edition drive home the point: this is art that goes hand in hand with its mortal and mortifying enemy. If experiences in time are not discrete entities, neither are the poems and sequences in these volumes, unless discreteness is defined only in terms of spatial limitation. If it is difficult to draw the line between experience and poetry in the first place, how much more difficult it must be to distinguish poem from poem. Lowell even insists upon the impossibility of such distinctions in his "Afterthought" in the first edition when he advises us that "the poems in this book are written as one poem." When he goes ahead to say that his plot "rolls with the seasons," he seems to have reached that point mentioned above at which the book becomes dependent upon the actual world for its form.

But, as Lowell himself suggests, there is again a circular movement through the *Notebooks*, and if the movement is modeled on the seasons, it is still a structural means. Indeed, the implications of the *Notebooks* are that the same principles underlie life and art, that there is a fructifying tension between flux and form in each realm, and perhaps even that art need be no less—or no more—than a reflection in small of this relationship as it exists in nature. In blurring these distinctions, however, Lowell weakens his aesthetic structures at almost every level. Surely such a recognition is at least partly responsible for the radical revision of his *Notebook*.

In the summer of 1973, Lowell published simultaneously three volumes of poetry, all written in the same fourteen-line blank verse form that he had used exclusively since 1967: *History*, a reworking of *Notebook; For Lizzie and Harriet*, a collection and revision of poems once scattered throughout *Notebook;* and *The Dolphin*, a new sequence. The two smaller volumes, dedicated respectively to the poet's second wife and their daughter and to his third wife, work the personal, journalistic vein that ran through *Notebook. History*, on the other hand, is a monumental structure built largely of what was quarried earlier. Perhaps still in progress, this volume promises or threatens to become Lowell's *Cantos*, or at least *His Toy, His Dream, His Rest*. It is structurally distinguished from these two works, however, as well as from its previous phases, by a chronological framework that shapes its dense reticulation of motifs, many of which derive from earlier volumes.

In fact, by including versions of poems from all of Lowell's preceding volumes (except the first, much of which was incorporated in the second), *History* testifies to and helps to establish a contextual relationship among all of these volumes that is comparable to the relationships among the poems within one of them. The book is a synecdoche for Lowell's work: what his poetry is to history, *History* is to his poetry. More than this, it is Lowell's most ambitious attempt to date to discover the whole of his life—which is to say its shape as well as much of its data—in a part of it.

If it still risks being lost, as one of its sections implies the *Cantos* risk being lost, "in the rockslide of history," *History* certainly better fits the conception of a book that is "one poem" than had either of the *Notebooks*. A troubling and troubled work, which takes chances that most of us did not even know could be taken, it nevertheless reassures us that Lowell has not lost touch with the formal desiderata of poetry, just as he has not lost touch with his earliest work. Perhaps there is little need to worry that he will ever do so. The principle that accounts for the nature of his development so far and betokens that of his future development also provides for the preservation of the shaping spirit. Lowell has stated this principle indirectly in the remark on Eliot quoted near the beginning of this introduction. More directly, in a statement that recalls that one and that the following chapters attempt to elucidate, he has said: "All your poems are in a sense one poem, and there's always the struggle of getting something that balances and comes out right, in which all the parts are good, and that has experience that you value."[13]

Words, as is well known, are the great foes of reality.
—JOSEPH CONRAD, *Under Western Eyes*

And that was why the catapulting fur,
A wooly lava of abstractions, flowed
Over my memory's inflated bag.
—"A Suicidal Nightmare"

THE WORD IN THE GARDEN:

Land of Unlikeness (1944)

From cover to cover *Land of Unlikeness* is an extraordinary volume. Printed in an edition of only 250 copies and published in July 1944 by the Cummington Press, the book bears in scarlet on a background of dusky blue its author's name on the spine and its title and epigraph on the cover; in a titlepage woodcut by Gustav Wolf, a striking summary of its tone and concerns; in one and one-half pages of italics, its credentials, an introduction by Allen Tate; in stanzas of verbal boullework on thirty-seven unnumbered pages, a total of twenty-one poems; and if it is one of the select twenty-six, the number of the copy and the signature of Robert Lowell. It is an elegant, confident publication that announces a proud, ambitious poet. There is nothing in it, however, that would have allowed one to predict the kind of poet its author would have become in ten years, let alone twenty and now thirty; and yet, in retrospect, this *Land of Unlikeness* seems the inevitable point of departure for Robert Lowell's peregrinations.[1]

Even if access were easier, the sign at the border of this small ultramontane kingdom would be almost sufficiently intimidating to account for an infrequency of visitors. Wolf's woodcut, the first evidence of Lowell's insistence that his work be accompanied, if at all, by meaningful graphic art, is a neo-Gothic horror.[2] It depicts a grotesque figure hanging on a Latin cross—not nailed to the cross, but clinging to it, as though to an object, like a church steeple, still elevated above the rising waters of a catastrophic flood. One's first impression is that the figure is the Old One himself: it has the hideous features of a gargoyle; the sharply ridged spine, visible behind and at first seemingly a part of its head, of some extinct rhynchocephalian; the wings of a bat; hands and feet that terminate in claws; and the tail of a jungle cat, which, as it coils around the cross, is intersected by the epigraph, culled from Gilson's *Mystical Theology of St. Bernard*, which has already appeared on the cover: "Inde anima dissimilis deo inde dissimilis est et sibi" ("When the soul is no longer like God then it is no longer like itself").[3] The placement of the epigraph is arresting, for the implication is perhaps that man himself, no longer the mirror image or the son of God, has become Satanic. Closer investigation of the woodcut first lends credence to this inference and then leads one to qualify it slightly but significantly. The body of the figure is after all human; the expression on the face, however repulsive, is very close to pitiable stupefaction; and the wings behind it are at such an odd angle in respect to the body that they do not really seem to belong to it. Moreover, both the lion's tail and the thorny spine behind the head might be oblique references to the figure one might expect to find on a cross. What we have, then, is a bizarre montage of demonic, human, and Christlike attributes, an emblem that fuses the qualities that Tate notes in his introduction, "spiritual decay" and "at least a memory of the spiritual dignity of man."

There is a wistful note in that "at least," and when one turns through the poems, he begins to see the occasion for it. In "The Drunken Fisherman," a poem singled out for its excellence by R. P. Blackmur, who judged the book as a whole to contain "not a loving rhythm,"[4] the memory that Tate mentions is further defined:

> Children, the raging memory drools
> Over the glory of past pools.

Such a memory, one would think, would hardly be capable of appreciating the glory it recalls, let alone of emulating it; indeed, the very recollection, with its positioning of the "pools" beneath "drools," seems to befoul the glory. Like Wolf's woodcut, and like many other passages in this volume, this one imputes to the inhabitants of the *Land of Unlikeness* an almost fantastically repellent quality. Here, for an extreme example, is the opening stanza of "Christ for Sale":

> In Greenwich Village, Christ the Drunkard brews
> Gall, or spiked bone-vat, siphons His bilged blood
> Into weak brain-pans and unseasons wood:
> His auctioneers are four hog-fatted Jews.
> In furs and bundlings of vitality,
> Cur ladies, ho, swill down the ichor in this Dye.

In a world in which spiritual decay is so pervasive, a mere glimmering of spiritual dignity would be a treasure indeed.

In truth, however, this passage repels not so much because of what is seen in this world as because of the way in which it is seen. The raging memory has become the raging imagination; and the images here (if a passage so far removed from actuality can be said to have images) attain an ugliness quite different from that achieved by, say, Baudelaire in poems such as "Une charogne" or "Un voyage à Cythère" because they arise not from description or apparent description but rather from abstraction and caricature.[5] It is the same kind of symbolic distortion that takes place in Wolf's woodcut, or in "The Crucifix":

> It's time; the worldly angels strip to tease
> And wring out bread and butter from their eyes
> To wipe away the past's idolatries. . . .

The worldly angels' are not the only remarkable eyes in this poem. As in "Christ for Sale," either the poet's loathing of his subject is so great that it overwhelms his powers of observation or the observations that he might make would be inadequate to convey his loathing. If perception of man's spiritual decay led Lowell to disgust, the disgust leads him away from the objects of his perception.

A foil—however unfair the comparison in the final analysis—might be useful. "Ubi amor ibi oculus est" might have been the motto, instead of just a piece in his mosaic, of another poet, an older contemporary (shortly to be awarded by a panel of judges including Lowell the first Bollingen Prize in poetry) whose eye was so sharp that it would notice the "green elegance" of a midge and the way the dawn sun trapped the shadows of some ants. "Ubi amor ibi oculus est"; or, as the Augustinian title of Richard Wilbur's poem has it, "Love Calls Us to the Things of this World." By implication, where there is no love there is no eye for concrete particulars; and if to Blackmur's ear there is not a loving rhythm in *Land of Unlikeness*, to many a reader's eye there must be hardly a loving glance. There are exceptions, of course, such as the conclusion of "Cistercians in Germany," the last lines of which Lowell preserved in altered form in a poem in *Lord Weary's Castle*, "At the Indian Killer's Grave":

> We lift our bloody hands to wizened Bernard,
> To Bernard gathering his canticle of flowers,
> His soul a bridal chamber fresh with flowers,
> And all his body one extatic womb,
> And through the trellis peers the sudden Bridegroom.

But exceptions are rare. More often than one comes upon such a miraculous pergola in *Land of Unlikeness* he stumbles into a "Slough of Despond":

> At sunset only swamp
> Afforded pursey tufts of grass . . . . these gave,
> I sank. Each humus-sallowed pool
> Rattled its cynic's lamp
> And croaked: "We lay Apollo in his grave;
> Narcissus is our fool."

This is familiar ground, though swampy. Although the passage begins with a close look at nature, at actuality, Lowell's eyes are soon elsewhere; and as soon as he has turned the stagnant pool into the lamp with which his Diogenes, in a world denied the objective light of Phoebus Apollo, discovers narcissists where he would find honest men, he puts the words of that acid-

tongued philosopher into the mouth of a bullfrog at the pool's
edge. It is this preference of the abstract, convoluted metaphor
to the image of the actual that suggests the kind of poet Lowell is at the beginning of his career.

Seven years after he wrote the introduction to Lowell's first
volume, in which he presented "a consciously Catholic poet,"
Tate published an essay called "The Symbolic Imagination."[6]
In this essay Tate distinguishes the faculty named in the title
from "the angelic imagination": "I call that human imagination angelic which tries to disintegrate or to circumvent the
image in the illusory pursuit of essence." Such an imagination "professes to know nature as essence at the same time
that it has become alienated from nature in the rejection of its
material forms." Tate proceeds to quote Charles Williams's
study of Dante, *The Figure of Beatrice:*

It was, however high the phrases, the common thing from which
Dante always started, as it was certainly the greatest and most common to which he came. His images were the natural inevitable images
—the girl in the street, the people he knew, the language he learned
as a child. In them the great diagrams were perceived; from them the
great myths open; by them he understands the final end.

According to Tate, an initiate, "the Catholic sensibility, as we
see it in modern Catholic poetry, from Thompson to Lowell,
has become angelic. . . . Catholic poets have lost, along with
their heretical friends, the power to start with the 'common
thing': they have lost the gift for concrete experience. The
abstraction of the modern mind has obscured their way into
the natural order." Whereas Dante's love of actuality encour-
aged him to begin with the observed world, and indeed never
to lose it in the process of his poetry, the angelic poet, so far
from thinking of the world as full of natural inevitable images
that he is likely to see it as a land of unlikeness to which he
has been exiled, begins with abstract means.

For the angelic poet the means is a language as disjunct
from nature as possible. If this kind of poet bothers to look at
nature, Tate observes, "he spreads the clear visual image in a
complex of metaphor, from one katachresis to another
through Aristotle's permutations of genus and species."[7]
And one thinks, for an example, of the katachresis by which

the pool becomes the cynic's lamp and the bullfrog's croak his voice. The poet who in pursuit of essence cannot turn part of his attention to nature turns it all upon his words and the figures that they make in the hope that the latter, more abstract than nature, will bring him nearer Reality.

Fifteen years later, in *Life Studies*, Lowell would go back to "the natural inevitable images—the girl in the street, the people he knew, the language he learned as a child." Twenty years later, as though recalling Tate's essay, he would say of Hawthorne, one of the figures most venerated in *For the Union Dead:*

> Leave him alone for a moment or two,
> and you'll see him with his head
> bent down, brooding, brooding,
> eyes fixed on some chip,
> some stone, some common plant,
> the commonest thing,
> as if it were the clue.

But that was to be twenty years later. In 1944, not long before Pound, in his cage near Pisa, would be meditating on midge and ant, lizard and wasp, Lowell, courageously serving his own sentence for evading the draft on grounds decreed by conscience, was truly confined in his *Land of Unlikeness*, twice removed from the natural world.[8]

Put most simply, then—for the rejection of nature in its material forms is inseparable from the verbal expression that constitutes that rejection—what stands between Lowell and the objects of his scorn and infrequent praise is his language itself. In one sense, of course, this is necessarily true of all writers, just as in another sense it is necessarily true of all people, and it is obviously neither of those senses that is intended here. For the Lowell of *Land of Unlikeness*, the nominal subject of a poem often seems subordinate to the concern with the potential of the verbal symbols ostensibly employed in the service of that subject. Correspondingly, this poetry consistently directs one's attention to symbols rather than to physical objects and to the composition of the poem rather than to the constitution of the world to which the poem would refer. The narrator in Conrad's *Under Western Eyes* speaks of the danger of a related preoccupation in this way:

If I have ever had these gifts in any sort of living form, they have been smothered out of existence a long time ago under a wilderness of words. Words, as is well known, are the great foes of reality. I have been for many years a teacher of languages. It is an occupation which at length becomes fatal to whatever share of imagination, observation, and insight an ordinary person may be heir to. To a teacher of languages there comes a time when the world is but a place of many words and man appears a mere talking animal not much more wonderful than a parrot.

It is a coincidence that in "Thanksgiving's Over," one of Lowell's later poems, a woman who is so at odds with actuality that she must be confined in an asylum manifests her madness thus:

"I hear the word
Of Brother Francis, child and bird, descend,
Calling the war of Michael a pretend;
The Lord is Brother Parrot, and a friend."

But the real subject of these poems, several of which purport to be about war, *is* the word, even as it is the Word. Lowell's perceptions here are primarily of the relationships among words and phrases, not of the relationships among people and things, and this characteristic is both the source of the deficiencies and the condition of the virtues of his early work.[9]

The symptoms of a preoccupation with verbal patterns at the expense of natural, narrative, and even thematic elements abound in *Land of Unlikeness*. In poem after poem, proverbial phrases, dead metaphors, clichés, and quotations seem almost to have been sought out for the sake of the novel twists that can be given them.[10] This technique, which is of course no more original with Lowell than the phrases themselves, can be responsible for some of his most effective passages, as in these lines from "The Bomber":

How can frail wings and clay
Beat down the biting dust
When Christ gives up the ghost?

There are at least two adaptations being made here, of which the italicized refrain is the most apparent. The expression that someone has "given up the ghost" acquires an ironic edge in this context, for the point is that the Bomber, having surrendered his means of salvation by violating the First Commandment, must now have his own spirit (his *Geist*) relinquished in turn. In this case, a phrase that has lost nearly all of its original force gains a new power because Lowell returns, with a vengeance, to a literal meaning. Somewhat less obtrusively, in the line preceding the refrain, Lowell has converted the worn-out expression "to bite the dust" into an incisive image by making the dust the active agent.

On other occasions it is hard to see the point of such recasting of idiom, and sometimes the technique seems self-defeating. This rhetorical question is from "Dunbarton," the second poem in the sequence "In Memory of Arthur Winslow":

> "Arthur, no one living has reached
> Dunbarton. Are only poor relations left
> To hold an empty bag of pine-cones?"

One surmises that the realization that an " 'empty bag' " should not hold anything, including pinecones, persuaded Lowell to revise these lines when he republished the poem in *Lord Weary's Castle*. Less flagrant, but distractingly superfluous, is the allusion to Mark Antony's oration in the opening lines of the third section of this elegy:

> This Easter, Arthur Winslow, five years gone,
> I come to bury you and not to praise
> The craft that netted a million dollars, late
> Mining in California's golden bays. . . .

When the poet calls upon one of the most belabored passages in English literature to carry the climax of "Concord Cemetery after the Tornado," it is difficult to avoid the conclusion that he is shirking his duty. In reference to Ralph Waldo Emerson, he prophesies that "Soon / Angels will fear to tread / On that dead Lion's bones." Because the recollection of Pope's line neither clarifies nor enriches what appears to be an image of resurrection on the Day of Judgment (history is

abridged throughout this volume: Judgment is always imminent, and at one point Bishop Ussher's dating of Creation
seems to be adopted), one can hardly help feeling that this is
a prime instance of Lowell's propensity to rely upon verbal
formulas.

The single-minded attentiveness to words is also witnessed
by the plethora of puns, ranging from the inspired to the
gratuitous and sometimes disconcerting ("the worldly angels
strip to tease"), that can be found in *Land of Unlikeness*. One of
the more admirable examples of extended punning here is in
the opening lines of "Dunbarton," quoted above, in which
"craft," "netted," "dollars," and "golden bays" all conjoin
images drawn from fishing with the vocabulary of the
capitalism, which, among other things, Arthur Winslow represents. In "The Boston Nativity," when Lowell says that
"Doctors pronounce him [Christ] dead," he succeeds in compressing into one line his grievances against emancipated
doctors of divinity and positivistic Biblical scholars. There is a
similar equivocation on "brass" in "Concord Cemetery after
the Tornado":

> Brain
> And brass are come to clay
> While the professors cart
> Our guts to Babylon. . . .

The use of "brass" to denote both "gall" and "eminent persons," however, verges upon the ingenious; and the double
significance in "Soon the Leviathan / Will spout American"
("The Boston Nativity") is dangerously close to the frivolous.

But the seemingly irresistible urge to create ambiguities,
like the compulsions to tinker with commonplaces and to
polish touchstones, is only an indication of the extent to
which Lowell's imagination is angelic, his sensibility verbal.
More important than the symptoms are the implications of
such a sensibility for fundamental procedures, for Lowell's
fascination with verbal pattern affects his means of construction at the most basic level, his concept of the organization of
the poem, his technical apparatus, and even the genres that
he chooses.

Of these areas, perhaps the most crucial is the first, the basic structural principles, the means of getting from one point to another within the bounds of a stanza or even within the confines of a line. Since one of the tendencies of a poetry as verbally centered as that in *Land of Unlikeness* is to prescind from the world of nature and society, one of the tasks that it must undertake is to relate its elements to one another without the full benefit of their referential functions. The problem—to get at the matter from a perverse angle, but one from which the young poet seems also to have got at it—is to find a method of connecting words and images that neither entails nor depends upon the conjunction of referents. As some of the passages quoted earlier must suggest, Lowell's response to the problem involves exploitation of the latent meanings of the verbal materials themselves: his words and phrases interact with one another by means of connotation and secondary meaning, and repetition or ramification of connotation becomes the cohesive force. The characteristic structural principle in *Land of Unlikeness* is what Tate has called "intension," that network of ambiguities and contradictions generated beneath the surface of the poetry.[11]

At the same time that it affords a means of unifying a poem on one level, the submerged verbal pattern invites disorganization on other levels. Too great a concentration upon the intension of a poem is liable to involve disruption or obfuscation of its "extension," or abstracted logical structure, which depends upon denotation. This seems to be what happens in this importunate address to the Virgin in "On the Eve of the Feast of the Immaculate Conception 1942":

> Freedom and Eisenhower have won
> Significant laurels where the Hun
>   And Roman kneel
> To lick the dust from Mars' bootheel
> Like foppish bloodhounds; yet you sleep
> Out our distemper's evil day
>   And hear no sheep
>   Or hangdog bay!

Much is adroitly accomplished here. The ambiguity of "Hun"

and "Roman" introduces a historical perspective, which, even as it alters the tone of the superficially triumphant initial line, prepares us for the bitter irony of the fourth and fifth lines, which in turn perhaps explains the "yet" of the second clause; and the second clause is bound tightly to the first by the several canine references, so that the whole stanza is integrated. The very phrasing responsible for this ulterior unity, however, raises questions that point to flaws in the stanza's surface. In what sense, for example, are Hitler and Mussolini (or their respective soldiers) "bloodhounds"? Are we not really to understand "bloodthirsty brutes" or the like, rather than skillful trackers of scents, most notably employed in running criminals to earth? Again: what is the relationship, precisely, between the Allied forces and Mars? Are the former really to be viewed as votaries of the latter? Or is it perhaps that the other connections permit no distinction to be made between Eisenhower and Hitler? Finally, and most obviously: what manner of beast is the "hangdog" (poet) that he can be alternatively identified as a "sheep" (of the flock)?

A briefer but more exaggerated instance of verbal pattern conflicting with surface structure concludes this stanza from "Satan's Confession, II":

> The laurels are cut down,
> The Son of Darkness cries;
>   Old Adam's mortal wreath,
>   The prize of Death,
> Is Jesus' Crown,
> Jack's beanstalk to the skies.

The startling image in the last line simply preempts the stanza's organization. The katachresis issues from the identification of "the skies" with a Christian heaven and the tenuous relationship among a laurel wreath, the crown of thorns, and the beanstalk. The allusion to the fairytale, however, adds nothing to the poem as a whole and can be justified almost solely on the grounds of these cross-references. Perhaps a more salient point—since justification is not necessarily required of every element in a poem—is that this allusion actually conflicts in tone with the rest of the stanza. Although the last line knots the various strands of imagery of the preceding lines, it is itself an unassimilated element.

It is partly because metaphors based on wordplay tend to round themselves out, to exhaust themselves quickly, that Lowell has difficulty unifying his early poems. Hence, too, his predilection for the tight stanza and perhaps his liking for the sequence, for to the extent that the section of the sequence and the stanza can be regarded as self-contained units, they provide spaces appropriate in their limitation to the short-winded figures. It is notable in this respect that Lowell's syntax almost never finds occasion to override the temporary conclusion inevitably suggested by the close of a stanza. Indeed, one's frequent impression is that a form has been blocked out and then (to the poet's relief) filled in, rather than that feelings have evolved and then tested a form. This is another way of saying that the poems in *Land of Unlikeness*, especially those that were not reprinted in *Lord Weary's Castle*, rarely exhibit a significant movement, a natural curve of emotion or thought.

If the concentration upon verbal patterns and the recurrent use of rigid stanzas make for a static quality, that quality is accentuated by other devices characteristic of this volume. Lowell's use of the refrain ("The Bomber," "Concord Cemetery after the Tornado"), for instance, can only point up the isolation of stanzas from one another and thereby emphasize the lack of structural development. In "Satan's Confession," the three main sections open with stanzas nearly identical; and the slight variations, instead of marking important shifts in subject or tone, seem different drafts of the same stanza. Lowell's handling of rhyme also calls attention to and reinforces this static quality. "The Boston Nativity" is a prosodic tour de force, in which what seems at first a poem of five tightly patterned six-line stanzas ($a_6b_8a_{10}b_8c_{10}c_8$) turns out to be an even more demanding form, since the second and fourth lines of each of stanzas 2 through 5 pick up the couplet rhyme of the preceding stanza, and the concluding stanza's rhymes have all been used before. In "A Suicidal Nightmare," three stanzas of six lines apiece operate on only five half-rhymes, and one of two rhyme words ("bag" and "bog") ends the third and sixth line of each stanza. Identical rhyme is also used in "Dea Roma," where the last word of the last line of each stanza repeats the last word in the first line, and in "Christ for Sale," where, in addition, only the rhyme in the first and fourth lines of a given stanza is not repeated elsewhere in the poem.

For many of the poems in *Land of Unlikeness*, then, the title of "Scenes from the Historic Comedy" is apt inasmuch as it suggests a static quality. Inasmuch as it directs one's attention to time and place, however, the title could hardly be more misleading. With a few exceptions (such as "The Park Street Cemetery," "The Drunken Fisherman," and "In Memory of Arthur Winslow"), these poems do not answer to "where?" any more adequately than they do to "when?" W. H. Auden has said that when a young poet dispraises some aspect of another writer's technique he is usually commenting on a flaw of his own, and Auden's aperçu might illuminate Lowell's criticism at about this time of Thomas Merton and Christina Rossetti for leaving their poems "precariously unlocated in time or place."[12]

This was also one of Lowell's main criticisms of Dylan Thomas, a poet for whom he had great admiration and with whom he had much in common, for he said in a review that "if Thomas kept his eye on the object and depended less on his rhetoric, his poems would be better organized and have more to say."[13] In this comment Lowell makes precisely the connection that his critic must make in regard to Lowell's own early work: most of the poetry is so verbally centered that it deprives itself of those dimensions—time and space— and those principles—conflict and development of either a mental or physical nature—that alone provide the means of organizing poems. Charles Feidelson, Jr., makes this point in more general terms in regard to other "symbolists" who carry their method to an extreme:

Poetic form presupposes the rational world at every point. And the more thoroughly the symbolist conceives of language as symbol, the more likely it is that he will lose touch with language as sign. . . . Deliberate symbolism is hazardous in its quest for a pure poetry, for poetry can be pure only by virtue of the impurities it assimilates. In the degree that the poem shakes loose from the poet himself and from the world of objects, in the degree that the poetic word is freed from logical bonds, poetry will be deprived of material; in performing its function, it will destroy its subject matter.[14]

At this point in his career, Lowell's work is frequently close to a "pure poetry" because it assumes a disjunction of the verbal symbol and the actual world, because it ignores the incorrigibly referential function of words.

At the same time, *Land of Unlikeness* evinces Lowell's knowledge of the structural problem by providing several responses to it. In the first place, as Lowell said disapprovingly of Thomas's lyrics, his own poems often substitute "repeated symbols or description for logic or narrative." This substitution is probably what Blackmur had in mind when he said that although Lowell's poems do not always exhibit structural movement, they do have things put in to give the appearance of it.[15] In "Leviathan," for example, in lieu of conflict or development there is a repetition of the central paradox that gives the illusion of structural movement. Here is the first and best stanza of the poem:

When the ruined farmer knocked out Abel's brains,
Our Father laid great cities on his soul,
    A monolithic mole
To bury man and yet to praise him. Cain's
Life-blood shall drown the Serpent in his Hole.

The "ruined farmer" is of course Cain, whose descendants are punished by banishment to the evils of the city and modern civilization; but besides being evidence of man's degeneracy ("To bury man"), the city bears witness to his worth ("to praise him"). Man is precipitately damned and saved— the "essence" of the matter is "grasped"—and it seems that there is little to do but to rephrase the paradox. The last sentence in this stanza does exactly that, as it makes Cain, the archetypal figure of the damned, a type of Christ, so that his life is here the expense of victory over Satan. A liberal theology can sanction this identification of sin and salvation, but a poem that begins with it might already be at its end, as "Leviathan" is. The paradox is echoed weakly in the second stanza ("He sent us Canaan or Exile, Ark or flood") and more faintly in the last line of the third and concluding stanza ("Go *down* with colors *flying* for the King"). With the sinking ship in the last line and the Ark in the second stanza, there seems at first to have been a development; but in fact, the concept is stated in its most complete form in the drowning image of the first stanza.

"Satan's Confession" is a more extreme and more clear-cut instance of the substitution of repeated symbols for logical or narrative development. This poem is divided into three main sections, the titles of which—"The Garden," "The Fruit," and "The Tree"—might suggest in this context a progression from innocence through temptation to knowledge and the Fall. On the other hand, "The Tree" might be that of Life, "The Fruit" might be that of Mary's womb, and "The Garden" might be otherworldly; or "The Tree" might be the Cross . . . What happens is that Lowell, because of his focus upon the verbal symbol apart from the possible referents, sees (or writes as though he sees) all of these meanings at once, and consequently there can be no true structural movement through the poem. Everything is said by the end of the first stanza of "The Garden":

> The laurels are cut down,
> The Son of Darkness mourns;
>   Old Adam's funeral wreath,
>   Once crossed with death,
>   Is Jesus' crown,
>   King Jesus' Crown of thorns.

Satan's temporary victory, Adam's defeat, and Christ's ultimate victory through defeat are compressed in the symbol of the garland, the circle of paradox; and the potential for conflict and development is obviated. Lowell has tried to justify the ways of God to man in six short lines without realizing, apparently, that the justification resides not in the paradox itself but in the poetic rationalization of it, not in the idea of *felix culpa* but in the working out in the plot and the imagery of the identity of rising and falling. What is missing is an analogue to the Christian view of history, a recognition of millennia of "common experience"; what we have instead is a God's-eye view of time, an attempt to seize "essence." Because he impetuously adopts his paradoxical resolution at the outset, Lowell is reduced to reiteration for the rest of the poem, the longest in the volume. "The Tree" concludes: "Adam's blood / Is a king's crown, / King Jesus' purple shroud."

The "Envoy" to this poem provides its only development, and even this development is more apparent than real:

> I praise the Trinity;
> From Death three Eagles fly;
>   Sire, Son and Paraclete
>   A blind world greet;
> One Charity
> Reverbs the three-fold I.

This stanza not only eulogizes the Trinity but also unites the speaker (the initial "I") with the Deity (the concluding "I"), as well as with the three figures discussed above (Satan, Adam, and Christ). Although the first of these unions might seem surprising out of context, it is after all but a facet of the second; and this "three-fold" nature of the speaker is implicit throughout the poem, for Satan, Adam, and Christ all seem to speak, although Lowell significantly omits all means of certain identification and allows the reader to view the pertinent stanzas as indirect quotations. In short, it is not so much the "One Charity"—which in this proof of the proverb begins at home—as it is this poem that "Reverbs the three-fold I."

Perhaps in no other poem in *Land of Unlikeness* is Lowell's structural problem so clear, and the "Envoy" can serve as an emblem of that problem. It is itself a tight circle of paradox, its last Word identical with its first word; and since that word—a mere single-letter pronoun—is the sum of existence, the circle cannot be broken or enlarged. It can only be inscribed over and over (as in this poem) or intrasected by various identifications; in Blackmur's terms, which Lowell was to quote approvingly in a poem of twenty-five years later, either the "vision turns the logic to zealotry" or the "logic lacerates the vision."[16]

A rather startling example of Lowell's logic's lacerating his vision (or of his ramifying "the clear visual image in a complex of metaphor, from one katachresis to another") is "A Suicidal Nightmare." On the whole not one of the finest poems in *Land of Unlikeness,* as Lowell admitted by excluding it from *Lord Weary's Castle,* it is still, in Tate's words, "more dramatic" and "richer in immediate experience than the explicitly religious poems." In other respects, too, it is a forerunner of some of the best poems in the next two volumes and therefore deserves to be quoted entire:

> Tonight and crouching in your jungle-bed,
> O tiger of the gutless heart, you spied
> The maimed man stooping with his bag;
> And there was none to help. Cat, you saw red,
> And like a grinning sphinx, you prophesied
> Cain's nine and outcast lives are in the bag.
>
> Watching the man, I spun my borrowed car
> Into the bog. I'd left the traveled road
> And crashed into a lower bog;
> And that was why the catapaulting fur,
> A wooly lava of abstractions, flowed
> Over my memory's inflated bag.
>
> The maimed man stooped and slung me on his back:
> My borrowed car flopped quacking in the flood,
> It foundered in the lowest bog.
> Man, why was it your rotten fabric broke?
> "Brother, I fattened a caged beast on blood
> And knowledge had let the cat out of the bag."

Unlike most of the poems in this volume, "A Suicidal Nightmare" is built of a succession of events, albeit oneiric events, that provide a rudimentary plot. The first of these events is the hungry or simply malicious spying of the tiger upon the undefended, maimed man. In the second stanza, the dreamer enters his dream as his car plunges off the road into a bog in the vicinity of the man. At the end of the poem, the dreamer is rescued, at least temporarily, by the maimed man, and the nightmare ends with an inscrutable quotation.

When it is stripped down to such a paraphrase, the poem is clearly a miniature allegory in which the driver of the "traveled road" is the individual soul, the accident the wages of sin, the maimed man Christ, and the tiger Satan. Only the climactic event in the narrative remains obscure; it does not seem determinable whether the rescue is permanent, for the concluding lines do not allow us to infer the result, or even the occurrence, of a confrontation between maimed man and tiger.

The source of the problem in the last lines is familiar: Lowell's penchant for adaptation of idiom leads him to install as the crucial part of the poem the expression "to let the cat out of the bag." Consequently, the figure that seems hitherto to have been spying upon the maimed man gathering "lives" must now be imagined to be inside the bag that the man holds. The enigma is not immediately resolved by a rereading of the poem, for upon rereading, if not before, one sees that Lowell is also playing, at the end of the first stanza, with the phrase "to be in the bag," with the result that it is unclear whether man's soul is "in the bag" from Christ's point of view or from Satan's. The earlier issue is even further confused by the realization that the reference to "nine . . . lives" makes of Cain's descendants a litter of kittens. Finally, in addition to being related to the cat, man is equated, by virtue of the phrase "your rotten fabric," either with the bag or with the maimed man who carries it or both—whatever that might mean.

The patient reader will have begun by now to see what it does, what it *must*, mean: that there is in this poem the same trinity (man, Satan, and Christ) that there is in "Satan's Confession" and Wolf's woodcut, for the tiger in his jungle-bed is the speaker in his own bed and jungle of allusions, just as the maimed man with his bag is man with his own "rotten fabric." The nightmare is thus "suicidal," not because the dreamer drives off the road on purpose (this event seems truly to be an accident, at least in the sense that any well-intentioned soul's fall is an accident, and this road is doubtless paved with good intentions), but because one part of the self must do in the other. Whether the unregenerate side or the divine side triumphs is uncertain, but the uncertainty is of no moment to the poet, for what he is concerned with is the paradox that all but obviates the conflict between them. Every phrase in the poem is bent to the paradoxical end. If the tiger seems at first to be Satan, one must remember the tradition behind Eliot's term "Christ the tiger" and must also observe that the speaker, like the tiger, is watching the man. If "the maimed man" is a likely symbol of Christ, he is also a possible symbol of fallen man and even of the cloven-hoofed devil. If the cat in the bag is the knowledge of evil, it is also a vengeful Christ and man as a newborn kitten about to be drowned (or saved). Once the logistics of paradox is evident, it all makes sense.

It makes too much sense. This is an ingeniously analytical poem whose very extremes of rationality necessitate the irrational setting of dream, whose very coherence destroys its subject, and whose very "logic" crucifies its vision. It ends in the verbal bog ("*cat*apaulting fur," indeed) that it has made. And at a level that is not the "lowest," Lowell, to his credit and advantage, knows this. The bog, the wooly lava of abstractions, and the foundering vehicle might not have been intended as descriptions of this poem; but when one discovers image after image of this sort in *Land of Unlikeness*, and when one recalls the self-consciousness implied by this poetry, he must suppose that the poet sees what he does. Such an insight would be the motivation behind "The Drunken Fisherman," a poem that comes near the end of the volume, in which the speaker first notes that once upon a time "The fisher's fluent and obscene / Catches kept his conscience clean" and then goes on to ask: "Is there no way to cast my hook / Out of this dynamited brook?"

To ask that question was to begin to find the way. When Lowell began to turn from "abstraction" and a quest for "essence" to his own "common experience," especially that of writing, he left the dynamited brook behind him. The capacity for the descendental experience, however, he took with him. Twenty years later, he found himself "long awash, / breaking against the surf, / touching bottom," and therefore finding the means of beginning the ascent.

Lowell's future work is more fully anticipated by another poem in this book. "Death from Cancer," the first poem in the sequence "In Memory of Arthur Winslow" and one which appears with little revision in *Lord Weary's Castle*, distinguishes itself from the more characteristic pieces here in two important ways. In the first place, it is firmly anchored (as are the next two poems in this sequence) in time and space; and in the second place, its structure is a movement, a series of metamorphosed images, rather than a repetition of essentially identical images. Now the relationship between situation and structure in this poem is not fortuitous, for it is in this world that things move and change. To view things *sub specie aeternitas*, to be preoccupied with essence and paradoxical unity, is to ignore the temporal process in the course of which development takes place; and correspondingly, to turn one's attention to this world is to notice painful oppositions (good and evil, life and death) and the processes that emerge from them.

In the beginning of "Death from Cancer," in sharp contrast to "Satan's Confession," Lowell is excruciatingly aware of the opposition between, rather than the unity of, antitheses:

> This Easter, Arthur Winslow, less than dead
> Your people set you up in Phillips House
> To settle off your wrestling with the crab
> Whose claws drop flesh on your serge
>   yatching-blouse [*sic*]. . . .

In being "set . . . up" so on Easter, the poet's grandfather might resemble Christ, but he reminds Lowell chiefly of the losing wrestler in a fixed match; and it is the painfully understated fact that Arthur Winslow is "less than dead" that Lowell stresses, not the possibility of resurrection. In the face of the image of the disease, which becomes a crab by virtue of the zodiacal sign for Cancer as well as by virtue of the pain undergone and the setting near the ocean, such a possibility might not be consoling; at any rate, "The coxes' squeakings dwarf / The *resurrexit Dominus* of all the bells."[17]

The reference to resurrection is amplified in the second and concluding stanza in a grimly ambiguous way:

> the mid-Sunday Irish scare
> The sun-struck shallows for the dusky chub,
> This Easter, and the Ghost
> Of risen Jesus walks the waves to run
> Arthur upon a trumpeting black swan
> Beyond Charles River to the Acheron
> Where the wide waters and their voyager are one.

These lines seem to echo Pound's "Homage to Sextus Propertius, VI," but the difference between the Pound and the Lowell is more instructive than the similarity. Pound's lines are:

> Moving naked over Acheron
> Upon the one raft, victor and conquered together. . . .

Pound puts his two figures, Marius and Jugurtha, together on the raft of death and stresses their bond, but the union is nothing like that accomplished by the metamorphoses in Lowell's lines. In the latter, a shadowy fish turns imperceptibly into the ghost of Jesus, and then that ghost fades into Charon; the Charles flows into the Acheron, and then the Acheron turns into "the wide waters"; and Arthur Winslow, as Lowell's inspired rhymes tell us by themselves, merges with both the ambiguous figure of his guide and the mysterious ocean.

Lowell's method, then, is to transform the actual into the symbolic and then to convert the symbolic into the ineffable. These metamorphoses are possible because in acknowledging the natural world, Lowell implicitly recognizes the distinctions necessitated by rationality; reconciliation and fusion presuppose opposition and discreteness, which are characteristics of this world. In Tate's terms, "nature offers to the symbolic poet [as distinct from the angelic poet] clearly denotable objects . . . which yield the analogies to the higher syntheses." By keeping in touch with the actual, Lowell gives himself the opportunity to develop his images, and the course of this development becomes the structure of the poem. If it is a coincidence that the movement of the river is analogous to that of the poem, it is a suggestive one.

A parallel development can be seen in the theme of life and death: the actual problematic situation (Arthur Winslow's dying) gives rise to the thought of a resolution (resurrection), and then that resolution gives way to a more comprehensive one (embodied in the Christ-Charon figure). The reconciliation that Lowell manages at the end of the poem is not the traditional Christian paradox of life-in-death, but a union of that concept and its antithesis; for Charon is clearly not a prototype of Christ the Savior, but his opposite, the ferryman of the dead. Perhaps Lowell means to condense this new paradox in the phrase "the Ghost / Of risen Jesus." In any event, these last lines, if not necessarily evidence of one early critic's contention that Lowell's images often run away with him, are surely testimony to another's warning that Roman Catholics should be less eager to preconize this spokesman.[18]

From one point of view, Lowell's conclusion might be considered none at all, since its fusion of Christ and Charon seems to amount to agnosticism; in other words, it might seem impossible that the speaker could be any less ignorant of the fate of his grandfather's soul at the end than he was at the beginning. From a different perspective, the conclusion might be regarded as an attempt to express an ineffable union, with the apparent contradiction the result of viewing that expression through the lens of logic. In either case, with the last line Lowell cuts the poem loose from the objective, rational world, and it is swept into "the irrationality of the fluid sea" of ambiguity.[19] In leaving the actual world behind, the poem abandons its means of organization, its channel, and therefore it is suitable that it ends where it does.[20] Indeed, it is almost aesthetically necessary that it end there; and while the last lines cannot prove the validity of Valéry's dictum that "le poème . . . n'a d'autre but que de préparer son dénouement," they certainly justify it. In poems like "Leviathan" and "Satan's Confession," there is no preparation, no development, because those poems exist in the world of multivalence and paradox, where there is no opposition or individuation. In those poems the concern with the medium is correlative with a neglect of this world; in "Death from Cancer," the same concern is redeemed by the recognition of the referential function of the language. "Death from Cancer" thus constitutes a process that takes place between the termini of the actual and the unknowable or the ineffable. Such a process is typical in *Lord Weary's Castle;* and as other writers have noticed, the title of the first poem in that volume—"The Exile's Return"—seems itself to acknowledge the escape from the actual world in this volume.[21]

But perhaps one does not have to look even that far afield to find Lowell commenting on this tendency in his own early work. The first poem in *Land of Unlikeness* is "The Park Street Cemetery," the first words of which place it firmly "In back of the Athenaeum." An even more remarkable thing about this poem is that contrary to repeated claims that all of the lyrics in this volume exhibit an intricate prosodic organization, "The Park Street Cemetery" is unrhymed and unmetered.[22] These hints that Lowell might have intended to revise this poem rather than include it as it is in his first book are perhaps supported by the fact that it was radically reworked, extended, and formalized when it appeared in the next book as "At the Indian Killer's Grave."[23] Now if Lowell did open his first volume with a poem that he all the while knew he would revise, it stands to reason that he did so primarily in order to provide that volume with an appropriate introduction. This speculation might be justified in part by the observation that "The Park Street Cemetery" is followed by "In Memory of Arthur Winslow," which is introduced by the concluding lines of the first poem:

> The graveyard's face is painted with facts
> And filagreed swaths of forget-me-nots.

The second of these lines, at least, might also describe the quality of the imagery in this whole first book, as might these lines earlier in the poem:

> Dusty leaves and the frizzled lilac
> Liven this elder's garden with baroque
> And prodigal embellishments. . . .

Like the recurrent images of bodies of stagnant water (for example, in "The Slough of Despond," "The Drunken Fisherman," "A Suicidal Nightmare") and like Wolf's woodcut emblem, the image of the garden-cemetery virtually acknowledges the static nature of these poems.

If one does not leave the "baroque / And prodigal embellishments" entirely behind in going from the garden to the castle, one does enter a world of consistently vital and organic forms. These forms are incipient in *Land of Unlikeness*—in the relationship among images and symbols in "Death from Cancer," on one level, and in the relationship between that poem and "The Park Street Cemetery," on another—but they are not developed until Lowell's second book.

this way that generates itself, leads itself on, and returns into itself. . . .
—HEGEL, "Preface" to *The Phenomenology of the Spirit*

the lurch
For forms to harness Heraclitus' stream!
—"Concord"

2

A DIALECTICAL SYMBOLISM:

Lord Weary's Castle (1946)

*T*he general development of Lowell's poetry after *Land of Unlikeness* can be adumbrated by a brief comparison of two of the most incisive commentaries on his early work: R. P. Blackmur's review of *Land of Unlikeness* and Randall Jarrell's review of *Lord Weary's Castle*.[1] Because these two critics seem compelled to use much the same vocabulary in discussing Lowell's methods, the discrepancies between their assessments of his achievement are illuminating.

Generally speaking, Blackmur points out certain deficiencies in the work of the young poet that Jarrell thinks do not exist. Blackmur observes that *Land of Unlikeness* displays "not examples of high formal organization achieved, but poems that are deliberately moving in that direction and that have things put in to give the appearance of the movement of form when the movement itself was not secured"; and Jarrell praises *Lord Weary's Castle* for the poems that have an extremely complex and effective "dramatic, dialectical internal organization." Again, the earlier volume seems to its reviewer marked by an antagonism between form and subject and a corresponding indecision whether "the Roman Catholic belief is the form of a force or the sentiment of a form." In the second book, on the other hand, Jarrell perceives an extraordinary congruence of the "outer shell" and

36

the "subject matter" of individual poems and suggests that the poet's particular brand of Catholicism is singularly suited to his literary sensibility.

Elsewhere in his notice, Blackmur suggests the development that explains the gap between these two appraisals. He hits upon a succinct formulation of the difficulty facing the young author of *Land of Unlikeness* when he remarks that unless his point of view is altered, Lowell will have "the special problem of maturing a medium, both of mind and verse, in which vision and logic combine." Perhaps Jarrell has such a medium in mind when he speaks of the "dialectical internal organization" of the poems in *Lord Weary's Castle*. "Dialectical" is apt, in any case, if we simply take that much-abused term to refer loosely to a method that resembles Hegel's in that it comprises the continuous metamorphosis and recombination of its elements, a method that seeks to break down the barriers of ordinary classification and to convert otherwise static entities into processes. Some such method accounts for much of the individuality and power of Lowell's second volume, from the nature of its imagery to its metrical "bumps and grinds."[2] The synaesthetic response, with the impressions of one sense fusing with those of another; the fluid description, in which observed details fade into one another; the Bergsonian view of history, with the past and present related like currents in a river; the shifting point of view, by means of which one speaker dissolves into another—all of these characteristics point to a poet uncommonly concerned with synthesizing his materials, with the dialectical organization of his work.

In fact, the more seriously the term "dialectical" is considered, the more precise its application to Lowell's second book appears, for it can be used, in a strict Hegelian sense, to indicate a speculative process that embodies its content in its structure, a process whose essence is its self-shaping activity; and the central accomplishment of *Lord Weary's Castle* is a mode in which the substance of poetic vision also functions as poetic logic. The "logic" involved here of course has little to do with philosophy, although more than might be thought; instead of a symbolic logic, one might say, it is a

logic of symbols, a dialectical symbolism. This method did
not spring full-blown from the poet's head at the time of the
composition of the new poems in this volume, however; on
the contrary, it was incipient in *Land of Unlikeness,* especially
in the structure of "Death from Cancer"; and beyond that, it
has its origins in one of the most important of recent literary
movements.

This movement can be associated less with the Elizabethan
and Metaphysical poets, who were strong influences upon
the earlier volume, than with a group of Lowell's mentors
and older contemporaries who can trace their own poetic
lineage back to the Renaissance.[3] Perhaps the word *group*
should be qualified, for the men whom it designates here
include Hart Crane and Dylan Thomas, Allen Tate and William Empson, and several others to whom the labels "neo-
symbolist poets" and "New Critics" are often attached.[4]
While Lowell's own theoretical comments are scattered and
scarce, his work, together with the few critical and autobiographical essays and the interviews that he has published,
makes it quite clear that his poetics owes much to these men.
He links Crane with Thomas, whom he considers one of the
greatest modern English poets;[5] he associates Empson,
Thomas, Tate, and Crane when he recollects his early
influences;[6] and he sees a similarity between the works of
Crane and one of his first poetic models, Allen Tate, in spite
of the latter's repudiation of what he considers the premises
of such writers as Crane and Thomas.[7]

It seems not unreasonable to claim, without forgetting the
differences among these writers, that neo-symbolism and
New Criticism share a concern with structural principles inherent in, or particularly adaptable to, literature, principles
comparable to those which underlie reason. Indeed, either in
explicit terms or by implication from a contrast between the
methods of imagination and reason, these writers often posit
a "poetic logic." Hart Crane says of the type of poetry that his
own work exemplifies that "its apparent illogic operates so
logically in conjunction with its context in the poem as to
establish its claim to another logic, quite independent of the
original definition of the word or phrase or image thus
employed."[8] Again, speaking specifically of his own work,

Crane contends that a certain metaphorical statement in "Faustus and Helen" is "pseudo in relation to formal logic" but nevertheless "*is* completely logical in relation to the truth of the imagination."[9] Similarly, Thomas describes his method as a "dialectical" one, contrasting its means of organization with that of the kind of poetry that "moves round one idea, from one logical point to another, making a full circle."[10] Empson, when trying to explain the nature of those "forces" which hold together a poem and relate its "ambiguities," surmises that logic operates on the basis of a parallel set of forces.[11]

The phrases "the logic of poetry" and "poetic logic," however, have attained such currency that there is little reason for reiterating instances of them and all the more reason for clarifying what is meant by them.[12] Clearly, whatever poetic logic might mean, it does not mean a science founded upon the traditional "laws of thought." A great deal of neo-symbolist poetry seems to ignore the law of noncontradiction and to maneuver in that middle ground that is supposed to be excluded as a possibility. In fact, any attempt to define a poetic logic in terms of its necessary and sufficient principles, which is itself a logical mode of definition, might be doomed from the outset; but it is nonetheless possible to infer from the writings of the neo-symbolists and New Critics some general attributes of the mode to which Lowell's work is indebted.

The most fundamental of these attributes is the assumption that verbal symbols imply their own potential development, that in a sense they contain within themselves in embryonic form other verbal symbols. Although this might seem at first a rather strange notion, it can be regarded as a version of a familiar metaphysical tenet applied at the level of aesthetics. As Tate puts it in another connection:

Chekhov said that a gun hanging on the wall at the beginning of a story has got to be fired off before the story ends: everything in potency awaits its completed purpose in act. If this is a metaphysical principle, it is also the prime necessity of the creative imagination.[13]

The existence of the gun implies its being fired; and in a less dramatic fashion, the existence of a word or an image in a

poem entails the development of its potential. This is a variation on the proposition that in art as in nature the whole is
implicit in the part. To some philosophers this proposition
would seem a flagrant case of a "category mistake," but it is
not without analogues in the history of philosophy either as
an axiom or as a method. It is identical, for example, with the
principle behind the subtitle of Nietzsche's *Ecce Homo: How
One Becomes What One Is*. The "prime necessity of the creative
imagination" is also remarkably similar to Leibniz's principle
that every true statement, whether logical or contingent, is
true by virtue of the hypothesis that the "predicate or consequent is always present in the subject or antecedent," even
if this kind of tautology is impossible for men to dem-
onstrate.[14] Perhaps most helpfully, as a means of exposition it is related to Hegel's dialectical self-movement, "this
way that generates itself, leads itself on, and returns into
itself" and that "makes of itself what it is implicitly."[15]
Hegel's statements may call to mind several recent descriptions of poetic composition, of which Dylan Thomas's is one
of the most famous. In the letter to Henry Treece, quoted
earlier, Thomas speaks of the "central seed" or "motivating
centre" of a poem that under application of his "intellectual
and critical forces" breeds a "contradictory image" which, in
conjunction with the first, produces another, and so on.[16]

The assumption that "words bring meaning to birth and
themselves contained the meaning as an imminent possibility
before the pangs of junction" gives rise to the neo-symbolist's
attention to each and every component of a poem, for each
implies another and is in turn implied by it.[17] In short, the
emphasis upon context as an important poetic factor seems to
derive from the idea that verbal symbols represent potential
meanings which can be realized only in other verbal symbols.
I. A. Richards discusses the relationship between these two
premises in "The Interactions of Words":

A word then by this sort of definition is a permanent set of possibilities of understanding, much as John Stuart Mill's table was a
permanent possibility of sensation. . . . It sounds nonsense to say
that a word is its interactions with other words; but that is a short
way of saying the thing which Poetics is most in danger always of
overlooking.[18]

Of course it does not "sound nonsense" at all to readers of Crane, Thomas, or Lowell, and probably only the superlative in the last clause is dubious. Crane has reference to the same idea when he describes an *"inflection* of language" by virtue of which a word or phrase means something "quite independent of the original definition," and Thomas talks of letting his images "interact" so that their meanings can be elicited.[19]

To say that a word is "its interactions with other words" or that a phrase is capable of a radical *"inflection"* according to the context in which it appears is to say that a word or phrase is more of a function than a sign.[20] Words act upon one another, and what they mean is determined by the ways in which they affect and are affected by other words. On this basis Crane can speak of the "dynamics of metaphor" and oppose his language to "logically rigid significations," and Tate can contrast the self-generated pattern of "intension" with the abstracted, logical arrangement of "extension." Consequently, poetic structure must be viewed as "logically circular" to a great extent and to that extent amenable only to paradoxical description.[21]

Now these principles—that a verbal symbol contains and implies its own development, that context serves a maieutic purpose in eliciting that potential, and that as a result a poem is a set of functions or a process rather than a sign—if not overtly subscribed to by Lowell, nevertheless epitomize that part of his poetics that he absorbed from his study of, and work with, the neo-symbolists and the New Critics. They can be called dialectical principles for the reason that they all have to do with converting content into structure. From the "prime necessity of the creative imagination" through the "dynamics of metaphor," they echo Hegel's definition of the method that is his subject: "The true is its own becoming, the circle that presupposes its end as its aim and thus has it for its beginning—that which is actual only through its execution and end."[22] *Lord Weary's Castle* evolves comparable circles time and time again.

Lowell's method cannot be adequately discussed in the abstract, however, precisely because it is part and parcel of a

process, because it is as wound into his lines as the serpent is
into the bowels of time in the opening of "Mother and Son,"
the first poem in the sequence entitled "Between the Porch
and the Altar":

> Meeting his mother makes him lose ten years,
> Or is it twenty? Time, no doubt, has ears
> That listen to the swallowed serpent, wound
> Into its bowels, but he thinks no sound
> Is possible before her, he thinks the past
> Is settled. It is honest to hold fast
> Merely to what one sees with one's own eyes
> When the red velvet curves and haunches rise
> To blot him from the pretty driftwood fire's
> Façade of welcome.

"Between the Porch and the Altar," which Jarrell seems to
have thought one of the four best poems in *Lord Weary's Castle*, has rarely been discussed in much detail.[23] This scarcity of
comment would put the sequence in a class by itself among
the longer poems in the book even if it were not distinguished by any other means. The fact of the matter is that
Jarrell was surely right about its quality; and for this reason,
as well as for the reason that the sequence exemplifies the
characteristic thematic and technical concerns in this volume,
it will be worth dwelling upon.

The lines quoted above convey much that is pertinent, including a basic change in Lowell's modes of perception since
Land of Unlikeness. Poems do, whether out of a sense of pride
or out of a need to confess, comment upon themselves, and
this passage tells us something about the aural and visual
qualities of this stage of Lowell's style. As for the latter, to an
extent hardly prepared for by the first volume, Lowell does
indeed hold fast to the concrete details of the observed things
that now compose his scenes. In sharp contrast to much of
Land of Unlikeness, this poetry is remarkable for its
Dinglichkeit, its homage to what Jarrell calls "the contrary,
persisting, and singular thinginess" of its particulars. As for
aural quality, one notices immediately how much more functional (and therefore natural) the metres are in this book. In

place of the short, self-contained stanzas whose willed intricacies often recalled Traherne and Taylor, *Lord Weary's Castle* frequently offers enjambed couplets and rhymed verse paragraphs the distinctive feature of which is fluidity. In the beginning of "Mother and Son," the caesura consistently interrupts the couplet in such a way that the lines themselves seem to follow a winding course, and the poem seems to uncoil, or to draw out into the open, if not to exorcise, the serpent, the theme of evil that works its way through this entire sequence.

The image of the serpent itself develops from the reference to the mother in the first line, for that surprising adjective "swallowed" reminds us that with the eating of the apple—which the earlier Lowell might have called "wormy" and installed in the poem forthwith—mankind's mother ingested, for all time, the evil that the serpent represents. Eve and the serpent and time itself, that is, are variations of one another. Hence the sinuous movements of the lines on time and the sensuality, summoned as much by the metrical motion as by the color and the quality of the material itself, of the "red velvet curves" that constitute the son's first image of his mother—which is also his first recollection of her, as the following passage suggests:

> Then the son retires
> Into the sack and selfhood of the boy
> Who clawed through fallen houses of his Troy,
> Homely and human only when the flames
> Crackle in recollection. Nothing shames
> Him more than this uncoiling, counterfeit
> Body presented as an idol. It
> Is something in a circus, big as life,
> The painted dragon, a mother and a wife
> With flat glass eyes pushed at him on a stick;
> The human mover crawls to make them click.

The retrogression has begun in the first line of the poem and continued, almost magically, in the lines in which the mother not only rises from her seat but also seems to grow in size even as her son diminishes. Here, as the son relives his childhood impressions of her, she becomes first an "uncoiling" body and then, by association, one of those accordion-like paper dragons that she must once have given her son. In the poem's concluding lines, the mother-serpent-time image undergoes a further metamorphosis:

> The forehead of her father's portrait peels
> With rosy dryness, and the schoolboy kneels
> To ask the benediction of the hand,
> Lifted as though to motion him to stand,
> Dangling its watch-chain on the Holy Book—
> A little golden snake that mouths a hook.

With the image of the watch chain, the poem perfects its movement—for it is the poem, not just the objects and figures in it, that has moved—by linking the generation preceding the mother with the one issuing from her at the same time that it links its opening and closing lines. Associated with the mother's father, whose portrait is scaly, the "little golden snake that mouths a hook" also clearly mirrors the son, who is about to be raised by the hand that has been extended in profane "benediction." The watch chain provides a consummate conclusion, for in addition to condensing the relationship among time, bondage, and evil, it sets forth in small both a catenation of guilty figures (grandfather-mother-son) and a closed circle of sin.[24] Although not literally represented, the image of Uroboros is inevitably conjured, not simply because of the presence of the snake, but also because the poem has its tail in its mouth. Retrospect shows us that the end (the "little golden snake") is there in the beginning (the "swallowed serpent"), and the shape of the poem acts upon the image of the snake as the organization of the opening lines acts upon that of the serpent. What the poem does, and does masterfully, in terms of both theme and technique, is to draw the end out of the beginning, or, alternatively, literally (which is to say figuratively, by means of figure) to turn the inside out. The snake in the grass at the beginning of the story, to modify Tate's maxim, must out at the end.

As we shall see later, this relationship between beginning and end characterizes this volume as a whole. The point to be made now is that the dialectical structure of "Mother and Son"—"this way that generates itself, leads itself on, and returns into itself," this circular process that "presupposes its end as its aim and thus has it for its beginning"—is not a peculiar one when it comes to the individual poems in *Lord Weary's Castle*, as an examination of the rest of "Between the Porch and the Altar" will suggest and a glance at some other poems will confirm.

When one stands back and surveys this sequence in its entirety, one of the first things that one notices about it is its symmetry. The four poems are of approximately the same length (they range from twenty-six to thirty-four lines); each is in pentameter couplets; each focuses on a relationship between a male and a female figure; and each concludes with an image suggestive of damnation. A fearful symmetry, perhaps one should say, since the nature and sequence of the relationships suggests rather strongly that Lowell might have had in mind the organization of "The Mental Traveller." Northrop Frye gives this concise paraphrase of Blake's poem in his *Anatomy of Criticism*:

In . . . *The Mental Traveller* we have a vision of the cycle of human life, from birth to death to rebirth. The two characters of the poem are a male and a female figure, moving in opposite directions, one growing old as the other grows young, and vice versa. The cyclical relation between them runs through four cardinal points: a son-mother phase, a husband-wife phase, a father-daughter phase, and a fourth phase of what Blake calls spectre and emanation, terms corresponding roughly to Shelley's alastor and epipsyche. None of these phases is quite true: the mother is only a nurse, the wife merely "bound down" for the male's delight, the daughter a changeling, and the emanation does not "emanate" but remains elusive. The male figure represents humanity. . . . The female figure represents the natural environment which man partially but never wholly subdues.[25]

Mutatis mutandis—"wife" would have to be changed to "mistress" and allowance would have to be made for the difference between Blake's eccentric and Lowell's more conventionally religious frames of reference—this paragraph could gloss the structure of Lowell's sequence.

There are of course some fundamental dissimilarities between the two poems which to minimize would be perverse. For one, Blake's is an allegory, whereas Lowell's is a series of quasi-dramatic, symbolic monologues. More important, Lowell's sequence is structured not only according to male-female relationships, but also according to the four major events, from the orthodox Christian point of view, that take place in human history. The poems treat in order, but with various degrees of emphasis and candor, a Creation, a Fall, a Crucifixion, and a Resurrection and Judgment. Thus, in "Mother and Son," while we are undeniably concerned with evil, which we might expect to be (as it is) the focus of the second poem, we are also concerned, as the title leads us to believe, with birth. The key lines in this respect are those which follow the first hints of a mental retrogression:

> Then the son retires
> Into the sack and selfhood of the boy
> Who clawed through fallen houses of his Troy,
> Homely and human only when the flames
> Crackle in recollection.

The question that one asks of these lines is what to make of the phrase "the sack and selfhood." Unless one wants to see in "selfhood" simply an appropriation of Blake's term for the original sin of egocentrism and in "sack" merely the influence of "Troy," the most likely explanation is that the phrase is a fleeting and punning reference to the prenatal stage, followed immediately by a symbolic description of birth and its consequences, entrance into necessarily "fallen houses."[26] It is certainly not the only time in this volume that Lowell equates the destruction of Troy with the end of innocence;[27] and in view of the relationship between life and sin in this poem (the "painted dragon" is exactly as "big as life"), innocence would seem to be lost with the amnion. The following lines, then, discover the first evidence of original sin—the Oedipal relationship between son and mother that "shames" the child—and the concluding lines, following his growth from the crawling to the schoolboy stage, parody an initiation, as he is confirmed in his evil ways by the "father," whose rubicund and peeling face does not inspire a great deal of trust. In the course of the poem, the son loses *first* ten and *then* twenty years and then returns, at its exact center, to his very origin, therewith to be "reborn" and to grow up into a schoolboy.

In "The Mental Traveller," too, the first phase is one of torment for the child, as the mother "nails him down upon a rock, / Catches his shrieks in cups of gold," "binds iron thorns around his head," and "grows young as he grows old." In the second phase, the relationship is inverted, as the female becomes first "a virgin bright" who is bound down for the delight of the male and then "his dwelling place / And Garden fruitful seventy fold." In the second poem in Lowell's sequence, "Adam and Eve," the grown and married son is the speaker, and he says to his mistress: "I quarreled with you, but am happy now." The happiness, however, is qualified not only by the circumstances surrounding the illicit relationship but also by the speaker's view of the human condition. He bitterly maintains that "Never to have lived is best" and goes on to point out that sex is but salt in the original wound:

> Man tasted Eve with death. I taste my wife
> And children while I hold your hands. I knife
> Their names into this elm. What is exempt?

The Garden is there, but it is hardly Blakean, let alone Edenic. Because the Fall has occurred and is bound to recur—not because this relationship is illicit but rather because (as the implied metamorphosis of mother into lover indicates) sexual longing is itself the sign of sin—the Garden is spoiled.

"Adam and Eve" opens with an ironic New England version of Michael, the guardian of the gate to Eden, whose last avatar must have been Falstaff and whose flaming sword has been beaten back into a ploughshare:

> The Farmer sizzles on his shaft all day.
> He is content and centuries away
> From white-hot Concord, and he stands on guard.
> Or is he melting down like sculptured lard?
> His hand is crisp and steady on the plough.

48 A DIALECTICAL SYMBOLISM

Corresponding to the fireplace-Troy complex in the first
poem, "white-hot Concord" is this poem's hell on earth,
which is to say anywhere on earth after the Fall. When the
speaker, thinking of sin and its wages, asks "What is
exempt?" the question is transparently rhetorical. First colonial America and then the Roman Catholic Church seem to
stand for what is exempt; but the rectitude of the Farmer will
shortly be seen to be phallic only, while the righteousness of
the church is but a façade that is itself "puritanical":

> I eye the statue with an awed contempt
> And see the puritanical façade
> Of the white church that Irish exiles made
> For Patrick—that Colonial from Rome
> Had magicked the charmed serpents from their home,
> As though he were the Piper. Will his breath
> Scorch the red dragon of my nerves to death?

Again the question is rhetorical. Blake writes of his young
lovers: "He plants himself in all her Nerves, / Just as a Hus-
bandman his mould; / And she becomes his dwelling
place. . . ." In "Adam and Eve," it is the "swallowed serpent" who has planted himself in the speaker's nerves, and
no combination of St. Patrick, St. George, and the Pied Piper
will charm him out. On the contrary, for Patrick (and, by
extension, Rome) seems able only to fight fire with fire,
which in this case is to feed the flames.

The son is still clawing his way through "fallen houses of
his Troy," and the "red dragon" of his nerves is but a
foretaste of the flames already consuming his ancestors. The
last lines of the poem take us back, by way of Milton, to the
first of those ancestors and then, like "Mother and Son," to
its own first lines:

> You cry for help. Your market-basket rolls
> With all its baking apples in the lake.
> You watch the whorish slither of a snake
> That chokes a duckling. When we try to kiss,
> Our eyes are slits and cringing, and we hiss;
> Scales glitter on our bodies as we fall.
> The Farmer melts upon his pedestal.[28]

The structure of "Adam and Eve" can be described either in terms of circularity or in terms of declivity, and in either case the critic finds himself describing as well the poem's view of the human condition. Lowell is expert at exploiting the inevitable movement of his lines *down* the page, and here he lets that movement (which culminates in the dropping of the basket, the sinking of the lovers to ground, and the melting of the Farmer) coincide with what is in effect the tearing down of the "puritanical façade" of St. Patrick's and the lovers' equally inevitable fall. Because the poem provides an analogue to the original sin, to point out the circular structure implied by the repetition of certain images (the "charmed serpents" and "red dragon" in the metamorphosis of the lovers, the heat of Concord in the "baking apples," the sizzling Farmer in the melting one) is also to verge on explication of content. Perhaps the two points of view can be accommodated by another, more abstract description: Lowell's images develop (or seem to develop, if one wants to think of himself as looking over the poet's shoulder) from one another in a manner analogous to that in which the contemporary predicament derives from and repeats the original lapse.

Whether this relationship is more than glibly analogical, whether some such terms as these might usefully amplify Jarrell's observation that Lowell's "rather odd and imaginative Catholicism is thoroughly suited to his mind . . . [and] to literature," can only be decided after more poems have been looked at in this light. Neither this light nor any other, of course, can make all of these poems appear circular and declivitous in structure; but then the proposition is not that the poems can be diagrammed in the same way but rather that there is an intimate relationship between Lowell's means of organizing a poem and his means of organizing reality. As it happens, however, neither "Katherine's Dream" nor "At the Altar," the last two poems in this sequence, will dissuade the zealous critic from employing compass and protractor.

Often singled out, and rightly so, for its candor and comparative simplicity, "Katherine's Dream" is nonetheless an intricate poem, especially if one has its predecessors in mind when reading it. Indeed, one important reason that "Katherine's Dream" is such a fine slice of life is that it is veined with motifs from the rest of the sequence. It is not that its opening lines, for example, are really less dense than anything in the other two poems, but rather that much of their work has already been done.

> It must have been a Friday. I could hear
> The top-floor typist's thunder and the beer
> That you had brought in cases hurt my head;
> I'd sent the pillows flying from my bed,
> I hugged my knees together and I gasped.
> The dangling telephone receiver rasped
> Like someone in a dream who cannot stop
> For breath or logic till his victim drop
> To darkness and the sheets.

In view of the fall that concludes "Adam and Eve," Lowell needs to do no more than refer to Katherine's physical position. More subtly, the symbolization of the watch chain that was "Dangling" from the hand of the grandfather in "Mother and Son" interprets in advance the "dangling telephone receiver" (just as the two together help to prepare us for the Miltonic overtones of a sentence in "At the Altar": "I turn and whisper in her ear"). In a slightly different way—for the connection is thematic rather than verbal—the first two poems permit the opening sentence in this one to be at once its most conversational and most symbolic. "It *must* have been a Friday" because, in the wake of the Creation and the Fall, the Crucifixion must occur. It is a matter no less of Lowell's poetic logic than of his theology.

The realization that it is Good Friday might or might not lend additional significance to the "top-floor typist's thunder" and the pain in Katherine's head; it will help us put the end of the poem in perspective, as will the memory of Blake's poem. In her dream, which constitutes exactly the last half of the poem, Katherine finds herself in the courtyard of St. Patrick's watching the penitents enter and leave "by twos" a building that is less the Ark than a speakeasy ("One / Must have a friend to enter there"); and although she is at first warmed "with love for others," she soon feels bereft. The dream and the poem conclude:

> I begin
> To cry and ask God's pardon of our sin.
> Where are you? You were with me and are gone.
> All the forgiven couples hurry on
> To dinner and their nights and none will stop.
> I run about in circles till I drop
> Against a padlocked bulkhead in a yard
> Where faces redden and the snow is hard.

In the dual light of Blake's third phase and the Crucifixion, the "you" of this passage discloses its importance. The third phase of Blake's poem ends with the changeling daughter's discovery of "the Man she loves" and the consequent exile of her stepfather, "the aged Host," who becomes "A beggar at another's door." While Katherine seems at first to be the beggar here, and rather reminiscent of Henry at Canossa, she certainly feels that she has banished her heavenly Father at the same time that she has been, as an earlier passage informs us, a "dishonor" to her earthly father. The juxtaposition of her supplication for "God's pardon" and her feeling of having been forsaken can hardly allay the suspicion thus aroused that the "you" is not only her lover. It is an "odd and imaginative Catholicism" indeed that can not only make of this girl a version of Christ but also leave her, abandoned by her God, her father, and her lover (the son of the first poem's mother), in such a region, for those "circles" and reddened faces (among which one expects to find that in the portrait) are unmistakably infernal. The effect is the more horrifying for the dream's being recounted in the narrative present tense.

Nor is the horror alleviated by the device of the dream-vision. On the contrary, one would think, for at least two reasons. In the first place, if it is a dream, it is a dream from which Katherine does not awake in the course of the poem—a terrible response, as it were, to the child's prayer "Now I lay me down to sleep." In the second place, if we imagine Katherine waking from the dream, we must imagine her as we find her at the beginning of the poem: alone and tormented physically and spiritually. The "circles" that Katherine runs about in are those of real and dreamed guilt and anguish. To put this another way: it is not easy to decide, once the question has been raised, which half of the poem constitutes the dream. It is in the first part of the poem that the telephone receiver is said to sound "Like someone in a dream"; and one sentence (ll. 9–15) could be a transition either to or from a nightmare. It is not necessary to argue that dream and reality are devised to be susceptible to transposition, however, to realize that the speaker is in the same position at the beginning of the poem that she is in at the conclusion, both of which ends evoke images of crucifixion and the tortures of the damned.

It will not be surprising that "At the Altar" follows the same general and ultimately circular pattern. Again there is a discernible narrative, but far from being the main integrating agent in the poem, the plot is almost obscured by the real unifying forces. Here we find the male speaker of "Adam and Eve" stepping out on his wife on the night before Easter, taking his mistress to what seems to be a nightclub in which a Norwegian girl performs a ballet on ice. The persona, like many of Lowell's speakers in this stage of his career, gets drunk; and following the performance there is a wild, careening drive through the city which ends, midway in the poem, as the car with its two occupants crashes into a church. The last half of the poem is epiphanic, as the speaker either deliriously envisions, or in fact goes through, his death, last rites, and judgment. Overlying this narrative, like the strings of Christmas decorations evoked by the imagery, there is a network of glowing symbols, or a series of symbols so closely related that they give the impression of having developed from one another. Thus the opening lines, in which the speaker's mistress's eyes "burn with brandy," contain implicitly the drunken vision of the "whirl / Of Easter eggs . . . colored by the lights," the flash of the skater's costume which gleams "Like Northern Lights," the "seven red-lights" (representing the deadly sins) that the car races through, the "lightning" that strikes in the vision of the Day of Judgment,

and the image of the Judgment itself in the poem's concluding lines:

> Here the Lord
> Is Lucifer in harness: hand on sword,
> He watches me for Mother, and will turn
> The bier and baby-carriage where I burn.

Just as this poem's analogue to Katherine's nightmare is its
apocalyptic vision, so its analogue to her running about in
circles is the turning of the speaker upon a spit; and just as
the "little golden snake" returns us to the "swallowed serpent," so the description of the speaker's punishment returns
us to the image of his mistress, "Whose eyelids burn with
brandy" (as though in parody of Blake's last female figure's
features, "The bread and wine of her sweet smile, / The wild
game of her roaming eye"). Finally, just as the "girl" of the
first line becomes the "Mother" of the penultimate, so the
latter becomes the "mother" of the opening of "Mother and
Son." "The Mental Traveller" also ends with allusions to its
opening stanzas that bring the poem full circle, as again
" 'The Babe is born!' " and again:

> none can touch that frowning form
> Except it be a Woman Old;
> She nails him down upon the Rock,
> And all is done as I have told.

In the case of a set of poems that is so fundamentally a
process, a matter of electrical current running through a
labyrinth of coils, summary treatment would have seemed a
factitious impertinence earlier in this essay. Some sorting and
generalizing, however, seems advisable at this point.

A bird's-eye view of the structures that constitute the sequence reveals an architect extraordinarily interested in, or
unable to evade, the circular form. Not only does the series as
a whole have such a shape, but so does each of the poems, and
so do many of the images, either by virtue of their literal
descriptions (the spit turning, Katherine's running) or by virtue of their semantic constructions (the speaker in II would
set a dragon, St. Patrick, to catch a dragon, sin). A closer view

of these images discovers a relationship such that its members seem to grow out of one another, as the poems themselves seem to emerge from one another, and as indeed (according to the theology espoused by them) the events that they reflect are born of one another.

Partly because of a context so highly charged with metaphor and partly because of overt comparison, the various figures in the sequence become virtually interchangeable. On the other hand, from the male figure's point of view his mother and wife are indistinguishable ("The painted dragon, a mother and a wife" in I; "Man tasted Eve with death; I taste my wife" in II; "I want to leave my mother and my wife" in IV), while it is soon clear to the reader that the mistress is but a surrogate mother-wife (she is the serpent in II that the mother is in I, for example). On the other hand, the man and his mistress's father tend to merge (the latter is also getting a divorce, and he keeps the "guilty presents" of the former), as do the "son" and his maternal grandfather. As the dialectic would seem to dictate, the male and female figures also converge: the grandfather of I lives on in his daughter; and the two lovers are both turned to serpents in II, both punished by parents of the opposite sex, and both victims of the wreck in IV. These diverse identifications come to their climax in the last lines of the sequence, where "Mother" and God are as inextricable as the Lord and Lucifer.

At this juncture, if that term can be meaningful in this context of confluences, the dialectical poet in Lowell is clearly at odds with the Catholic convert. "Two angels fought with billhooks for his soul," Lowell writes in "The Soldier," a poem based on Dante's meeting with Buonconte da Montefeltro in the *Purgatorio*, but he could be speaking of himself. Having availed himself of Catholic symbolism to provide his sequence with a means of organizing itself, to give his particulars a significance beyond themselves, and to measure evil against good, Lowell exploits it to such an extent that the poems are processes of internal transactions, the details melt into one another, and his good and evil wear each other's aspects. The fused figures—and from one point of view the circular structures as well—are products of a dialectical mill for which all subject matter is grist. Even more obviously than in "Death from Cancer," where the relationship between Christ and Charon was established indirectly and less insistently, the method threatens to swallow up the doctrine that, inasmuch as it afforded the terms, facilitated it. A foreshadowing of that threat is implicit in the title of the sequence, which derives from Joel 2:17, where the prophet declares: "Let the priests, the ministers of the Lord, weep between the porch and the altar, and let them say, Spare thy people, O Lord, and give not thine heritage to reproach, that the heathen should rule over them; wherefore should they say among the people, Where is their God?"[29] By viewing every one of the four major events in the lurid light of damnation, by giving his figures no choice but to persist in their evil ways, and above all by turning the baby-sitter into Lucifer, Lowell implies that God's heritage has indeed been given to reproach and that therefore the question "Where is their God?" which a politic Joel attributes to the heathen, is not impertinent.

Instead of expounding or justifying dogma, "Between the Porch and the Altar" struggles, however heretically, to define it. For Hegel, the true is an activity continuously defining itself by bringing itself into being, both in the form of his system of thought and in the form of the evolution of the world. Something analogous happens in this sequence, which is less a proponent than an instrument of knowledge and which finds it difficult to abide such static entities or "rigid significations" as "the Lord" and "Lucifer." Unlike such poems as "Satan's Confession" and "Leviathan," which seized upon and gloried in paradoxes and consequently had little capacity for development, these poems, grounded in reality and the recognition of apparent oppositions that stand in need of reconciliation, constitute a heuristic process. It is a process, moreover, that is so energetic that it is terminable only when Lowell can bring together momentarily its farthest origins and ends; and consequently the resolution reached can only be tentative and temporary—as indeed the reader's sense of the form of the whole must be. To impose a strict structure upon such a poem would be to refuse to recognize

exactly half of its achievement, the whole of which consists in
the reconciliation of what Lowell has referred to as "the flux
of experience" (temporal existence with all of its currents and
crosscurrents and motion) with the form that experience
yearns for.[30] The sequence, in other words, might be viewed
as a response to the dilemma defined by A. R. Ammons in
"Summer Session": "The problem is / how / to keep shape
and flow." In turning us back to its beginning in its last lines,
it establishes not only the relationship of past to present—
thus creating, as in Blake's poem, the shape of temporal experience (both historical and biographical in Lowell's case) as
well as its own shape—but also the continuation of the
struggle to define that relationship, not only the cyclical form
but also the process of discovering it. A veritable Katherine
wheel, the sequence keeps the reader, as well as its heroine,
who recalls St. Catherine of Alexandria herself, going in circles.

It keeps him, that is—and this is so whether one emphasizes
the process or the cycle—in the temporal world. It is significant
that the infernal fires of its conclusion are sanctioned by the
mother of its beginning and are virtually inseparable from the
"flames" that "crackle in recollection." Even the eternal
appears here in the guise of the temporal; or to put that the
other way around, the temporal is preserved, sublated, in the
image of the eternal. Like "Death from Cancer" ("Mother" is
to the Lord-Lucifer figure as the implicit swanboat operator is
to the Christ-Charon figure), the new poems in this volume
are rooted in the actual world; and it is because they are so
rooted that they can develop as they do, that they can "yield
their analogies to higher syntheses." In the review of Dylan
Thomas's poetry quoted earlier, Lowell notes that Thomas
"usually develops his action by means of Freudian or Christian symbols" and that "icons and objects are often hard to
tell apart" in his work.[31] The remarks are relevant to "Between the Porch and the Altar," not only because of the combination of Freudian and Christian perspectives especially
noticeable in the first and third poems, but also because of the
means by which the poems develop their actions. Even more
effectively than Thomas, whom Lowell perceptively criticized

for not paying enough attention to the actual aspect of his phenomena, Lowell plots his poems by turning objects into icons, by converting his characters into archetypes. Common experience is the sine qua non of the kind of movement referred to here as dialectical because by delimiting the nature of its elements, it permits them to possess and eventually to disclose their potentials, to be inflected, to discover their ends.

"At the Indian Killer's Grave," the poem that grew out of "The Park Street Cemetery" and the coda of "Cistercians in Germany," testifies to the importance of the actual world to Lowell's new structures. One of the longer poems in this volume, it is built mainly of two "plot lines," or of two images, also the central elements in the setting, which unfold their meanings in the course of the poem. The first of these mentioned is King's Chapel in Boston, behind which there is a cemetery, dating from colonial days, where the meditation that constitutes the poem takes place. Even before the poem per se has begun, with an epigraph from Hawthorne's "Gray Champion" that informs us that the colonialists buried here were the murderers of Indian natives, including King Philip, the famous sachem of the Wampanoag tribe, the chapel starts to enlarge its meaning. It is as though the chapel were named for the Indian chief, and the opening lines insist, however circuitously, upon the connection:

> Behind King's Chapel what the earth has kept
> Whole from the jerking noose of time extends
> Its dark enigma to Jehoshaphat;
> Or will King Philip plait
> The just man's scalp in the wailing valley!

At the same time that these lines connect the Indian king with the chapel, they associate him with King Jehoshaphat, the greatest leader of Israel after Solomon; further, because of the juxtaposition with the epigraph, they link the cemetery with the Valley of Jehoshaphat, the site of the Last Judgment, which Joel seems to have named for the King of Israel. King's Chapel is to King Philip, one deduces, as the Valley of Jehoshaphat is to Israel's monarch.[32]

The implications of the analogy are not clear, however,

until other changes have been rung upon it, as they are with the allusions to Charles II, the restored British King, and to John the Baptist, to whose execution King Philip's is implicitly likened, and even to "John and Mary Winslow," two of the poet's ancestors. In the last lines of the poem, the opening analogy and the subsequent allusions suddenly come into focus:

> John, Matthew, Luke and Mark,
> Gospel me to the Garden, let me come
> Where Mary twists the warlock with her flowers—
> Her soul a bridal chamber fresh with flowers
> And her whole body an ecstatic womb,
> As through the trellis peers the sudden Bridegroom.

Compressing suggestions of rebirth, spiritual marriage, and Armageddon, this passage is the culmination and explication of the preceding references. King Philip, executed like Charles I, John the Baptist, and Jesus, is to be restored, like Charles II and like all of "the just," with the restoration at the end of time of Heaven's King, whom all mortal monarchs only attempt to rival or, like Jehoshaphat and Philip, prefigure. Thus the poem moves from the actual to the imminent, from King Philip to Christ, from King's Chapel and the cemetery to the Valley of Judgment and the Garden, the latter being developments or higher syntheses of the terms at the level of the former, just as the Lord-Lucifer figure evolves from the mother and grandfather figures in "Between the Porch and the Altar."

The movement is not, of course, quite as progressively synthetic as this brief analysis makes it appear. In fact, all of the levels exist simultaneously once one understands that the figures imply one another, so it is not disruptive for the anticipatory figure most grounded in the actual world to appear in the penultimate section, where, behind King's Chapel, "A public servant putters with a knife / And paints the railing red / Forever." If the workman is more immediately a product of common experience than King Philip is, he is still an intermediary figure between the latter and the returning Lord of Hosts, the taker of scalps, in the last section. What is impor-

tant is that the anchoring of the poem in the actual world
gives Lowell a vertical range, an opportunity to move up and
down a scale, or rather to strike a chord; the overarching
horizontal development of the poem, the way it unfolds in
time between the concrete present and the symbolic future,
simply schematizes or turns to particular structural use the
general capacity.

The second plot line in "At the Indian Killer's Grave" develops, in a manner which might owe something to the third
section of Eliot's "Burnt Norton," from the poem's second
sentence:

> Friends,
> Blacker than these black stones the subway bends
> About the dirty elm roots and the well
> For the unchristened infants in the waste
> Of the great garden rotten to its root. . . .

In the third section, the image takes on more definitely symbolic features and then becomes a full-fledged symbol:

> A green train grinds along its buried tracks
> And screeches. When the great mutation racks
> The Pilgrim Fathers' relics, will these placques
> Harness the spare-ribbed persons of the dead
> To battle with the dragon?

The metamorphoses of the "subway" into the "green train"
and of the latter into the "dragon" outline particularly neatly
the steps by which Lowell's objects become icons. The latest
form of the image is augmented in the fourth section:

> When you go down this man-hole to the drains,
> The doorman barricades you in and out;
> You wait upon his pleasure.

As the public servant is to Christ, so the gatekeeper is to
Cerberus. The underground image is then given one last,
surprisingly significant twist in the first lines of the final stanza:

> I ponder on the railing at this park:
> Who was the man who sowed the dragon's teeth,

That fabulous or fancied patriarch
Who sowed so ill for his descent, beneath
King's Chapel in this underworld and dark?

One imagines first that the patriarch was Cadmus, who, having slain a dragon descended from Ares, at the advice of
Athene sowed the dragon's teeth only to harvest a legion of
armed soldiers, most of whom he then had to dispatch by
setting them fighting among themselves, and who was, along
with his wife Harmonia, eventually turned into a serpent.
Because he is not named here, however, he merges with the
Christian patriarch, Adam, whose descendants—King Philip
and the Pilgrim Fathers among them—have always fought
among themselves. Indeed, murder is the very hallmark of
man, the pun on "descent" suggests: to be of Adam's lineage
is to be damned. For the reason set forth by the pun, the
subway of the previous passages becomes in these lines "this
underworld and dark," and with the demonstrative the main
function of the cemetery setting appears. Having transformed the underground into hell, Lowell fuses hell with this
world, thereby giving spiritual death substance and damnation immanence.

   Whether one wants to call such a synthesis a higher one is
dubious; but that the synthesizing process structures the
poem is obvious. At the same time that the poem turns King's
Chapel into the Valley of Judgment, it turns "the great garden rotten to its root" into "this underworld." Lowell declines the overt synthesis that would correspond to that in the
last lines of "At the Altar," although with the image of Christ
as Warrior and with the question of identity in the last stanza,
he is on the verge of it. The circle is not so obviously inclusive
here, but it is nonetheless clearly limned. The temporal world
at the beginning of the poem is the underworld at the end,
which is also to say that the world of the patriarch is the
world of the Pilgrim Fathers and the world of today. "Nothing underneath the sun / Has bettered," as Lowell phrases
it in "The Death of the Sheriff"; and by returning into itself at
the end, this poem ties in its own way the "noose of time."

   The actual world affords Lowell his means of organization,

then; but it is also fraught with special dangers, one of which is that its particulars *are* potentially so volatile. When Jarrell says that "the things in Mr. Lowell's poems have, necessarily, been wrenched into formal shape, organized under terrific pressure," he does not quite say what is sometimes the case, and what is the expense of Lowell's new power, that the iconic objects are distorted beyond reason or recognition.[33] Besides lending themselves to distortion, the things that Lowell wants to work with are often parts of wildly diverse settings, and so he must often have recourse to such dreams and drunken visions as will quickly transport his speakers. But perhaps the greatest peril to be encountered by the neo-symbolist poet in the actual world is that world's very abundance. The chief danger entailed by Lowell's method is simply that the poetry might acquire a homogeneous texture, that the very unity of a poem might preclude a structure. If every object is a potential icon, and if the primary means of developing action is through symbolic connections, then the logical end is a poetry in which each detail develops the action and all details are of equal weight.

This is the end for which Lowell seems to be striving in one of the more famous poems in this volume, "The Quaker Graveyard in Nantucket." The dynamism and rhetorical power of this poem are undeniable, but there is something that is dragging at even the most energetic passages and dulls the edges of the finest rhetoric, and that is the poet's desire to élicit from each observation its full potential regardless of consequences. Frequently, the result does not seem to justify the effort, as in the first section, when the image of the ocean leads to the thought that "the heel-headed dogfish barks its nose / On Ahab's void and forehead." If Ahab is a symbol of evil, then the "dogfish" is legitimately "heel-headed" not only because of the shape of its head but also because it prefigures Christ, who is to bruise his heel on the head of the serpent of evil. On the other hand, Ahab seems to represent man's past, not Satan, so that the religious allusion seems incongruous. Moreover, the main justification for the verb "barks" seems to be that the subject is "dogfish." If it is objected that Lowell meant "heel-headed" only as a literal

description and "barks" only in the sense of "abrades," it
must be remembered that a poet whose ambiguities are of
such importance to his work has to be responsible for those
puns that he does not make—or at least for the most obvious
ones. In the wordplay in the lines that open the third section—

> All you recovered from Poseidon died
> With you, my cousin, and the harrowed brine
> Is fruitless on the blue beard of the god

—the lament that Warren Winslow's achievements died with
him is undercut by the whimsical allusion to the homicidal
chevalier. This baroque treatment of detail is common in
"The Quaker Graveyard," and sometimes one wishes that
Lowell had not developed his action so scrupulously.

"The Quaker Graveyard" has been the subject of a number
of structural analyses and there is no need to discuss it at
length here, but it is important to notice that the general
movement of this poem has something in common with
those of "At the Indian Killer's Grave" and "Between the
Porch and the Altar."[34] In Richard J. Fein's terms, the last
lines "return us not only to the first lines of the poem, which
describe the drowning of a sailor, but also to the opening of
Genesis. The poem strives to unite the past and the present,
the beginning and the end, the origins of sorrow and its
present forms."[35] Fein is quite right to point out the circle that
the poem makes. What, for his purposes, he does not need to
say is that the very last line—"The Lord survives the rainbow
of His will"—does not contribute to, but rather transcends
and therefore sets off, that circular structure. A complete sentence, this line stands aloof from the temporal process (the
cycle of "rot and renewal" as Lowell will call it in *For the
Union Dead*) that is the main subject of the poem and from the
process that *is* the poem. It is to the seventh section, in other
words, what "Our Lady of Walsingham," the sixth section, is
to the poem as a whole and what its last lines are to "At the
Indian Killer's Grave": a moment of terrible stillness that
points to a realm outside the temporal cycle reflected in the
structure.

The apprehension of such a realm, however, is less common in this volume than the surprisingly frequent relationship between circular structure and cyclical existence. Blake's "same dull round" appears everywhere after these lines in the first poem, "The Exile's Return," the very title of which suggests a circular movement:

> Fall
> And winter, spring and summer, guns unlimber
> And lumber down the narrow gabled street
> Past your gray, sorry and ancestral house. . . .

"Christmas in Black Rock," the fourth poem, is framed by the following passages:

> Christ God's red shadow hangs upon the wall
> The dead leaf's echo on these hours
> Whose burden spindles to no breath at all. . . .
>
> . . . .
>
> O Christ, the spiralling years
> Slither with child and manger to a ball
> Of ice; and what is man? We tear our rags
> To hang the Furies by their itching ears,
> And the green needles nail us to the wall.

The ball of ice is this poem's analogue to Katherine's circles or to the "noose of time," the image that condenses the shape of the poem, which is in its turn the embodiment of a cyclical existence, in which new life is but a prelude to more death. Set on Christmas, this poem begins and ends with an image of crucifixion, and the evergreens here promise not life but death.

In "New Year's Day," the fifth poem in the volume, the title of which is also ironic, the initial image is again one of birth in terms of death: "Again and then again . . . the year is born / To ice and death. . . ." Throughout the poem, Lowell uses the device of simple repetition, employed in the opening phrase, to accentuate his theme: "While we live, we live / To snuff the smoke of victims"; "the church whose double locks / Wait for St. Peter, the distorted key. / Under St. Peter's

bell. . . ." The device is so integral to the poem that it functions even when it is not quite there, in the reference to man as
the beast of a special burden in the last lines of the poem:

> Joseph plucks his hand-lines like a harp,
> And hears the fearful *Puer natus est*
> Of Circumcision, and relives the wrack
> And howls of Jesus whom he holds. How sharp
> The burden of the Law before the beast:
> Time and the grindstone and the knife of God.
> The Child is born in blood, O child of blood.

In this marvelously succinct conclusion, the turning
grindstone epitomizes the temporal world, its apparently
futile cycle of birth and death and its pain. Time is the
grindstone upon which the knife of God is whetted; and the
ritual of circumcision, a symbol of the pain, exacted by God,
that accompanies even the beginning of life. All of the previous repetitions foreshadow the last line, which not only unites
the pain of the world with that suffered by Christ, but
also sets forth the reason for both: as Christ had to suffer for
man, so man must suffer for causing Christ's pain. Much of
the poignancy of the poem derives from the difference between the first, capitalized figure and the second, lowercased
figure. It is almost suggested that the one is the Law, whereas
the other is the mere beast that carries the "burden" (both the
weight and the continual reminder of the weight, the refrain)
of the Law. The last line, again a complete sentence that bares
the radical difference between man and God, might be seen
as a transition between the last line of "Christmas in Black
Rock" and that of "The Quaker Graveyard," which is the
sixth poem.

Again and again Lowell varies the basic form-content pattern. "Christmas Eve Under Hooker's Statue," like "Christmas in Black Rock," opens with an image of the hanged man:

> Tonight a blackout. Twenty years ago
> I hung my stocking on the tree, and hell's
> Serpent entwined the apple in the toe
> To sting the child with knowledge. Hooker's heels
> Kicking at nothing in the shifting snow. . . .

It is a condensation of the opening of "Mother and Son," with its sudden loss of "Twenty years" and its association of the serpent with childhood. Even as the child's first stocking was hung, he was hanged, or so the juxtaposition of the present "blackout" and the seemingly executed general intimates. At its conclusion, the poem resurrects this complex of imagery:

> When Chancellorsville mowed down the volunteer,
> "All wars are boyish," Herman Melville said;
> But we are old, our fields are running wild:
> Till Christ again turn wanderer and child.

"Never to have lived is best," for to be born is to be stung with knowledge, to be stunted inevitably in one's growth, to remain one of the "children" responsible for war and evil. One's end is in his origin, as the poem tells us partly by returning at its conclusion to its beginning. Paradoxically, the last line stands apart, isolated by the colon and by the very repetition in its last word of the term used for the speaker as a boy. Superficial identity is as effective as capitalization in indicating the essential distinction.

Examples could be multiplied. They would include the first poem in "The Death of the Sheriff," which begins with a sky of stars that *"wheels"* from the moon and concludes with "The thirsty Dipper on the *arc* of night," as well as its second poem, "The Portrait," which opens with the phrase "The whiskey *circulates*" and closes with mourners' cars that *"Wheel"* toward home; "Winter in Dunbarton," which begins with "Time smiling on this sundial of a world"; and "The Ferris Wheel," the second poem in "The First Sunday in Lent," which begins, "This world, this ferris wheel. . . ." In each instance, these miniature circles ("The little wheel is turning on the great," the poet says with a turn of his own in "The Ferris Wheel") are intimations of the larger circle of mortality that the poem draws simultaneously in structure and argument. Rather than catalog all of the occurrences of circular structure in *Lord Weary's Castle*, however, perhaps we should examine in some detail an instance of it in a poem that is slightly but instructively different from "At the Indian Kill-

er's Grave," in the way that the latter is different from "At
the Altar."

If it affords a less ambitious and less dramatic example than
those other poems, "In the Attic," the first poem in "The First
Sunday in Lent," also provides a somewhat clearer one of the
relationship between Lowell's poetics and his view of time.
As the analyses above have suggested, just as a verbal symbol implies its predecessor and successor for Lowell, so the
image of the present implies those of the past and the future;
and just as the expounding of a verbal image is one of Lowell's chief structural means, so the unfolding of the present is
another. "In the Attic" begins in what seems to be the present, a Sunday in March, with the poet-speaker looking out
from his attic window upon "The crooked family chestnut" in
the yard and his townspeople returning home "From ser-
mons in a scolded, sober mob." This first of three stanzas
concludes with the question:

> What will clamp
> The weak-kneed roots together when the damp
> Aches like a conscience, and they grope to rob
> The hero under his triumphal arch?

This image probably tries to evoke, without wanting to define
precisely, the ideas of castration and necrophilia, the gist
being that the present townspeople lack the courage of the
dead heroes from whom they descend. What is quite clear is
that "The weak-kneed roots," an image that develops from
that of "The crooked family chestnut," provides a transition
to a consideration of the speaker's past, his own "roots"; and
that the second stanza then regresses (or seems to regress,
because of the change in tense) first to the speaker's immediate past, his youth, thence to the nation's past, and finally to the history of the Western World:

> This is the fifth floor attic where I hid
> My stolen agates and the cannister
> Preserved from Bunker Hill—feathers and guns,
> Matchlock and flintlock and percussion-cap;
> Gettysburg etched upon the cylinder
> Of Father's Colt. A Luger of a Hun,

> Once blue as Satan, breaks Napoleon,
> My china pitcher. Cartridge boxes trap
> A chipmunk on the saber where they slid.

How much like the stanza quoted earlier from "On the Eve
of the Feast of the Immaculate Conception 1942," yet how
much more lucid and richer, this stanza is. A fine example of
what Lowell's descriptive passages can accomplish when un-
hindered by the impulse to add "baroque / And prodigal
embellishments," it brings together World War I, the Civil
War, and the Napoleonic Wars and implies that they constitute the matrix (and the prison) of the present. That the
speaker belongs in the attic of the ancestral house or the limbs
of the crooked family chestnut tree, that he is one of the
townspeople who "grope to rob / The hero," the "stolen
agates" assure us. The poem elaborates these points in the
last stanza, which takes us even deeper into the past:

> On Troy's last day, alas, the populous
> Shrines held carnival, and girls and boys
> Flung garlands to the wooden horse; so we
> Burrow into the lion's mouth to die.

These lines make the deeper past a prototype as well as a
matrix. As the Trojan youths were to the horse, so we are to
the "lion's mouth" of our own wars and presumed victories:
the common denominator is the acceptance of the invitation
to disaster. The identity of those times and these, on the one
hand, and the allure that self-destruction holds for man, on
the other, are cleverly compressed in an image that associates
the speaker with the Trojan youths by virtue of age and with
the Greeks by virtue of the enclosure in a wooden structure.
The past is thus the imminent future as well as the source of
the present.

The beginning and end of things can be drawn even a bit
closer together, but to do so is also to destroy the frame of
reference. The poem concludes:

> Lord, from the lust and dust thy will destroys
> Raise an unblemished Adam who will see
> The limbs of the tormented chestnut tree

> Tingle, and hear the March-winds lift and cry:
> "The Lord of Hosts will overshadow us."

As the poem comes full circle with the references to the chestnut and the March storm, it also plunges deeper into the past (Adam) and the future (the new Adam); and even as it identifies them, it explodes the temporal framework and transcends it.

Described in general terms, the movement of this poem sounds much like that of "Death from Cancer," "At the Altar," and "At the Indian Killer's Grave": beginning with the actual, it moves through the symbolic to the ineffable. Just as there are different sorts of infinity, however, so there are different kinds of ineffability, and that of "In the Attic" can be distinguished from that of the other poems. What is unutterable in this poem, the nature of the Eternal God who "will overshadow us," appears in the other poems in potentially or flatly contradictory but nonetheless spoken terms (the Christ who is Charon, the Bridegroom who is a warrior, the Lord who is Lucifer). In the other poems, contradiction is either purely symbolic of ineffability or is its negation, whereas in this poem contradiction is avoided altogether. The difference is that between an illogical but hypothesized convergence of good and evil and a transcendence of such categories.

While these two kinds of ineffability can be distinguished in the abstract, they seem in Lowell's practice to be near allied. "In the Attic" contains the germ of the conclusion of "At the Altar" in its second stanza's juxtaposition of "Father's Colt" and the "Luger . . ./ Once blue as Satan," in which a pun on "Father" and more stress than the poem warrants on the pertinent lines would identify God not only with the incomprehensible "will" that "destroys" but also with the particular, Satanic instruments of destruction. It is one thing to say that God foresaw and permitted the Fall and another to say that he handed Eve the apple, or so we have been told by centuries of theologians. But the distinction is harder to grasp than the apple, especially in poetry, and even more especially in a poetry whose stock-in-trade is the iconic object. In this stanza Lowell almost brings his God within the range of his technique. Once he has done so, the dialectic can make poetic hash of the religion, as it threatens to do in "At the Indian Killer's Grave," as it begins to do in "At the Altar," and as it does, with the vengeance of the disappointed convert behind it, in "The Mills of the Kavanaughs."

"Really," Henry James wrote, "universally, relations stop nowhere, and the exquisite problem of the artist is eternally but to draw, by a geometry of his own, the circle within which they shall happily *appear* to do so."[36] There are obviously other ways in which to define the problem of the artist and therefore other standards by which to measure him; but in James's terms, "In the Attic" succeeds because even as Lowell links his opening and penultimate lines, he draws a temporal circle that unites the beginning and the end of history. The independence of the last line from the rest of the poem, an independence that is comparable to that of several other concluding passages noted above, stands metaphorically for what Lowell, at this stage in his career, can still sometimes exclude from the circle of his dialectic.

Because Lowell's poetics does cut across the joints of his Catholic framework, it is at least an overstatement of the case to say, even of the early Lowell, that "religion . . . is the bone and blood, the structure and the spirit of the poetry."[37] In later poems, beginning with "Thanksgiving's Over" (*The Mills of the Kavanaughs*) and "Beyond the Alps" (*Life Studies*), Lowell attacks Catholicism outright, and several poems in this volume might best be described as heretical. The attacks are but an outgrowth of the heresy, however, and the heresy itself seems rooted in Lowell's dialectic, which is the true "structure and spirit of the poetry." To make that claim is not, of course, to challenge Lowell's former commitment. It is simply to say that to read Lowell, as to read Yeats (or Blake or Shelley, both of whom Yeats studied in published detail), is to realize that the poet availed himself of certain religio-philosophical concepts and symbols and then proceeded to make over his appropriations in order that he might, as Yeats's communicator put it, have metaphors for his poetry.[38]

Lowell's comments on his own religious symbolism sometimes seem to echo Yeats's remarks, as when he notes: "I
won't say the Catholicism gave me subject matter, but it
gave me some kind of form, and I could begin a poem and
build it to a climax."[39] Like Yeats's "metaphors" (as well as
Thomas's iconic and Freudian objects), Lowell's Catholic
symbols permit the organization of the experiences in a poem
in terms that are at least partly external to the poem itself. If
this comparison is pushed a little further, it will be found that
these two poets have similar views about the problem of belief. Yeats knew that "some will ask whether I believe in the
actual existence of my circuits of sun and moon"; and he
replied that some of his notions were "plainly symbolical"
even in the beginning, while others, although he may have
taken them "literally" when first struck by them, became less
demanding of belief as time went on, and his "reason . . .
soon recovered." He concluded his introduction to *A Vision*
with these words about the historical periods that were at the
core of his symbolism: "Now that the system stands out
clearly in my imagination I regard them as stylistic arrange-
ments of experience. . . . They have helped me to hold in a
single thought reality and justice."[40] Lowell, as though following suit, has said:

Then there is a question whether my poems are religious, or whether
they just use religious imagery. I haven't really any idea. . . . I'm
sure the symbols and the Catholic framework didn't make the early
poems religious experiences. Yet I don't feel my experience changed
very much. It seems to me it's clearer to me now than it was then,
but it's very much the same sort of thing that went into the religious
poems—the same sort of struggle, light and darkness, the flux of
experience.[41]

Lowell's religion compares with Yeats's system in that it
provides a framework for experience. At the same time, this
similarity itself is not sufficient grounds for maintaining that
the two poets have much in common, especially in view of
the fact that Yeats's system is both very personal and integral
to the poetry. Whereas Yeats virtually built a mythology by
himself, and moreover constructed much of it in the poetry
itself, Lowell took over a Catholic framework and made a few

minor adjustments. Or so it might be argued. Such an argument, however, would overlook the importance to *Lord
Weary's Castle* of precisely its groups of subsidiary symbols,
not the least of which is the circle, which are established by
the poems themselves.

Yeats's method is pertinent, that is, not only because of the
system behind the poems but also because of the supplemen-
tary symbolism created within them. In fact, several of Yeats's
most significant motifs recur in Lowell's work. The Irish
"fisherman," for instance, might be compared with Lowell's
"Drunken Fisherman," who is a kind of negative image of the
former; Yeats's use of the tree in certain passages anticipates
Lowell's image of the "dynamited walnut tree," the "mined
root," "the dirty elm roots," and the "crooked family
chestnut"; both poets are particularly fond of the swan; both
make of Troy a prototype; and so on. Besides functioning as
nodal or pivotal elements that help to organize the dense
material of the individual poems, these recurrent symbols
unite the poems in *Lord Weary's Castle* in somewhat the same
way that Yeats's draw together those in his volumes. It must
be admitted at the outset, however, that Lowell is less systematic than Yeats, and less systematic than he himself is in
later volumes. In any case, the point is not that Lowell was
influenced by the Irish poet but rather that their symbologies
have a feature in common, that the Tower and the Castle,
both of which are related to Herbert's Temple, are not unrelated structures themselves.

That the architectural structure itself is a centripetal symbol
for Lowell is guaranteed by the poet's quotation, in his prefatory note, from the old Scottish ballad, "Lamkin," that inspired his title:

> "It's Lambkin was a mason good
>   As ever built wi' stane:
> He built Lord Wearie's castle
>   But payment gat he nane. . . ."

In the ballad Lamkin avenges himself upon his ungrateful
employer when the latter is "o'er the sea" by murdering his
son and his wife, for which crimes he is executed when his

lord returns; but this stanza, lifted from its context, is probably intentionally ambiguous.[42] The "mason good" might be the creative power of God or Christ if the "castle" is identified with the world and man is conceived of as the debtor. Alternatively, the "mason" can be thought a stand-in for the poet if "Lord Wearie's castle" is taken as a reference to this volume of poetry, in which case the lack of payment alludes either to the poet's failure to gain a sense of grace or to his failure to achieve a lasting resolution of the conflicts that he faces in these poems.[43]

While the symbol of the castle need not be charted in great detail, its function may not emerge as it should without more commentary. The introductory poem, "The Exile's Return," provides material for more commentary than is necessary here, but a word about the "gray, sorry and ancestral house" in this poem may shed some light on Lowell's method. That this house is to be associated with the castle of the title and the ballad is suggested by several details in this vignette based on Thomas Mann's *Tonio Kröger*.[44] Just as Lord Wearie returns from "o'er the sea" to the spectacle of his murdered child and wife, so this exile returns to find a war-ravaged town from which the familiar faces of children and public officials are ominously absent. A more important parallel, although perhaps a less obvious one, exists in the similar connections established between the dwellings and the families who occupy them. In the ballad, instead of destroying his work, Lamkin destroys his lord's family, and the connection between house and inhabitants remains implicit; but in his poem Lowell latensifies this relationship in the lines in which the returning exile describes his

> gray, sorry and ancestral house
> Where the dynamited walnut tree
> Shadows a squat, old, wind-torn gate. . . .

The adjective "ancestral" intimates that the "house" represents a family and its heritage, as it does in the phrase "the Trojan royal house," to which Lowell continually refers; and this intimation is enforced by a related pun in the next line, where the walnut tree (like the "crooked family chestnut," which itself corresponds to the family house) might also be a family tree. Like Lord Wearie, the exile is returning to a desperate situation, and the "wind-torn gate" (another version of the subway turnstile in "At the Indian Killer's Grave") leads him to associate his home with hell itself by means of the allusion to Dante's *superliminare* (*Inferno*, III. 9) in the last line. The same lines also point back to the beginning of the poem and a similarly symbolic structure, the Hôtel de Ville, where the "braced pig-iron dragons" guard the entrance like a pair of infernal beasts.

The images of the ancestral house and the dynamited tree, which occur exactly in the middle of the poem, are central in more than one sense. They constitute a real crux in that they both compress the theme of the poem and connect its opening and closing lines. Each of these symbols, the house and the tree, repeatedly functions as both synapse and synapsis in *Lord Weary's Castle*, although the particular ramifications of each vary according to context. In "Colloquy in Black Rock," for example, the house symbol both contracts and expands its meaning, standing in one line for the poet-speaker and in the next for the entire world:

> the dust
> Is on this skipping heart that shakes my house,
> House of our Savior who was hanged till death.

If in "The Exile's Return" the decadence of the familial house implies that of the individual and that of the world, here the same decadence is presented in microcosm and macrocosm by means of the deft repetition of the word "house," with the carefully fortuitous change from the lowercase to the uppercase *h*.

The relationship between the house and the poet-speaker's forebears is explicitly stated in "Children of Light," in which the subject is the "Pilgrims unhouseled by Geneva's light" who left to their heirs "The riotous glass houses built on rock." In addition to an ironic allusion to the founding of the Old World religion, this line makes use of a popular synonym for *ridiculous* and a hackneyed proverb to suggest the threat to the American heritage: the "glass houses," set between

"riotous" and "rock," appear remarkably fragile. In the poem
that follows this one, "Rebellion," Lowell stresses the culpability of his speaker, who is after all a descendant of the guilty
Pilgrims, by employing the same symbol:

> You damned
> My arm that cast your house upon your head
> And broke the chimney flintlock on your skull.

The house appears in numerous other forms, including
"King's Chapel," but there is no need to gloss each of these
appearances. The point to be made here—a point which will
be made in more detail in discussions of later volumes—is
that the repetition of such a symbol has a cumulative effect,
which not only links various poems but also permits the poet
to give an otherwise casual reference the force of an allusion.
When we come to a phrase like "the fallen houses of his
Troy" or to a line like "The wastes of snow about my house
stare in" ("Winter in Dunbarton"), we hear it echo in the
context of other uses of the same image.

The house is just one of a cluster of symbols whose natural
interrelationships Lowell exploits repeatedly. One of the
others set forth in the ballad stanza quoted above is that of
the skilled but evil mason. In the elegy for Arthur Winslow
we have

> the faith
> That made the Pilgrim Makers take a lathe
> And point their wooden steeples lest the Word be dumb.

The betrayal of their own Lord by these builders is suggested
by the blasphemous view of themselves—again Lowell's
capitalization is significant—and hammered home by the
purblindness of their motivations for raising their churches.
Surely the Word was not dependent upon the skills of the
Puritan architects and carpenters. All this would doubtless be
plain enough without recollecting Lamkin, who, if under-
standably aggrieved, is nonetheless treacherous; but to remember the ballad is to put the Pilgrims' failings and their
fates into what other poems here would suggest is their
proper perspective. Nor are these failings and fates preroga-

tives of the Protestant builders alone, as we learn from a passage in "Adam and Eve":

> I eye the statue with an awed contempt
> And see the puritanical façade
> Of the white church that Irish exiles made
> For Patrick. . . .

Admittedly, in view of the predominantly Catholic context established by this volume (one aspect of which allows us to see in "puritanical" a synonym for "damned"), the "contempt" expressed at first seems at least as odd as it is "awed." But the Irish builders—who are, like the poet's ancestors ("Children of Light") and the poet himself, exiles or wanderes and descendants of Cain[45]—are undeniably objects of scorn; and here, as elsewhere, the recognition of the symbol and the use to which it has been put helps to guard against a narrow Catholic interpretation—and to see, for example, the irony in the last two words of the quoted sentence.

This symbol reappears in "As a Plane Tree by the Water," where

>   the devil's long
> Dirge of the people detonates the hour
> For floating cities where his golden tongue
> Enchants the masons of the Babel Tower
> To raise tomorrow's city to the sun
> That never sets upon these hell-fire streets
> Of Boston. . . .

This passage reveals again Lowell's urge toward the generalization: the Masons are symbols as soon as they are apprehended; the Tower of Babel immediately turns into a city; and the city, by way of ironic allusions to Campanella's *City of the Sun* and St. Augustine's City of God, becomes the world. The expansion is temporal as well as spatial, as the lines encompass ancient Babylon, contemporary Boston, and the end of time. The city is also one of Lowell's major symbols, but it will not require commentary here. It is sufficient to note that in such poems as "In the Attic," "To Peter Taylor on the Feast of the Epiphany," and this one he does what he said Williams did in *Paterson*:

First, the City is his: all its aspects, its past, its present, its natural features, its population and its activities are available for him to interrelate and make dramatic. But also he can use his whole life in the City—every detail is an experience, a memory, or a symbol.[46]

Because such symbols are typical of the book as a whole, individual poems gain a support and a potential scope that they might not have on their own, as those in "Between the Porch and the Altar" do from one another. This is particularly true of those poems which, because of their ostensibly personal nature and more casual language, are invariably singled out as forerunners of *Life Studies*. "In the Cage," often viewed as confessional, is a highly compressed vision of the human condition which depends partly upon its context, or rather upon the reader's memory of symbols used elsewhere in the book. The "Cage" is no more easily reducible to the penitentiary in which Lowell served several months for his conscientious objection during World War II than the Hôtel de Ville or "the blackened Statehouse" or "King's Chapel" is to an actual building. The ambiguity of the title itself should warn against a limited interpretation, even though it is legitimate slang for serving time in prison, and the first lines, which recall the description of the "good people" entering the church in "Katherine's Dream," bear out that ambiguity:

> The lifers file into the hall,
> According to their houses—twos
> Of laundered denim.

The "lifers" in their respective "houses" are not simply convicts with life sentences, but men sentenced to live, and therefore men analogous to those creatures who entered the Ark "two and two." This hint of the Ark is developed by the assortment of types represented here: "Canaries" as well as "lifers," a "colored fairy" as well as a "Bible-twisting Israelite." By unobtrusively supplying a Biblical analogue, Lowell turns virtually inside out the notion of a prison as a place of isolation for a few maladjusted individuals; and at the same time he converts an extremely personal recollection into an experience that is truly typical.

Oddly enough (but the contradiction is superficial), Lowell's method also permits a kind of intermittent autobiography. If "In the Cage" is not so simply personal as is sometimes supposed, several of these poems are more intimate than they seem, and some contain sly allusions to the poet's own craft. When Lowell says in "At the Indian Killer's Grave," "I ponder on this railing at the park," the pun ironically alludes to his own poem—as the next lines indicate, when he turns from "railing" to supplication. "Salem" can be read as the poet's admonition to himself not to forget—as though Lowell ever could—the duties that have devolved upon him because of his heritage, and in this perspective the poem is seen to contain a miniature portrait of its author in the guise of "the knitting sailor" who "stabs at ships / Nosing like sheep of Morpheus through his brain's / Asylum." "Concord," the companion sonnet of "Salem," is perhaps also a more personal poem than it might appear, since it presents a small compendium of the literary heroes of New England, who then serve as foils for the poet. It is not only the "Fords" who are "idle here in search / Of a tradition," but one of the Lowells, too. Given the context of the references to Thoreau and the allusion to Emerson in the last lines, the "ruined bridge"—which was the "ruined Bridge" in *Land of Unlikeness*, where, like "Salem," the poem first appeared—might well be a memory of another poet who sought his tradition. In the center of the sonnet is a rhetorical question that must also be that of the poet in regard to the validity of his own work:

> Crucifix,
> How can your whited spindling arms transfix
> Mammon's unbridled industry, the lurch
> For forms to harness Heraclitus' stream!

The query is perhaps more applicable to the problems of *Land of Unlikeness*, but the method of which these poems are a microcosm is that of *Lord Weary's Castle*. Placed on facing pages, they reflect one another in form and subject—both are sonnets (although of different types), and in the title of each there is hidden a pun on "peace" or "harmony" that mocks the actual situation—and in doing so they epitomize the closely knit nature of the whole volume.[47]

Taken together with such poems as "In the Cage," "Butter-
cups," and "Rebellion," obliquely personal poems like these
constitute a portrait, or rather a sketch, of the artist himself. A
striking instance of both this uninsistent autobiography and
Lowell's ability to bring a variety of his symbols to bear simultaneously is "After the Surprising Conversions."[48] Commentary on this poem is usually (and justifiably) confined to Lowell's brilliant transformation of Jonathan Edwards's prose, but
the title almost demands to be related to the poet, whose own
conversion to Catholicism during his college days must have
been surprising, to say the least, to a family descended from
the Puritans. The poem's description of a suicide fits Lowell
closely enough, particularly if allowance is made for a little
self-directed irony:

> A gentleman
> Of more than common understanding, strict
> In morals, pious in behavior, kicked
> Against our goad. A man of some renown,
> An useful, honored person in the town,
> He came of melancholy parents; prone
> To secret spells, for years they kept alone. . . .

The "melancholy parents" do not put in a significant appearance until *Life Studies*, but other relatives with a similar disposition populate this volume; and when Lowell goes ahead
to remark apropos the "secret spells" that "His uncle, I believe, was killed of it," it is difficult to avoid thinking of "The
Death of the Sheriff." In the next line but one—"I preached
one Sabbath on a text from Kings"—we may be reminded of
"As a Plane Tree by the Water," where there is in fact an
allusion to 3 Kings 16:34. The possibility that the poem has an
autobiographical dimension certainly enhances the irony of
these lines farther on:

> though a thirst
> For loving shook him like a snake, he durst
> Not entertain much hope of his estate
> In heaven.

And immediately after this passage comes a series of possible allusions to "In the Attic," "At a Bible House," and "To Peter Taylor on the Feast of the Epiphany," or perhaps "Concord":

> Once we saw him sitting late
> Behind his attic window by a light
> That guttered on his Bible; through that night
> He meditated terror, and he seemed
> Beyond advice or reason, for he dreamed
> That he was called to trumpet Judgment Day
> To Concord.

Some might say that these last lines could refer to almost any of these poems, but it must be granted that these possible allusions are not specific enough to assure us of the presence of autobiographical elements in this poem. One does have to credit Lowell with some deviousness in order to think that it is intentionally ambiguous, and therefore perhaps one ought to have better grounds for doing so than the mere presence of other autobiographical poems in this book. For this reason, it seems worth the risk of asserting as a conclusion what is still a hypothesis: namely, that it is not uncommon to find in Lowell's future work barely veiled references both to others of his poet-speakers and to himself as poet and that indeed such references form the bases of the structures of *Imitations* and *For the Union Dead*.[49]

There is one other dimension to *Lord Weary's Castle* that deserves comment because it anticipates a development in later volumes, and that is the relationship between the individual poems and the collection. In view of the connections among the poems, it is not surprising that *Lord Weary's Castle* has an organization looser than, but in general outline very like, that of several of the poems. "The Exile's Return," in particular, with its movement from the Hôtel de Ville through the ancestral house to the cathedral, is almost a microcosm of this volume, as well as an introduction to it. It will be remembered that the initial poem ended with the grimly anticipatory lines adapted from the *Inferno:* "Pleasant enough, / *Voi ch'entrate,* and your life is in your hands." This Inferno is "Pleasant enough," presumably, because it is to be identified with "your life," which is tolerable in the ironic sense that there is no alternative. At the same time, however, the phrase seems to refer to the "rough / Cathedral" that "lifts its eye" in the preceding sentence, and in view of one aspect of the house symbol as interpreted above, the "rough / Cathedral" might be the book itself.

Such a reading is consistent with the structure of the volume, for the cathedral recurs in significant forms in its approximate center and at its end. Midway through the volume, looming above what are known as "lesser attempts," there is "Between the Porch and the Altar"; and if the "Porch" of this title is identified with the entrance implied by Dante's inscription and the initial position of "The Exile's Return," then halfway through the book one expects to be "Between the Porch and the Altar." While it is true that the last poem in this sequence is entitled "At the Altar," it is also true that the altar recurs in the last stanza of the last poem, "Where the Rainbow Ends":

> At the high altar, gold
> And a fair cloth. I kneel and the wings beat
> My cheek. What can the dove of Jesus give
> You now but wisdom, exile? Stand and live,
> The dove has brought an olive branch to eat.

Since the "exile" of this poem is surely that of the first poem, this arrival at the altar must be intended to conclude the journey begun in the first poem, just as the title of the central sequence must be meant to indicate the middle of the journey.

The term *journey*, however, might give a false impression of the organization of this volume, for the concluding poem is hardly different in outlook from "The Exile's Return." The return to a war-ravaged Germany in that poem is echoed here in the "scorched-earth miles" that stretch out before the speaker, the "dynamited walnut tree" in the "wild ingrafted olive" and the withered root, and the ambiguous statement that "your life is in your hands" in the injunction to "Stand and live." The journey might be thought of as circular, with the title of the first poem constituting the closing of the circle and the reinauguration of the process. *Plus ça change, plus c'est la même chose.*

Do I contradict myself?
Very well then, I contradict myself,
(I am large, I contain multitudes.)
—WALT WHITMAN, *Song of Myself*

In the writing of a poem all our compulsions and
biases should get in, so that finally we don't
know what we mean. . . .
—"A Talk [with Stanley Kunitz]"

3

THE LOGIC OF CONTRADICTION:

The Mills of the Kavanaughs (1951)

What can the dove of Jesus give
You now but wisdom, exile? Stand and live,
The dove has brought an olive branch to eat.

It is indicative of the complex problems posed by Lowell's early work that the question raised at the end of *Lord Weary's Castle* is but superficially rhetorical, since it does not determine whether "wisdom" is to be the poet-speaker's certain reward or his only possible reward, and that the injunction that follows admits of contradictory interpretations, since the dove's gift could be either sweet or bitter.[1]

Given such irreducible ambiguities, the obvious alternatives are to regard these lines as purposefully ambivalent or to view them as unintentionally imprecise. Because the lines conclude *Lord Weary's Castle* and thus point to an unknown future, the former alternative seems justifiable. That alternative would be misleading only if it were taken to imply that Lowell's use of the ambivalent and the contradictory is a local rather than a general strategy. In his work there are many similar cruxes, very few of which, of course, can be explained in terms of temporal reference; and the existence of these

81

other passages, while it might keep us from deciding that the quoted lines are just unintentionally imprecise, might also discourage the thought that the ambiguities of these lines derive solely from their contemplation of the future. In any case, the struggle between meanings exemplified by these lines characterizes Lowell's poetry; and the sooner we recognize that fact, the sooner we can come to grips with the reasons that lie behind, and the techniques that create, such conflict.

If there are any doubts about the extent to which Lowell sanctions ambiguity and even antilogy, his comment on the subject will dispel them quickly.

A poem needs to include a man's contradictions. One side of me, for example, is a conventional liberal, concerned with causes, agitated about peace and justice and equality, as so many people are. My other side is deeply conservative, wanting to get at the roots of things, wanting to slow down the whole modern process of mechanization and dehumanization, knowing that liberalism can be a form of death too. In the writing of a poem all our compulsions and biases should get in, so that finally we don't know what we mean.[2]

The pragmatic critic might find it convenient to regard that last statement as an exaggeration; but if it is, it is an exaggeration of an attitude which any reader of these early volumes will do well to recognize, since many of their distinctive techniques are means of expressing "a man's contradictions." If Lowell's earnest declaration recalls Whitman's rather more insouciant admission, very well then, it does.

Lowell's comment is probably no less true of his first two volumes than of this one, but it can be true in the different cases because it is broad enough to permit a variety of techniques, not because the techniques remain unaltered. Perhaps the point is worthy of some emphasis in view of the critical consensus that Lowell's early work is pretty much of a piece, at least in strategy and style, and that the third volume in particular is imitative of a mode developed earlier.[3] *The Mills of the Kavanaughs* is of course a lineal descendant of *Lord Weary's Castle*. Lowell's rhythms still seem frequently willed and frenetic and the rhymes sometimes riveted into the stanzas. Less noticeable, but more significant in light of the poetry to come, are Lowell's continued experimentation in the use of personae and his persisting interest in larger canvases.[4] Along with these other features, the metaphorical density and the attendant thematic ambiguity of this volume certainly recall *Lord Weary's Castle,* although there is nothing in the earlier volume so obsessively complicated as a couple of these poems, and thus there is no sense in denying that these poems hark back to the earlier ones. There are distinctions worth noting, however, and the chief one of these has to do with Lowell's increased tendency to contradict himself, to get the process of thought rather than its product into the poetry.

At least one of these poems looks as though it were written just too late for publication in the earlier book, and a brief examination of it can provide a review of Lowell's former position as well as an introduction to, and a foil for, his new one. "Her Dead Brother" bears several remarkable resemblances to the preceding volume's "The Death of the Sheriff" in both form and content. Each poem has two sections of three ten-line stanzas apiece, and with the exception of the last two stanzas in the earlier poem, the rhyme scheme is varied from stanza to stanza. Both poems involve a persona who has apparently commited incest and who has a desperate need for expiation, a suicide, and a portrait that figures almost as a personality; and both poems move from the objective world to the lurid dream world of the poet-speaker, with its bizarre revery, guilt-ridden memory, and apocalyptic vision.

The opening description in "Her Dead Brother" is luminous with symbolic import:

> The Lion of St. Mark's upon the glass
> Shield in my window reddens, as the night
> Enchants the swinging dories to its terrors. . . .

Both of these opening images, we realize at the end of the second section, "Three Months Later," are expressions of a mind contemplating death: the night "Enchants the swinging dories" much as death is to charm the self-condemned woman; and the emblem of St. Mark "reddens" in the sunset to recall the flames in which her brother died when his cruiser was torpedoed in the war, as well as to signify the divine wrath which is provoked by their sins and against which "the glass / Shield" is hardly protection. The trappings of the brother's portrait, described later in the first stanza, work in a similar and complementary manner, for the "German-silver hawsers" that are coiled about the painting suggest not only the cause of his physical death but also the coils of Satan.

The festooned and varnished portrait, which "mirrors / The sunset as a dragon," is the image from which the rest of the first section unwinds. In the second stanza, the speaker figures her dead brother as "a wintering dragon" and then recalls an outing that they had made as children:

> Remember riding, scotching with your spur
> That four-foot milk-snake in a juniper?
> Father shellacked it to the ice-house door.

A transformation that would be extremely strange in the work of another poet but that should not surprise us by now in Lowell's takes place in these three lines. Even as the milk snake is a metaphor for the brother, whose incest with his sister, intimated in the following stanza, turns him into a likeness of the serpent, the brother becomes a type of the child Jesus, who is often portrayed in medieval art in the act of bruising his heel upon the head of the serpent. The involuted figure is summed up in the last of the quoted lines, where the "shellacked" snake, which echos the varnished portrait, is emblematic of both the defeat of Satan and the crucifixion of Christ. The passage is thus contradictory not only on the emotional level, at which the speaker both hates and loves the brother with whom she slept on "that August twenty-third," but also on the theological level, at which the principles of good and evil are indistinguishable and together constitute the coils that enmesh the portrait of man.[5] The appropriate legend is the anguished question uttered in one of the best-known poems in this volume, "Falling Asleep over the Aeneid": " 'Who and I, and why?' "

The inextricable problems of the natures of God and man are the focal points of "Three Months Later," where the combination of devotion to her brother and guilt from the commission of incest drives the speaker to suicide. Her suicide and its ramifications are set forth by means of three metaphors, all of which develop from the imagery invoked at the end of the first section: the *Water Witch*, a replica of a knockabout constructed by the brother and abandoned by him, which is, as the name suggests, a projection of the persona; the ship of death, manned at the moment that she begins to inhale the gas from the oven by the suicidal speaker and her brother; and the ships "by the Stygian Landing," envisioned by the speaker in her last few seconds, which are flaming and confused to the point that enemy and ally cannot be told apart. This last, chthonic scene is a memory of the brother's death in the war, and it is an image of the speaker's death in the present, but it is also a vision of the future devastation of that "Babel of Boston," as Lowell called the city in "At a Plane Tree by the Water," responsible for incest, war, and suicide. The vision of the chaos at "the Stygian Landing" is to this poem what the razing of Troy is to "The Death of the Sheriff."

Although the way in which the apocalypse is obscured by the other considerations is one of the things about "Her Dead Brother" that indicates an affinity with "Falling Asleep over the Aeneid," the source of the ambiguity of the attendant image of God relates this poem closely to those in *Lord Weary's Castle*. The ambiguity here first manifests itself in the sails that puff out and "tell / The colors of the rainbow," thereby recalling the Covenant, only to slacken and hang limp as the wind dies in the canvas, and then in a vision of "The Lord" himself, which is really but a brief glimpse, hardly sufficient to disclose his nature:

> His stick is tapping on the millwheel-step,
> He lights a match, another and another—
> The Lord is dark, and holy is His name. . . .

A composite of a blind man searching for someone and an arsonist, the Lord is at once a potentially redemptive but helpless deity and the implacable Yaweh. The paradox is reflected in the last stanza of the poem in an image that compresses the theme of the first section: when the brother appears in the vision of Armageddon, shouting as though rallying his forces and cupping his "broken sword-hand," the speaker says of him, "You are black." Whether he is good or evil, victor or vanquished, is as undecided as the nature of the Lord, who is "dark." The sins of the world—for the "New England town" is surely no more nor less than a synecdoche[6]—will doubtless be repaid; but as in "The Quaker Graveyard," "The Lord survives the rainbow of His will," and man's ultimate fate is consequently unknown and unknowable.

These crucial ambiguities are achieved by familiar means; the poet presents us with images that encourage contradictory interpretations, presumably because the mystery of God defies comprehension. The ambivalence, in other words, springs from human ignorance—"The Lord is dark"—and in this respect this poem is not representative of *The Mills of the Kavanaughs*. Although these poems are ambivalent, their ambivalence usually derives, not from tacit admission of ignorance, but from assertions of contradictory ideas; and it is not so much that the poems come to ambiguous conclusions as it is that they consist of the interaction, the transactions of conflicting thoughts.

In this book, in short, the poetry moves further away from an insight into the unity of things in order to incorporate even more of the struggle involved in obtaining such an insight. Both the increasingly dramatic character and the increasing length of these poems testify to this shift in emphasis, for conflict facilitates different points of view, which in turn lend themselves to embodiment and guarantee a certain extension of the occasion. As in *Lord Weary's Castle*, where the first movement in this direction took place, conflict, drama, and length go hand in hand with an increasingly homocentric view of things. If in this volume Lowell is more concerned with the contradictions within paradoxes than with paradoxical unity, it is partly because he focuses more steadily on a sphere in which the contradictions are more apparent than the unity.

Because the difference between *The Mills of the Kavanaughs* and the earlier volume is thus a matter of a shift in emphasis and a correspondingly subtle evolution of technique, it is difficult to apprehend in the abstract. It is this difference, however, that emerges from a comparison of the conclusions of both "In the Attic" and "At the Altar" with that of "Bathsheba's Lament in the Public Garden" (the second poem in "David and Bathsheba in the Public Garden"). While "In the Attic" waives the option of analyzing the nature of God, "At the Altar" exercises it, with the result that the poem concludes with an enigma: the Lord and Lucifer are inexplicably one figure, who solicitously rocks the baby's carriage and sadistically roasts the soul upon a spit. The burden of the former poem is that while this life is death, God absolutely transcends it, and consequently we can know nothing of his desires and purposes. The latter poem tells us not only that this life is death (the baby carriage is a bier); but also that death is life (the bier is a baby carriage); and it even suggests that life-in-death and death-in-life (the tortures of the damned and the trials of this life) are inseparable. The one poem refuses to explicate God's nature; the other offers a radical explication in the name of unity, presenting the reader with a necessarily obscure reconciliation of contradictory ideas. "Bathsheba's Lament," however, ends with the unequivocal statement " 'I must surely die.' " Now the point is not that "David and Bathsheba in the Public Garden" is less ambivalent than "Between the Porch and the Altar," for the last statement in the first section of the poem is David's boast " 'Surely, I will not die,' " and on an eschatological level either might be true. The point is rather that the second poem's conclusion stands in direct opposition to that of the preceding one and that consequently the reader is presented not with a vision of transcendence, and not with a resolution or even an apparent resolution of a contradiction, but with the contradiction itself.

In terms of religious belief, the difference is that between one which accepts paradox in the name of a faith and one which calls a faith into question because it is paradoxical; in terms of poetic method, the difference is that between one which synthesizes or unites contraries and one which analyzes or insists upon distinctions. Since a large part of poetry consists of analogy, the union of superficially dissimi- lar things, the notion of a poetry of analysis itself verges on being contradictory, and therefore it needs to be stated at once that Lowell's chief means of analysis is multiplication of analogy. It is precisely by comparing one person or event to several others that he is able both to disclose the contradic- tions inherent in his subject and to express his own conflict- ing feelings. This multiplication of analogy is responsible for the rich texture and the complicated point of view in one of this volume's most moving and intricate poems, "Falling Asleep over the Aeneid."

This poem, which is to "In the Attic" what the latter is to "On the Eve of the Feast of the Immaculate Conception 1942," has five main focuses in time. Chronologically ar- ranged, as they are not in the poem, they are: (1) Aeneas's interlude with Dido (*Aeneid*, IV); (2) the funeral of Pallas (*Aeneid*, XI); (3) the Second Punic War; (4) the funeral of Charles, the poet-speaker's uncle, shortly after the American Civil War; (5) the present, when the poet-speaker is a man of eighty-some years. To put it another way, there are two cen- tral situations in the poem—the old man asleep in his chair in Concord and Aeneas at the funeral of Pallas—and these merge in the dream to form one center, which then reaches out through other dreams, memories, and visions to touch all of the other situations. The result is that in eighty-six lines we have a selective history of Western culture from about 1000 B.C. (the Italian Civil War) through 200 B.C. (the Second Punic War) and 1865 (the American Civil War) to 1950–1951. The latter period seems to be distinguished by the prevailing peace, for what is peculiar about this history is its obstinate recurrence to scenes of war and its insistence upon their similarity.

This similarity is conveyed primarily by the imagery; just as the war scenes recur, so do the images of fire, birds, and swords, among others, so that the various vignettes flow into one another.[7] An even more striking instance of Lowell's

Ovidian attitude is the treatment of the gods and the historical figures in this poem. Both the Greek and the Roman ap-
pellations are used for the gods, for example; and at one point
Ares (or is it Jupiter?) fades into the figure of Father Time:

> the King,
> Vain-glorious Turnus, carried off the rest.
> "I was myself, but Ares thought it best
> The way it happened." At the end of time
> He sets his spear, as my descendants climb
> The knees of Father Time. . . .[8]

The old man becomes Aeneas in his dream, but then Aeneas
is inextricably linked with Turnus, his mortal enemy, when
"a boy's face" mirrored in the Trojan's sword asks a question
actually voiced by a confused Turnus in the *Aeneid:* " 'Who
am I, and why?' " The question is trenchant, for the old man,
Aeneas, Turnus, and the boy—who could be Pallas, or
Lausus (his Etruscan counterpart who is slain by Aeneas as
Pallas is by Turnus), or Ascanius (Aeneas's son, the founder
of the *gens Iulia* and thus a link between Aeneas and Augustus), or the poet-speaker as a youth, or all of these at once—
are brought together with these words, and consequently
each has the right to ask it. Again, there is an obvious identification of Pallas and Uncle Charles toward the end of the
poem.

But perhaps the most important of these relationships
among personae is that among the old man, Augustus, and
Vergil. The last lines of the poem make the old man mirror
Augustus:

> It is I, I hold
> His sword to keep from falling, for the dust
> On the stuffed birds is breathless, for the bust
> Of young Augustus weighs on Vergil's shelf:
> It scowls into my glasses at itself.

The last lines have often been understood simply as an ironic
comparison of the emperor with the old man, the point being
that modern man is at best a dreamer, incapable of the heroic
exploits of his illustrious ancestors. But the bust of Augustus

is scowling, it seems, not so much at the speaker as at his own reflection; and one reason for the scowl is not far to seek, for it is implicit in the sonics, which link "dust" (with its overtones of mortality) and "bust" (with its pun) to "Augustus" (a title that is therefore ironic). The disillusionment here derives not from contemplation of the least of mankind, as modern man tends to see himself, but rather from consideration of the greatest, as Octavius, Augustus Caesar, in fact saw himself. Augustus is Lowell's enlightened Ozymandias, and the theme of the poem is, not the demise of heroism, but its apparent futility.

The theme is expressed as well in the comparison of Vergil, who predicted a new Golden Age in his fourth eclogue and redacted the mythological foundations of the ultimate state in his epic, to the poet-speaker, who has had his own dreams of the past and the future.[9] While Vergil wrote of the grandeur that was *Roma aeterna,* however, the old man seems to dream of her destruction. The import of his dream becomes clearer when it is realized that even in this poem Lowell has exploited religious imagery. From the rainbow colors with which the poem begins, through the "drunken God," "the returning bridegroom," and the "King [who] . . . carried off the rest," there are a number of references that have Christian overtones. The setting is of importance too, for the old man has forgotten to attend morning service, and the church bell chimes in the background to rouse him from his dreams; significantly, "Church is over" immediately after the vision that the poet-speaker dreams he had as Aeneas. This vision is prompted by Vergil and deals, on the surface at least, with a battle with Hannibal's Carthaginian troops in the Second Punic War:

> At the end of time,
> He sets his spear, as my descendants climb
> The knees of Father Time, his beard of scalps,
> His scythe, the arc of steel that crowns the Alps.
> The elephants of Carthage hold those snows,
> Turms of Numidian horse unsling their bows,
> The flaming turkey-feathered arrows swarm
> Beyond the Alps.

The surface, however, is transparent, and beneath it, as a result of a kind of *sortes Vergilianae,* is an intimation of the mortality of earthly kingdoms that contrasts ironically with Vergil's confidence in Rome. Hannibal seems to be defeating the Romans, a historical detail that Vergil only touches upon in passing (*Aeneid,* X, 6 ff.) and that could never have occupied a climactic position in his poem. Further, while "the end of time" might have implied international Roman domination for Vergil, it has a different meaning in the context of the foregoing Christian allusions. Similarly, although the antecedent of "He" in the passage quoted above might first seem to be "Ares," it is ambiguous (and we will suspect Lowell of capitalizing once more on his line break); so are the "Turms of Numidian horse" armed with flaming arrows, which call up images from Revelation. Finally, an image that the reader of Lowell will be attentive to is "the arc of steel that crowns the Alps": in addition to the scythe of Father Time, the arc recalls the cutting edge of God's Covenant, symbolized for exegetes by the color of fire in the rainbow. In sum: this passage is the poet-speaker's apocalypse cast in the form of Vergil's prophecy of Roman hegemony.

That Lowell intends Aeneas's last vision to be at best of ambiguous portent seems certain. At the same time, it must be kept in mind that this poem's vision of Armageddon is inseparable from that significantly altered prophecy. The dialectic going on here is difficult to grasp, but the implication is that the apocalyptic dimension of the vision is as implausible as Vergil's prediction. Vergil, through the eyes of Aeneas, foresaw Roman conquest, not Roman defeat; yet Lowell suggests that the prophecy is (as it should have been) one of ultimate Roman defeat, and he even hints that the defeat is Armageddon itself; but then that Armageddon is nullified in turn by its being part of a dream of time past instead of the true "end of time."

So Lowell suggests and denies, on the one hand, the existence of Pax Augusta, that short-lived goddess who was virtually invented with the new title of the *imperator;* and he suggests and denies, on the other hand, the possibility of a Day of Judgment. If there can be neither a lasting peace nor a Judgment, there can only be an endless succession of wars.[10]

That is why the advice that Aeneas and the poet-speaker are given is so tantalizing:

> "Brother, try,
> O Child of Aphrodite, try to die:
> To die is life."

Aeneas cannot die, not only because he is the son of a goddess, which is but a convenient metaphor for the point that Lowell wants to make, but also because he is incarnate in Uncle Charles, and the poet-speaker, and so on *ad infinitum*. Man is plagued with war and passion, with "whoring Mars / And Venus," to whom "Our cost / Is nothing"; but for this very reason he is also burdened with a responsibility that has the potential of being converted to heroism. Like the poet-speaker in the last lines, he must inherit and hold the "sword" of his ancestors, but that sword is what keeps him "from falling."[11]

One critic has held it a "great flaw" in a poem otherwise "brilliantly intricate" that while the various historical figures and vignettes in "Falling Asleep over the Aeneid" are all "brought into analogy . . . we can only see that there is *some* analogy. We cannot quite identify what it is."[12] John Holloway goes ahead to complain that each time we think that we are about to grasp the analogy, "a farther likeness or a farther discrimination takes shape before us, and holds us off from it." These are acute remarks, and they can be helpful, especially if they are pointed in a different direction. As long as the assumptions are, first, that there should be *an* analogy at the base of a poem and, second, that the use of one analogy should preclude the use of others, the necessary conclusion is that "Falling Asleep over the Aeneid" is gravely flawed.

Once the foregoing assumptions have been articulated, however, it is clear that neither they nor the conclusion to which they point need be shared. How better to say that man is his own worst enemy than by transforming the speaker into both Aeneas and Turnus? If that double analogy vitalizes Wordsworth's phrase "man's inhumanity to man," the parallels between the speaker and Augustus, on the one hand, and the speaker and Vergil, on the other, give a concrete form-to the proverbial rivalry of sword and pen. And how better to represent the awesome weight of accomplishment and evil of the past than by a weapon that has been passed down, as it were, from Aeneas to Augustus to Grant to the present? As for the superimposition of a vision of *Dies Irae* upon a vision of a war wrongly supposed to have been a step on the way to the establishment of universal peace—why, the interlacings of desire for knowledge of the nature and end *(telos)* of humanity (" 'Who am I, and why?' ") and fear that there can only be what there has been, the shades of irony and hope permitted by Lowell's method, seem virtually inseparable from that method. " 'Who am I, and why?' " Lowell's epyllion does as much as any work of comparable length that comes to mind to respond to the first question; and if there are always farther likenesses and discriminations to keep us from exactly defining his answer, perhaps we ought to ask ourselves whether we would be satisfied to be formulated in a phrase. One of the poem's triumphs, in other words, is its justification of an inability to answer the second question.

Holloway's remarks would be useful, then, if taken as a description of a consistent method instead of as a criticism of a departure from an acceptable method. Several of the other major poems here rest, not on simple analogies, but on sets of overlapping and contradictory analogies. Consequently, the problem lies not in identifying an analogy but in discerning the ways in which analogies are extended and modified. Since the plot and the framework of the title poem have been discussed at some length by Hugh Staples, and discussed in terms that are compatible for the most part with those employed here, it can be examined fairly succinctly and with particular attention to Lowell's mutually modifying analogies. [13]

The most patient and attentive reader will probably have to confess, along with William Arrowsmith, that at least parts of this long, hermetically complicated poem escape his understanding. [14] Its motivating tensions, its objectives, and its methods are nevertheless not difficult to find out. A comparison of the first and last words of Anne Kavanaugh, Lowell's main speaker, suggests the poem's general drift. In the last

lines of the opening stanza, after the scene has been set in an
objective narrative, Anne addresses Harry, her brother by her
adoption and her husband as well, who went mad during
their marriage after serving a stint in the Navy and has been
dead, perhaps by suicide, for about a year:

> She kneels to furl
> Her husband's flag, and thinks his mound and stone
> Are like a buried bed. "This is the throne
> They must have willed us. Harry, not a thing
> Was missing: We were children of a king. . . ."

Since " 'This' " is apparently Harry's grave, the references to
plenitude and royal prerogative seem ironic. That this is not
exclusively the case, that death is a legacy which Anne is
willing and even eager to accept, is the sense of the poem's
concluding lines, in which she compares herself for one last
time to Persephone, the goddess whose statue stands by the
mill pond at Kavanaugh, the family house, and whose myth
is at the center of the poem:

> "And yet we think the virgin took no harm:
> She gave herself because her blood was warm—
> And for no other reason, Love, I gave
> Whatever brought me gladness to the grave."

Anne accepts death as she thinks Persephone must have accepted death or Hades, and she accepts it for the same
reason: because she is alive and passionate and loving
enough, her blood is warm enough, to make her want to die.
The statement is paradoxical but unequivocal; " 'her blood
was warm' " and there was " 'no other reason.' "

Now this is not an example of that perverse hedonism
under the aegis of which one rushes to embrace the ultimate
experience, but an intuitive recognition of the paradox that
" 'To die is life.' " It is because it is intuitive, because it is
secular and esoteric rather than sectarian and in-
stitutionalized, that these lines are so hard to formulate in
other terms. The concept is one we associate with religion,
and there is a religious vocabulary with which to express
it—the resurrection of the soul, the union with Christ, and so

on—but Lowell has declined to use this vocabulary.[15] Instead, he has created one of his own—for he has not simply borrowed a Greek myth—to express the ogygian impulse to believe that, as the Kavanaughs' motto has it, " *'Cut down we flourish.'* "

Like so much else in this poem, these last lines, and therefore the preceding commentary on them, depend upon an understanding of some odd joints and strangely twisted members in a fascinating and awkward Goldbergian infrastructure. It should be understood, for example, although this narrative coup has apparently gone unnoticed, that Anne commits suicide at the end of the poem and that these lines in the past tense cannot have been uttered by a living person. This feature of Lowell's machinery is perhaps not as unique as it might seem at first. As Sartre pointed out years ago, the entire Quentin section of *The Sound and the Fury* presumes a vantage point outside this life. Moreover, some of Lowell's other poems involve comparable situations; there is "At the Altar" in *Lord Weary's Castle*, and there is "Her Dead Brother" in this volume. The first-person description of the suicide in the latter poem even bears some striking resemblances to these lines in the thirty-seventh stanza of "The Mills of the Kavanaughs":

> "I think we row together, for the stern
> Jumps from my weaker stroke, and down the cove
> Our house is floating, and the windows burn,
> As if its underpinnings fed the stove."

Randall Jarrell was speaking of instances like this one, in which Harry is an exact reflection of the dead brother and in which the combination of water and fire and stove is repeated from the other poem, when he said that it was sometimes difficult to remember which poem one was reading.[16]

The water imagery has a more natural source in the narrative here, for Anne has put her cards away and taken a "metal boat" out into the mill pond, whence, rather like Arthur Winslow, she is not to return. It is not quite clear how the suicide is accomplished, but one imagines that Anne must drown herself:

> She can hardly row
> Against these whitecaps—surely never lulled
> For man and woman. Washing to and fro,
> The floorboards bruise the lilies that she pulled.

As maladroit as the image is, that last sentence probably alludes to Ophelia. The suspect image in the first clause, of "whitecaps" on a mill pond, can be partly exculpated by the point of the following phrase, which is that this voyage is not only a literal one. If after due consideration of that phrase one can remain unpersuaded that Anne is a suicide, there are other similar passages that must be taken into account. Here is one of them, which recalls Cordelia as much as Ophelia:

> Now her matches fall
> In dozens by her bobber to expire
> As target-circles on the mirrored fire-
> Escapes of *Kavanaugh*. She sees they hold
> Her mirror to her—just a little cold. . . .

Anne's own escape from the House of Kavanaugh is her death, an event symbolized also by the expiring matches.

There is another, less extraordinary context within which to interpret the very last lines of this poem. It is just possible that Anne has reference there to her *past* decision to remain with Harry even after he has gone berserk, that she is speaking more as Persephone than as the widowed Anne Kavanaugh and recalling that she sacrificed her life to stay with her husband in the underworld of his madness.[17] Even if the phrase " 'gave . . . to the grave' " could be stretched enough to accommodate this second interpretation, that interpretation would not exclude the first. Indeed, once the implications of this second interpretation have been noted, it seems likely that Lowell intends the two to support one another. If we take Anne to be playing Persephone to Harry's Hades in these lines, we might also recall that Anne has outlived Harry; and thus from the convergence of the "real" relationship with the mythological one, there issues a modified myth whose import, like that of Donne's sonnet, is "Death, thou shalt die." Anne's future, or the meaning of her suicide, is thus to be discovered in her past as well as in her final words.

This modification of the central myth is the other salient feature in the poem's last lines. The view of the Persephone myth that Lowell attributes to Anne, which is that instead of being raped by Hades she gave herself to him, is an unprecedented one.[18] He employs a similar combination of ancient myth and original interpretation earlier in the poem, when Anne implicitly compares herself with another heroine:

> She thinks of Daphne—Daphne could outrun
> The birds, and saw her swiftness tire the sun,
> And yet, perhaps, saw nothing to admire
> Beneath Apollo, when his crackling fire
> Stood rooted, half unwilling to undo
> Her laurel branches dropping from the blue.

It is unorthodox to see Daphne as the type of woman so self-esteeming that she could think the gods alone were worthy of her and so casual about Apollo that she permitted him to overtake her; nor is it ordinary to think of Apollo himself as so struck by her beauty even after her metamorphosis that he hesitates to touch her and is himself half-transfigured. Yet these seem to be the implications of this passage, which is the more extraordinary because there is but a modest "perhaps" to indicate those radical emendations. In fact, this new interpretation is strange enough, and this version of it ambiguous enough, that one might let it pass if it were not clear that the Daphne myth thus altered coincides with the Persephone parallel. In each case the heroine is changed from hapless victim to willing accomplice, and in each case her fate is one which she chooses; and this description applies to Anne Kavanaugh both at the time of her decision to stay with Harry and at the time of her decision to commit suicide. It is significant that Anne's thoughts on Daphne are triggered when she "feels her husband's fingers touch her neck," for Harry's touch—whether in memory, imagination, or fact—transforms her as Hades' did Persephone and Apollo's did Daphne.

At the same time, there is a difference between the analogies with Persephone and Daphne that is as obvious as the distinction between Hades and Apollo. Just as the former, the power of darkness, is an ancestor of Satan, so the latter, as the sun-god, is a type of Christ; and if the Daphne analogy reinforces the Persephone analogy on one level, it is its exact antithesis on another. On this second level, the Anne-Daphne parallel is a projection of a faith that the forces of life will triumph, while the Anne-Persephone parallel is a metaphor for the inexorable law of mortality. These two parallels under this second aspect constitute this poem's analysis of death. The complexity of Lowell's method can be glimpsed when we recall that there is beyond this analysis a synthesis which is embodied in the primary analogy as it appears under the other aspect; that is, as we have seen, the betrothal of Anne-Persephone to death or Hades is also a projection of an intuitive belief that man transcends his mortality. To put the same thing a different way, any passage of the several in which Lowell refers to the rape of Persephone as a symbol of death is a synecdoche for the concept that death is life. We need not " 'mistrust / Ourselves with Death' " because death, a part of the whole, is also an ineffable transcendental state that embodies that whole.

It is typical of this poem, and of this volume, that the synthesis is a tenuous one at best, that it is formulated most conclusively only in the last lines, where its position prohibits further challenge, and that elsewhere it is continually breaking up into the conflicting assertions and contradictory analogies that it would reconcile. These analogies proliferate to reinforce, obscure, and nullify one another in stanza after stanza.

At times, one finds a single analogy virtually disintegrating in its attempt to comprehend two or more different meanings at once, as in this passage at the end of the eleventh stanza in one of Anne's visions of Persephone:

> "[Persephone] curbed her horses as if serpent-stung,
> While shadows massed in earnest to rebel.
> Weary and glorious, once, when time was young,
> She ran from Hades. All Avernus burned.
> Black horse and chariot thundered at her heel.
> She, fleeting earthward, nothing seemed to steal,
> But the fruition that her hell had earned."

The burdens of this passage are many. In the first place,

Persephone, in an invention of Anne's that is not consistent with her final one, has lost her desire to escape the under-world, for some reason that is not explicitly stated. That reason, one gathers from context, is that she became recon-ciled to Hades in the same way that Anne became reconciled to Harry. The point of both reconciliations is that death, once understood in the sense that was explained in the last para-graph, will be elected over life. In the second place, Anne, by virtue of Lowell's mythological scheme, was in hell when married to Harry; and the choice to remain with Harry earned her fruition. Now, since Anne flees life as Persephone fled hell, it would seem that her fruition is in death, which is again to be understood in the sense outlined above. The two figures come to the same end, but they arrive by different routes.

In addition to Anne and Persephone, there is another figure involved in the lines quoted above, and involved in a very complicated way. Although the analogy is not as appar-ent here as in some other passages, the heiress of Perseph-one and Daphne is also a latter-day Eve, as the reference to the serpent in the first line above might suggest. With this passage in mind, we can look quickly at some others where the Anne-Eve parallel is more apparent.

This is a part of Anne's recollection of her childhood with Harry:

> Here bubbles filled
> Their basin, and the children splashed. They died
> In Adam, while the grass snake slid appalled
> To summer, while Jehovah's grass-green lyre
> Was rustling all about them in the leaves
> That gurgled by them turning upside down;
> The time of marriage!

In these highly compressed lines, the description of a prelap-sarian childhood overlies the knowledge of the destruction of that Edenic existence, and that knowledge includes that of the identity of God and his Adversary. As in adjacent sec-tions, there is a fairly obvious pun on "died" here, and the leaves that were "turning upside down" hint at the reversal in store for Anne and Harry as the course of their lives recapitulates that of Eve and Adam. Even the enormity of the effect of the original sin, *la petite mort,* is intimated: the snake was "appalled" not only because it was concealed by the grass but also because even Satan could be horrified by the Fall. As for the identity of God and Satan, if "lyre" is read as "liar" the description in the last lines applies exactly to the "grass snake," the snake in the grass who is of course the serpent of evil. When the serpent appears in Anne's vision of Persephone, it is in such a way as to equate Persephone's sojourn in Avernus and the results of Eve's consumption of the apple. The implication—soon to be contradicted—is that the Fall is tantamount to damnation and spiritual death.

The parallel of Anne and Eve is employed less obtrusively in stanza 5 in another passage that has implications for the vision under consideration. Anne thinks that

> She hears her husband, and she tries to call
> Him, then remembers. Burning stubble roars
> About the garden. Columns fill the life
> Insurance calendar on which she scores.

In view of the general chthonic atmosphere of the poem and the omnipresence of Hades, this scene is primarily an infernal one. At the same time, the "garden" is postlapsarian Eden, in the flaming light of which the "Him" of these lines (how *often* Lowell manages to get his pronouns in uppercase!) is also God, whom Eve lost as Anne has lost Harry, so that the life insurance policy is ironically worthless. Even more certainly than in the last quoted passage, God and his opposite number are identified. The same equation is effected in the tenth stanza:

> She listens to his feared
> Footsteps, no longer muffled by the green
> Torrent, that serpents up and down between
> Them, while she sprints along the shelf.

Literally, the male figure here is Harry in a memory of their youth; but because she is running from him, he is Hades; and the "feared / Footsteps" no longer drowned out by the serpentine stream are also those of God in the Garden after the Fall (Gen. 3:8). In the excerpt from the opening stanza quoted earlier in this chapter, both the "throne" and the "king" have an exactly parallel ambivalence.[19] The equation of Avernus and Eden by means of the imagery of conflagration is established in the lines, quoted earlier, in which Anne leaves her sanctuary by boat:

> "I think we row together, for the stern
> Jumps from my weaker stroke, and down the cove
> Our house is floating and our windows burn."

The house, a favorite symbol of Lowell's ever since *Lord Weary's Castle*, represents Anne's heritage and accommodates the thrones of both Hades and God. When Persephone ran from Hades and a burning Avernus in Anne's vision, she was also running from God and Eden; hence, her reconciliation with Hades is a reconciliation with God, and the implication that the Fall is the passage to Avernus or hell is reversed.

To move from this web of connections among metaphors back to its center, one can follow the old idea of *felix culpa*. In terms better adapted to this poem, since sin does not necessarily entail salvation and since the life-in-death adumbrated here is hardly angelic, Anne-Eve's fruition earns her hell and Anne-Persephone's hell earns her fruition. In the final analysis, life and death are interlocked in a dialectical process in which nothing is left behind, and that is why Anne's past prefigures her future without being a definition of that future. In the spiral of Lowell's dialectic, Anne's life at Kavanaugh was both Avernal and Edenic, and in giving herself again to death she is repeating that life at a different level.

That is, at least, the combined force of the analogies in view of the last lines of the poem. The poem itself is an arena where the various analogies constitute a welter of conflicts. The whole is grasped, if at all, only at the end, only when the poem is put by. Within the poem there is a disjunction of parts that Anne herself comments on in the sixth stanza, in a memory of her youthful relationship with Harry:

> "We are tumbling through
> The chalk-pits to our rural demigod,
> Old skull-and-horns, the bullock Father slew
> There on the sky-line. Let the offal sod

Our field with Ceres. Here is piety;
Ceres is here replenished to the full—
Green the clairvoyance of her deity,
Although the landscape's like a bullock's skull . . .
Things held together once," she thinks. "But where?
Not the life of me! How can I see
Things as they are, my Love, while April steals
Through bog and chalk-pit, till these boulders bear
Persephone—illusory, perhaps,
Yet her renewal, no illusion, for this air
Is orgied, Harry, and your setter yaps
About the goddess, while it nips her heels."

The " 'Things held together once' " but sundered in Anne's view of them until the end of the poem are the " 'Green . . . clairvoyance' " of life and the " 'skull' " of death. At this point early in the poem, Anne is unable to understand that " 'To die is life.' " Apparently life and death are intimately connected for her only in the cycle of nature, in the operation of which the offal of slaughter becomes the fertilizer of fields. " 'Things as they are' " in reality—the Reality in which contradictions are reconciled—are particularly incomprehensible in a spring so pervaded by natural life that Anne can almost believe in Ceres and Persephone.

In the poem's last lines, when these things come together for Anne, the diverse mythologies that have expressed confidence in such a reality are vindicated; but these mythologies do not cohere through the poem, and this incoherence is reflected here in the jumble of allusions to pagan ritualistic sacrifices, the Eleusinian mysteries, and most notably the Christian atonement and its mystery. The " 'Father' " who slew the bullock is her natural father, from whom she was separated at a very early age, or perhaps her father by adoption, Red Kavanaugh himself; but he is also God the Father, from whom she has also been removed, and by whom she will perhaps be "adopted." The " 'landscape' " that is itself " 'like a bullock's skull,' " is, although she does not recognize it, an emblem of Golgotha, literally the "place of the skull" and the site of another immolation which was purported to reconcile life and death.[20] Better than any other passage in "The Mills of the Kavanaughs," this one articulates the poem's motivating tension and its objective. The source of the poem is not the idea that " 'To die is life' " but rather that to die ought to be life; and its purpose is not so much to present " 'Things as they are' " in their ultimate unity as it is to unite the " 'Things [that] held together once.' " To this end Lowell lays parallel athwart parallel until the whole model of parallelism must be exchanged for that of a maze of intersecting analogies. The single entrance to the maze is Anne's recognition that these myths and the life and death with which they deal no longer seem to form a whole; its center—the point at which the whole can be intuited—is, if " 'Not the life' " of Anne, her death.

The things to be united are present in Lowell's landscape, and this contrivance of an elaborate setting, which weds the actual situation of the speaker to its historico-mythological analogues, is one of the most remarkable and revealing things about "The Mills of the Kavanaughs." In spite of Lowell's insistence upon the importance of observation to the poet,[21] and regardless of the capacity that he developed in *Lord Weary's Castle* to get objects into his poems, he characteristically puts things in his poems for his personae to see, instead of seeing things and attributing sight of them to his personae. If the distinction is not immediately apparent, one need only compare his use of physical detail in the title poem of this volume to the recording of particulars in, say, several of Elizabeth Bishop's poems, such as "The Fish" or "The Bight." In Bishop's poems, whatever symbolic import there is emerges from the minutiae which she observes only when these minutiae are subjected to the most intense intellectual pressure; the objects are retentive of their individualities. For Lowell, on the other hand, the symbolic potential of an object is its primary recommendation.

"The Mills of the Kavanaughs" and "Thanksgiving's Over" represent the extreme to which the concern can run. In "Her Dead Brother" and "Falling Asleep over the Aeneid," although the pressure of the historico-mythological contexts can be felt at virtually every point, the symbolic details are less self-assertive. In this respect, these poems resemble "Mother Marie Therese," a poem which is in turn closest to those in *Life Studies* in the subtlety of its symbolism.

Only the reader versed in classical sources and searching for allusions to them would notice immediately that the seemingly unportentous phrase "our narrow Bay" is a reminder that the Maris Stella House of "Mother Marie Therese" is supposed to be located at a place in New Brunswick named "Carthage." This "fossil convent," an enclave established by religious exiles, fortified by faith, and surrounded by a hostile world, is a modern type of the citadel founded by Dido and her Tyrians. Indeed the mother superior bears some resemblance to that mythological queen (as well as to Anne Kavanaugh), who was " 'An emigrée,' " who vowed eternal fidelity to a murdered husband, and who was exalted almost to the status of a divinity after her death. Similarly, the Punic Wars that finally destroyed Carthage seem to have perceptible echoes in the scattered allusions to the Seven Years' War and the Franco-Prussian War. The French, with whom the convent has identified itself in the past, were defeated in both cases.

These parallels are not exact or consistent, however, and they are sporadically interrupted by others. The mother superior's name, for example, is perhaps intended to recall Maria Theresa, the archduchess of Austria and queen of Hungary, whose combination of physical beauty and political sagacity would have made her a rival of Queen Elizabeth I or of Dido herself. Although the facts that she got her husband elected Holy Roman Emperor and that she allied herself with the Bourbons in the Seven Years' War tend to strengthen the connection, one hesitates to say that there is anything as definite as a parallel here. Lowell probably associates the nun with the empress for much the same reason that he has her "parroting the *Action Française*," the right-wing French daily that espoused an extreme form of nationalism: to emphasize her worldly interests.

In the case of nuns, of course, worldly interests are likely to issue in actions that are unbecoming, and that is why the old nun who is the speaker in this poem can say:

The good old times, ah yes! But good, that all's
Forgotten like our Province's cabals;
And Jesus, smiling earthward, finds it good;
For we were friends of Cato, not of God.

To be a friend of Cato the Censor is to be passionately concerned with the public welfare, and to be involved in political
cabals in the Canadian provinces of the late nineteenth century was to plot to overthrow British governors. What we
have here is a group of sisters concocting revolutionary plans
within the walls of an essentially reactionary institution. The
vitality and passion of the mother superior and her associates
were responsible for allegiances that were *au fond* contradictory. Like Pius IX, a print of whom adorned the wall in the
sitting room when she was the mother superior, Mother
Marie Therese was both a reformer and an archconservative;
but unlike the pope, whose conservatism developed only
after he had been driven from Rome by Mazzini, she was
both at once. A modern Teresa of Avila, the saint who
seemed to Crashaw to incorporate both "eagle" and "dove,"
she is exactly the sort of figure one might expect to be drawn
by a poet who believes that a poem should include all of a
man's contradictions.

In a world that is fundamentally ambivalent, to have but
one point of view is perhaps to falsify; it is perhaps to become, in Stevens's words, a "lunatic of one idea." People,
institutions, and even the gods, at least in the perspective
framed by mortals, are complex and self-contradictory, Lowell implies, and therefore only a certain ambivalence can keep
one from oversimplifying.[22] One of Lowell's means of dem-
onstrating the complexity and contrariness of things is to
set up certain traditional oppositions and then show that the
opposing terms themselves are comparable unions of contraries. If this strategy—which is apparent even in the statement quoted near the beginning of this chapter, in which
Lowell characterizes himself as a conventional liberal and a
radical conservative—lies behind the conception of a mother
superior who resembles an empress, it is also responsible for
the views of the Church and its God that are worked out in

the course of "Mother Marie Therese."[23] It produces some of
its most dramatic effects in these lines:

> Like Proserpina, who fell
> Six months a year from earth to flower in hell;
> She half-renounced by Candle, Book and Bell
> Her flowers and fowling pieces for the Church.

At first this passage seems merely an indulgent description of
a nun who could or would not renounce her worldly concerns altogether just because she had taken orders. A closer
look at the syntax reveals a more polemical attitude. Her
sequestration, such as it is, is compared to falling, and the
religious implications of that idea can hardly be ignored in
this context. Even more striking is the simile "Like Proserpina," for what follows is her entrance into the order, and the
implied comparison is between hell and the Church. Unless it
is assumed that the construction of the sentence is faulty, that
what Lowell means is that she was like Proserpina only in
leading a double life, this passage can be read no other way.

Once the ambivalence of this passage has been emphasized, that of the preceding lines is latensified:

> Was it not fated that the sweat of Christ
> Would wash the worldly serpent? Christ enticed
> Her heart that fluttered, while she whipped her hounds
> Into the quicksands of her manor grounds,
> A lordly child, her habit fleur-de-lys'd
> There she dismounted, sick; with little heed,
> Surrendered.

In view of the reference to Proserpina in the following lines, it
is clear that the comparison to be drawn here is between
Christ and Hades. The nun-to-be, with "her habit fleur-de-
lys'd," is a daughter of Demeter, "enticed" from earth to the
underworld while gathering flowers. Other details in this
passage support the heretical comparison. The juxtaposition
of "the worldly serpent" and "Christ enticed" and the internal rhyme in the latter are provocative, as is the image of
"Her heart that fluttered," which recalls "the Mother's
strangled grouse" and thereby implies that she was herself a
victim.

The ambiguity in passages such as this has two effects: in the first place, it blurs the distinction between the worldly and the religious; and in the second place, partly as a result of the implication that such a dichotomy is fallacious, it deprecates the ascetic life, the justification of which depends upon the distinction. The grouse, alluded to in a passage just discussed, are recurrent symbols in this poem, and another of their appearances can be cited to exemplify these effects. Near the end of the poem, the speaker, reflecting on the sisters now living in the convent, says that they

>   wish the times were love,
> And their hysterical hosannahs rouse
> The loveless harems of the buck ruffed grouse,
> Who drums, untroubled now, beside the sea—
> As if he found our stern virginity
> *Contra naturam.*

The buck grouse is "untroubled" only in the sense that the former mother is no longer around to take potshots at him. To the speaker he seems very troubled indeed by the unnatural virginity of the nuns. If one could avoid the theological ramifications of these lines, they might seem simply, albeit grimly, humorous. But the religious terminology makes those ramifications virtually impossible to avoid, and once considered they can only lead to the conclusion that the speaker is inclined to the point of view that she attributes to the bird.

Actually, it could hardly be otherwise, since "the buck ruffed grouse" is an all but blasphemous figure for Christ as Bridegroom, just as "loveless harems" is a burlesque of the nuns awaiting union with him. The "hysterical" quality of the prayers might be ascribed to the nuns' fear that their virginity (and by implication their whole way of life) is pointless just as easily as it might be ascribed to their religious passion. Indeed, this *hysterica passio* might have one of its sources in desperation. At any rate, the speaker has such fears, for in the following lines images of a perverse abstinence ("now we freeze," "warped trees") and religious death ("our nunnery slab") merge to imply a spiritual sterility ("Now all the bells are tongueless"). This sterility entails the end of the religious heritage, and while "A new year" or a new era "swells and stirs," the "narrow Bay / Freezes itself and us."[24] Without flatly denying the worth of the ascetic life, the old nun knows that spiritual sterility is not confined to the secular world alone.

Lowell suggests that chastity is not necessarily a virtue in another less characteristic passage. In the last line—"My mother's hollow sockets fill with tears"[25]—the poem's only use of the singular possessive and the uncapitalized noun might be intended to induce speculation on the reader's part and thereby to keep the "Mother's" character richly ambiguous. Such speculation certainly reminds us that there was another poet who enjoyed commending in unobtrusive ways his personae's deviations from their ascetic paths and that Browning's monologues were obviously models for several of those in this book.

On the whole, however, this poem is more likely to recall another Victorian poet, whose "Dover Beach" supplied one epigraph for the title poem. Like Arnold in both that poem and "Stanzas from the Grande Chartreuse," Lowell is ambivalent about the ascetic life; but whereas Arnold was skeptical of its philosophical foundations, Lowell is also convinced of the corruptibility of its adherents. This corruptibility is suggested, with the result that the contrast between the contemplative life and the active life is further weakened, in these lines:

> "O disregard
> Time's wings and armor, when it flutters down
> Papal tiaras and the Bourbon crown;
> For quickly, priest and prince will stand, their shields
> Before each others faces, in the fields,
> Where, as I promised, virtue will compel
> Michael and all his angels to repel
> Satan's advances, till his forces lie
> Beside the Lamb in blissful fealty."

The " 'Papal tiaras' " and " 'the Bourbon crown' " are equated by the conjunction, so that the sponsor of the nunnery appears every bit as involved in the struggle for power as the

French kings, with the possible difference that the latter are less hypocritical. The yoking of " 'priest and prince' " serves the same purpose, except that there is an ambiguity that makes this reference even more provocative. These lines are imagined to have been spoken by "Heaven's Prince," or Christ, and it is implied that worldly priests, who just might lead " 'Satan's advances,' " might find themselves opposed to "Heaven's Prince" and "Michael and all his angels'" in the end. In any case, this passage lays bare the inconsistency. of a church that condemns worldly politics and secular force, on the one hand, and images its ultimate justification in exactly those terms, on the other.

Lest there be some doubt about his meaning here, Lowell makes the point again along with another in a section that echos both Yeats and Blake:

> "A sword," said Father Turbot, "not a saint";
> Yet he who made the Virgin without taint,
> Chastised our Mother to the Rule's restraint.

The sanctimonious character of the priest is revealed not only by his name (which is also that of a flatfish with eyes on the upper side that spends much of its time on the bottom of the sea) but also by his formulation of Mother Marie Therese in a phrase that is falsely dichotomous, both in that it oversimplifies her nature and in that it oversimplifies the nature of God. She *was* "Chastised . . . to the Rule's restraint" and she was "*Chastised* . . . to the Rule's restraint." The same God that made the Lamb and the Virgin made the Tygre and the Mother, and consequently his nature and desires remain obscure. It was their unblinking acceptance of this fact that enabled the old nun and her mother superior to deride the other sisters for their orthodoxy and to hold their ears when they "heard the spheres / Whirring *venite*"; and it is by means of these two figures, and by means of the mutually qualifying analogies that they make and call forth respectively, that Lowell gets all of his biases into this marvelously sympathetic and subtly humorous and sensual monologue.

Until the last poem in *The Mills of the Kavanaughs*, the biases against Christianity and its God are very nearly balanced by those in favor of it; or it might be more accurate to say that the agnosticism takes the form of alternating attacks upon and defenses of the religion. Nevertheless, in keeping with Lowell's tendency to organize his volumes around a crucial center—a tendency that becomes an important strategy with his next volume—"Mother Marie Therese" does seem to epitomize this ambivalence, and perhaps the scales begin to tip in the poem following it.

"David and Bathsheba in the Public Garden," it had better be said at the outset, is undoubtedly one of the least successful and least intelligible poems that Lowell has published. There are three major sources of obscurity here, and once they have been spotted it is possible to understand at least the poem's gist. The first of these is the incomplete revetment of parts of the Biblical story of David's life (especially 2 Sam. 11–14), which results in children punting footballs in Judah and the king mouthing sentiments that might have been criticized by Eliot's "young man carbuncular." Since the contemporary setting recedes, rather inexplicably, after the opening lines, and since David gives way to a more perceptive Bathsheba after the first poem, and since the attitude that one is to take toward David is finally made clear, this problem is not insurmountable. The second problem is that Lowell's puns are more gratuitous and frivolous here than in anything since *Land of Unlikeness*. The double meanings in " 'the *gravity* / Of reaching for the moon,' " in "the *wood-winds* of the North," and in the "prows" that "Were *sworded*" contribute little; but once the reader realizes that one meaning at the most is really relevant, these puns are no longer obstacles either.

The ambiguities that cannot be reduced if the poem is to be understood at all are those which enshroud God and the fate of the sinful soul. These two ambiguities are of course one to the extent that the fate of the soul depends upon the nature of God. It is David's belief, maintained in the face of Bathsheba's hesitant but sincere doubts and timid queries, that in spite of his adulterous betrayal and virtual execution of Uriah, he is immortal. In looking into the pond he sees in

" 'The Lion's' " face that is reflected there not only the emblem of Judah's courage but also the image of God. David ignores what his queen in "Bathsheba's Lament in the Garden" realizes: that traditionally the lion's cruelty also renders it "an appropriate metaphor for a fierce and malignant enemy . . . and hence for the arch-fiend himself."[26] Besides associating the lion with David, Bathsheba identifies the lion with the victimized Uriah, who

>   found
> Jehovah, the whale's belly of the pit.
> He is the childless, the unreconciled
> Master of darkness. Will Uriah sit
> And judge?

In these lines, Uriah is both Jehovah and the Prince of Darkness, as Harry is both Hades and the Son, and consequently he is "Always a stranger."

In these passages, the poet clearly goes beyond the question of David's salvation to call into question the existence of the New Testament God. As in "Her Dead Brother," "The Lord is dark"; but if there is a difference between the questioning here and that in the poem on the other side of "Mother Marie Therese," it is that this time Lowell's female persona does not claim that his name is "holy." He is the Lion that David sees reflected in the pond, but he is the Lion with all of his attributes. In the imitation of Franz Werfel's "Der Dicke Mann Im Spiegel," Lowell posits a universe that is either controlled solely by the powers of darkness or entirely godless. In this sometimes opaque allegory, "the mad King's zoo" and "the royal grotto" stand for a world afflicted with violent events such as wars and political executions: "The bullies wrestled on the royal bowling green; / Hammers and sickles on their hoods of black sateen." This world is also envisioned as a capriciously run penitentiary in which man is subjected to the continual torture of his own mutability—the painful realizations that the "apples" of youth have turned into the "ashes" of middle age and that the gaily mischievous boy has become the repulsive figure in the mirror—so that the speaker "serves / Time" in two senses.[27]

This pun is one of the three or four upon which this whole poem turns. Another is "swinging," which refers to the game of the speaker's childhood and repeats the motif of execution. If the first meaning dominates in the initial stanza's recollection that "Nurse was swinging me so high, so high," the second emerges in the last stanza's thought that "Nurse and I were swinging in the Old One's eye." The change, hardly noticeable at first, from the transitive to the intransitive use of the verb is crucial. The other important pun here is that on "eye" and "I", which Lowell was to make much of in several of the best poems in *For the Union Dead*.[28] Lowell rhymes "eye" and "I" in both the opening and the closing stanzas in order to stress this pun, which seems to have two implications that are not necessarily compatible. The most apparent of these implications is that the speaker is the tool of the Devil, "the old dog" or "the Old One." The second implication, stemming from the situation in which the "I" of the poem is staring into his own "eye" in the mirror, is that the speaker himself is in effect "the mad King" or "the Old One." Since the associations, the lacunae, and the rhythms in the poem are all designed to convey the impression of madness, this interpretation seems plausible; and its plausibility increases when one recalls Bathsheba's interpretation of David's reflection in the water and the implications of the old man's observation that the bust of Augustus scowls into his glasses at itself. In "The Fat Man in the Mirror" the point seems to be that the only possible supernatural powers are projections or reflections of mad individuals. It is as though Lowell were using the Pauline metaphor of no longer seeing through a glass darkly but seeing face to face in order to attack the object of that metaphor.

The recognition that this poem is fundamentally anti-Christian helps to explain its inclusion in this volume and its particular position here, for "Thanksgiving's Over," the poem that concludes *The Mills of the Kavanaughs*, is a vicarious exorcism of the poet's Catholicism. In somewhat the same way that Pound's Mauberley's art parodies the art of E. P., who is a projection of the poet, Lowell's female figure's religion parodies that of her husband, who is an extension of his creator. If one imagines that Pound caricatured some of his own poetic inclinations in order to shed them, then the parallel is fairly precise, for here Lowell presents under the guise of the beliefs of a madwoman his most bizarre version of the religion that he was to abandon altogether after this volume.[29] The title of the poem, a quotation of an observation made by Michael's wife, is the poet's most explicit dismissal of his religion in this book.

Unfortunately, Lowell's poem recalls Pound's in its obscurities as well as in its framework, if indeed the latter can be thought of as other than the origin of the former. As in "Mother Marie Therese" and "Falling Asleep over the Aeneid," one of the chief sources of difficulty here is the lack of distinct divisions between different times. The other difficulty, one which is certainly expected by now, consists in the poem's labyrinth of analogies and repetitions. In one respect this difficulty is of a different sort from that encountered in most of the other poems in this volume. In addition to the legitimately imposed problem of working out the relationship among various associated images and allusions, there is the pseudoproblem of deciphering the meaning of basically inexplicable echoes. In other words, one suspects that in "Thanksgiving's Over" Lowell's dialectic is more habit than method. After puzzling over the possible significance of the connection between the "numskull" cockatoo and the "skullcaps" on the mountains or of the "bell" in the asylum and the "belled" pigtails of the madwoman, one will probably decide that these echoes are hollow.

Many others are functional; and as usual in these first volumes, the metamorphoses in the imagery constitute the equivalent of plot. Since this function might not be immediately apparent and since the potpourri of dreams and visions can be confusing, a section-by-section commentary might be worthwhile. Characteristically, the poem begins with a setting in which the details are obliquely symbolic:

> Thanksgiving night: Third Avenue was dead;
> My fowl was soupbones. Fathoms overhead,
> Snow warred on the El's world in the blank snow.

It is night because the time for the giving of thanks is nearly over, and this because there is no longer anything for which to give thanks. Indeed, as the reference to the Trinity suggests, Michael no longer believes that there is anything *to* which to give thanks, and consequently the "soupbones" are not only a substitute for the traditional turkey but also a travesty of the symbol of the Holy Ghost. The odd use of "Fathoms" can be explained on the same basis when it is realized that the second line contains an odd echo of the first lines of Ariel's song: "Full *fathom* five thy father lies; / Of his *bones* are coral made."[30] The next line reiterates the "death" of Michael's "father" both in the image of the natural world storming the ramparts of heaven and in the implied vacuity of the latter.[31] Michael's loss of faith can be attributed at least in part to the paranoia that hers has helped to inspire in his wife, whose recollected speech opens normally enough but soon indicates her insanity, as she first envisions herself as a new Mother of God pregnant with the Word (" 'garblings' ") and then as a Bride of Christ who offers, in the manner of the old London street vendors immortalized by Campion, to sell her virginity.

Whether her madness prompted the teeming associations that overwhelm the last part of this first stanza, or whether, as one sometimes suspects, the latter were partly responsible for the choice of a mad speaker, the passage jumbles together the Holy Ghost as dove, St. Francis's pigeons, Christ as the Word and therefore " 'Brother Parrot,' " and Michael's wife in her room with barred windows as a caged " 'Bird of Paradise.' " The bird motif reappears in the second stanza, where her "celluloid and bargain cockatoo" seems to be an icon of Christ and where a candle's flame ("A bluebird in a tumbler") is a symbol of her because she thinks of herself as Mary confined. Her confinement was either cause or effect of a desire to kill Michael; unable to do so, she somehow hurled herself through the barred window "Into the neon" in a parody of a union with Light that recalls ironically her earlier dream of a "new life." After the attempted suicide, as we learn in the third stanza, she was put in an asylum, again surrounded by birds and again in a cell. There she sees herself as a combination of Maid Marian, whose name and unlikely but legendary virginity have obvious analogues in this context, a sequestered nun, and an incarcerated criminal.

Time passes in a blur, and in the autumn her need to escape her suffering persuades her at every point that the end of the world (" 'El Dorado' ") is at hand. The bird symbol recurs in the form of the " 'golden weathercocks,' " which for her are heaven-sent messengers that crow the beginning of the end and for the reader are reminders of her insanity.

Her concentration upon the Final Things inspires a confusion of her husband with the archangel who would lead the heavenly host into combat at Armageddon, a confusion which affects every reference to " 'Michael' " in the fourth stanza of this poem. Even more suggestive of both her state of mind and the state of her religion is her confusion of chastity with erotic love. She interprets the locking of her cell as the locking of a chastity belt emblematic of her own virtue; but she also conceives of the cell as a " 'lying-in-house' " in which she is waiting to be delivered of her soul, worthy of deliverance because of her chastity.[32] In a similar vein, Venus, goddess of love, is her pagan patron saint, when Diana, the virgin goddess, would seem to be indicated. She thinks she is visited by angels that are also incubae, and to them she reports her husband's supposed cruelty.

At some proximate point, probably early in the fifth stanza, the scene shifts back to the time when she was confined at home and Michael could find almost no relief from her mad harangues. For the most part this stanza deals with details of her virtual captivity that seem either redundant or misplaced, and for this reason it is probably the weakest section of the poem. Nevertheless, the concluding lines, which bring Michael's voice back into the poem and begin the transition to the last stanza, establish firmly the symbolic relationship between man and wife:

> Sleep dispelled
> The burden of her spirit. But the cars
> Rattled my window. *Where am I to go?* She yelled:
> "Let go my apron!" And I saw them shine,
> Her eyeballs—like a lion at the bars
> Across my open window—like the stars!

This passage recalls an earlier one, which describes the same period in their lives:

                                 the bars
Still caged her window—half a foot from mine,
It mirrored mine:
My window's window.

Lowell has apparently designed a house with a strange floor
plan in order to employ, again, the mirror image. In looking
out of his window and into hers during the dark night remembered in the fifth stanza, Michael is seeing face to face a
terrifying figure that is either an image of God or a distorted
image of himself; or rather it is a symbol of both a mysteriously cruel deity and the madness that belief in such a deity
entails.

   Michael is an Irish Catholic, or so his name and the
"cowhorn beads from Dublin" that are mentioned in the last
stanza suggest, and not unnaturally his repudiation of his
faith leaves him with no place "*to go.*" Unlike his wife, who
would follow the example of Henry's penitential journey to
Canossa and " 'go / Barefooted through the snow' " to ask
forgiveness, Michael cannot return to the church. Although
the phrase " 'bootless Brothers' " means "humble Franciscans" to his wife, who might well confuse the Franciscans
with the "discalced" Carmelites, it means "helpless" or
"worthless monks" to him. Similarly, for the brothers and his
wife the contention that " '*our burden's light*' " signifies that
tasks set by God should not be difficult and that the refrain of
their religion is the Light of God, while for him it means that
the Light of God is a weight that man might not be able to
bear. Appropriately, then, the poem ends with his memory
of visiting the Franciscan church with his wife and sitting, at
her insistence, to listen to nothing in the empty building, for
only she can "hear" the intoning of the Psalm from the Vul-
gate. Having renounced his God, he must indeed " 'join this
deaf and dumb / Breadline for children,' " as must the poet,
and *The Mills of the Kavanaughs* concludes with "Not a sound."

   Yet in the very silence of its conclusion, this poem begins to
turn back upon itself; Lowell's dialectic, his attempt to include a man's contradictions, goes on, in effect, even though
the poem and the volume have ended. If Michael must " 'join
this deaf and dumb / Breadline for children,' " it is also true,

according to the belief that he has renounced, that one must become as a child again. This is the principle symbolized by the sculpture group of St. Francis feeding a row of "toga'd boys with birds beneath a Child" that stands before the Church. Moreover, although Michael presumably scorns the " 'bootless' " Franciscans, his own image for his snow-encrusted boots is that of feet wrapped "In sheepskins."

One remembers, too, that Ariel's song, alluded to in the opening lines of "Thanksgiving's Over," has as its theme not death so much as metamorphosis. Thus, from beginning to end, there is an undercurrent that would pull the poem back into the area of faith. Eliot once argued of someone's poetry that it evinced faith, not because of any belief that it professed, but rather because of the despair that it implied, and it might be mentioned in regard to this poem that Lowell hints that Michael's renunciation is itself religious. Be that as it may, the importance of contradiction in this poem can hardly be denied; it is not until "Beyond the Alps," the first poem in *Life Studies*, that Lowell definitely puts Rome behind him. Even there, he does not reject Christianity so much as he shifts his focus to other subjects, which he continues to treat in terms that accommodate and foster contradictory inclina- tions.

Divorce is
the sign of knowledge in our time
divorce! divorce!
—WILLIAM CARLOS WILLIAMS, *Paterson*

hanging like an oasis in his air
of lost connections. . . .
—"Memories of West Street and Lepke"

4

DIVORCE AND RECONCILIATION:

Life Studies (1959)

*T*he years between 1951 and 1959, as everyone knows, form the first watershed in Lowell's career. As Thomas Parkinson says, "The breaking point comes with *The Mills of the Kavanaughs*, for with that book the specifically Catholic content of the poetry stops, as does the poetic style that is early Lowell."[1] That is certainly correct, at least in regard to the specific content and the stylistic surface, and the reasons for the divorce are not far to seek. In the first place, Lowell's Roman Catholicism justified itself poetically inasmuch as it provided him with a vehicle for themes not necessarily Catholic; and when Catholicism itself came under review and was found wanting, Lowell had either to modify the vehicle or to resort to another means of conveyance. The former alternative, chosen on several occasions in *Lord Weary's Castle* and frequently in *The Mills of the Kavanaughs*, involved Lowell in a messy business indeed. Some of the poems discussed in the preceding two chapters must today make Lowell himself smile wryly when he recollects Stevens's criterion: a poem must resist the intelligence almost successfully.

In the second place, Lowell was writing longer poems in

The Mills of the Kavanaughs—just as he had written poems longer than those of *Land of Unlikeness* in his second volume—and in the course of doing so he put himself in a position very near that in which Hart Crane put himself in writing *The Bridge*. In phrases that reveal the plight of at least a generation of American poets, R. P. Blackmur has defined that position. Crane wrote, he said, "in a language of which it was the virtue to accrete, modify, and interrelate moments of emotional vision" and yet "attempted to apply his language, in his major effort, to a theme that required a sweeping, discrete, indicative, anecdotal language. . . . He used the private lyric to write the cultural epic."[2] As a preceding chapter indicated and as Blackmur's description of Crane's language suggests, Lowell's earlier mode is closely related to Crane's; and while none of the poems in *The Mills of the Kavanaughs* has the scope that *The Bridge* has, even "Falling Asleep over the Aeneid" might be said to exemplify the same problem. Lowell recognized the dilemma: he could not have both such density and such length.

Life Studies is a characteristically stubborn reaction to this recognition. Taken as whole, it can be regarded as an alternative response to the desire to escape the confines of the short poem without surrendering the advantages of the language that Blackmur describes. In other words, during the period after *The Mills of the Kavanaughs*, while Lowell's poetry changes in certain obvious ways with the decisive rejection of the religious symbology and the stunningly effective appropriation of personal subjects, the transformation is more a matter of style than of method. Lowell is fundamentally a lyric poet, and he still writes in a language of which it is precisely "the virtue to accrete, modify, and interrelate moments of emotional vision," although the vocabulary and the measures have altered drastically. They will alter again—most notably in *Near the Ocean*—but this fundamental language, this method, remains constant. The most important difference between the preceding volumes and *Life Studies* is that the latter, like the volumes that follow it, constitutes a coherent whole.

The nature of the unity of *Life Studies* can be illuminated by

J. V. Cunningham's comments on the predicament of the poet "committed by temperament and habit to the shorter poem," yet in need of the "world" readily available to the longer poem.[3] There are basically two means by which a group of short poems can attain this end: either the poet "sets the poems in a matrix of relevant prose" or he builds a sequence, "a series of short poems in whose succession there is an implicit structure." *Life Studies* makes use of both of these methods, although it would not be strictly accurate to refer to "91 Revere Street" as a matrix. The most pertinent of Cunningham's remarks is that "length, however, is only a means; what one wants is a situation in which the several items can lend each other context, reference, and resonance, in which this short poem will be something more than it would be in isolation by belonging to a whole."

In his development of exactly this kind of "situation" in *Life Studies*, Lowell may not have had any particular model in mind. Nevertheless, there is some indication that he might have learned a part of his technique from William Carlos Williams's *Paterson* (Book One), another volume which incorporates prose passages, albeit in a way different from *Life Studies*. Lowell reviewed the first book of *Paterson* in 1947 and found it the most important volume of poetry to be published in the previous year. Moreover, he had read Randall Jarrell's review and regarded it as the best possible introduction to *Paterson*, and in Jarrell's review there is a commentary on Williams's method that is relevant to Lowell's.[4] After speaking of "theme" and "movement" in *Paterson*, Jarrell says:

I have used this simile deliberately because—over and above the organization of argument or exposition—the organization of *Paterson* is musical to an almost unprecedented degree: Dr. Williams introduces a theme that stands for an idea, repeats it over and over in varied forms, develops it side by side with two or three more themes that are being developed, recurs to it time and time again throughout the poem and echoes it for ironic or grotesque effects in thoroughly incongruous contexts. Sometimes this is done with the greatest complication and delicacy. . . . [5]

Such a method might be exemplified by following any one of numerous images and themes through *Life Studies*. To take just one such image at this point, there is "the mustard spire" of "A Mad Negro Soldier Confined at Munich," which is faintly echoed two sections later in the description of Ford Madox Ford, who was "mustard gassed voiceless some seven miles / behind the lines at Nancy or Belleau Wood," and is further developed in "To Delmore Schwartz," where Lowell recalls that "the antiquated / refrigerator gurgled mustard gas / through your mustard-yellow house." Lowell's purpose here is twofold: first, he wants to establish a line of alienated figures whose plights enforce and illuminate one another; and second, he wishes to associate madness, war, and art. These purposes can be elaborated in the following discussions of individual poems; the point to be made here is that this method allows the poems to "lend each other context, reference, and resonance" and therefore permits Lowell to construct a long work without relying upon an external frame of reference.

The prevalence of this strategy in *Life Studies* encourages the suspicion that after *The Mills of the Kavanaughs* Lowell took advantage of Jarrell's advice: "If you want to write a long poem which doesn't stick to one subject, but which unifies a dozen, you can learn a good deal from *Paterson*."[6] This suspicion can only be increased by one passage in "Ford Madox Ford":

> you emerged in your "worn uniform,
> gilt dragons on the revers of the tunic,"
> a Jonah—O divorced, divorced
> from the whale-fat of post-war London!

These lines, which focus on the estrangement of the artist from a culture that has devoted itself to commerce and profit, are reminiscent of the lines in *Paterson*, quoted in Jarrell's review, where the academic language that separates the educated elite from the common man is judged

> perfect
> in justice and substance but divorced, divorced
> from its fellows, fallen low—
> Divorce is
> the sign of knowledge in our time
> divorce! divorce!

Although his immediate subject is different, Williams's lines are enough like Lowell's to have inspired them; but more important, as the following pages will attempt to show, Lowell's method has in common with Williams's the use of motif to draw together passages that are pages and even sections apart.[7]

While there can be no thought of influence where fundamental concerns are involved, these two poets also share a painful awareness of the extent to which "divorce" is characteristic of our time. In *Life Studies*, this basic theme is set forth in its most extreme form in the first poem, "Beyond the Alps," which concludes with this couplet:

> Now Paris, our black classic, breaking up
> like killer kings on an Etruscan cup.

This vision of the sundering of the modern world epitomizes the concerns of a volume too often considered the prime example of confessional poetry.[8] The theme is reiterated at the beginning of each of the following parts of the book, although it is modified in each case according to the nature of that part. Part two opens with the account of the mysterious Major Mordecai Myers, "Grandmother Lowell's grandfather," who represents a romantic past with which the sophisticated present has all but lost contact: "Undoubtedly Major Mordecai had lived in a more ritualistic, gaudy, and animal world than twentieth-century Boston." The third part begins with the poem on Ford Madox Ford that includes the lines quoted above on the divorce of the artist from the public. The first line of "My Last Afternoon with Uncle Devereux Winslow," the poem with which part four begins, is " 'I won't go with you. I want to stay with Grandpa!' " which suggests a division within the poet's own family.

The theme of divorce or disintegration is thus the matrix of the other themes in *Life Studies*. The "breaking up" occurs on four levels, related in such a way that they might be called the twentieth-century version, or rather perversion, of the chain of being. In the first place, there is the disintegration of the old order of culture in both the religious and the political realms, which is primarily the subject of the poems in part one. This condition is mirrored in the decay of the love relationships and familial connections that constitutes the subject of the prose of part two and one main concern in part four. What results from the severing of the ordinary bonds of love and the destruction of cultural values is the isolation and alienation of the individual artist, which is the focal point of the poems in part three. Finally, the exaggerated nature of this alienation is responsible for the "breaking up" of the individual himself, for the many forms of insanity explored in part three and part four.

Over against these centrifugal forces, especially in the last two parts of *Life Studies*, Lowell sets the ability of man, or rather of individual men, to absorb the shock of cultural disintegration. Most often, his shaky confidence in men is revealed by his insistence on their capacity to abide conflict within themselves, to encompass antinomies and therefore to unite them.[9] This response to the problem—and it is a response rather than a solution—can be found close to the surface in only a few poems, but it is latent in several key "studies." In "For George Santayana," for instance, it is the philosopher's personal reconciliation of Christianity and atheism with which Lowell counters the breakdown of religious values as it is exemplified in "Beyond the Alps"; and in "Skunk Hour" it is the poet-speaker's recognition of both the dignity and the degradation of human nature with which he responds to the various perversions typified by "A Mad Negro Soldier Confined at Munich." At a further remove this attempt to reconcile contradictory tendencies informs "Memories of West Street and Lepke," where the poet-speaker, who elsewhere describes himself as "part criminal and yet a Phi Bete," combines criminal inclinations and an honest and "agonizing reappraisal." Implications such as these, however, depend greatly upon the interaction of individual poems, upon the "situation" that Lowell creates, and that situation cannot be understood apart from a more detailed examination of these poems.

"Beyond the Alps," the introductory poem in part one, is a series of three sonnets that treat the theme of the disintegration of Western culture in the areas of politics and religion.[10] As in "Falling Asleep over the Aeneid," Lowell's historical allusions are to five distinct eras (in this case, the Hellenic era, Etruscan civilization, the Roman Empire, the period of World War II, and the present); and as in "Her Dead Brother," he quickly converts setting to symbol. If in the earlier poem death was changed to seascape, here we find "Life changed to landscape." Because "Beyond the Alps" is partly a *de casibus* poem, the imagery forms a rise-and-fall pattern: the Swiss mountaineers climb but fail to gain the summit of Mt. Everest and are forced to descend again; the train in which the poet-speaker travels from Rome to Paris first winds up the Alps and then returns "to earth"; and the same motif recurs in the reference to the papal definition of the dogma of Mary's bodily assumption, as well as in the vignette of the papal guards who "sloped their pikes to push" the crowds from the doors of the Vatican.

Taken in conjunction, the historical scheme and this pattern of imagery seem at first to provide the structure of the poem; that is, it seems that Lowell is presenting a cyclical theory of history in terms of which civilizations rise and fall and so are analogous to one another and to the mountainous landscape.[11] If one tries to correlate this idea of the structure with the details of the poem, however, it will be found that some of those details must either be ignored or wrenched out of shape. For example, the idea that every civilization reaches a peak and then destroys itself, which is suggested in the image of "each backward, wasted Alp, a Parthenon, / fire-branded socket of the Cyclops' eye" is difficult to reconcile with the succeeding lines:

> There were no tickets for that altitude
> once held by Hellas, when the Goddess stood,
> prince, pope, philosopher and golden bough. . . .

Here the culture of classical Greece seems to be identified with the Golden Age, a norm by which all subsequent civilizations must be measured, rather than representative of one high point in the cycle of civilization. In other words, there is a hint of the Renaissance theory of the "running down" of history which is not easily combined with a cyclical theory.

But there is no need to debate this point, for in the lines following those just quoted, Greece suddenly turns into Rome, and neither of the above interpretations is any longer applicable:

> There were no tickets for that altitude
> once held by Hellas, when the Goddess stood,
> prince, pope, philosopher and golden bough,
> pure mind and murder at the scything prow—
> Minerva, the miscarriage of the brain.

Lowell seems to merge the image of "the Goddess" Pallas Athene with that of Nike as she appears in the famous Winged Victory of Samothrace, which is in the form of a figurehead from the prow of a ship; and then, on the basis of the irony of "the scything prow" of Victory (Victoria was her next name) and the equivalence of Athene and Minerva, the Roman goddess of war and wisdom, he fuses Greece with Rome and implies that both civilizations mirror ours. The "pure mind and murder" that are the links between Athene and Minerva are to be associated with Mussolini's "pure prose" and his "lynched, bare, booted skull." Consequently, the attitude toward history seems less that of Spengler or the Renaissance than that of the speaker in "The Death of the Sheriff":

> Nothing underneath the sun
> Has bettered, Uncle, since the scaffolds flamed
> On butchered Troy. . . .

In the earlier poem, a Christian concept of history as a process in time that would end with the Day of Judgment was also advanced. In "Beyond the Alps" there may be an allusion to this concept in the difficult lines in the third section, where the description of dawn seems to merge the Greek sun-god and an image drawn from Rev. 10:1-3. This one possible allusion, however, is not enough to make this poem teleologically oriented, and there is nothing even as ambiguously apocalyptic as the reference to "the end of time" in "Falling Asleep over the Aeneid." If there is any coherent theory of history behind this poem, it seems that it must be linear rather than cyclical, entropic, or teleological.

One need not insist, however, that "Beyond the Alps" affords a coherent theory of history; in fact, to realize that it does not is important for an understanding of Lowell's method. Just as his metaphors are in a state of continual flux, so his concepts are continually being transformed; and usually, as in the figures of Athene and Minerva in this poem, the metamorphosis in the one area entails that in the other. Any attempt to marshall the views of history in this poem into a theoretical structure would be tantamount to an effort to analyze the figure of "the Goddess" (Athene-Minerva-Mary) in strict analogical terms.

In "Beyond the Alps" an explanation of the relationship among the different historiographical views depends upon the recognition that the main subject of the poem is not the course of history but the condition of contemporary civilization; and if there is a hint of *Dies Irae*, it only serves to reinforce the poet-speaker's own condemnation.[12] The points of view that on one level seem conflicting are perfectly compatible on another.

One reason for the abandonment of the visionary mode is suggested by the title and the note on the setting that prefaces the poem. "Beyond the Alps" is a quotation from "Falling Asleep over the Aeneid" (l. 68) intended to inform us that the poet's religious position has altered, that he has gone beyond the sanctuary of the Catholic Church;[13] and the note that puts the speaker "On the train from Rome to Paris" indicates the same change. This movement away from the Church becomes a subject of the poem proper in the first section:

> *O bella Roma!* I saw our stewards go
> forward on tiptoe banging on their gongs.
> Life changed to landscape. Much against my will
> I left the City of God where it belongs.

"Stewards" is of course a Biblical term meaning "servants of God" as well as the name for the hosts on a Pullman car, and their incongruous actions here imply a motivation for the speaker's willingness to let them "go / forward" without him. The same subject—the motivation for the poet-speaker's de-

sertion of the Church—is implicit throughout the second section of the poem, which traduces Pope Pius XII by providing
an intimate glimpse of him in his private apartments at the
Vatican, where he has his hands full with an "electric razor"
instead of a scepter and a "pet canary" instead of a dove. If
the "electric razor" suggests that the Church has been cor-
rupted by the very "lights of science" with which it is in
conflict, the exotic description of "Mary risen—at one
miraculous stroke, / angel-wing'd, glorious as a jungle bird!"
suggests that it has erred equally in the opposite direction.
Moreover, the thought that "God herded his people to the
coup de grâce"—with the ironic allusion to the shepherd of the
flock and the bitter pun on *grace*—points to the speaker's
repudiation of Christian dogma.

By stressing the speaker's disillusionment with present religious and political forces,[14] Lowell suggests a causal relationship between the "breaking up" of the culture and the
isolation of the individual, so that the transition to the poems
on the collateral theme of alienation has already begun. The
theme of disintegration is transposed to the level of the family
in the second poem, "The Banker's Daughter," which concentrates on the failure of the marriage of Marie de Medici
and King Henry IV of France. Her "brutal girlish mood-
swings" that drove her husband "wrenched and giddy, from
the Louvre, / to sleep in single lodgings on the town" anticipate Charlotte Lowell's nagging and Commander Lowell's
escapes into the solitude of "the Maritime Museum" and his
midnight "speculations," as well as the situation in " 'To
Speak of Woe That Is in Marriage.' " Also woven into this
poem are the themes of alienation—Marie was "exiled by her
son [Louis XIII] and lived in a house lent to her by
Rubens"—and religious and political corruption:

> Your great nerve gone, Sire, sleep without a care.
> No Hapsburg galleon coasts off Finisterre
> with bars of bullion now to subsidize
> the pilfering, pillaging democracies,
> the pin-head priest, the nihilist grandee.

There is probably a pun on "great nerve" in the first line here, since Henry IV was assassinated by the religious fanatic Ravaillac in 1610: "Murder cut him short— / a kitchen-knife honed on a carriage-wheel." In any case, the reference to the assassination underscores the political chaos with which Lowell is concerned. This theme links "The Banker's Daughter" to the following poem, "Inauguration Day: January 1953": *Le roi est mort; vive le roi*, but conditions have still not bettered.[15] This terse sonnet recapitulates the political theme of "Beyond the Alps" and does so in similar terms. Instead of the "breaking up" of "killer kings," here there is a splitting apart:

> Ice, ice. Our wheels no longer move.
> Look, the fixed stars, all just alike
> as lack-land atoms, split apart,
> and the Republic summons Ike,
> the mausoleum in her heart.

Eisenhower, a general, is also worthy of the title that Lowell gives Grant: "God of our armies." As Hugh Staples has pointed out, Eisenhower is just the latest in the poem's succession of warrior-administrators that includes Grant and Stuyvesant, all impotent in spite of the military power that they command.[16] This impotence is conveyed not only by the freezing moral cold that pervades the poem—the "mausoleum" in the "heart," the "ice," the "snow"—but also by the physiological overtones of such phrases as "Manhattan's truss of adamant" and "the fixed stars"; and it is in stark contrast to the frank warmth and sexuality of Marie de Medici, a secular counterpart of Mother Marie Therese:

> And so I press my lover's palm to mine;
> I am his vintage, and his living vine
> entangles me, and oozes mortal wine
> moment to moment. By repeated crime,
> even a queen survives her little time.

A virtual incarnation of the *élan vital*, Marie de Medici is one of the first of this volume's "exiles"—the speaker of "Beyond the Alps" is another descendant of the exile in *Lord Weary's Castle*—who succeed in personally overcoming the conditions in a world of which the image of "atoms, split apart," captures both the fragmentation and the violence.

The bacchanalian quality of Marie de Medici's image of herself and her lover, the Marquis d'Ancre, is just one aspect of the life force which she as *magna mater* represents. For the "Mad Negro Soldier Confined at Munich," however, love has dwindled or hardened into sex alone:

> "Her German language made my arteries harden—
> I've no annuity from the pay we blew.
> I chartered an aluminum canoe,
> I had her six times in the English Garden."

An exact inversion of Marie de Medici, the black soldier is the man fallen victim to the disordered and disordering world. His alienation is witnessed not only by his confinement following World War II, and not only by his color, but also and most poignantly by the drubbing given to him by two other black American inmates. That insanity is the nature of his environment as well as the state of his mind is indicated by his claim that he receives attention only from those with whom he was supposed to be at war, "'a Kraut DP'" and a " 'Fraulein.' " In his isolation, madness, and tendency to violence, he foreshadows the poet-speaker in later poems in *Life Studies;* and in some respects he is a forerunner of the persona of *For the Union Dead*. At the same time, he is less a model for Lowell's later speakers than a spectre of what they might conceivably become, an image of the threat with which they are faced.

"A Mad Negro Soldier Confined at Munich" is an energetic if not frenetic conclusion to part one. The second part of *Life Studies*, in sharp contrast, is a slow, lyrical autobiographical sketch in prose. This section is the backdrop for much of part four and will be touched upon when the poems in that section are discussed. Part three of *Life Studies*, comprising four poems on different kinds of writers, extends the autobiographical second section as Lowell calls up the figures of men whom he has known or admired, and it also prepares for the figure of the poet-speaker as he emerges in the fourth part.[17] These four poems are closely related by several motifs, with the result that what we have is less a gallery of portraits than a composite picture of the writer as hero. Just as cultural disintegration is the crux of part one and family conflict is the main subject of part two, so the isolation of the artist is the focal point of this part.

In "Ford Madox Ford," this theme inspires the comparison of the novelist to "a Jonah" who was lost and forgotten in "the whale-fat of post-war London" and therefore "divorced" from his public. When he recalls Ford's lecture to a new audience on the other side of the Atlantic—in Boulder, Colorado, where the altitude left him breathless—Lowell inverts the motif:

> your audience, almost football-size,
> shrank to a dozen, while you stood
> mumbling, with fish-blue-eyes,
> and mouth pushed out
> fish-fashion, as if you gagged for air. . . .

A fish out of water, or a stranded whale, Ford painfully exemplifies the neglected and exploited artist. Because this image also recalls the last quatrain in "A Mad Negro Soldier Confined at Munich," it underscores Ford's own confinement, which is of a different kind but just as pathetic. If we are inclined to regard this connection as accidental, we should also be reminded that this poem makes much of Ford's *Good Soldier* and of his tales of his own tour of duty in World War I; and although he was hardly insane, Ford's infamous "lies" were nearly pathological. His imprisonment by a culture inimical to art is implied by the reference to "Washington / and Stuyvesant, your Lilliputian squares," which brings to mind not only Gulliver's stature among the little people but also his bondage. This reference is related to that of the stranded fish by virtue of Gulliver's having been tied down on the beach; and if Gulliver's pockets were emptied by the Lilliputians, Ford's have been "turned . . . inside out" by an equally ungrateful public.

Both the strength and the bondage of Gulliver are echoed in the epithets "Wheel-horse, O unforgetting elephant": the wheelhorse is the stronger of the two in a tandem harness, the one that turns the vehicle; and the elephant's proverbially prodigious memory indicates the extent to which Ford possessed one basic prerequisite to being a good novelist. Another of these talents is the capacity to believe one's fantasies, whether they are the personal fantasies of one day achieving recognition or the public fantasies that constitute the writings, and this capacity is condensed in Lowell's tribute: "Sandman! Your face, a childish *O*." This image is the transition between that of Ford's mouth, "pushed out / fish-fashion," and that of "The sun," to which Ford's intoxicating and perhaps intoxicated joviality is implicitly compared.

As the references to "A Mad Negro Soldier Confined at Munich" indicate, however, Ford was not all childishness and Falstaffian joviality. The allusion to Timon, near the end of the poem, emphasizes the shabby treatment accorded the novelist by his potential public, the isolation that is a result of that treatment, and the threat of madness that accompanies such isolation and lack of understanding. The next poem turns on an even sharper conflict. "For George Santayana" limns a man who is "divorced" both from his public and his religious tradition; the philosopher is not only segregated from the world by the walls of "the monastery hospital" in which he is dying, but is also estranged from the "geese-girl sisters" inside, the Blue Sisters of the Little Company of Mary, by virtue of his atheism. Like Mother Marie Therese in *The Mills of the Kavanaughs*, Santayana is doomed to be an émigré in this world and the next. Santayana also resembles the speaker of the poems in the group "Life Studies," and his cell anticipates that of the poet in the West Street Jail. That he, like others who repudiate the church, is buried "outside the consecrated ground" in Rome's Verano Catholic Cemetery, having died "still unbelieving, unconfessed and unreceived," is further evidence of his alienation.

Santayana's ultimate triumph consists in his personal reconciliation of those forces—religion and atheism—whose conflict is evidence of the "breaking up" of the modern world. Lowell describes him as a "free-thinking Catholic infidel"; and in the quotation of the philosopher's paradoxical belief, " 'There is no God and Mary is His Mother,' " the poet

offers further testimony to this rapprochement. But Santayana's transcendence of categories like "Catholic" and
"atheist," his victory over the apparent contradiction, is most
conclusively, movingly expressed in the poem's final lines,
which give rise to Frank Parker's title-page illustration of a
lion, apparently fatally wounded, in a passageway beneath
the Forum, and in which Lowell pictures the old philosopher,
his sight failing, making some final revisions:

> Old trooper, I see your child's red crayon pass,
> bleeding deletions on the galleys you hold
> under your throbbing magnifying glass,
> that worn arena, where the whirling sand
> and broken-hearted lions lick your hand
> refined by bile as yellow as a lump of gold.

Having recurred, in the first words here, to the soldier motif
that we have noted above, Lowell proceeds to modulate this
motif into that of the Christian Soldier by likening the proof
sheets under the magnifying glass to a gladiatorial arena. The
philosopher, far from being simply an atheist, or perhaps
victorious in his atheism, appears as a Christian gladiator
who is so brave and sympathetic a figure that his most fero-
cious opponents are "broken-hearted" by his death. The
Christian side of Santayana colors other phrases, such as the
allusion to the Biblical dictum that one must "become as a
child" to enter the kingdom of heaven, a dictum that is rein-
forced by the alchemical image in the last line (the common
denominator is the reduction to purity). At the same time that
he asserts Santayana's essentially religious nature, Lowell
does not ignore his atheism; instead, the two are reconciled in
the philosopher's work, the tortuous struggle in which each
deletion is comparable to a battle wound. As was the case
with Ford, that "Timon and Falstaff," Santayana's victory is
the forging of a character from seemingly contradictory
elements—a victory which, to borrow from Eliot, costs not
less than everything.

   In this poem Lowell's own presence makes itself strongly
felt, and he introduces himself frankly in "To Delmore
Schwartz," the third poem in part three and one which has

been the object of both praise and disapproval.[18] The latter attitude seems to derive from the notions that this poem is primarily autobiographical data and that it substitutes levity for an effort to deal with problems that are of general interest. Its closing lines have been cited as indicative of the poem's tone:

> The Charles
> River was turning silver. In the ebb-
> light of morning, we stuck
> the duck
> -'s web-
> foot, like a candle, in a quart of gin we'd killed.

Surely only a gloomy academicism could condemn the apparently careless gaiety and inspired frivolity of these lines. A closer look at them, however, shows that the gaiety is more careful than careless and that Lowell was inspired to more than frivolity. The action depicted is a rather bizarre one, even in view of the presumption that Schwartz and Lowell, unlike their "furnace," were well lit. Moreover, the word "killed" gets more emphasis than it would otherwise because it is the last in the poem and because it comes at the end of a long line after a series of short ones. Again, an acquaintance with Lowell's method, his evolving of "a situation in which the several items can lend each other context, reference, and resonance," is helpful. Looking back over the poem, we find that killing has been mentioned explicitly twice before in connection with the duck: "It was your first kill" and "it looked through us, as if it'd died dead drunk." In addition to these previous references, there is the related image that suggests war:

> the antiquated
> refrigerator gurgled mustard gas
> through your mustard-yellow house,
> and spoiled our long maneuvered visit
> from T. S. Eliot's brother, Henry Ware. . . .

These lines relate this poem to "Ford Madox Ford" and to "A Mad Negro Soldier Confined at Munich," and as a result the subjects of those other poems are drawn into "To Delmore Schwartz." Given this context, perhaps the last sentence in this poem seems ominous; it certainly does when the context is broadened to include the rest of the poems in this volume that are concerned in one way or another with the conjunction of drugs and death.

The motivation for such a tone discloses itself in the central part of the poem, and most candidly in Schwartz's intentional misquotation of Wordsworth's "Resolution and Independence": "'We poets in our youth begin in sadness; / thereof in the end come despondency and madness.'"[19] It is this association of poetry and madness that informs the tone of those last lines; and throughout, the implication is that some form of madness is the expense, the condition, of writing. This "mania," as Lowell terms it in *Imitations,* is the real theme of the poem, for it is the solvent of both the "'Joy'" of which the two young poets speak and the suppressed violence of which they do not. "'Joyce and Freud'" might be their "'Masters of Joy'" (the Joycean connection is that "joy" is *Freude* in German), but Coleridge, whose portrait is in the room, is their patron saint, much as the duck is their talisman. In fact, there is a pointed similarity between the portrait and the dead duck. The latter is depicted in this way:

its bill was a black whistle, and its brow
was high and thinner than a baby's thumb;
. . . .
it looked through us, as if it'd died dead drunk.
You must have propped its eyelids with a nail,
and yet it lived with us and met our stare,
Rabelaisian, lubricious, drugged.

Coleridge's face is remarkably like the duck's:

The room was filled
with cigarette smoke circling the paranoid,
inert gaze of Coleridge, back
from Malta—his eyes lost in flesh, lips baked and black.

Coleridge paid for his joy with paranoia and laudanum addiction; the duck seems drugged and drunk; and Schwartz and

Lowell, "Underseas fellows, nobly mad" who are afflicted with a "universal / *Angst*," are in the process of getting thoroughly drunk themselves. If creative madness is the condition that precariously reconciles joy and violence, Schwartz's "tiger kitten, *Oranges*," who "cart-wheeled for joy in a ball of snarls," is made—however playfully—in his owner's image.

"Words for Hart Crane" presents with a candor that borders on brutality another writer whose creative and destructive energies are closely allied; and as the conclusion to this section, it also echos the first two poems. Like Ford, Crane suffers neglect of his talent with scorn; and like Santayana, he refuses to compromise with the powers that be. Just as Santayana was interpreted as at least as religious as the "geese-girl sisters" who flocked about him, so Crane turns out to be essentially more American than any "'dope / or screw'" who has won a Pulitzer. The violence, love, and perversion, the genius and the arrogance that make him up, are all condensed in these lines, with their puns on "'rage'" and "'wolfing'" and their paradox that, although an exile, Crane can claim the right to address the reader as though the latter were the foreigner:

> "Because I knew my Whitman like a book,
> stranger in America, tell my country: I,
> *Catullus redivivus*, once the rage
> of the Village and Paris, used to play my role
> of homosexual, wolfing the stray lambs
> who hungered by the Place de la Concorde."

Whitman is to Crane what Coleridge is to Schwartz and Lowell; homosexuality is evidence of alienation just as madness is. By having Crane proclaim himself "'the Shelley of my age'" at the end of the poem, Lowell continues the series of allusions to the Romantic poets and the political exile and perhaps recalls Santayana's atheism.

Inasmuch as "Words for Hart Crane" does recall the other poems in this third section, it provides a model of the method of the whole volume, the method that makes the volume a whole; for although the sections are individually more highly integrated than the book, they are continually related to one another as well. In its tempo, its use of a persona whose sexual needs testify to estrangement from society, its mood of barely restrained violence, and its acerbic tone, and even in its position at the end of a section, "Words for Hart Crane" is related to "A Mad Negro Soldier Confined at Munich"; and at the same time, by virtue of all of these features except the tempo, it is a forerunner of "Skunk Hour." If the relationships among these particular poems are matters of theme and mood, rather than of word and phrase as in several instances pointed out above, they are nonetheless unifying factors. The more specific relationships, in addition to contributing to the book's unity, remind us that the unity is not simply a result of an individual sensibility.

The intricate interrelationships among the poems of the first and third parts of *Life Studies* might warn us against relying upon our most likely first impressions of "My Last Afternoon with Uncle Devereux Winslow," the introductory poem in the fourth part, for at an initial reading it seems nonchalantly, almost carelessly done.[20] The idiom is casual, the verse is free, the structure is unobtrusive enough to make the poem appear a desultory recollection of loosely associated events, and even short passages sometimes seem extraordinarily confused or literally self-effacing. Take this description of Uncle Devereux Winslow, for example:

> He was as brushed as Bayard, our riding horse.
> His face was putty.
> His blue coat and white trousers
> grew sharper and straighter.
> His coat was a blue jay's tail,
> his trousers were solid cream from the top of the bottle.
> He was animated, hierarchical,
> like a ginger snap man in a clothes-press.
> He was dying of the incurable Hodgkin's disease. . . .

The peculiarity of these lines seems at first almost opposite that of Lowell's earlier poetry, where the images were welded to one another and the problem was separating them in order to understand what was going on. Here the images are laid next to one another like bricks, and the difficulty is discovering what relationship they have to one another.

The absence of explicit connectives, together with the nearly formulaic parallelism, has persuaded one critic to explain this passage in terms of "the quality of a black-magic incantation."[21] It might very well have this quality, although it would seem that the relevance of black magic to an elegiac poem would still require some explanation; but a better interpretation of the tone of these lines would take into account the circumstance that although the poem is in the past tense, the persona's point of view often approximates that of a boy of "five and a half," as the image of the "ginger snap man" suggests. The curiously detached tone of this description, then, might derive from the child's lack of experience with death and could be summarized as a combination of innocence and fascination. On the other hand, the poem *is* in the past tense, and the words "animated, hierarchical" are as indicative of sophistication as the "ginger snap man" is of naiveté. Even more to the point are these lines earlier in the fourth section:

> I cowered in terror.
> I wasn't a child at all—
> unseen and all-seeing, I was Agrippina
> in the Golden House of Nero. . . .

According to Tacitus, Agrippina, Nero's mother, schemed and connived to advance her son to the position of emperor, which devotion he rewarded by assassinating her.[22] Agrippina, guilty of murder herself, lived "in terror" because she knew of the plots against her own life. This poem is not about innocence, but about loss of innocence; and the fascination in the tone is not the product of ignorance, but of knowledge.

In any case, it is not sufficient to explain the first quoted passage in terms of tonal quality, for each of the images has a specific function, and they are all intimately related. An understanding of this relationship discourages the notion that this poem consists of the unfathomable musings of a child and reveals the advisability of paying careful attention to the intricate network of details in this volume. A poem of the same number of sections as the volume itself, situated at the beginning of the title section, and longer than any other poem in the book, "My Last Afternoon with Uncle Devereux Winslow" epitomizes the method of *Life Studies*, just as the "incantation" toward the end summarizes the poem. That passage occurs only toward the end, however, and to understand its elements it is necessary to have in mind their previous uses.

The prerequisite is underscored by the fact that Uncle Devereux does not even appear until near the end of the poem, and the event that would seem to be its *raison d'être*—that he was "dying at twenty-nine"—is withheld until the next to the last stanza. Once this unusual arrangement of things is taken note of, the reason for it is at hand; for if it is correct to assume that Uncle Devereux's dying is the subject of the poem, then the general function of the first three sections must be to create a context by means of which his imminent death takes on a greater significance. In each section, and in almost every image in the poem, the relationship between life and death is the fundamental subject, but everywhere this relationship is reflected from a slightly different angle so that it has many different forms, some less immediately recognizable than others.

The central symbols in the poem are of course the piles of "black earth" and "white lime," with which he remembers playing and which were the ingredients of the concrete the resident farmer was using for "cementing a root-house under the hill" on Lowell's grandfather's farm. Black earth, popularly regarded as fertile soil, is patently symbolic of life; while lime, an extremely caustic substance which in one of its forms is used to destroy the bodies of dead farm stock, is just as obviously symbolic of death. The young Lowell's mixing of earth and lime, then, reflects the crucial situation, in which the process of living is most clearly identifiable with that of dying. So, too, does the "cementing" of the "root-house," a cellarlike structure not dissimilar to a tomb. The interpenetration of death and life is suggested also by Uncle Devereux's dying in summer, a detail that points up the irony of the fact that he is dying in the prime of his life.

It is important to realize that the poem concerns itself with the dying, not with the death, of Uncle Devereux. The number of present participles—"mixing," "cementing," "dying," "blending," and so on—indicates that it is the presence of death in life, the incomplete process, that is Lowell's subject. This process is mirrored in several scattered images, like the homebrew "which Grandpa made by blending half and half / yeasty, wheezing homemade sarsaparilla with beer." The apparent incongruity of the acts of concocting a drink and preparing to die might make us reluctant at first to suppose that there is any parallel intended, but the choice of the verb in the last line of the poem seems significant:

> My hands were warm, then cool, on the piles
> of earth and lime,
> a black pile and a white pile. . . .
> Come winter,
> Uncle Devereux would blend to the one color.

Comparable images abound. For example, Lowell remembers the pond,

> *Assawompset*, halved by "the Island,"
> where my Uncle's duck blind
> floated in a barrage of smoke-clouds.

As with the reference to the shandygaff, it would be easy to discount the memory that "'the Island'" was "halved" if it occurred in a different context. As it happens, the half-and-half shandygaff and the cement that is half earth and half lime are elements in the context. Moreover, that the description of *"Assawompset"* is not meant to be discounted is the point of these lines, which come shortly after it:

> At the cabin between the waters,
> the nearest windows were already boarded.
> Uncle Devereux was closing camp for the winter.

The first line here confirms the form of the preceding image, and the next two lines assert its force. Both the boarding of some of the windows and the note that the camp was closing can be easily related to Uncle Devereux's condition.

Now it is not that each of these details is flatly symbolic of

Uncle Devereux's state; on the contrary, they are oblique and often distorted reflections of that central concern. Their function is to make the theme of dying or of death-in-life permeate the whole poem. The consequences of this method can be elaborated after the examination of a few more details, including those relating to marriage.

The marriage symbol differs from the earlier symbol in that the basic concept, the theme on which the variations are performed, is not positively present in the poem; instead, there are only the variations, only the reflections. Nevertheless, it is not difficult to determine what that basic concept is, partly because it played such an important role in Lowell's earlier poetry and partly because this poem does present what is nearly a parody of it. Here, the Catholic concept of death as coincident with the union with God—"the sudden Bridegroom" of "At the Indian Killer's Grave" and "the returning bridegroom" of "Falling Asleep over the Aeneid"—reappears in this guise:

> Uncle Devereux was closing camp for the winter.
> As if posed for "the engagement photograph,"
> he was wearing his severe
> war-uniform of a volunteer Canadian officer.

There are other variations on this concept, like the passage where Uncle Devereux and his wife "left their three baby daughters / and sailed for Europe on a last honeymoon." At a further remove, this motif is heard in the gossip about Aunt Sarah, who once "tilted her archaic Athenian nose / and jilted an Astor." This seemingly gratuitous detail is itself repeated and developed in the observation that although she practiced long and hard in order to become a concert musician, "On the recital day, she failed to appear." Uncle Devereux cannot jilt the Bridegroom nor fail to appear.

Indeed, Aunt Sarah, who is sixty years old and "risen like the phoenix" and to whom the third section of this poem is devoted, is a foil for Uncle Devereux, who is dying at half her age and to whom the fourth section belongs. The brief second section, a snapshot of the poet as a boy of "five and a half," who was "a stuffed toucan / with a bibulous, multicolored beak," provides another contrast with the dying man; but more important than the contrast between the boy and his fatally ill uncle is the subtle connection that is established between them. Lowell's chief means of making this connection is the manipulation of the motifs of colors and clothes.

The color white, for instance, which is that of lime and New England winters, enters into the memory of this scene in Grandfather Winslow's summer house:

> Near me was the white measuring-door
> my Grandfather had pencilled with my Uncle's heights.
> In 1911, he had stopped growing at just six feet.
> While I sat on the tiles,
> and dug at the anchor on my sailor blouse,
> Uncle Devereux stood behind me.

The white "measuring-door" and the white sailor blouse both link Lowell, who has already identified himself with Agrippina, with his uncle, and the association is ominous. Uncle Devereux had stopped growing, according to the marks on the door where his nephew is doubtless to be measured also, when he had reached the height that is the traditional depth of burial. Eleven years later, dying of Hodgkin's disease, in which the later stages are accompanied by anemia and a consequent grayish pallor, he is significantly dressed half in white. Besides the color of his clothes, Lowell stresses the severity of Uncle Devereux's dress and the rigidity of his posture, which suggest a precocious *rigor mortis:* "His blue coat and white trousers / grew sharper and straighter." This image demands recollection of that of Uncle Devereux "As if posed for 'the engagement photograph' " in his "severe" uniform, and it turns us back to other details earlier in this section:

> Daylight from the doorway riddled his student posters,
> tacked helter-skelter on walls as raw as a board-walk.
>
> . . . .
>
> The finest poster was two or three young men in khaki kilts
> being bushwhacked on the veldt—
> they were almost life-size. . . .

After all of the other references to dying, the young men "being bushwhacked" need no gloss. Uncle Devereux had other posters, and the clothes imagery is again significant; and if properly understood, it is horribly so in the case of "Mr. Punch, a water melon in hockey tights, / [who] was tossing off a decanter of Scotch." What seems at first a humorous description of a cheap student poster turns out to be an almost unbearably grotesque image of Uncle Devereux himself, for Hodgkin's disease is the less formal term for lymphoreticuloma, in which the lymph glands swell uncontrollably.

Another passage involving clothes implicitly links the young Lowell with his uncle:

> My perfection was the Olympian
> poise of my models in the imperishable autumn
> display windows
> of Rogers Peet's boys' store. . . .

In the present context, to emulate the poise of the mannequins is to rival Uncle Devereux's own stiff "pose." The same relationship is suggested by this part of the catalog of the interior of the "stone porch" on which Lowell sat:

> a Rocky Mountain chaise longue,
> its legs, shellacked saplings.
> A pastel-pale Huckleberry Finn
> fished with a broom straw in a basin
> hollowed out of a millstone.

While the "pastel-pale" figurine certainly suggests Uncle Devereux, whose condition is accompanied by anemia, it might also suggest his young nephew (who would later compare himself with all manner of fishermen). The most direct connection between the boy and his uncle, however, is made in these lines at the beginning of the fourth section:

> I picked with a clean finger nail at the blue anchor
> on my sailor blouse washed white as a spinnaker.
> What in the world was I wishing?
> . . . A sail-colored horse browsing in the bullrushes . . .

A fluff of the west wind puffing
my blouse, kiting me over our seven chimneys,
troubling the waters. . . .

Like most of the details in this poem, these are usually passed
off as the vague thoughts of a child, but they can be explained
and indeed must be if the theme of the poem is to be apprehended. The blue and white of the sailor blouse repeat the
blue and white in Uncle Devereux's clothes, which in turn
parallel the black earth and the white lime. The "sailor
blouse" and the "sail-colored horse" are also to be associated
with Uncle Devereux, since later he "sailed for Europe on a
last honeymoon," a reference that has been glossed above.
The last lines quoted are based on at least one Biblical passage, John 5:3-4, where what were probably thermal springs
are interpreted in miraculous terms:

> In these lay a great multitude of impotent folk, blind, halt, with-
> ered, waiting for the moving of the water.
> For an angel went down at a certain season into the pool, and
> troubled the water: whosoever then first after the troubling of the
> water stepped in was made whole of whatsoever disease he had.

With this much background, it is possible to answer the
question that the young Lowell asked himself, or rather to
extrapolate from his own answer, and to discover his connection with Uncle Devereux. His wish, which the language of
the answer suggests could not have been articulated at the
time, was a form of a death wish, a wish to be no longer
"anchored" to life; and as it seems to have been the only
marking on the blouse, otherwise "washed white as a spin-
naker," the anchor suggests the imperfection, the stain that is
unavoidable this side of "the one color." The image of the
"sail-colored horse" captures the boy's idea of Uncle Devereux's journey into death and his idea of the escape from
the process of which disease and death are a part. That the
two ideas are not identical is the burden of the following
lines, in which the young Lowell sees himself as a combination of a sort of angel and one who has been "made whole of
whatsoever disease" he might have. He dreams of "the west
wind . . . kiting" him over the fire and smoke of life and over

the waters that are associated with the voyage to death. In brief, he was wishing that he might escape becoming one of the "great multitude of impotent folk," who include his Grandmother Winslow ("tone-deaf, quick as a cricket") and Aunt Sarah (whom he associates with a "grasshopper") as well as Uncle Devereux. This is why he speaks of the "perfection" of the "models" in the boys' store; it is why they are *his* models, and it is also why he notices the "imperishable autumn" of the "display windows" in which they stand. Much as in Yeats's "Sailing to Byzantium," imperishability is associated with death, whereas the "dying generations" of his ancestors are proof of the imperfection of life. The theme might be illuminated by a pivotal passage in "91 Revere Street," where Lowell identifies completion with perfection and implicitly opposes them to incompletion and imperfection: "because finished," Lowell says, the things and their owners in his memory of the Revere Street house "are endurable and perfect."

At this point it is probably unnecessary to explicate at much length those lines, near the end of the poem, with which this discussion began. The "blue coat and white trousers" that "grew sharper and straighter" suggest Uncle Devereux's death-in-life. The description of his face as "putty" supports the color symbolism, as does the "blue jay's tail" of his coat; and the vision of him as a "ginger snap man in a clothes press" caps the references to his rigorous carriage. The memory that he was "as brushed as Bayard, our riding horse" recalls both his imminent "engagement" and the "sail-colored horse" of the boy's revery. The densest line, and one which serves as a summary of Uncle Devereux, is: "He was animated, hierarchical." On the one hand, both animation and hierarchy connote a stiffness that enforces the image of the "ginger snap man." On the other hand, "animated" might be taken to mean "full of life" and "hierarchical" to mean "angelic." On this interpretation, the two adjectives sum up the contradictory aspects of the process that Uncle Devereux represents.

The process terrifies the young Lowell, for it makes him see for the first time that his life entails his death, that living and

dying can be synonymous; and this realization makes him
yearn for flight into a realm where things are immutable and
perfect, where there is only "the one color"; and, finally, the
force of this realization accounts for the tendency for everything in this poem to be seen in terms of the opposition of life
and death.

This has been a rather lengthy analysis, but it has seemed
justifiable partly because the method in this poem has never
been attended to and partly because "My Last Afternoon
with Uncle Devereux Winslow" is the most comprehensive
expression in *Life Studies* of the need to endure in a world so
riddled with contradictory forces that life itself is an "incura-
ble . . . disease." In the rest of the poems in "Life Studies, I,"
Lowell turns more directly to the theme of the decline and fall
of the Lowell family and the conflicts between and within the
characters of its members.

"Dunbarton" and "Grandparents" deal mainly with the
poet-to-be and his maternal grandfather, whose figure,
romanticized by the age gap between him and his protégé,
becomes the measure of other men in the family. After the
literary heroes of the third part, Grandfather Winslow is the
only figure to come close to embodying a norm, and therefore
it is not surprising that his own isolation is the point of departure in "Dunbarton":

> My Grandfather found
> his grandchild's fogbound solitudes
> sweeter than human society.

Coupled by their distaste for the family and social circles,
Lowell and his grandfather made "yearly autumn get-aways
from Boston." The word "get-aways," with its connotations
of heroic outlawry, indicates the tone of this poem and the
view of his grandfather. With Uncle Devereux recently de-
ceased and Lowell senior "on sea-duty in the Pacific," the old
man becomes a surrogate father: "He was my Father. I was
his son." Characteristically, Lowell extends the relationship
beyond the situation and turns it into an element in the structure of the volume. On their trips together to the graveyard
Grandfather Winslow

took the wheel himself—
like an admiral at the helm.
. . . .
We stopped at the *Priscilla* in Nashua
for brownies and root-beer,
and later "pumped ship" together in the Indian summer. . . .

The implication is that unlike his real father, nominally a "Commander," his grandfather is essentially a sailor. This implication is borne out by the various other heroic allusions in "Dunbarton." There is occasion to refer to "the ever-blackening wine-dark coat / in our portrait of Edward Winslow" and thus to suggest the quasi-epical stature of his grandfather's family. Similarly, Lowell remembers the ritualistic service that he and his grandfather performed for their ancestors:

> Grandfather and I
> raked leaves from our dead forebears,
> defied the dank weather
> with "dragon" bonfires.

Even the ellipsis and heavy alliteration contribute to the effect by suggesting some Old English poem of heroes or exiles. Then, too, there are their accomplice, a Mr. Burroughs who "had stood with Sherman at Shiloh," and his grandfather's cane, which was "carved with the names and altitudes / of Norwegian mountains he had scaled— / more a weapon than a crutch." The reference to the "altitudes" that his grandfather had attained looks back to the "altitudes" of "Ford Madox Ford" and "Beyond the Alps" and forward to the "hill" of "Skunk Hour."

But Grandfather Winslow's status is more—or less—than heroic. As always in this volume, other poems must be kept in mind lest the irony be overlooked. For example, if it is recalled that it was Grandfather Winslow who scolded Uncle Devereux and his wife for "'behaving like children,'" these lines in "Dunbarton" can be seen in a new light:

> Freed from Karl and chuckling over the gas he was saving,
> he let his motor roller-coaster
> out of control down each hill.

It is true that being "Freed" or "out of control" is more likely than not to meet with Lowell's approbation, as we know from Mr. Burroughs's "illegal home-made claret" and the view of himself "as a young newt, neurasthenic, scarlet / and wild in the wild coffee-colored water." Nevertheless, Grandfather Winslow is clearly in need of his own admonition. Similarly, the lines from "Dunbarton" undercut the picture of him in "Grandparents":

> Back in my throw-away and shaggy span
> of adolescence, Grandpa still waves his stick
> like a policeman. . . .

In fact, this poem, the next in the book and its most un- abashedly emotional, is shot through with ironic references in spite of its last stanza. Although there can be little doubt about the poignancy of that stanza, elsewhere in this poem there are evocations of his grandfather that are both cooler and more equivocal. The opening sentence itself exhibits that "wry, humorous indulgence" that one reviewer regards as the home key of this volume:[23]

> They're altogether otherworldly now,
> those adults champing for their ritual Friday spin
> to pharmacist and five-and-ten in Brockton.

The phrase "those adults" questions the very maturity that it ascribes to the Winslows. Consequently, the line "the nineteenth century, tired of children, is gone" acquires an additional ambiguity: besides implying that his grandparents were weary of their descendants and perhaps unappreciative of children in general, it also suggests that the century itself was tired of its childish adults. A mild irony also modifies what might otherwise be maudlin in this passage:

> I hear the rattley little country gramophone
> racking its five foot horn:
> "O Summer Time!"
> Even at noon here the formidable
> *Ancien Régime* still keeps nature at a distance. Five
> green shaded light bulbs spider the billiards-table;
> no field is greener than its cloth,

where Grandpa, dipping sugar for us both,
once spilled his demitasse.

A "rattley little country gramophone" and a "demitasse"
hardly consitute an old order formidable enough to keep "nature at a distance"—as the poet acknowledges, perhaps, in
noting that the lights "spider" the table, which is covered by
a cloth greener than a "field." This last image recalls Ser
Brunetto and the green cloth at Verona ("For George Santayana") and thus approaches being a mock-epic device—as
does the statement that "They're all gone into a world of
light; the farm's my own," in which Lowell quotes the title
line of one of Henry Vaughan's more melancholy elegies and
then juxtaposes it with the more mundane (but ultimately
terrifying) consideration that he has inherited the land.[24]

The figure of Grandfather Winslow thus serves a double
function in terms of the structure of the "Life Studies": he
provides a norm by which his descendants may be judged;
and he is the earliest of the poet's ancestors about whom
Lowell is able to be objective and even slightly critical. Grandfather Winslow can serve both purposes because the
idealized view of him is the most pronounced. The emphasis
shifts in the portraits of Lowell's parents and himself, as the
defects in the family become more and more the subject of the
poems. Nevertheless, all of these family figures are complex,
and it simply does not seem true that in these poems Lowell
renders harsh verdicts that are final or conclusive. The opin-
ion that these poems do make conclusive judgments encourages the acceptance of either Stephen Spender's notion that
the only problem with the "Life Studies" is that Lowell's air
of certainty crowds out the possibility of a certain freedom of
interpretation on which poetry thrives or M. L. Rosenthal's
view that the "Life Studies" are the disclosures of "the naked
psyche of a suffering man."[25] If these poems were indeed
what Rosenthal says, then one might expect to find the
weakness that Spender does.

Since Lowell's recollections of his father are usually viewed
as the most caustic in Life Studies,[26] "Commander Lowell"
should provide an adequate test case. One of Lowell's critics

regards the Commander as "an image of failure and embarrassment to his son and finally to his wife and himself,"[27] and
if this were the case it might seem strange that Lowell should
suggest, by setting his father's dates (1887–1950) beneath the
title, that the poem is an elegy. Of course there is no denying
that Lowell's "study" of his father is not wholly complimen-
tary. A Navy man whose interest in ships is basically
academic, whose main connection with Pearl Harbor is that
he once bought "white ducks" at the commissary there, and
whose way of celebrating giving up naval life for a position
with Lever Brothers' Soap is to sing " 'Anchors aweigh' " in
the bathtub, he is bound to appear somewhat ridiculous. The
only time he displays a "seamanlike celerity" is when he
leaves the Navy—only to squander a small fortune in the less
secure civilian world. A revelation of facts such as these constitutes an indictment, and Lowell is not stingy with them.

At the same time, these observations are placed in a context
that takes the edges off them and that even manages to return
to the Commander some of the dignity that his rank implies.
One of Lowell's resources here is the memory of the characters of the people who surrounded his father, so that the
latter's weaknesses are in part explained and in part transformed. For example, we know from numerous references
that his father was not altogether a satisfactory husband, and
we may be inclined to read as further confirmation of this
inadequacy the comment that "Mother dragged to bed alone,
/ read Menninger, / and grew more and more suspicious"; but
our response to this comment must be qualified by the opening lines of the poem:

> There were no undesirables or girls in my set,
> when I was a boy at Mattapoisett—
> only Mother, still her Father's daughter.
> Her voice was still electric
> with a hysterical, unmarried panic,
> when she read to me from the Napoleon book.

The barely suppressed Freudian interpretation of his mother
does much to explain and perhaps even to justify his father's
fecklessness. The fact that *she* read "the Napoleon book" to

her son is not meant to go unnoticed; and the very circumstance that a poem purporting to be about his father
opens with such pointed remarks about his mother is significant. If it will not do to see the older Lowell as a hapless
victim of a domineering wife, neither will it do to view him as
the family liability. The situation is too complex to be reduced
to such stock explanations; and what Lowell does is to play
one character against the other, letting the real situation
emerge in the course of this interplay. Much the same thing
happens in the second stanza, where the Commander's inability to mix with his contemporaries is set forth. Not to fit in
with the country club set, who incongruously regard golf as
the game of professionals, and not to be one of the yachting
crowd, who ludicrously see themselves as "seadogs" on
Sundays, are almost laudable characteristics. It is easy to
think it a blacker mark that he was "once successful enough
to be lost / in the mob of ruling-class Bostonians." Rather than
a type of failure, Commander Lowell might be regarded as a
type of hero, although a decidedly Quixotic type. But even
the humor of condescension that is accorded a Quixote is
banished from the last lines of this poem:

> nineteen, the youngest ensign in his class,
> he was "the old man" of a gunboat on the Yangtze.

The conclusion of "Commander Lowell" embodies that
kind of ambiguity that issues from the poet's apprehension of
complexity. "Terminal Days at Beverly Farms," on the other
hand, concludes with an ambiguity that seems owing—
whether it is in fact the case or no—to the poet's own indeci-
siveness:

> Father's death was abrupt and unprotesting.
> His vision was still twenty-twenty.
> After a morning of anxious, repetitive smiling,
> his last words to Mother were:
> "I feel awful."

Is there a hint of courage in his father's way of meeting death,
or is the lack of protest expressive of a typically submissive
and not wholly admirable cast of mind? Or is there an implicit

recognition by the Commander of his past failures that makes him find death less disagreeable than he might otherwise? Lowell refrains from committing himself to any of these options while he suggests all of them, and consequently it is uncertain whether "'I feel awful'" is an intentional understatement by his father or simply a literal truth. The difference is crucial, for therein lies the distinction between a knowledge of what is about to happen and an ignorance of it, between a sort of bravado and a sort of buffoonery. Perhaps the point, again, is that Lowell's father will not fit comfortably into either pigeonhole, and if so, it is a point to be respected in regard to both the father's character and the poet's understanding of it; but the ambiguity itself may be misplaced, since it would be impossible for the poet's father to be both stoical in the face of death and unaware of its approach at the same time.

Regardless of what his last words convey, Commander Lowell is to be contrasted with his wife's father and with Uncle Devereux. The first image in the poem suggests that he is a different kind of man from Grandfather Winslow. Lowell's "Grandfather's farm" has already been described in terms that suggested that "more ritualistic, gaudy, and animal world" that Major Mordecai Myers knew:

> Diamond-pointed, athirst and Norman,
> its alley of poplars
> paraded from Grandmother's rose garden
> to a scarey stand of virgin pine,
> scrub, and paths forever pioneering.

At his father's Beverly Farms things are so civilized that "a portly, uncomfortable boulder" is remarkable precisely because it is "an irregular Japanese touch." Even Commander Lowell's automobile is to be contrasted with Grandfather Winslow's Pierce Arrow. The brand name of the latter combines with the fact that it was kept in a horse stall to connote a naive but romantic past; Commander Lowell's car, on the other hand, is "garaged like a sacrificial steer / with gilded hooves." Its gilded and gelded qualities make the "*Chevie*" a symbol of the vitiation of the culture.[28]

Like "Commander Lowell," this poem moves from an adverse although never humorless view of his father to a more
balanced one. Although it is less marked in "Father's Bedroom," the same structure can be seen in that poem. Beginning with a description of his father's bedroom that emphasizes its unbecoming femininity and should be contrasted
with the description of his mother's "master-bedroom" in
"During Fever," this poem nevertheless hints at the more
romantic and vigorous side of his father's life by noting the
copy of Lafcadio Hearn's *Glimpses of Unfamiliar Japan*, Volume
II, with its "warped olive cover" that has been "punished like
a rhinoceros hide."[29] The summarizing comment again
comes in the last lines, where Lowell quotes the note in the
flyleaf of the book:

> "This book has had hard usage
> on the Yangtze River, China.
> It was left under an open
> porthole in a storm."

The " 'hard usage' " was obviously not due to reading, and the
book's cover was clearly not "punished like a rhinoceros
hide" in the course of fulfillment of a dangerous assignment;
nevertheless, Lowell implies, his father was on the Yangtze
during the Chinese civil war.

Just as the first three poems in "Life Studies, I" focus on his
parents' families, and just as the next three deal with his
father, so the following three poems are devoted to the poet's
mother. In "For Sale" we learn that the relationship between
Commander Lowell and his wife was not quite as uncom-
promisingly antagonistic as is sometimes implied in the previous poems. Like many couples who have lived together for
a long time, their mutual animosity was a part of their dependence upon one another, and waiting for the furniture to
be moved out of Beverly Farms, Mrs. Lowell

> mooned in a window,
> as if she had stayed on a train
> one stop past her destination.

The "double-barrelled shotgun" of the train tracks has been

associated with the death of her husband, and this image forecasts Mrs. Lowell's own death. Her "destination" has been reached by the next poem, which depicts the poet "Sailing Home from Rapallo," where he has gone to claim his mother's body and to provide an escort home. Mrs. Lowell is still compared to Napoleon, as her casket resembles that of the emperor in the Hôtel des Invalides in Paris, but the pose of hauteur that she assumed in life has been brutally reduced by death: in her coffin she is "wrapped like *panetone* in Italian tinfoil." This image of a loaf of bread *en papillote* provides a bizarre companion for that of her husband's tombstone, an "unweathered pink-veined slice of marble." Both the grandeur to which she aspired in life and her failure to achieve it are summed up in death by the "grandiloquent lettering" on her coffin that misspells the family name "LOVEL."

The last poem in Lowell's elegiac series for his mother, "During Fever" also forms the transition to the final poems of "Life Studies, 1," for its initial stanza concerns the past and his daughter, the second and third return to Lowell's childhood, and the fourth goes all the way back to his mother's youth. The structure of this poem provides a fitting conclusion to those devoted to Lowell's ancestors, for it recapitulates in reverse order the generations that are the subject of this section. The tripartite organization is also a means of implying comparisons among three relationships: one between the poet and his daughter, another between the poet and his mother, and the last between his mother and her father. These three relationships are interlocked by the reappearance of the poet and his mother and by the recurrence of the different types of "sickness" that are the main subjects of the poem. The poet's daughter's "fever" is the physical counterpart of what is plainly an Oedipal relationship in the second stanza:

> Often with unadulterated joy,
> Mother, we bent by the fire
> rehashing Father's character. . . .

Lowell's language throws a special light on the psychological relationship that Freud considered unavoidable: the word

"unadulterated" naturally—or unnaturally—suggests "inces-
tuous" instead; and the conspiratorial overtones of the image
in the second line accent the word "rehashing" in the third,
so that the confrontation of Oedipus and Laius actually is
conjured.

The third stanza elaborates the psychological theme in its
description of his mother's "master-bedroom." The
"master-bedroom" and the "hot water bottle / monogram-
med like a hip-flask," with their connotations of masculinity,
impute to the mother an unyielding nature, while the combination of the "electric blanket" and the "hot water bottle"
suggest frigidity. Again, the description of "the nuptial
bed"—"as big as a bathroom"—implies an aversion to sex;
and the word "fruity" has connotations that mesh with these
other references. The sterility of the bedroom is also indicated
by the artificial "bunches and berries / and proper *putti*" on
the "Italian china."

The vignette in the fourth stanza of the poem accounts for
the abnormality implied in the third, as it concerns the relationship between the poet's mother and her "Freudian papá."
The obverse of that intimated in the second stanza, this relationship between Grandfather Winslow and his daughter
was at least partly responsible for her inability to enjoy marriage. The "National Geographic Magazine" that her father
read as he kept an ear on her suitors and her is an ironic
comment on her own colorless and provincial life. Although
apparently straightforward enough, the lines that summarize
this last relationship are rather complicated:

> Terrible that old life of decency
> without unseemly intimacy
> or quarrels, when the unemancipated woman
> still had her Freudian papá and maids!

In the first place, of course, "that old life" was hardly a "life
of decency," in terms of Lowell's interpretation, but rather a
life of repressed sexuality. But more important, and more
complicating, is that the speaker himself has reconstructed
this vignette of "that old life" on the basis of a smile that he
remembers seeing on his mother's face. In other words, the

poet-speaker is imagining his mother imagining her father; and in view of the Oedipal overtones of stanza 2, it is not difficult to arrive at a motive for his condemnation of "the unemancipated woman" and "her Freudian papá." Thus this last exclamation cuts two ways: it not only explains his mother's character to some extent, but it also witnesses his own "dim-bulb" view.

The perspective in this poem can be traced back through the opening section of "Commander Lowell," with its Freudian interpretation of the poet's mother, through the Thanatos theme of "My Last Afternoon with Uncle Devereux Winslow," to the main concern of "To Delmore Schwartz" and "A Mad Negro Soldier Confined at Munich." Until "During Fever," where it takes the form of an obstacle to the establishment of satisfactory love relationships, the theme of psychological instability has been subordinate in part four; but from this point on, it becomes a major concern again. The titles of the last two poems in this section, "Waking in the Blue" and "Home after Three Months Away," indicate the direction that the rest of the poems in *Life Studies* will take. Leaving the problems of his ancestors, Lowell focuses on himself and his immediate family and begins using the present tense for the first time in part four.

The "Blue" of the title of the first of these poems has at least three meanings relevant to the setting of the poem: it refers to the "Azure day" (and perhaps to Mallarmé's "L'azur,"[30]); it suggests the "blue mood" of the speaker (manifest in "my agonized blue window"); and it alludes to the dreamlike, unreal quality of life in "the house for the 'mentally ill' " (as in the saying that someone is "off in the blue"). Two of the techniques with which Lowell captures this quality deserve particular attention. The first of these techniques, which might owe something to Eliot's "Hollow Men" and might derive from Elizabeth Bishop's "Visits to St. Elizabeth's," a poem about Ezra Pound's confinement in that institution, is the incorporation of a formula from a children's song.[31] The song to which Lowell alludes begins with the line "This is the way we wash our clothes" and concludes with the line "So early in the morning." In Lowell's hands these lines become: "This is the way day breaks in Bowditch Hall at McLean's," the mental institution near Boston in which he was confined. The echoes of the children's song are not strong; and in fact this last line, which is very similar to Bishop's "This is the house of Bedlam," might even allude to a different song. Nevertheless, these lines serve an important function, as they incorporate in the quality of the verse the idea that the minds of the men in McLean's are childlike, an idea that Lowell presents explicitly in the marvelous line: "These victorious figures of bravado ossified young." If "Stanley, now sunk in his sixties" is "still hoarding the build of a boy in his twenties," men like "'Bobbie'" still have the minds of boys much younger.

The second technique referred to above is more peculiar to Lowell and more commonly employed in *Life Studies*. This is the intentionally mixed metaphor, which in its most characteristic form combines phrases involving different animals in such a way that the incongruity thrusts itself upon the reader. The first lines of the poem afford an example of this technique:

> The night attendant, a B. U. sophomore,
> rouses from the mare's-nest of his drowsy head
> propped on *The Meaning of Meaning*.
> He catwalks down our corridor.

Now "mare's-nest" is doubtless a pun, signifying both the mussed hair of the student and the confusion of his mind after his encounter with Ogden and Richards, and "catwalks" nicely condenses the images of a lithe stride and a narrow hallway, so that the words are easily justifiable in themselves; but the mixed metaphor they produce is striking. It might still be passed over if it were not for other instances of the same kind of image, several of which are more remarkable. There is, for example, this description of "'Bobbie,'" who also seems to be associated somehow, in this poetry of "lost connections," with both Ford Madox Ford and the poet:

> redolent and roly-poly as a sperm whale,
> as he swashbuckles about in his birthday suit
> and horses at chairs.

The verb "horses" is vividly descriptive, but it clashes with the image of the "sperm whale" and thus suggests a slightly abnormal point of view.

Several other examples of this kind of thing can be adduced: the "Mad Negro Soldier" says that "'Cat-houses talk cold-turkey to my guards'"; in "To Delmore Schwartz" the "stuffed duck craned toward Harvard"; in "Home after Three Months Away" the nurse is seen as "a lioness who ruled the roost"; and so on. Nor will it do to write such language off as "animal imagery" that suggests a pessimistic view of human nature, for it is not the animal imagery per se that is so remarkable but rather the persistent mixing within and among the images. Surely it is more to the point to note that each of the poems just mentioned employs a persona who is or has recently been unbalanced and to suggest that one of the purposes of this technique—which was employed to a greater extent in the speeches of Michael's wife in "'Thanksgiving's Over"—is to convey the distortion in perspective that accompanies this state.

Along with most of the rest of the poems in *Life Studies*, "Waking in the Blue" also makes use of the oblique and imprecise analogy that is omnipresent in "My Last Afternoon with Uncle Devereux Winslow." A pertinent passage is this one:

> He ·catwalks down our corridor.
> Azure day
> makes my agonized blue window bleaker.
> Crows maunder on the petrified fairway.
> Absence! My heart grows tense
> as though a harpoon were sparring for the kill.

The metaphor in the last two lines is clear enough, as is its glittering point: the poet-speaker, threatened by his commitment to McLean's and fearful of not being "Cured," thinks of himself as a whale (or a seal) about to be killed. It is perhaps not so apparent that the same feeling of being threatened by his surroundings, which might be either the cause or the result of his commitment, finds expression in the preceding lines as well. The "petrified fairway," because it anticipates the "granite profile" of Stanley and the "ossified" figures, is to be associated with the inmates; and the inmates, or at least the poet-speaker, might be said to "maunder"; and consequently, by a strange addition, they might be likened to "Crows" upon which "the night attendant" advances like a cat. Such an analysis is bound to give a false impression of the total effect of the analogy, but it can at least expose the elements that make it up.

The poem that concludes this section, "Home after Three Months Away," turns on several analogies of the same kind. Thus the image of the "gobbets of porkrind" that "hung" on the magnolia tree for exactly the length of time that the poet-speaker was in McLean's Hospital prefigures the end of the poem—"I keep no rank nor station. / Cured, I am frizzled, stale, and small"—where the puns confirm the implied analogy. Again, there can be little doubt but that Lowell means the image of the tulips to reflect the poet-speaker:

> Bushed by the late spring snow,
> they cannot meet
> another year's snowballing enervation.

Similarly, the poet-speaker keeps "no station" (from the Latin *stare*), and the tulips, once upright, are now "horizontal."

A comparable metaphor, on a larger scale, frames "Memories of West Street and Lepke," the first poem in the second sequence in "Life Studies." The first stanza of this poem is given over mostly to the speaker, who is living in a house on " 'hardly passionate Marlborough Street,' "

> where even the man
> scavenging filth in the back alley trash cans,
> has two children, a beach wagon, a helpmate,
> and is a "young Republican."

The situation is reflected in the last stanza, where Lepke is seen "dawdling off to his little segregated cell full / of things forbidden the common man." Like the speaker, Lepke is isolated from other men; and in the fine lines that end the poem, this association is both confirmed and denied:

> Flabby, bald, lobotomized,
> he drifted in a sheepish calm,

where no agonizing reappraisal
jarred his concentration on the electric chair—
hanging like an oasis in his air
of lost connections. . . .

"Memories of West Street and Lepke" is itself an "agonizing reappraisal," as is the whole of *Life Studies;* but this more or less explicit contrast serves almost to link the two men rather than to separate them, while the concentration on death and the "air / of lost connections" are remarkably applicable to the poetry of this volume. The same relationship obtains between Lepke and Lowell as does between the "lost connections" and the "sooty clothesline entanglements" that the poet saw from the roof of the West Street Jail. The figure of Lepke is more a mirage than a mirror image—as the "oasis" suggests—and consequently the technique of the poem itself exemplifies the "air / of lost connections." That there is a connection at some level between the poet-speaker and the gangster is intimated by Lowell's recollection of himself in "During Fever" as "part criminal and yet a Phi Bete." That description of himself is relevant to "During Fever" because the poem goes ahead to recall the "rehashing" of his father's character, but both the description and the "rehashing" are also relevant to this poem; if Lepke is a murderer in fact, the poet-speaker is one in intent. This is to put the matter too bluntly, perhaps, but what Lowell seems to suspect in these poems is that any man's murder taints other men.

Should there be any doubt about the validity of the association of *"Murder Incorporated's* Czar" and the poet, it will be dispelled by the numerous references to violence in the succeeding poems. In "Man and Wife" the setting and the landscape are vividly colored by the filter of tranquilized derangement through which the poet sees them. The initial lines, which in effect if not in intention parody Donne's "The Sunne Rising," owe much of their power to just this kind of distortion:

Tamed by *Miltown,* we lie on Mother's bed;
the rising sun in war paint dyes us red;
in broad daylight her gilded bed-posts shine,
abandoned, almost Dionysian.

The submerged violence rises to the surface of the poem in the description of the magnolia blossoms that "ignite / the morning with their murderous five days' white." A few lines later, where the speaker sees himself as having been "dragged . . . home alive" from "the kingdom of the mad" by his wife, Lowell glances back at the confinement in McLean's Hospital and the incarceration in the West Street Jail, each of which testifies to both the poet's isolation from the world and the problems of living in that world. " 'To Speak of Woe That Is in Marriage,' " which seems to have begun with a translation of Catullus,[32] shifts to the wife's point of view and reiterates the possibility of violence: " 'This screwball might kill his wife, then take the pledge.' " Her own febrile temperament, as well as her husband's tortured mind, is implied in her conception of his moonlighting: " 'free-lancing out along the razor's edge.' "

The poem that concludes *Life Studies* exhibits a style slightly but significantly distinctive.[33] Dedicated to Elizabeth Bishop, a writer whom Lowell has admired for years, this poem bears more than traces of her influence upon him. Composed in five-line stanzas and a delicately irregular and overlapping rhyme scheme and built of images that are at once vivid and evanescent, "Skunk Hour" itself qualifies for the praise that Lowell gave those poems by Bishop that seemed to him representative of poetry from some future century.[34]

As "Skunk Hour" has received extensive and expert commentary elsewhere, this discussion can be confined to those aspects of the poem that substantiate the claims that we have been making about the volume as a whole.[35] As Lowell has made a point of saying, " 'Skunk Hour' is not entirely independent, but the anchor poem in its sequence."[36] Although it is not certain whether Lowell has in mind the second section of part four, or the whole "Life Studies" group, or the volume, it is clear that this poem in a sense reviews all of *Life Studies*. The voyeuristic poet-speaker could very well be the " 'hopped up husband' " of the preceding poem; and the mother skunk who "swills the garbage pail" by the back steps echos "Memories of West Street and Lepke" and the figure of "the man / scavenging filth in the back alley trash cans."

Again, the poet-speaker's perverse love recalls several preceding poems, and his perilous mental balance repeats a theme in "To Delmore Schwartz" and "A Mad Negro Soldier Confined at Munich." There are even motifs from "Beyond the Alps," such as the reference to "Queen Victoria's century" and the images at the beginning of the fifth stanza: "One dark night, / my Tudor Ford climbed the hill's skull."

"Skunk Hour" provides an appropriate conclusion to *Life Studies* because it draws together such motifs, but this is not the only reason that it is the last poem; a more important reason is that it reasserts with more force than ever before Lowell's affirmative response to a world that is "breaking up." That the world is doing so, of course, is the burden of the first seven stanzas. The "chalk-dry and spar spire / of the Trinitarian Church" hints at the sterility of religion; and the "dotage" of the ancient heiress who purchases all of the ugly buildings "facing her shore" and "lets them fall" suggests the inadequacy of traditional provincial attitudes in the modern world, just as "the eyesores" point up the inadequacy of that world itself. The alienation of the individual is set forth not only in the figure of the poet-speaker—"I myself am hell; / nobody's here"—but also in that of the "fairy / decorator" who would like to marry and live on his wife's earnings, in that of the "hermit" heiress, and even in that of the town's patron (nearly a religious symbol):

> The season's ill—
> we've lost our summer millionaire,
> who seemed to leap from an L. L. Bean
> catalogue. His nine-knot yawl
> was auctioned off to lobstermen.
> A red fox stain covers Blue Hill.

This stanza intimates that "the summer millionaire" was a suicide. "Lost" hints that he is "dead" as well as "gone," and the passive voice in the next to the last sentence implies that its owner was not around to sell the yawl himself. The means of suicide is implicit in "leap" and in the "red fox stain" on the hill. Suicide, as well as the madness usually associated with that act, also throws its shadow on the poet-speaker:

                               I hear
     my ill-spirit sob in each blood cell, ˙
     as if my hand were at its throat. . . .

In brief, all of the levels of the disintegration of the culture
that have been exposed in this volume are included in this
final poem; in fact, the range of this disintegration is encom-
passed by two related phrases from "Skunk Hour," "The
season's ill" and "my ill-spirit."

At the same time, this poem sets out Lowell's most affirmative response to the fragmentation of his world. It is perhaps
surprising, at first, to realize that this response is framed in
religious terms, partly because religion has been so noticeably
absent from most of the preceding poems and partly because
it is not so noticeably present in this one. A few words and
images early on—such as the "hermit / heiress" whose son is
"a bishop" and the grazing "sheep"—are the only hints of
Christianity until the fifth stanza of the poem, and in this
crucial stanza the religious framework remains latent.
Nevertheless, the "One dark night," by Lowell's own testimony, alludes to "the dark night of the soul."[37] Similarly,
"the hill's skull" might be a rendering of "Golgotha." Taken
together, these allusions imply a trial of the poet-speaker's
"ill-spirit." In addition to these allusions, the grammar might
be evidence of the pivotal nature of this stanza, for this stanza
alone is in the past tense.

The location of the dark night in the past might well be an
indication of the outcome of that night. The skunks certainly
are. It is easier to see that the skunks are symbolic, however,
than to define precisely the nature of the symbol, for it has a
built-in resistance to being analyzed as a simple analogy. In
John Berryman's terms, which we will find especially applicable to the poems in For the Union Dead, the skunks are
parabolic rather than allegorical; or, in Lowell's terms, the
skunks' march is "ambiguous" as well as an "affirmation."[38]
The skunks are perhaps "ambiguous" because they represent
both the speaker's condition and the moral norm to which he
would like to adhere, with the one meaning shading off into
the other as the poem moves from the seventh to the eighth
stanza. Like the poet-speaker, and perhaps like the couples

in the "love-cars," the skunks upon their first appearance are searching "in the moonlight for a bite to eat." In other words, the persona's spiritual deprivation—suggested by both the quotation from Milton's Satan and Lowell's recollection that he had in mind "a passage from Sartre or Camus about reaching some point of final darkness where the one free act was suicide"[39]—seems to be objectified in the skunks' physical hunger. In a comparable manner, the image of the "moonstruck eyes' red fire" suggests insomnia and his own mental instability.

The merging of the physical and the spiritual is implicit also in the pun on "soles," the secondary meaning of which is drawn out by the reference to "the Trinitarian Church." The same method is employed in the last stanza, but here the mother skunk seems more "affirmative" than "ambiguous," a source of inspiration rather than a reflection of the speaker. The "rich air" and the "column of kittens" give evidence of the potential of life and can be contrasted respectively with the sterile wealth and the frustrated love in the village. The "rich air" is not necessarily pleasant, of course, and the mother skunk's swilling of "the garbage pail" indicates even more emphatically the unpleasantness one accepts when he refuses that "one free act." Although the position of the poet-speaker "on top / of our back steps" suggests the mystical ladder of St. John of the Cross, the subject of this last stanza is not the achievement of divine love or grace but rather the recognition of the possibility of accepting the frequently revolting conditions of this world. The last lines of the poem summarize the affirmative aspect of the mother skunk:

> She jabs her wedge-head in a cup
> of sour cream, drops her ostrich tail,
> and will not scare.

This emblem is not free of irony, since the second line suggests that even the skunk is capable of a proverbial trepidity, but determination seems her dominant quality. Indeed, the very possibility for such irony—rather than the pathetic self-pity of the fifth and sixth stanzas—indicates that the speaker has come through the dark night.

Like the last poem in *Lord Weary's Castle,* the last poem in *Life Studies* demands of the poet that he stand and live; but instead of a dove and an olive branch, he is confronted with a skunk and a cup of sour cream. The difference is crucial, but it does not consist merely in a more pessimistic point of view nor even in a less religious attitude. For one thing, on the basis of the image of the mother skunk with her "white stripes, moonstruck eyes' red fire," and "ostrich tail," it would be possible to argue that this poem is more optimistic than "Where the Rainbow Ends" simply because it recognizes the beautiful and the exotic in the disgusting and ordinary instead of waiting for it to descend from above. For another thing, religion has not been discarded so much as subsumed. Lowell has said that the night in the poem "is not gracious, but secular, puritan, and agnostical. An Existentialist night." Nevertheless, it is a "dark night of the soul," and because the vehicle of the agnosticism is a mystical framework, the poem might be said to incorporate the lesson of the skunks as well as the image of them, for it combines seemingly contradictory elements. For this reason, the poet might be compared to George Santayana on the very terms that he establishes, for they both succeed in uniting in their work forces that are antagonistic elsewhere.

(Let us speak of the osmosis of persons)
—EZRA POUND, *Canto XXIX*

the dissolution of ourselves into others,
like a wedding party approaching a window. . . .
—"The Landlord"

5

MANY PERSONALITIES, ONE VOICE:

Imitations (1961)

The opening paragraph of the introduction to *Imitations* includes these pointed statements:

> This book is partly self-sufficient and separate from its sources, and should be first read as a sequence, one voice running through many personalities, contrasts and repetitions. I have hoped somehow for a whole. . . . The dark and against the grain stand out, but there are other modifying strands.

If one were not acquainted with Lowell's habit of constructing whole books of poems, as distinct from collecting poems and placing them between two covers, these claims might seem enigmatic or pretentious. It is certain that in spite of these remarks, many reviewers and critics have regarded *Imitations* as a collection of more or less free translations that bear little relationship to one another. Ben Belitt, himself a translator and poet and one of Lowell's most competent critics, is typical in this respect. After declaring that the first sentence quoted above is a "startling expectation" for a poet-translator to have, Belitt simply disregards it and proceeds to discuss (quite perceptively) several individual imitations.[1] Frequently, even the claim about the independence of individual poems is not taken quite seriously, and perhaps partly for this reason *Imitations* has not had the undivided critical attention that most of Lowell's other volumes have received.[2]

165

At least two recent critics, however, have paid heed to Lowell's plea that the book be considered "a whole." In a review of *Near the Ocean*, Daniel Hoffman has described *Imitations* as "a long, fragmented poem of the self, struggling in its engagements with history." As Lowell struggles with the poets whom he imitates, "with their vision, their style, their problems, they become his doppelgängers in their times and he theirs in our time."[3] Basing his own discussion upon Lowell's comments and Hoffman's translation of them, Richard J. Fein has cataloged and discussed several of the themes— including war, infinity, the quest, and nature—that recur through this volume.[4] Fein's discussion concerns itself with texture rather than structure, however, and not even his sensitive reading discloses the intricacy of the interrelationships among the imitations. Nor will this chapter, one suspects, for *Imitations* is a work of such dimensions that it warrants a small book. Perhaps the best that can be hoped for is an indication of the form that such a study might take.

Lowell's *Imitations* have been brilliantly chosen and scrupulously arranged. The organization of this book resembles that of *Lord Weary's Castle* in that emphases are placed upon the beginning, middle, and concluding poems; in both cases, by repeating key words and images at these points, Lowell calls attention to the generally symmetrical structure of the books. But if in the placing of emphases by means of motif *Imitations* recalls *Lord Weary's Castle*, the extent of the use of motif reminds us of *Life Studies*. The title of this volume itself indicates its relationship to its predecessor, for in addition to its literary meaning, *imitation* has a pertinent musical denotation. According to the *Harvard Brief Dictionary of Music*, imitation is "the restatement in close succession of a musical idea (theme, subject, motive, or figure) in different voice parts of a contrapuntal texture," and it "may involve certain modifications of the musical idea, e.g., inversion, augmentation, dimunition, etc." From the concept of modified "restatement" of materials to that of "different voice parts," this definition is parallel to Lowell's talk of "modifying strands" and of "one voice running through many personalities, contrasts and repetitions."[5]

The organization of *Imitations* is thus more closely related to that of *Life Studies* than to that of *Lord Weary's Castle*, but it is probably most closely related to that of the book that succeeds this one in Lowell's canon. As the brief comparison with *Lord Weary's Castle* has suggested, *Imitations* has a basically symmetrical structure in which the central section is the crux; and as we shall see in the next chapter, the profile of *For the Union Dead* is remarkably similar. Moreover, within the symmetrical framework of each book, there is a series of interrelated groups of poems which function in the manner of a narrative.

One can distinguish two principles upon which the narrative of *Imitations* rests, the most important of which corresponds to the development of character in a more conventional narrative and the other of which corresponds to the development of action or plot. The first of these principles, which is the one upon which Lowell's introduction focuses, provides for the changes in the outlook of a persona who, depending upon one's immediate point of view, either undergoes or emerges from the experiences reported in these poems; for if it is true that there are "many personalities" in this volume, it is also true that there is but this "one voice." Lowell's two phrases, which seem contradictory at first glance, can be reconciled easily enough by means of a simple but unorthodox distinction. This distinction is between the two terms, often considered synonymous, *poet-speaker* and *persona*. For present purposes, the former term refers to the speaking figure in any single poem, while the latter designates the figure who is capable of speaking in all of these voices. The poet-speaker in a given poem, then, although not identical with the persona, is one facet of the latter, or one of the instances from which we infer his development. The other instances include all of the other poet-speakers and a few of the more properly dramatic figures, such as Achilles in the imitation of Homer, who seem to be projections of the persona. If the persona is not identical with any of the poet-speakers or dramatic figures, neither is it identical with the poet, since the poet is the creator of this collective mask just as he is the imitator of the individual masks. Lowell's "many personalities" are the points that comprise the curve of his "one voice."

Perhaps the mixture in that last metaphor indicates the advisability of positing a second principle upon which this poetic narrative operates. The course of the persona's experience is frequently best described in terms of spatial metaphors, and one reason for this is that there is something like a plot in *Imitations*. This principle is harder to analyze than the first because it is both less consistently and more variously invoked. Since thought and feeling rather than deed and event are the concerns of the lyric, action is as necessarily intermittent as character is unavoidably present in this volume; and since lyric themes are fewer than the settings that they involve, action at this most rudimentary level is bound to be more diverse than the "personalities" in *Imitations*. Nevertheless, there are enough references to similar events to constitute a sketchy plot, and this plot is demonstrably of the epic variety. These poems were selected and arranged with an eye to the events and the settings which they involve, and their events and settings are often those one would expect to encounter in a heroic poem—battles, shipwrecks, descents to hell, and the like. *Imitations* opens with Achilles at Troy, and its next to last stanza concerns Leonidas at Thermopylae. But the clearest instance of the use of such a plot is in the central section, which is the nadir of the persona's development, the dark night of the soul, and in which the most important poems describe voyages and shipwrecks. If Ovid, whose *Metamorphoses* is the source of the drawing on the title page, provides the model for the changing personalities in this book, then Homer, whose *Iliad* is the source of the first poem, is the guiding spirit for its ghost of a plot.[6]

To catch these two principles at their point of intersection, one might say that *Imitations* presents the metamorphosis of Achilles, the type of the warrior, into Odysseus, the type of the voyager. Such a description, however, would still be limited, not only because many of the poems are not concerned with wars or voyages, but also because even the combination of the two heroic figures would only be symbolic of the fundamental subject of the book. Another type that might be singled out as representative of this subject, and which would be more comprehensive than either of the heroic figures because it would conceivably include them, is that of the poet. Almost as many of these imitations are concerned with poets and writing as are concerned with wars and voyages; moreover, as E. R. Curtius has pointed out, there is a seemingly inherent connection between composing poetry and voyaging, and the "boat of the mind" was a commonplace in antiquity.[7] Indeed, just to mention the metaphor is to call to mind a host of poems in English much older than Pound's *Cantos*, Crane's "Voyages," and Stevens's "Prologues to What Is Possible," as well as several of those imitated in this volume, including Baudelaire's "Voyage" and Rimbaud's "Bateau ivre." Lowell's volume is another of these symbolic voyages, but it is to be distinguished from most other such symbols in that what it signifies (the life of the poet) is virtually identical with what it is (a series of closely related, many-voiced poems). *Imitations* is a particularly apt synecdoche for the poet's life because the poet, be he Homer or Ovid or Lowell, undergoes in the course of his work those changes of personality which Lowell insists are at the heart of this book.

Because it is an intricately organized whole with the requisite beginning, middle, and end, it seems that the volume must remain a symbol for the poet's life rather than a reflection of any particular life. The persona, it will be remembered, is not necessarily Robert Lowell. At the same time, as we shall see, the structure of *Imitations* is not such as to preclude its being a reflection of Lowell's own life as well as a symbol of the life of the poet.

With these general observations in the background, it is possible to examine the structure of *Imitations* in more detail. Although any such analysis must ignore some of the more subtle transitions between poems and the quite natural deviations from the overriding scheme, *Imitations* can be divided into seven sections. The ordering of these sections constitutes both a symmetrical arrangement, in which poems and short sequences approximately equidistant from the center counterbalance one another, and a progressive structure, in which a spiritual descent turns into an ascent and an affirmative conclusion grows out of a nihilistic beginning. On several occasions, Lowell goes out of his way to indicate some of the more salient points of this scheme, and it is mildly surprising that almost no one has yet taken his hints. The earliest of these indications, and the one which has been admirably glossed, appears in the first line of the first poem, "The Killing of Lykaon," which is based on two separate passages from the *Iliad*.[8] In Lowell's translation, Homer's line becomes "Sing for me, Muse, the mania of Achilles." The remarkable aspect of this line is that the Greek word which corresponds to Lowell's "mania" is "ménin," which means "enduring anger" or "divine wrath" and is invariably rendered as such by Homer's translators. While the Greek word is cognate with "mania" and Lowell is therefore more "literal" in a peculiar sense than other translators, the denotations of the two words in their respective languages are significantly different. Lowell's choice, then, enables him to declare in the opening line of the volume his imitative license. That it has an even more important function might be suggested by quotation of another line, this time from one of the poems at the center of the book. In Rimbaud's "Les poètes des sept ans" there is the line "Vertige, écroulements, déroutes et pitié," which in Lowell's version becomes "dizziness, mania, revulsions, pity." Since neither "écroulements" ("ruins" or "failings") nor "déroutes" ("routs" or "confusions") would ordinarily be rendered with "mania," one might suspect a connection of some sort between this line and the one in "The Killing of Lykaon." Nonetheless, it is likely that the suspicion would be dismissed if one were not to notice that Lowell makes a similar alteration in translating the last line of Rilke's "Die Tauben" in the poem that ends the book. In the course of transfiguring Rilke's entire last stanza, Lowell turns the last line into "miraculously multiplied by its mania to return." Especially since this imitation has been conspicuously displaced from the chronological order that obtains almost everywhere else, it is clear that Lowell intends "to return" us to the volume's initial line; and once this connection of end and beginning has been noticed, it is likely that we will pay more attention to the line in the Rimbaud poem in the middle of the book.[9]

Simply by placing the word "mania" in these critical positions, Lowell outlines the general curve of *Imitations*, or designates three of the seven sections noted above: the introductory poem, the central sequence, and the concluding
poem. Comparable devices are used to designate other
groups of poems and the relationships among them. Just
after the imitation of Homer and just before the imitation of
Rilke, there are short sequences (selections from Sappho and
Der Wilde Alexander, on the one end, and from Annensky
and Pasternak, on the other) which serve as transitions between these poems and the core of the volume; and Lowell
points up the parallelism of these sequences (our second and
sixth sections) by making them reflect one another. The concluding lines of the third poem based on Sappho and some
lines near the end of "Hamlet in Russia, A Soliloquy," based
on several poems by Pasternak, stand in such a relationship.
Lowell's version of Sappho runs:

> The moon slides west,
> it is midnight,
> the time is gone—
> I lie alone!

The poem derived from Pasternak recalls the preceding lines
with this image:

> The sequence of scenes was well thought out;
> the last bow is in the cards, or the stars—
> but I am alone, and there is none. . . .

Both passages deal with the solitariness of the speaker, both
address themselves to a darkness not only of the night, and
both stress the passing of time. The chief difference between
them is that "The sequence of scenes," which is to say the
majority of these imitations, has passed. The significance of
this distinction, which involves a discussion of the progressive or incremental structure of the volume, is the subject of a
later inquiry. At this point, it is necessary to touch upon some
of the other indications of our tentative division of this
"sequence of scenes."

The transitional sections under consideration reflect one

another by means of several other anticipations and echoes, the most important of which concern a symbolic forest. In "Children," the forest is a mysteriously dangerous place, " 'alive with snakes,' " which must be avoided if one is not to be lost. As the herdsman admonished the children:

> "Well then, get out of the woods!
> If you don't hurry away quickly,
> I'll tell you what will happen—
> if you don't leave the forest
> behind you by daylight,
> you'll lose yourselves;
> your pleasure will end in bawling."

The children, however, did not leave the woods, and the poem intimates that they did indeed lose themselves:

> Where we picked up violets
> on lucky days,
> you can now see cattle gadding about.

In a note in *The Penguin Book of German Verse*, whose prose translation Lowell seems to have consulted, the editor remarks that "this poem is probably an allegory." Like the lyric itself, this note is probably disingenuous, since the former is certainly allegorical; but the specific subject is sufficiently ambiguous to justify editorial reticence, and it is this ambiguity which Lowell exploits later by means of oblique allusions. When we find, near the end of the book, one poem in which the speaker enters the woods and is advised by them, and several poems set in the forest, and one poem entitled "In the Woods," we must suspect that the persona was one of the children who never got "out of the woods" and that Lowell is bending the allegory to his own purposes. The suspicion is enforced and more specifically directed by the reference to the woods as a place where one must suffer strange transformations, where " 'you'll lose yourselves,' " a reference that is recalled by the last stanza of "The Landlord," another imitation of Pasternak:

> as if life were only an instant, of course,
> the dissolution of ourselves into others,
> like a wedding party approaching the window.

This loss of the self repeats but radically revises the notion as it is allegorized in "Children." More will be said of the nature of this revision in connection with the progressive structure of the book; what is important to notice here is that "The Landlord" and "Children" parallel one another by virtue of both position and subject and thus help to establish the ordonnance of the *Imitations*.

The titles of several key poems exemplify most simply this structural use of parallelism. The beginning of what might be called the third section of *Imitations*, for example, is marked by an imitation of Villon's "Le grand testament," a title that is translated by Lowell's "The Great Testament." Lowell's title, apparently unremarkable, assumes some importance when it is realized, first, that the adjective "grand," while often interpolated, was not originally in Villon's title and, second, that its inclusion and translation as "Great" suggests more immediately a relationship between this poem and an imitation of Montale called "Little Testament." Since it occurs late in this volume, at the end of the Montale poems, and since it and the poems just preceding provide a thematic response to "The Great Testament" and the poems succeeding it, "Little Testament" concludes our fifth section.

Similarly, if more dramatically, Lowell translates Hugo's "A Théophile Gautier" as "At Gautier's Grave" and then alters the title of Mallarmé's "Toast funébre" to "At Gautier's Grave" too. The clear implication is that these poems are to be paired, and this implication is strengthened by the positions of the two poems: on either side of the long selections of poems from Baudelaire and Rimbaud. Just as the two "testaments" seem to begin a third section and conclude a fifth, so the two poems on Gautier seem to conclude the third and begin the fifth.

Between the two poems on Gautier, there are twenty-six poems based on Baudelaire and Rimbaud. Since the number of imitations of Baudelaire (fourteen) is the largest of any author, while the number of imitations of Rimbaud (twelve) is second, and since these two are the ninth and tenth of eighteen authors, there is no doubt that what we will call the fourth section is the heart of this volume. Throughout this section there are so many repetitions of phrase and image that it is difficult not to regard them as allusions intended to lace these two sets of imitations together. Of course it might be coincidental that the first Baudelaire poem opens with the indictment that "we spoonfeed our adorable remorse, / like whores and beggars nourishing their lice," while the last Rimbaud poem is "The Lice-Hunters"; and that in the one poem the devil sat by the sickbeds and "hissed," while in the other "the royal sisters" sat there and "hissed";[10] and that the tone of the first poem, which occurs before the spiritual crisis discussed below, is summarized in the phrase "yawning for the guillotine," while that of the second, which follows this book's dark night, is epitomized by the phrase "begged the fairies for his life"; and so on through the other poems. But even if these echoes are considered accidental, the whole question of whether they are so could not have suggested itself without a recognition of such definite structural indicators as have been noted. From one point of view, *Imitations* is a dense reticulation of internal allusions; and once this self-allusive quality has been noticed, the problem is not so much in showing how the allusions create a structure as in keeping that structure from seeming to fade into the texture of allusions.

The symmetry of that structure, however, might not be as sharply limned as it might appear from the preceding adumbration. The *Imitations* fall almost as easily into five or nine sections as into seven; and once the principle of balanced arrangement has been discerned, it might even be advisable to dispense with references to sections altogether. Nevertheless, the outline sketched above does have the merit of providing a framework for a discussion of the narrative or progressive aspect of that structure. In the course of tracing the plot that this narrative involves, there will be no attempt to deal with each of the poems individually, as there has been and will be in the cases of other volumes, both because the length of *Imitations* is prohibitive and because the themes and devices here are often akin to those discussed elsewhere. Nor will there be many comparisons of Lowell's poems with the originals, although some of the more significant and characteristic deviations will be touched upon in passing, for the assumption is that Lowell's suggestion about how to read his book can be fruitfully pursued. Finally, the last half of this book will receive more comment than the first half, since it is in the later poems that we find the preponderance of comments on the methods with which we are concerned. In brief, our strategy will be to summarize certain groups of poems whose themes and relationships seem apparent or only indirectly contributory to the main stream of thought and to dwell upon those which are more complicated or crucial to the narrative element, and meanwhile to take note of the original texts when such notice facilitates discussion of the latter poems.

The first poem in *Imitations*, "The Killing of Lykaon," is apt to seem a perfunctory exercise, an acknowledgement of the virtual necessity of beginning "a small anthology of European poetry" at the beginning. Actually it warrants its position as "prologue" for at least three allied reasons. Since it translates the invocation to the muse that opens the *Iliad*, it implies that what follows is similarly a coherent whole that turns on the attitudes and actions of a single figure. Second, because "The Killing of Lykaon" brings together short passages from the first and the twenty-first books of the *Iliad*, it constitutes a microcosm of Lowell's volume, in which widely separated poems are intimately connected. Finally, the passages that Lowell chooses from Homer condense a complex of themes woven throughout *Imitations*.

Nominally, the "mania" of Lowell's first line refers to Achilles' anger at Agamemnon and his consequent refusal to join the fighting at Troy, and this withdrawal of himself from the arena of action has analogues in the implied experience of the poet. On the one hand, Achilles' self-imposed moratorium conceivably refers to the period after the publication of *Life Studies* in which Lowell seemed to turn from his "original" work to "imitations" and his translation of Racine's *Phèdre* (a period of the sort that we often but insensibly regard as "silence" on the poet's part), so that even on the first page Lowell might be insinuating himself into the narrative or dramatizing his life. On the other hand, and more certainly,

Achilles' abnegation of his position and duties anticipates the defeatism and the death wish that become increasingly prominent as the poems get closer to the center of the volume.

It soon becomes evident that the real referent of "mania" is broader than "anger" or "wrath"; and as the more comprehensive meaning discovers itself, the further aptness of the position of this poem is also revealed. Partly because "mania" is a term that describes a general condition rather than a specific emotion, and partly because both Homer and Lowell find in Achilles' disgust with his fellow Greeks the seeds of Patroklos's death and Achilles' resumption of his duties and his own death, the implications of the word cannot be closely circumscribed. In positive terms, it denotes his wrathful return to battle, as well as his petulant withdrawal from it. This extension of the meaning of the word is justified not only by the merging of Achilles' indignation at Agamemnon with his killing of Lykaon in this poem, but also by the "mania to return" of the last poem in the book. So if Achilles' retreat from combat foreshadows the persona's later escapism, his return to the war anticipates the persona's final acceptance of this world with all of its certain frustrations.

In other words, Lykaon's offer of "'ransom,'" based as it is on the notion that one can eschew the "'destiny and death'" meted out to him, parallels exactly Achilles' fond attempt to renege on his vows. Lowell emphasizes the pertinence of this parallel, the impertinence of both warriors, not only by including Achilles' speech on the universality of the rule of *moira* but also by adding a small detail to that speech. Homer's hero says nothing of being shot "'with an arrow through the heel,'" and by lending his figure this bit of ironic foreknowledge just before he notes that "Achilles hurled Lykaon by his heel / in the Skamander," Lowell sharpens the point of the comparison. Lykaon's death prefigures Achilles' own; but Lykaon, who "lost his heart," is also the perfect foil for Achilles, who has just regained his.

In his wholehearted compliance with fate, his acceptance of what a later speaker calls "'the mulishness of Providence,'" Lowell's Achilles resembles the persona as he emerges at the end of *Imitations*. Recognition of that resemblance should not, however, blind us to the ambiguity that Lowell bestows upon him by use of an epithet stronger than any to be found in the Greek. The purpose of the phrase "that god, Achilles," begins to materialize in the almost unbearably bloodthirsty last lines of this poem:

> "Die, Trojans—you must die till I reach Troy—
> you'll run in front, I'll scythe you down behind,
> nor will the azure Skamander save your lives,
> whirling and silver, though you kill your bulls
> and sheep, and throw a thousand one-hoofed horse,
> still living, in the ripples. You must die,
> and die and die and die. . . ."

If it complicates things to realize that Achilles is an executive agent of Nemesis as well as a victim of that goddess, the complication is part of what makes "The Killing of Lykaon" a suitable prologue, for during most of the first half of the volume the powers that be appear under just this dreadful aspect, while the speakers display not unwarranted and remarkably consistent pessimistic attitudes.

The transition to this more pessimistic point of view is effected through the imitations of Sappho and Der Wilde Alexander, which deal with the theme of transience. In the "Three Letters to Anaktoria" Lowell converts three fragments, in two of which Sappho expressed her love for a young bride and a woman named Anaktoria, into a brief sequence in which the primary object of the speaker's love is a third party, a man.[11] Although it is not clear exactly what the poet gains by supplementing homosexual love with heterosexual, it is apparent that the net effect of this sequence is to impress upon us the fleeting nature of fulfilling love. In the first selection, the man is in love with Anaktoria, the speaker's intimate companion and rival, and in the second selection he has already been the speaker's lover and departed, so that whatever satisfactory relationship there was has been squeezed, as it were, into that briefest of intervals between the two laments. The tone of these imitations is fairly represented by the third section, quoted in full earlier,

while the thoughts that could motivate such lonely desperation are summed up in the last stanza of the second:

> A woman seldom finds what is best—
> no, never in this world,
> Anaktoria! Pray
> for his magnificence I once pined to share . . .
> to have lived is better than to live!

Just as the versions of Sappho end with this realization that
"the time is gone," so "Children" opens on this nostalgic
note:

> Years back here we were children
> and at the stage of running
> in gangs about the meadows. . . .

"So times passes" and with it the "lucky days," the "dancing
round," and the "new green sheaths" the children wore, to
say nothing of the children themselves. The theme of mutability, its universal application barely disguised by the personal circumstances in the "Three Letters to Anaktoria" and
by the whimsical surface of "Children," assumes the status of
a first principle with the initial poem of the third section. The
ubi sunt and *memento mori* motifs that pervade the following
poems are set out in these lines from "The Great Testament":

> My Father (God have mercy!)
> is in the ground, and soon
> my mother also must die—
> poor soul, she knows it well,
> her son must follow her.

This is an adequate summary, that is, as long as the irony of
the parenthetical phrase is recognized. Although it might be
true that Lowell's imitations of Villon are so good partly because the Christian tradition serves as a common denominator,[12] it is nonetheless certain that Lowell mines the
vein of skepticism in the medieval poet's work. This passage,
which occurs much earlier in Lowell's "Testament" than in
Villon's, is symptomatic:

> Where are those gallant men
> I ran with in my youth?
> They sang and spoke so well!
> Ah nothing can survive
> after the last amen;
> some are perhaps in hell.
> May they sleep in God's truth;
> God save those still alive!
>
> Some have risen—are grave
> merchants, lords, divines. . . .

The restriction of God's powers of salvation to those who are alive, the distortion of resurrection so that it denotes the elevation of men to "grave" positions, and the unequivocal claim that nothing survives death—these are not the most prominent characteristics of poetry in the Christian tradition.

The good wishes here extended to fellow poets still alive suggest one reason for Lowell's dedication of this poem to William Carlos Williams. It seems likely that there is another reason, since the other four poems in this volume dedicated to well-known writers are all nodes in its organization; but whether or not the dedication is Lowell's imitation of an asterisk, "The Great Testament" marks a crucial point in this narrative.[13] In the first place, it gathers up several motifs from the earlier poems, the isolation of the speaker in the lines quoted above being just one such motif. The speaker in "Children," in a phrase original with Lowell and characteristic of his particularizing tendency, refers to his "day burning down,"[14] and the same image recurs here in conjunction with the *ubi sunt* motif:

> How quickly my youth went,
> like ravellings of cloth
> the weaver holds to cut
> with wisps of burning straws!

And more bluntly:

> I was less ripe than black!
> nothing left on horseback

or foot, alas! What then?
My life suddenly burned.

The imitations of Sappho are also brought to mind at several points, as in the speaker's declaration that "I have loved—all I could!" and in his order to "sell love to someone else."

"The Great Testament" not only repeats these motifs but also provides a slightly different perspective on them. This perspective is the result partly of a shift in emphasis—whereas the Sappho imitations stressed her feelings for her lover and that of Der Wilde Alexander stressed the joy of childhood, the Villon concentrates on the miserable present—and partly of a change in point of view. The sex of the speaker in the "Three Letters to Anaktoria" and the mode of the expression in "Children" forestall an attribution of these poems even to a stylized version of the poet himself. In "The Great Testament" Lowell naturally adopts the autobiographical mask that Villon chose to wear, and it is suddenly quite difficult to identify the figure behind that mask:

> I am thirty this year;
> near Christmas, the dead season,
> when wolves live off the wind,
> and the poor peasants fear
> the icy firmament.
> Sound in body and mind,
> I write my testament,
> but the ink has frozen.

Even more than the opening lines of the imitation of Homer, the imitation of Villon has to have an autobiographical ring; to adapt the terms that Lowell uses in his introduction, the one voice of the persona meets with less interference from the personality of the speaker in this poem.

The change in point of view or voice, combined with the reiteration of motifs, is calculated to create the impression of a continuum of experience, in which the present is an extension of, and response to, the past. It is as though the resignation of Villon's speaker were rooted in the experiences of the preceding speakers. The narrative has advanced, and it continues almost imperceptibly as Lowell's persona becomes more complex and his fatalism turns into a more desperate attitude. Both of these developments are hinted at as early as the last lines of the imitation of Leopardi's "L'Infinito." The speaker has been musing on the "silence that passes / beyond man's possibility":

> and when the wind lifts roughing through the trees,
> I set about comparing my silence to those voices,
> and I think about the eternal, the dead seasons,
> things here at hand and alive,
> and all their reasons and choices.
> It's sweet to destroy my mind
> and go down
> and wreck in this sea where I drown.

The first thing to notice here is that the contrast between "the dead seasons" and the "things here at hand and alive" was the main concern of the imitations of Villon, that one voice does seem to speak through the two different masks. But it is even more difficult here than in the earlier poems to distinguish between the voice of the poet-speaker and that of the imitator. The chief reason for this difficulty is that Lowell has altered his source in such a way that the lines apply more immediately to *Imitations* itself than to Leopardi's original subject. Leopardi compared the "infinite silence" ("Infinito silenzio") of the universe "to this voice" ("a questa voce") of "the wind" ("il vento") in order to bring about the intersection of past and present. While the end might be the same, Lowell's means are notably different, for the speaker here compares his own silence to voices which, if they are supposed to be those of the leaves, are nevertheless ambiguous. As these "voices" are associated with "the eternal, the dead seasons," it is probably legitimate to assume that they are also those of the poets imitated in this volume. In fact, Lowell's merging of his silence and those voices, of the dead and the living, recalls his introductory statement that his imitations were done when he found himself incapable of writing anything original. What happens, then, is that Lowell's own work becomes a strand in his narrative, the writing of these poems becomes one of the subjects of them. Because the poems do constitute a narrative, the process of creating form, to the degree that it is one with the flow of experience that the poem transcends, becomes a part of that form. In terms perhaps less abstract but still paradoxical, the narrative that Lowell has composed incorporates as events in it the composition. The intersection here is not just of past and present, but also of form and flux.

The subject of the reconciliation of the flux of experience and the formality of art will come up more frequently when poetry becomes more frequently the subject of the poems. Meanwhile it is necessary to note the general change in attitude that first becomes apparent in "The Infinite." A literal translation of its last three lines runs like this: "So among this immensity my thought is drowned: and foundering is sweet to me in this sea."[15] As usual, Lowell's translation accents whatever suggestion of melancholy and violence there is in the original, and the effect here is to endow the speaker with a longing for death that is perhaps more redolent of the *fin de siècle* than suggestive of Leopardi's neoclassical awe of the sublime. In this instance, at least, Lowell's sensibility accords perfectly with the narrative that he is developing, for the most remarkable feature of the following poems is the persistence with which they express a death wish. The disillusionment with life characteristic of the poems based on Sappho ("to have lived is better than to live") becomes a positive desire for death in "Heine Dying in Paris" ("sleep is lovely, death is better still, / not to have been born is of course the miracle"). By the point of the imitation of Hugo, the last poem in our third section, the Thanatos motif dominates the poetry. The reverberations of the "rocklike, unhinging effort to die" of "The Flawed Bell" continue throughout the imitations of Baudelaire and are heard in those of Rimbaud, as in the exclamation "Oh that my keel might break, and I might drown" toward the end of Lowell's elliptical version of "The Drunken Boat."

Concommitant with these repeated death wishes, there are numerous indications that the narrative is approaching its midpoint. In the translation of Hebel, which has as its setting "the Basel road between Steinen and Bromback, at night," there are these lines to remind us of the course of things ever since "Children":

"Things start out young and new, and then they slide
gently downhill. They ache and age to their end. . . ."

And at the end of the poem the father, who is the projection of the persona here, describes the town in which he spent a laborious youth in terms that perhaps recall Achilles' repudiation of his duty:

"there's where I plowed and drained the bottom land,
scared rabbits through the brush, made splints for torches. . .
That's where I learned to drudge away my life.
All the king's horses cannot drag me back!"

Because the middle of the volume and of the narrative is an end, in the sense that it is the beginnning of a new life, the concluding lines of the translation of Hugo's "L'expiation" can also be interpreted as an indication of a turning point to come. The outcry forced by defeat from an atheistic Napoleon is " 'God of our armies, is this the end?' " and the chilling response is simply " 'No, Napoleon.' " The terrible irony is of course that Napoleon would regard the end as a blessing—and so, apparently, would God. Finally, or additionally, there are the lines from the first of the Baudelaire imitations, "To the Reader," where the devil's

flattery makes us eat a toad,
and each step forward is a step to hell,
unmoved, though previous corpses and their smell
asphyxiate our progress on this road.

As it turns out, to arrive in hell is to begin to escape from it.

Although it would be futile to attempt to designate the lowest circle of hell, the exact center of this volume, it lies somewhere between "The Voyage" and "The Drunken Boat." Indeed, the combination of the position of, and the contrast between, these two poems suggests that *Imitations*, unlike *For the Union Dead*, has no single poem as fulcrum. Because "The Voyage," which is dedicated to T. S. Eliot, embodies a qualified affirmation that anticipates later poems, while "The Drunken Boat" presents an experience of vertigo and loss of direction that we associate with earlier poems, it looks at first as though Lowell might have allowed his general chronological arrangement to subvert his narrative pattern. To assume that this is the case, however, would be to impose on the book a more rigorously symmetrical organization than actually informs it. Moreover, the element of similarity between the two poems is almost as strong as that of contrast. In addition to the death wish, the images of shipwreck and drowning figure prominently in both poems. In "The Voyage," drowning is the symbol that represents the conversion of the death wish into the desire to push forward:

> Only when we drink poison are we well—
> we want, this fire so burns our brain tissue,
> to drown in the abyss—heaven or hell,
> who cares? Through the unknown we'll find the *new*.

This is of course the famous end of "The Voyage," and perhaps, since it points so definitely to a beginning, it is the end for which the persona as represented by Napoleon was hoping earlier.[16]

This stanza is also a crucial link in one catenation of images that makes it possible to speak of a narrative in *Imitations*. It looks back through the image at the end of "The Game" of "those who scuttle character, / and crowd full sail into the blue abyss" and through the last lines of "The Infinite" to the first poem and Patroklos, " 'killed by the running ships when I was gone.' " At the same time, it looks forward through the conclusion of "Nostalgia" ("My boat stuck fast; its anchor dug for bottom") and that of "The Poet at Seven" ("he lay alone on pieces of unbleached canvas, / violently breaking into sail") to the penultimate stanza of "The Drunken Boat":

> Shrunken and black against a twilight sky,
> our Europe has no water. Only a pond
> the cows have left, and a boy wades to launch
> his paper boat frail as a butterfly.

The "boy" of this stanza is no less the poet—either Rimbaud

or Lowell—than the "voyager" of Baudelaire's poem; and if the latter knows that he must eschew the "spectre" that entices him with idle ease, Rimbaud's figure recognizes the need to continue the struggle that must end in his defeat. It is true that the temptation to surrender the struggle seems to have won out in the last stanza:

> Bathed in your languors, Waves, I have no wings
> to cut across the wakes of cotton ships,
> or fly against the flags of merchant kings,
> or swim beneath the guns of prison ships.

But if the speaker, the boat, has "no wings," the boy's paper boat (which is "frail as a butterfly") does, even though they might seem ineffectual. It is possible that Lowell sees in the penultimate stanza of Rimbaud's poem the slightest hint of rejuvenation. If so, this might explain why he adds the detail that the boat of the last stanza has "no wings" even at the expense of the mixed metaphor that results in the last line.[17] However unfortunate it might be in this respect, this detail does succeed in conveying a sense of contrast between the two boats and therefore a certain ambiguity that is barely if at all present in Rimbaud.

For our purposes, it does not really make a great deal of difference whether "The Drunken Boat" is considered a less emphatic restatement of the affirmation at the end of "The Voyage" or a relapse into the hopelessness that afflicted the persona in, say, "Heine Dying in Paris." For one thing, as the composite nature of the book and Lowell's refusal to adhere to a rigid scheme should both lead us to suspect, there are several such relapses in the second half of the book. "The Cadet Picture of My Father," after Rilke, and "Winter Noon," after Saba, would both have fit more neatly into earlier sections. To omit all traces of pessimism from this part of the book, however, would be to imply that there can only be one dark night of the soul, and Lowell wishes to suggest the contrary. The other reason that an unequivocal interpretation of "The Drunken Boat" is unnecessary is that the general thrust of the poems following this central section would remain virtually unaffected in any case.

The upward movement of the volume may be said to begin

for certain with the imitation of Mallarmé's "Toast funèbre," the first poem after those derived from Rimbaud. If Gautier's death is emblematic of "the bright times that changed to worse" in Lowell's Hugo, it is the occasion for a eulogy for the poet's ability to endure tribulation and therewith "reclaim / the restless miracle of paradise" in his Mallarmé. As in *For the Union Dead,* the section into which the central poems lead concerns the artist and his struggle; and as in that later volume, an exploration of this struggle discovers the means by which nihilism can be countered. Valéry's "Hélène" suits Lowell's purposes here not only because the Greek beauty represents an ideal for which "the gods" and "the kings" and, by extension, the poets must strive, but, more importantly, because she becomes the symbol of the poet's ability to infuse the dead past with life. By making Helen the speaker and the object, in the present as well as in the past, Valéry and Lowell through him resurrect "from the lower world" the figure whose death Lowell's Villon cited as evidence of the transience of all mortal things. That Lowell is as concerned with the fine points of his translations as with their general import and position this poem proves by its happy rendering of "antique" as "archaic." The adjective is particularly striking in the English because it refers to a specific period in the history of Greek art and therefore attributes an extraordinary perspective to a figure who lived in that period herself. Since the word has the effect of removing Helen altogether from her historical context and placing her in the present, it is one of the poet's chief means of bringing the past to life.

In "Helen" this regenerative process goes on beneath the surface of the poetry, but in the following poems, based on Rilke's work, it works its way up. In "A Roman Sarcophagus" the "terrible Etruscan mater familias" on the lid of the stone coffin is comparable to Helen before she was vitalized by the poet, and in the last stanza but one the speaker puts the question that Valéry might have asked himself before he began his sonnet:

> Where's the intelligence
> to galvanize this dead presence,

> to put her to use
> just once?

Of course the irony is that "the intelligence" is the one behind the poem, for it is only in the poem that the "pleats"
sculpted in the stone can become "whirling water," the
poem's symbol of life-giving power.[18] The last lines of
"Self-Portrait" make the same point, as the poet gazes at
himself in a mirror or photograph instead of at a figure on a
sarcophagus and sees that "Out of this distant and disordered thing / something in earnest labors to unroll." The
labor, which is not without its parturient meaning here, and
the unrolling are aspects of the poet's struggle to articulate
and shape his experience.

One of Lowell's symbols for this experience, for the poet's
task, is the journey, whether it is over the sea or on the road.
In "The Voyage" the speaker described the trials necessitated
by the course that he and others like him had set in terms of
"Sailors discovering new Americas, / who drown in a mirage
of agony," and in the poem based on Rilke's "Orpheus, Eur-
dike, Hermes," the journey and its pain are condensed in the
image of "the single road . . . unwinding like a bandage"
before the singer. The parallel between these two images
perhaps extends even further, since each suggests the positive side of the creative struggle even as it delimits the negative. (In the Baudelaire imitation, the discovering and the
drowning are inextricable; and in the Rilke, the unwinding
bandage signifies the completion of a healing process as well
as the revelation of a wound or a scar.) Nevertheless, the pain
and the loss attendant upon his journey clearly set Orpheus
apart from Eurydice, "a root, self-rooted," who enjoys the
ultimate tranquillity and perfection attainable only in death:

> She was drowned in herself, as in a higher hope,
> and she didn't give the man in front of her a thought,
> nor the road climbing to life.
> She was in herself. Being dead
> fulfilled her beyond fulfillment.
> . . . .
> She was still in her marble maidenhood,
> untouchable.

The first line here echos the shipwreck imagery of the central section, while the last image connects Eurydice with the "terrible Etruscan mater familias" whose "dead presence" in this case cannot be "galvanized" to life. In other words, she is the exact opposite of "Helen"; or, to borrow from "91 Revere Street," "because finished" she is "rocklike," "endurable and perfect," and Orpheus's attempt to retrieve her from the underworld is tantamount to an attempt to make her "come back urgent with life and meaning."

In the end, the implication is, this attempt cannot entirely succeed. The point, essential to an understanding of this volume, receives its fullest expression in this poem in the lines on Orpheus's moment of loss:

> Couldn't he turn round? (Yet a single back-look
> would be the ruin of this work
> so near perfection.) And as a matter of fact,
> he knew he must now turn to them. . . .

It is literally "a matter of fact," a phrase not in the original, that Orpheus "must" turn around precisely because perfection is possible only in death. Imperfection or "ruin," if not the measure of life and poetry, is the perquisite of both; the perfect life or the perfect poem is the end of living or the end of writing. From this proposition, which cannot be too strongly emphasized, it follows that imperfection alone can be fertile and reproductive. The idea is, of course, as old as Longinus and as famous as Browning; and, properly ramified, it is the response given in the last parts of *Imitations* to the desire for death that informs the earlier parts. In fact, *Imitations* as a whole embodies this response, since these poems are continually looking back, continually commenting on and revising the themes and images of earlier poems; and in the course of that commentary and revision, which are in effect necessitated by the poems' original incompleteness, Lowell admits their imperfection. At the same time, he is perfecting those poems, and this process extends his narrative, which gives further shape to the necessarily flawed experience that comprises it *and* creates the necessity for further shaping. Again, we are at the intersection of form and flux.

All of this can be put compactly by saying that Lowell's method is identical with the journey of Rilke's lyrist, whose ascent from the underworld naturally follows the descent to hell in the central section. Perhaps it is no accident, then, that this poem, which Lowell says was the beginning of the book and which he dedicates to William Meredith, contains one of the finest glosses available on his own use of anticipatory and recapitulating devices in the form of a description of Orpheus (in which, significantly, he adds the detail of the doglike "outlook" worrying *behind* him):

> It was as though his intelligence were cut in two.
> His outlook worried like a dog behind him,
> now diving ahead, now romping back,
> now yawning on its haunches at an elbow of the road.

The effect of Lowell's "outlook" can be seen in the positioning of "Little Testament," the poem that provides structural equivalence and thematic opposition to "The Great Testament." Instead of warning of the inevitability of death, the later poem reminds us of the continuation of life and of the ability of men to affect the future course of events:

> I have only this rainbow
> to leave you, this testimonial
> of a faith, often invaded,
> of a hope that burned more slowly
> than a green log on the fire.

The rainbow, an almost monotonously recurrent symbol in Lowell's earlier poetry, is invoked here to symbolize not the covenant between God and man but that between man and man. Still, the religious connotation seems to influence this passage, in which the speaker names the two capacities ("faith" and "hope") which enable men to reach into and alter their futures. The fire promised by the rainbow here seems to represent the creative intensity of the poetic sensibility; and the "green log" (which is "un duro ceppo," "a hard log," in Montale), a durable if not immutable aspiration. The fire symbol recurs in the last lines, which are representative

of the affirmative inclination that has been building throughout the poems derived from Montale:

> Each knows his own: his pride
> was not an escape, his humility
> was not a meanness, his obscure
> earth-bound flash
> was not the fizzle of a wet match.

The insistence, albeit in negative terms, on the significance of
the "obscure / earth-bound flash" of a man's achievement
implicitly contradicts the melancholy defeatism of the early
poems. Transience receives its due in this poem, but it is
coordinate with, and perhaps subordinate to, its opposite
number, for "an autobiography can only survive in ashes, /
persistence is extinction." The creative power must burn itself out, and the life of which it was a part only endures in the
form of the effects of that power, in the changes that it has
wrought. Although persistence leads inevitably to the extinction of the creative power, the ashes that manifest that extinction also witness the existence of the original force and therefore assure its survival.[19] As R. P. Blackmur puts it in a sentence that compresses the idea that is being elaborated here,
"death is the expense of life, and failure is the expense of
greatness."[20]

These lines are particularly relevant to *Imitations*, which is
an "autobiography" of the spirit whose power survives in the
poems or "ashes" that mark the path of the journey that the
poet undertook. Lowell is pointing up the further relevance
of this testimonial, this poem, to the strategy of the book of
which it is a part when he has his speaker claim that "It is
certainly a sign: whoever has seen it, / will always return to
you." Indeed, Lowell has returned to Montale, as poets and
critics return to Lowell and to Montale; and so again the
method of this volume, which consists in returning to the
theme of struggle and persistence as suggested by the works
and lives of other poets, becomes its subject.

With "Black Spring," the only imitation of Annensky and
perhaps the last major turning point in the volume, a bleak
but wise acceptance of the poet's task begins to appear, as the
typical new beginning and the necessary end meet vis-à-vis

in the image of the "dumb, black springtime" that "must look
into the chilly eye" of the past winter. The title of this poem
itself connotes the union of death and rebirth on which the
persona bases his resolution to persist. Two lines in the opening stanza of "September," the first poem derived from Pasternak, embody the union of opposites in a complex form that
has ramifications for several other poems in the book. The
pertinent lines are these: "Isn't it time to board up the summer house? / The carpenter's gavel pounds for new and
naked roof-ribs." The first line seems to be closely related to
an image in "My Last Afternoon with Uncle Devereux
Winslow" in *Life Studies*, and in any case its force is the same
because it suggests the passing of the fertile time of the year,
vacancy, and the approach of death. On one level, however,
this line conflicts with its successor, where the demand for
"new and naked roof-ribs" implies a renovation of the summer house rather than a closing of it and where both adjective
and noun suggest birth instead of death. The logic of the
metaphor, then, implies that death and birth are inextricable,
or more precisely, that death necessitates birth.

If their full meaning is to be felt, these lines must be viewed
in the context of related passages in other poems; and the
concept of "related passages" must be broad enough to include more than such obviously apposite images as these in
"Black Spring":

> from under the mould
> on the roof-shingles, the liquid oatmeal
> of the roads, the green stubble of life
> on our faces!

Particularly because of the almost allegorical nature of the last
line and a half, the house, an old symbol in Lowell's work,
might here be associated with the self or the mind affected by
the mold of age or decay—the imagery suggests a second
childhood—and consequently these lines can be seen as
causally related to the demand for renovation in "September."
This connection between the two poems is confirmed by
the similarity of their conclusions, in each of which the road
again symbolizes the course of life.

But the "modifying strands" woven through "September"

can be traced much further than the preceding poem. The speaker of this poem hears summer "mumbling . . . 'A lifetime of looking back,' " and the description is applicable to Lowell's persona as well. In the passage with which we are immediately concerned, he seems to look back to other references to houses and carpenters, among which two of the most notable are in "Autumn" and "Saturday Night in the Village." In the poem based on Baudelaire's "Chant d'automne" the speaker presents the approach of death in terms of winter entering his citadel and of his "heart-beat" destroying his body "like a slow battering ram crumbling a wall." Both images support the interpretation of the house symbol offered above, and the second makes living and dying synonymous processes and thus complements the inextricability of death and life in "September." Even more to our purposes is the last stanza of "Autumn":

> I think this is the season's funeral,
> some one is nailing a coffin hurriedly.
> For whom? Yesterday summer, today fall—
> the steady progress sounds like a goodbye.

The voiced question is easy enough to answer; it is more important to discern the unvoiced query: who is the "some one" nailing the coffin? The perhaps unsurprising answer to this query (as well as to the first one) is: the speaker himself. The carpenter is no less an aspect of the speaker in the earlier autumnal poem than he is in the later; and the carpenter in "September," literally boarding up a summer house, is also completing his own coffin, just as he is in "Autumn."

In light of the phrase "the steady progress" in the last line of the one poem and the connotations of "new and naked roof-ribs" in the other, and in light of the unavoidable association of carpenters and constructions, it can be suggested that both the building of the coffin and the work on the summer house are the writing of poetry. Lowell makes the first of these identifications explicitly in a poem in *History*, "Reading Myself," when he refers to "my open book . . . my open coffin." Just as an autobiography can survive only in the ashes of a life, so an idea can live only in the coffin of a poem, and a poet can survive only in the abandoned house of his

works. Whether the poet is seen in romantic terms as a flaming spirit or considered in classical terms as an architect, the
relationship between the man and the work is the same. If
further confirmation of the carpenter-poet correspondence is
needed, this stanza from an imitation of Leopardi provides it:

> Then all's at peace;
> the lights are out;
> I hear the rasp of shavings,
> and the rapping hammer
> of the carpenter, working all night
> by lanternlight—
> hurrying and straining himself
> to increase his savings
> before the whitening day.

Since the poet-speaker is also up late "Saturday Night" working over his verse—the imagery suggests such things as delet-
ing unnecessary words and driving rhymes like "night" and
"lanternlight" into place—the parallel seems sound.

The "new and naked roof-ribs" can thus be seen as fresh
poems and the "summer house" as the oeuvre; and since it is
the business of this volume to mirror the life of the poet,
these two symbols also represent respectively the successive
poems in the book and the book itself. Of course it is certain
that new roof shingles will get moldy, that new beams will
one day have to be replaced, and that new poems will ultimately prove imperfect. For this reason, *Imitations* might be
said to make the raison d'être of poetry the subject of its
poems; everywhere the knowledge of the reason that one
writes, or of the unreasonable need to write, becomes itself
the object of that need. Failure is self-generating; perseverance has its tail in its mouth. This is the force of the line in the
next poem, "For Anna Akmatova," where the speaker says,
"I must persist in my errors." It is not just that the poet feels
that he has to go on writing; nor is it even that he sees himself
as an inveterate failure; it is rather that persisting and erring
are the same.[21]

The structure of "The Seasons" reflects this theme of the
poet's persistence in error. Beginning with spring, the poem
moves through the cycle of the four seasons, and then in the

fifth section it returns to spring. This overlapping of the beginning and the end of "The Seasons" is significant, for it reveals the affirmative aspect of Lowell's book. By returning to the season of spring, Lowell not only redoubles his emphasis upon creativity or "resurrection" but also implies a transcendence of the "simmer of rot and renewal" that depresses the poet-speaker in several poems in *For the Union Dead* and is one of the factors responsible for the death wish early in *Imitations* itself. The cycle of life and death is surmounted each time the cycle begins anew; and although one can be certain that death follows life, it is a condition of life to attempt to triumph over death. In the same way, while it is true that poems must be imperfect, it is the nature of writing that the perfect poem be the target. The only means by which such a philosophy can be lived is by inexorably beginning again; and the only way in which it can be embodied in poetry, as distinct from being expressed, is in the making of new poems. It is this concept that Lowell indicates by returning to spring after he has run through the cycle of the seasons, and it is this concept itself that preempts the critical commentary that attributes to *Imitations* a philosophy of "cyclicism and moral decay" and a "cosmic pessimism."[22] In the last line of this poem, a line that echos the conclusion of "Self-Portrait" and recalls a pivotal image in *Life Studies*, the speaker asserts that "The overpaid gladiator must die in earnest."[23] It is difficult to see how this line could be squared with any "cosmic pessimism." In the terms of this book, "dying in earnest" entails living in earnest, or, as Lowell's Rilke says, laboring in earnest; and laboring in earnest precludes a view that has no means of accommodating faith, hope, and creativity.

If an "overpaid gladiator" is not the cosmic pessimist's idea of the poet, neither is the concluding stanza of the next poem his notion of the world:

"The world is always like this," say the woods,
as they mix the midday glare, Whitsunday and walking.
All's planned with checkerberry couches, inspired with clearings—
the piebald clouds spill down on us like a country woman's
house-dress.

For just a moment, this stanza from "Sparrow Hills" has the overtones of a pessimism, or at least of a view of the world in terms of the ennui that afflicted the persona in the Baudelaire imitations, but the last three lines first undercut and then positively make fun of that idea. To say that " 'The world is always like this' " is to say nothing at all suggestive of fatalism or weltschmerz if " 'this' " signifies a changing mélange of the most disparate elements. And if the last line is taken to be the final judgment, one has to praise, rather than deprecate, the continuity of life.

The structure of "The Seasons" is significant also in that it contributes to and summarizes the increasing emphasis upon spring through the last part of this volume. In addition to such poems as "Hitlerian Spring" and "Black Spring," admittedly poems of mixed emotions, others of these later lyrics are set in the juvenescence of the year. "Wild Vines," a brief poem that manages to be both delicate and bacchanalian, is only the most overt of several celebrations of "resurrection in the spring." The repetition of images of rebirth, youth, and love through this part of *Imitations* has a cumulative effect comparable with, but opposite to, the recurrent images of death (in "The Killing of Lykaon," "Villon's Epitaph," "Heine Dying in Paris," "At Gautier's Grave," "The Sleeper in the Valley," and so on) in the first half of the volume.

Some of the last poems respond to earlier ones in more specific terms. Take the last lines of "The Landlord":

> as if life were only an instant, of course,
> the dissolution of ourselves into others,
> like a wedding party approaching the window.

Instead of being conceived of as a punishment in the form of a grotesque metamorphosis, as it is in "Children," the loss of self is presented, paradoxically, as a marriage. The reason for the use of this symbol is that here, as in the lines on the planned chaos of the world in "Sparrow Hills," Lowell has his book in mind. The marriage is not only of the poet-speaker and his subjects, and not only of those subjects in the presence of the poet-speaker, although these meanings are implied; it is also of the imitator and the poets whom he is imitating, and of those poets in the hands of the imitator. The

second set of meanings is exactly parallel to the first; and if
the first involves a transformation of the individual into a
union, the second involves the conversion of the flux of the
experience of the imitator into the form of the relationship he
creates among his originals. Lowell dissolves for the moment
into the figures of those whom he unites in his narrative, and
in that narrative he provides a symbol of the experience of the
poet.

   In "Hamlet in Russia, A Soliloquy," and "Pigeons," the
"epilogue," Lowell gives fullest expression to the poet's experience. In some respects the first of these poems is the
more complex, since it epitomizes and glosses the idea of
"the dissolution of ourselves into others." As in several of the
Rilke imitations and as in "The Landlord," the complexity
and the importance of this version of Pasternak issue from
the relationships established between this poem and the volume as a whole, on the one hand, and the original poet and
the translator, on the other. These relationships are even
more complex here than usual because Pasternak's original is
also an imitation, a conflation of voices. The masks superim-
posed upon one another include Lowell's speaker, the Russian "Hamlet," and the Elizabethan figure; and the poets
involved include Lowell, Pasternak, Shakespeare, and even
Shakespeare's hero, a poet of sorts himself. Thus Lowell's
imitation presents in condensed form the "many personalities" through which the "one voice" of this volume
speaks. It epitomizes the first of the principles mentioned at
the beginning of this chapter.
   Inasmuch as the other principle, that pertaining to the "action" in the book, can be separated from the principle that
provides for the changes in the persona, it is also commented
upon in this poem:

"The sequence of scenes was well thought out;
the last bow is in the cards, or the stars—
but I am alone, and there is none . . .
All's drowned in the sperm and spittle of the Pharisee—

To live a life is not to cross a field."

In the guise of Hamlet, the poet-speaker is commenting not only upon his life, but also upon the sequence of poems in this volume that represent a life. As in the imitations of Sappho toward the beginning of the book, the speaker is alone, and the litotes of the final line suggests the trials that have been undergone; but the reaction to his loneliness and tribulation is a far cry from the temptation to reject life that characterized the earlier sections. Although " 'To live a life' " is more akin to undertaking an epic quest than to crossing a field, there is no thought here of preempting Fate or of giving up the quest. In fact, earlier in the poem, in lines reminiscent of Yeats's "Dialogue of Self and Soul," the persona makes the strongest affirmative statement in the whole of *Imitations:*

> "I love the mulishness of Providence,
> I am content to play the one part I was born for. . . ."

Even this affirmation is not unmitigated, however, and there is a finality to this poem that makes it a fitting conclusion. Although the speaker is " 'content to play the one part' " that he was born for, he finds that " 'quite another play is running now' " and implies that it is time for him to leave the stage. Since the stage is both his life and his poetry, there is an element of the farewell here that counterbalances the notes of affirmation and acceptance.

Characteristically, however, Lowell tips the balance in the epilogue, "Pigeons," which is dedicated to Hannah Arendt, both by means of his overt thematic statement and by incorporation of a symbolic gesture. As in the preceding poem, the thinly veiled subject in "Pigeons" is the character of the poet; but the emphasis shifts here from the composition of this volume and the persona's considered view of life to the creative urge involved in the writing of any poem and the irrational need to live in a certain manner. This irrationality is implicit not only in the "mania to return" to writing, but also in the description of inspiration:

> What is home, but a feeling of homesickness
> for the flight's lost moment of fluttering terror?

The "homesickness" here is a weariness of the quotidian and

a longing for the giddy flights of the imagination; while "The same old flights, the same old homecomings" are the poetic insights and the labor to which they invariably lead, which may or may not give rise to a poem, a clearing of "the pigeon-house." The unreasonable need to persist in one's calling despite the knowledge that one must fail, which is the need that defeats the temptations of ennui and the wish for death, is the focal point of the second stanza. The last two lines of this stanza—"Still, only by suffering the rat-race in the arena / can the heart learn to beat"—constitute this poem's equivalent of the autobiography that "can only survive in ashes." The bird "Back in the dovecote," on the other hand, is comparable to the flame of inspiration that never burns itself out and therefore never has any effect or to the perfect poem that can exist as the object of desire only and never as fait accompli. Nevertheless, it is the inability ever to write this work, or the failure to escape from "non-existence" into "the all-being" for more than a "lost moment," that accounts for the "mania to return" and for the miraculous multiplication of the poems.

As was pointed out above, the mania to return, the ceaseless rededication and effort, is Lowell's means of negating the pessimism which would seduce him. The negation informs the relationship between the epilogue to *Imitations* and the body of the book, for "Pigeons" cancels out, or rather sublates, one theme of "Hamlet in Russia, A Soliloquy," by ignoring, by virtue of its very existence, the conclusion and conclusiveness that the preceding poem implies. In other words, as the fifth section of "The Seasons" is to the other four, so the last poem of *Imitations* is to its predecessors: both embody not only the theme, but also the impulse, of perseverance. Although the last line of the volume returns us to the first line, Lowell's notion of returning—as these "partly self-sufficient and separate" poems themselves indicate— entails reconstructing and therefore denies the inevitability of *mere* cycles of rot and renewal.

Its third stanza, which stands in the same relationship to this poem as the poem itself does to *Imitations*, emphasizes the renewal rather than the cycle. This stanza, the burden of which is that death is liberation and liberation is life, is not in the Rilke poem at all. As a stanza original with Lowell, it too suggests the negation of a cyclical determinism or "cosmic pessimism"; it points away from the system established in this volume toward another. The interpolation of an original stanza into this last imitation signifies the imperfection of the method and thereby assures a return to composition in the future. That it reappears as a poem complete in itself under the title "Epigram" in *For the Union Dead* is evidence of the centrality of the themes of persistence and returning in Lowell's work; and it is also an indication of the fact that Lowell's books, like his personae, his poems, and his metaphors, are continually turning into one another.

Before any great task that begins a new life and calls upon untried resources of character, the need seems to arise for some introversion of the mind upon itself and upon its past—a plunging into the depths, to gain knowledge and power over self and destiny.
—MAUDE BODKIN, *Archetypal Patterns in Poetry*

The things of the eye are done.
On the illuminated black dial,
green ciphers of a new moon. . . .
—"Myopia: a Night"

6

PARABOLIC STRUCTURES:

For The Union Dead (1964)

On *For the Union Dead,* Lowell continues to work the personal vein that he first struck in *Lord Weary's Castle* and returned to with new equipment in *Life Studies;* but just as it led him away from the world at large and to the family in his fourth volume, so now it leads him away from the family and even deeper into the individual psyche, or deeper into "the dark / unconscious bowels of the nerves," to borrow a phrase from this book. In fact, his pursuit of this narrowing and deepening lode defines not only the course of this part of his career but also the structure of the first half of this collection of poems. To recognize the second of these movements is to begin to respond to the questions that a consideration of the results of the first must provoke in the mind of any reader of Lowell's work.

Through many of these poems, the speakers are alienated, neurasthenic, and ineffectual, and as a result Lowell has been charged with apotheosizing the hypersensitive intellectual instead of formulating "any clear view of modern literature or politics."[1] Even when this aspect of his sensibility is admired, the praise is liable to seem an approval of masochism, as in

200

William Stafford's comment that "Lowell is like a magnet for pain; he is the artist as victim. . . . He can sweep his programmed attention through the air and pick up signals that will elegantly terrorize the reader."[2] Because a number of the poems here are indisputably among the most excruciatingly introspective that Lowell has yet produced, the view that this volume is so confessional as to be egocentric and self-indulgent is not without foundation. At the same time, poems like "July in Washington," "Buenos Aires," the expanded version of "Beyond the Alps," and the title poem itself are clearly written in a "public" mode.[3] Consequently, Lowell has also been taken to task less for egocentric confession than for inconsistency, on the grounds that he "runs the . . . risk of . . . vacillating between a private and public voice."[4] This objection—like that noted first, of which it is really an augmented version—would surely be more telling if this volume were unified only at the level of style.

The recognition that Lowell has organized *For the Union Dead* just as carefully as he had *Life Studies* and *Imitations* is important for at least two closely related reasons. First of all, to turn briefly to the other criticism most frequently made of this volume, such a recognition might forestall the risky accusation that Lowell has relinquished, along with his religious framework, the "shaping spirit" that is the poet's sine qua non.[5] Although the charge of formal laxness might still be brought against individual poems, the realization that Lowell has taken pains to arrange his poems in meaningful sequences might serve as a worthwhile caveat. In the second place, the structure of this volume is such as to modify the subjective orientation of some of the poems and to account for the relationship between these poems and the more objective ones. In short, the point to be made is virtually the opposite of that argued by Jerome Mazzaro, who maintains that in this volume the poet "permits the isolated and fragmented experiences described to become even more isolated and fragmented in an onslaught of disparate, chaotic reactions."[6]

Although Herbert Leibowitz has categorized the poems in *For the Union Dead* according to subject matter and Mazzaro himself has pointed out a general difference between the first and second halves of the book, its basic means of structure and the details of that structure have yet to be investigated.[7] In spite of their apparently casual arrangement, these poems fall into groups that in turn constitute a larger structure. Curiously enough, Robert Bly, one of Lowell's most intransigent critics, has unintentionally characterized the organization of *For the Union Dead*. In an essay on the possibility of a meaningful political poetry in America, Bly has written:

> The truth is that most American poets do not bother to penetrate the husk around their own personalities, and therefore cannot penetrate the husk that has grown around the psyche of the country either. When a poet succeeds in driving inward, he develops new energy that carries him through the polished outside husk that deflects most meditation. Once inside the psyche, he can speak of inward and political things with the same assurance. . . . Paradoxically, what is needed to write true poems about the outward world is inwardness.[8]

The problem of the general validity of Bly's theory apart, it is remarkable how applicable this statement of it seems to the form of *For the Union Dead*.

The poems in *For the Union Dead* are organized on the basis of the persona's various degrees of awareness of, and ability to cope with, the world outside himself. In the first few poems in the book, he reviews some past relationships with other people in an attempt to define his present predicament, and in doing so he becomes a natural successor to the retrospective figure of *Life Studies*. As the poems unfold, however, he begins to lose contact with other people and with his surroundings until, almost imperceptibly, toward the middle of the book, subject displaces object as the focal point of the poetry. As the persona's psychological reactions become the main consideration, two other related changes occur. In philosophical terms, this part of the volume presents a view of the world that is almost solipsistic; in terms of technique, the imagery here tends toward the impressionistic and sometimes verges upon the oneiric. In either set of terms, in the middle of the book the objective world either seems illusory or is disregarded entirely. After passing through a "dark night of the soul" that is nonetheless terrifying for being secular, the persona manages to extricate himself at least partly from the inner world that threatened to engulf him. The emphasis in the volume then shifts from the irrevocable enmity between the world's condition and man's sensibility to the need for man to endure vicissitude and anguish; other people—especially artists—again figure in the poems; and Lowell begins to reassert his concern with traditional social values.

In Bly's terms, the movement is from outwardness to inwardness and back to outwardness. From one point of view the exchange of the "public" for the "personal" voice might be seen as vacillation, but from another it can be viewed as calculated to produce the effect of a personal development or of an experience that bears a resemblance to the archetypal withdrawal described by Maude Bodkin in the passage quoted as an epigraph at the beginning of this chapter, as well as to Bergson's "intuitive" experience as it is described by Wylie Sypher:

In his effort to "touch bottom," Bergson turns inward to contemplate how the self exists within the flow of time, how it endures behind or within change. . . . If the self is to be known, it must be intuited in the dim and quiet eddies streaming like quicksands far below the mechanism of the rational mind.[9]

If this second point of view is adopted, then Lowell's sequence of speakers, as in *Imitations*, can be regarded somewhat as one would regard a single autobiographical persona. Such a view facilitates an understanding of the relationship between poet and poet-speakers in this volume, for in a number of poems, as in *Lord Weary's Castle* and *Imitations*, the latter are only disguised versions of the former. In other words, the persona is a combination of the personality created in the course of this book and the poet as we know him from his other works. This is the case not only in such obvious instances as "The Old Flame" and "Caligula," but also in such enigmatic poems as "The Scream" and "Myopia: a Night."

Evidence of this kind of structure in *For the Union Dead* should also make Lowell less vulnerable to the charge of representing a chaotic world by reproducing it, for even if the poems represented "fragmented experiences," these would be significant parts of the form of the whole. At the same time, there is reason not to accede readily to the idea that the individual poems in *For the Union Dead* do represent "fragmented experiences" or an abandonment of the "shaping spirit." These judgments might derive in part from misapprehensions of certain aspects of the technique in this book; or at least the critics who have made them have not paid sufficient attention to two important features of several of the more difficult poems here.

The first of these features involves the relationship between poet and poet-speaker that has been touched upon above; several of these poems may seem more complete when it is realized that some of the apparently obscure imagery refers to Lowell's own past. The second feature of some of these poems has to do directly with the manipulation of symbols, for in this volume Lowell develops a mode that is even more subtle than that in *Life Studies*. In *For the Union Dead*, ambivalence almost always wins out over equivalence; symbols continually shift their meanings, even in the course of a single short poem, and occasionally they imply contradictory meanings. Once this tendency is recognized, the form of poems like "Water" and "The Neo-Classical Urn" is more evident. Like the hypothesis of the structure of this volume, however, these are claims that cannot be substantiated apart from an examination of specific poems.

The first poems in *For the Union Dead* look back in two respects: they reflect upon the persona's past relationships, and they recall the retrospective and understated, conversational mode of the fourth part of *Life Studies*, especially as it appears in "Skunk Hour." "Water" and "The Old Flame," the first two of these poems, almost constitute a subgroup of their own, for they are linked both by the symbols of purgation and rebirth in their titles, which are partly ironic, and by the attitudes that they take toward the past. Moreover, at first glance, both appear to be based upon Lowell's first marriage. That "Water" has a different origin than has been supposed is an arresting fact, for it helps us to realize the extent to which Lowell is willing to "plot" his life in retrospect—or to allow context to be a maieutic factor—and to begin to understand the relationship between sequence and narrative in this volume.

Because revised versions of "Water" have appeared in *Notebook* and *History* in groups of poems dedicated to Elizabeth Bishop, it now seems that Lowell's old friend, rather than his first wife, the writer Jean Stafford, is the other figure in the poem and that the relationship between the woman in the first poem and the old flame of the second was obscure in the first place simply because they were different people. As soon as one has so conjectured, however, he begins to wonder why Lowell did not attempt to forestall a possible confusion—by dedicating the poem in *For the Union Dead* to Bishop, for example, or by removing it to another part of the book. The possible confusion must have been obvious to Lowell, who has always been very sensitive to the potential of juxtaposition, for at least two of his most perceptive readers have taken it for granted that these first two poems deal with the same relationship.[10] When the problem is put in this way, of course, a likely solution immediately presents itself; Lowell sought the confusion precisely because he wanted to establish a narrative at the outset. Years later, in the last poem in *The Dolphin*, a sequence so personal that he even quotes extensively from private correspondence, Lowell confesses that he has "plotted perhaps too freely with [his] life." Whether he has been too libertarian or not is of no moment here, but it is essential to see that Lowell must have been similarly fictionalizing for the sake of form in the first version of "Water."

"Water" is fraught with other ambiguities and equivocations, although its main theme is set out clearly in the speaker's companion's dream, in which she saw herself as "a mermaid clinging to a wharf-pile / and trying to pull / off the barnacles with [her] hands." Since barnacles are motile only when young, attaching themselves to rocks or logs when mature, and since they develop sharp shells that can lacerate those who would detach them, it seems that Lowell is suggesting the impossibility of, and the pain contingent upon, any attempt to oppose the natural course of events by refusing to accept the changes wrought by time. Not all of this poem is so easily paraphrased, however, for it is a work in the vein of "Skunk Hour," a sort of parable, in which, instead of a reliable point for point correspondence between symbolic detail and meaning, there is a general correspondence of situations and forces. Interpretation is further complicated because this poem is virtually a chain of parables, with almost every stanza presenting a self-contained symbolic situation, and because an element that is used in one way in one stanza might be turned to another account in a following one.

The first stanza presents an image of departure, the ominous tone of which derives from the combination of several factors. In the first place, if the setting is "a Maine lobster town," there is no apparent reason for the journeys to the "granite / quarries on the islands"; precisely because these journeys do not fit the description of the town, there is something odd about them, particularly since there is no mention made of return trips. Moreover, the commonplace synecdoche for workers, "hands," acquires a macabre quality in the phrase "boatloads of hands," especially since this phrase follows the reference to the lobster fishing. Given the tone of these images, it is natural to recall that "quarries" are excavations and that "granite" is frequently used in headstones; and these recollections are relevant to the next stanza, with its description of the apparently empty "houses" that the "hands" have left behind them. These skeletal structures, which are comparable to the barnacles in that they are "stuck / like oyster shells / on a hill of rock," suggest positions that have been occupied and are now vacated—a ghost town, perhaps, or that string of dwellings that any restless person leaves behind him. But they need not be taken so literally; it is enough to realize that they represent what is left behind when people have "pushed off" for those ambiguous islands.

The following stanzas focus on the specific situation that was the present when the poet-speaker was involved in the relationship that he is remembering, when the fish "trapped" in the "mazes of a weir" reflected the two people. Had they been more sagacious they might have seen that the "slab of rock" on which they sat would one day serve as the cenotaph commemorating their relationship; but it is only in retrospect that the poet-speaker sees the gradual decay. Then the situation seemed ordinary enough, "the usual gray" of the quotidian with "the usual green" of enthusiasm or rededication; but if the inevitable effect of the waves is the wearing away of the rocks they wash, the unavoidable result of the monotony was the erosion of the relationship. Eventually, the rock, the relationship, or that phase of it, had to be abandoned, as the "white frame houses" had to be abandoned; and the only "return" conceivable is in some other life.

"The Old Flame" also focuses on the dissolution of a relationship—this one explicitly that of Lowell and his first wife and it extends the theme of the difficulty and necessity of relinquishing the past and accepting the natural course of events. The house symbol, established in the first poem, becomes the center of this one, the point at which three phases of the marriage intersect. The "new people" who are now living in the poet-speaker's former home, "the old / restored house on the hill," repeat the actions of the couple who preceded them, the poet-speaker and his "old wife," who presumably moved in with the same enthusiasm. Like the rock of the earlier poem, however, that period of initial exuberance takes on a different appearance in retrospect, and the very neo-Colonial style in which the house has been refurbished foretells the course of the relationship between the "new landlord" and his "new wife" at the same time that it symbolizes for the poet-speaker the fate that was built into the beginning of his own marriage. The new flag is already, as it were, an "Old Glory," and the new paint is "old-red." The second phase of the marriage as it is presented here also recalls a symbol from "Water": the trapped fish in that poem become in this one the "snowbound" couple who were "simmering like wasps" in a "tent of books." By tossing the snow from the road, the plow presumably freed the "snowbound" couple, but in this case freedom entailed separation, the last phase of the relationship.

It is the last phase, that is, unless one considers the "return" of these "two souls" to the house; for the poet-speaker and his wife do return in a sense, although as houseghosts rather than as "gulls." The poet-speaker describes himself as a "ghostly / imaginary lover" with suicidal tendencies and invokes his former wife as "Poor ghost, old love" and Lowell thus suggests again the difficulty of accepting the necessary transitoriness of the relationship.[11]

That a new beginning is not so easily made is also implied by the line "Everything's changed for the best," which is perhaps too trite and too flippant to be taken at face value. The uncertainty that naturally accompanies a decision to begin again is the subject of the following poem, "Middle Age," in which the poet-speaker reassesses his relationship with his dead father in much the same way that he has reviewed that with his divorced wife.[12] "Middle Age" is linked to the preceding poem by the season, the symbol of the road, and the appearance of another ghostly figure. Although the streets in this poem are not blocked, they are "chewed up" and difficult to negotiate, and what the trip itself might entail remains a mystery. The only prospect that is certain is his own death, as he finds that his father

> never climbed
> Mount Sion, yet left
> dinosaur
> death-steps on the crust,
> where I must walk.

The first lines here, which recall the "altitude" symbol of *Life Studies*, imply that his father never achieved very much, while the last suggest that a standard of achievement is less important than the common denominator of death.

Like the "new landlord" of "The Old Flame," the figure of the poet-speaker's father, whom he encounters at every turn in his life, is a sort of doppelgänger; but he is also, like the "Poor ghost" of the other poem, evidence of the tenacity of the past. For the speaker this tenacity takes the form of memories of those to whom he was close. As indicated above, however, these poems reflect a double image, like a windowpane backed by a storm window: there is the personality of the speaker in the foreground, and behind him there is the fainter figure of the poet. For the poet, the tenacity of the past takes the form of the framework of his earlier "Life Studies." As the speaker admits the difficult necessity of turning from his past to an uncreated future, Lowell acknowledges the necessity of discarding a former subject matter and discovering a new one: "At forty-five, / what next, what next?"

At the very least, this interpretation helps to explain the motivation for and the position of "The Scream," the fourth and last poem in what might be designated the first sequence in this volume. As Lowell indicates in the note that prefaces *For the Union Dead,* this poem "owes everything to Elizabeth Bishop's beautiful, calm story, *In the Village.*"[13] With the exception of the two lines that, perhaps partly out of a sense of irony, he places in quotation marks, Lowell has taken the poem almost verbatim from the short story. Even for a poet so given to borrowing phrases and situations, this versifying of Bishop's unimprovable prose comes as a surprise, especially if the poem is taken only on its own terms. Within the context of the book and this first sequence, however, "The Scream" is explicable, for both the poem and the short story treat family relationships in the light of the theme of transience. Because of these considerations, "The Scream" constitutes an apt farewell to the past and to the world that Lowell had created in the "Life Studies" and thus provides a doubly fitting conclusion to the opening set of poems. If the figures of his former wife and his father attenuated to shades of themselves in the earlier poems, the "Scream" that is the anguish of a whole family is but "a thinning echo" in the first stanza of this poem. And here is the last stanza:

> A scream! But they are all gone,
> those aunts and aunts, a grandfather,
> a grandmother, my mother—
> even her scream—too frail
> for us to hear their voices long.

The first line of this last stanza seems itself a "thinning echo" of the line in "Grandparents" which itself echoed one of Vaughan's elegies: "They're all gone into a world of light; the farm's my own." In effect, the rest of the stanza calls up and abruptly dismisses the figures of Aunt Sarah and Uncle Devereux's wife, Grandfather and Grandmother Winslow, and Charlotte Lowell. To a greater extent than any poem discussed thus far, "The Scream" connects the speaker with the poet; in other words, this poem makes of the combination of Robert Lowell and the speaker a figure who is neither wholly fictional nor wholly autobiographical.

Besides establishing a motivation for "The Scream" and providing an explanation of its position in this volume, the proposed relationship between poet and persona affords a stronger rationale for the subsequent emphasis upon the theme of alienation. If these first poems represent a covert severing of the connection with the stable "world" that the "Life Studies" constructed, then the reason for the isolation of the persona is clearer; for if the persona is cut off from other people, the poet has forsaken the setting and situations that gave him the subject matter of his earlier work. Almost paradoxically, the poet's biography helps to create this projection of himself as a dramatic figure.

In the series of poems following this introductory sequence, those from "The Mouth of the Hudson" through "Florence," Lowell's poet-speaker is detached from his family and alienated from his social and physical environment, with the result that he begins to regard himself as something of a shuttlecock, buffeted about by forces which are themselves uncontrolled. As a combination of solipsism and anomie invades the poetry, the imagery alters accordingly. In addition to an increasing amount of visual imagery, which perhaps suggests a passive, observing nature as opposed to one capable of effective action, there are images of unbalanced states of one kind or another, of enclosures of various sorts, and of desultory movement. These images connote, respectively, a mental instability, an irrevocable isolation, and a purposelessness that is applicable to both the persona and his universe.

"The Mouth of the Hudson" is virtually an emblem of the precarious position of man as the persona has come to see him. The poem opens with "A single man," who stands on an outcrop above a railroad siding and watches the trains switching beneath him:

                         They jolt and jar
and junk in the siding below him.
He has trouble with his balance.
His eyes drop,
and he drifts with the wild ice
ticking seaward down the Hudson
like the blank sides of a jig-saw puzzle.

These lines sum up the random violence of the poet-speaker's world, his lack of control over that world, and the scrambled puzzle that it seems to him. The fact that the train is a mechanical, and the ice floe a natural, phenomenon suggests the ubiquity of anomie and implies the impossibility of self-determination; in a world in which neither nature nor civilization is ordered, the individual has no choice but to drift. This theme is all the more remarkable in "The Mouth of the Hudson" because several of its details recall, ironically, "The River" section of *The Bridge*. Lowell seems to repudiate implicitly the optimistic vision of Crane; and the poem ends, not with Crane's "Passion" and promise of deliverance, but with "the unforgivable landscape."

The man who has difficulty keeping his "balance" in this poem shades off into the speaker in "Fall 1961." The worlds of the two poems are identical, although the jolting and jarring is more specific here, as the poet-speaker suffers "the chafe and jar / of nuclear war." If the ice "drifts" and "ticks seaward like a clock" or a time bomb in the one poem, "Our end drifts nearer" to the accompaniment of the "tock, tock, tock" of the grandfather clock in the other. Like the pendulum of this clock, the restive speaker of "Fall 1961" moves "Back and forth, back and forth" and finds that even his "one point of rest / is the orange and black / oriole's swinging nest." This detail suggests the coming of a spring that would relieve the "Fall" of nuclear war, and it also connotes an extreme form of the insecurity that has been a condition of Lowell's protagonists since "Where the Rainbow Ends"; but it is probably primarily a symbol of either poetry (the rhythmic swinging of the nest and the song of the oriole intimate this) or life itself (in which case the "one point of rest" is ironic). The last meaning is more important, partly because the movement of the "nest" mirrors that of the grandfather clock and therefore asks to be thematically related to it.

The pendulum symbol may well derive from a source that Lowell quoted in *Life Studies*, for Schopenhauer says of life that it "swings like a pendulum backwards and forwards between pain and ennui."[14] Ennui, as it is for Schopenhauer and Baudelaire, is one of Lowell's bêtes noires; and it, along with pain, is a motivating force in this poem. The ennui is behind lines like "We have talked our extinction to death," while the pain prompts such images as this one, which is reminiscent of "The Death of the Sheriff":

> We are like a lot of wild
> spiders crying together,
> but without tears.

A strange mixture of these seemingly mutually exclusive states inspires the images at the beginning of the third stanza:

> Our end drifts nearer,
> the moon lifts,
> radiant with terror.

Here, the terror is more applicable to the poet-speaker and his society than the grammar indicates; as a line in a later stanza has it, in these poems Shakespeare's art is reversed and "Nature holds up a mirror."

In the preceding poem, the knocking of the ice was compared to the ticking of a clock in order to suggest that final ruin was only a matter of the passing of a little time; similarly, in this poem, the moon is associated with the passage of time, as the face of the clock turns into the "orange, bland, ambassadorial / face of the moon," and the adjective "ambassadorial" points to the chief agent of devastation, named explicitly in another image: "The state / is a diver under a glass bell." The "state" is this poem's equivalent of the "Whore and Beast and Dragon" that "rise for air / from allegoric waters" in a much earlier work;[15] a frightening shape, it "lifts" a moonlike but unnatural face from the allegoric waters of this poem to threaten the world with nuclear war. In comparison to this sea monster, the poet-speaker feels "like a minnow" who swims, presumably "Back and forth," behind his "studio window," as if behind the plate glass of an aquarium.

The forboding movement recurs in the last lines of "Florence," in which the decapitated head of the Gorgon swings "like a lantern" in the hand of Cellini's Perseus. As other critics have pointed out, the Gorgon is one of the adverse forces necessary to the forging of heroes, and her death is thus indicative of the destruction of a mythological system that assumed and nourished the concept of heroism.[16] The extinction of such monsters is a tragedy for both the imagination and the will, for what has been substituted is both inaccessible to description and incapable of defeat. On one level, the new enemy is the state with its unpredictable and invincible powers. The Gorgon was at least an "erotic terror," a concrete and fascinating embodiment of the opposition, whereas the modern state is coldly and abstractly "radiant with terror"; and moreover, she was capable of "staring the despot to stone." There are no more "lovely tyranicides" because there are no more tyrants, and there are no more "lords and ladies of the Blood" because there are no more monsters. On a higher level, the new enemy is the demythologized universe, whose forces are equally capricious and indomitable. The persona, then, is cut off not only from his family and his immediate past, but also from his traditional heritage. Just where the destruction of all mythological systems leaves us, in Lowell's eyes, the passive, nostalgic speaker of this and the following nine poems suggests.

If these nine poems, from "The Lesson" through "The Public Garden," seem at first less closely related to one another than those in the preceding two groups are, there is no doubt about the general direction that they are taking. That direction is downward, in terms of the persona's morale and emotional stamina, and inward, in terms of his relationship to the world about him. This direction is only the more apparent after one has reached the middle of the volume, for the poems that stand in the center are also at the midpoint of the speaker's journey into and out of himself.

Like "Florence," the following poems view the past in the context of the present; but in these poems the absence of a meaningful mythological framework is taken for granted, and the poet-speaker attempts to relate himself to the world without the benefit of any transcendental schema. The first three of the poems following "Florence" are meditations on transience and immutability. As in "My Last Afternoon with Uncle Devereux Winslow" and "91 Revere Street," permanence and perfection are perquisites of death, while transience and mutability are attributes of life. This dichotomy is blurred, however, by further considerations: that what is in one's personal past is in effect dead and therefore durable and perfect; that transience itself is manifest in an eternally enduring cycle of life and death; and that the nature of man does not change.

These considerations lend "The Lesson" an almost impenetrable ambiguity in places, as in the third stanza:

> The green leaf cushions the same dry footprint,
> or the child's boat luffs in the same dry chop,
> and we are where we were.

Each of the three lines here says two things: that everything is the same now as in the past because death and renewal are continually revolving; and that one's past is unalterable in the memory. "We are where we were" both in the sense that our lives show no cumulative meaning but only cyclical repetition and in the sense that our past actions are frozen and no longer parts of time. This last sense is the one that is emphasized in the fifth stanza:

> Ah the light lights the window of my young night,
> and you never turn off the light,
> while books lie in the library, and go on reading.

The "you" here is himself as a boy, and he can literally "never turn off the light" since this scene, being past, is immutable. The first sense, on the other hand, is the one stressed in the last stanza:

> The barberry berry sticks on the small hedge,
> cold slits the same crease in the finger,
> the same thorn hurts. The leaf repeats the lesson.

As in the preceding stanza, and as in "New Year's Day" in *Lord Weary's Castle*, Lowell "repeats" words and phrases to

underscore the unchanging nature of life, but in this concluding stanza what does not change is change itself. The bar-
berry berry and the thorn and the leaf appear each summer in
just the form that they took in the previous summer. If nature
herself does not alter, neither does the nature of man; he is
always imperfect and vulnerable, subject to the cycle of life
and death, and his imperfection is always a source of pain, a
thorn in his side.

"The Lesson" adumbrates "Those Before Us" in both
theme and phrase. The thought that "we are where we were.
We were!" is counterpointed in the next poem by the phrase
"They never were." This phrase, which may refer to our past
selves as well as to our ancestors, seems not to mean that
"they" never existed, but rather that "they" never existed in
the past tense. In other words, the main point of "Those
Before Us" is one part of "The Lesson": the paradox that the
past, because finished, is durable and perfect. Incidents and
figures from that past work their ways to the surface of the
mind as arrowheads eventually work their way to the surface
of the ground; and they are "unregenerate" both because
they are not capable of being reconstructed or reformed in
any manner and because they are no longer parts of the process of degeneration and regeneration. The word "still"
fulfills much the same function in this poem that "same" did
in the preceding one, as in the second stanza:

Wormwood on the veranda! Plodding needles
still prod the coarse pink yarn into a dress.
The muskrat that took a slice of your thumb still huddles,
a mop of hair and a heart beat on the porch. . . .

The muskrat is "still" there and very much alive in the poet-
speaker's memory in spite of the fact that he remembers also
that it "furiously slashed" the packing crate in which it was
kept and eventually escaped. The same is true of those other
"all outline, uniformly gray," and mysteriously unnamed
figures who played cards in a room of the house that the
poet-speaker recalls: the "blinds" that we can "draw back"
are those that ordinarily close out the scenes in our
memories, and their card table is "still leaf-green" because it
is now imperishable.

This very imperishability, ironically enough, separates the poet-speaker from his past, for his life is still one of "stagnant growth"; he must still follow "the path" or "the trail" down which they have already gone, just as in "Middle Age" he had to follow in his father's "dinosaur / death-steps on the crust." His part in the "simmer of rot and renewal" is central to "Eye and Tooth," the next of these three tightly interwoven poems. As its title, with its reference to the Old Testament law, perhaps indicates, "Eye and Tooth" couples the themes of cyclical existence and man's unchangeable nature.[17] The flaw in man's nature appears here as "the old cut cornea," just as it did in "Those Before Us" as the sliced thumb and just as it did in "The Lesson" as the slit finger. If in the preceding poems he could see himself reading in his room and see his relatives playing cards in the house, in this poem he sees himself lying on his bed, chain-smoking through the night, and spying through a keyhole:

> No ease for the boy at the keyhole,
> his telescope,
> when the women's white bodies flashed
> in the bathroom. Young, my eyes began to fail.

This image makes this the most complex of these three poems in one respect, for the poet-speaker is peeping at himself peeping at the women. The implication is that even when he was a boy he was solitary, an implication that is even stronger when he says "I saw things darkly, / as through an unwashed goldfish globe." The parody of I Corinthians 13:12—which is particularly ironic in view of the eleventh verse, where Paul states that "when I became a man, I put away childish things"—suggests the poet-speaker's early inability to understand the world about him; and the image of the goldfish bowl, like that of the aquarium in "Fall 1961" and the title poem at the end of the volume, emphasizes his early isolation from that world. The difficulty in "seeing" the world clearly, and the alienation from it, along with the necessary participation in the cycle where "Even new life is fuel," result from the flaw in man's nature, original sin, which "Nothing can dislodge."

Lowell employs this last phrase twice; and along with the

other recurrent negative, "No ease," it is this poem's counterpart of "still" and "the same" in that it signifies the lack of change in the conditions of life. An abbreviated form of this refrain introduces the last stanza:

> Nothing! No oil
> for the eye, nothing to pour
> on those waters or flames.
> I am tired. Everyone's tired of my turmoil.

Like "the summer rain, / a simmer of rot and renewal," the "waters or flames," which look back to the opening poems, embody the ceaseless cycle of life and death that consumes the poet-speaker's energy. At this point in the volume, he would either pour oil on the waters of life and therefore still them or feed its flames and consequently have done with them.

The next five poems in this third group elaborate the themes set forth in these three and concentrate on the contrast between the turmoil of life and the peaceful perfection of death. "Alfred Corning Clark," a school friend of Lowell's who died at forty-five, represents the latter state. Since the poet, according to "Middle Age," is forty-five himself, Clark provides a foil for the persona of the volume. In describing Clark as he was some thirty years before, Lowell also depicts that timeless condition that he associates with death. The catalog of Clark's youthful qualities—

> your triumphant diffidence,
> your refusal of exertion,
> the intelligence
> that pulsed in the sensitive,
> pale concavities of your forehead

—anticipates in its praise of simultaneous peacefulness and intensity the concluding image:

> You usually won—
> motionless
> as a lizard in the sun.

The implication is that Clark, triumphant in his personal virtues and victorious at chess, has won again. The paradox of transience in life and permanence in death is succinctly summarized in the line "You were alive. You are dead." Given Lowell's previous uses of the copulative verb, the line might be read: "Alive, you were. Dead, you are."

The "Child's Song," a rather ugly poem whose form recalls Blake but whose tone almost parodies him, is a plea for freedom from the vicissitudes of life, for an escape to an "island" where "the white sand shines." Brightness is again associated with "liberation" and death in "Epigram," the six-line poem which Lowell incorporated in his imitation of Rilke's "Die Tauben," and in "Law." Mazzaro sees this last poem as one in which man is equated with animals by means of a "parallel of lawlessness," for "the natural inclinations of the narrator violate the laws of man," while "a man-made Norman canal violates the natural green lawn."[18] The crux of this poem, however, is not the similarity between man and animals but the conflict between the poet-speaker's apprehension of the natural cycle and his vision of something beyond that cycle or "outside the law" of nature; that is, the thematic opposition in "Law" is again that between "the simmer of rot and renewal" and whatever is finished and therefore perfect. On the one hand, the poet-speaker remembers seeing "only the looping shore" of the river and "nature's monotonous backlash," which he describes in now familiar terms: "The same. The same." On the other hand, he recalls seeing "once, in a flash" an artificial landscape (rather like Marie Antoinette's hamlet at Versailles) which has managed to remain outside the cycle. The "Norman canal" and environs are thus comparable to the "island" of the "Child's Song," the card room of "Those Before Us," the reading room of "The Lesson," and so on. "The Public Garden" emphasizes the same opposition. In the last section of this poem, a former "summer" in "Eden" with "Jehovah's grass-green lyre" is contrasted with the present, which is described in terms reminiscent of "Eye and Tooth": "The fountain's failing waters flash around / the garden. Nothing catches fire."

The imagery in the concluding lines again summons up the first two poems in For the Union Dead; and so does the question "Remember summer?" (In "Water" the poet-speaker asked, "Remember?" and in "The Old Flame," "Remember our lists of birds?") These echoes are appropriate, for "The Public Garden" concludes the first of the three major sections of this volume. In fact, this poem's structure conveniently, if accidentally, recapitulates the structure of the volume to this point: it moves from the time of day when "All's alive" in "The Public Garden" to the time of night when "Everything's aground" and "Nothing catches fire." These last images summarize the plight of the persona, who has been unable to establish a significant relationship between the self and "nature's monotonous backlash" and has become increasingly alienated as a result.

"Lady Ralegh's Lament," a brief poem on the theme of *sic transit gloria mundi*, can be viewed as the prologue to the poems that are at the core of this volume and that represent the lowest points in the volume's (doubly) parabolic structure. Although the last lines of "Lady Ralegh's Lament" do not seem closely related to the rest of the poem, they do indicate precisely the direction of the following poems. The last line is "Down and down; the compass needle dead on terror," and the image points inexorably forward to "Myopia: a Night."

The way to "Myopia: a Night" is through "Going to and fro," the title of which recalls the caged pacing of the poet-speaker in "Fall 1961" and the search that has been going on throughout the volume for a view of the universe as an intelligible creation. The title might also be a quotation from Arnold's "Summer Night" or from Job 1:7, where it is spoken by Satan in response to God's query about his recent whereabouts, and it suggests the damnation that is the fate of the speaker, the "pain, / suffering without purgation, / the backtrack of the screw," and the imprisonment that gives rise to suicidal impulses.[19] Even more than with Satan, however, he identifies himself with a Faustian figure. By playing on an everyday phrase, Lowell splits the speaker's personality and makes him talk to himself as though he were both Faust and his tempter:

> But you had instants,
> to give the devil his due—

he and you
once dug it all out of the dark
unconscious bowels of the nerves;
pure gold, the root of evil,
sunshine that gave the day a scheme.

The "evil" and "sunshine" in this passage are perhaps allusions to the axes of Lowell's religious framework, which "gave the day a scheme" for him at the time of *Land of Unlikeness* and *Lord Weary's Castle*. Or perhaps the reference to "the dark / unconscious bowels of the nerves" is intended to recall the confessional poetry of *Life Studies*. In either case, as we have seen, that such frameworks are no longer available is one reason for his pain and confusion; and it is also the motivation for the following poem, in which the day has become a night.

The feeling of futility and aimlessness sketched dramatically and ironically in "Going to and fro" finds a subjective presentation in "Myopia: a Night." Again the title is of special significance, for both of its elements stress the poet-speaker's inability to see clearly, and the vision that is obstructed is more metaphysical than physical. Moreover, the title calls to mind the metaphor that Lowell had employed to great advantage in "Skunk Hour." The experience of this poem is the solipsistic night into which the persona has been gradually descending since the beginning of the volume, when he let go his last hold on the objective world, in the form of the people who had been close to him, and began to consider his personal relationship to the "simmer of rot and renewal" in the world.

As in many of Lowell's poems, the setting of "Myopia: a Night" incorporates the theme; but what is notable about this poem is that instead of projecting concepts onto the objective world, it internalizes and subjectifies that world. Something of this sort has been going on ever since the statement in "Fall 1961" that "Nature holds up a mirror." From the premise that nature mirrors the self nothing can follow but the conclusion that only knowledge of the self is possible. The "landscape" in "The Mouth of the Hudson" is "unforgivable" precisely because it reflects the speaker, and "Nothing catches fire" in "The Public Garden" for a comparable reason. The rooms into which the poet-speaker keeps looking are not actual rooms but compartments of the mind. Because whatever the poet-speaker sees is interpreted in personal terms, the "eye" and the "I" become synonymous. In "Those Before Us" the figures and incidents from the past are "in the corners of the eye"; and in "Eye and Tooth" there are several puns that make this identification. In "Myopia: a Night" the scene is "ramshackle, streaky, weird" only nominally because the nearsighted poet-speaker has removed his glasses, turned off the light, and gone to bed. The essential reason for the phantasmagoria is his estrangement from the world. Although the pun is less insistent here than in "Eye and Tooth," the "I" and the "eye" merge, and the myopia of the latter signifies the solipsism of the former.

In this condition, which is itself a continuation of that in "Going to and fro," the poet carries the themes of the preceding poem through to a hard-won and barely retained resolution. Again he revisits his past in metaphoric terms: the "light" of his study in his youth, which he remembered in "The Lesson"; the "books" with their "blurred titles," among which might be the Bible and *Land of Unlikeness*; the "dull and alien room" which was his "cell of learning" when he was the "consciously Catholic poet" whom Allen Tate introduced with no little excitement; and the "white pipes" with their "ramrods of steam," an apt description of Lowell's earlier, visionary verse. His youth was "the departure strip" he imagines now as having led to "the dream-road" down which he has traveled only to find that it is almost literally a blind alley. This reverie ends with a reference to "lonely metal" pipes which "gurgle like the sick" and could be in either room, that of the past or that of the present. Perhaps they are in both, for, given the poet-speaker's present point of view, "sickness" is the common denominator for all of the stages of his life.

After renouncing the "blank, foregoing whiteness" of his youthful cloister because its brightness could not "burn away the blur" of the problem of man's relationship to the universe, the poet-speaker returns to considering Satan. Again Satan seems to be an aspect of himself, as "all that blinding brightness," which he has associated with his early work, was "changed into a serpent, lay grovelling on its gut," which might suggest the less dogmatic and less "triumphant" poetry of Life Studies and For the Union Dead itself. His currently confused point of view leads again to the idea of suicide, intimated in the last lines of the penultimate stanza: "At fifty we're so fragile, / a feather . . ." As in the preceding poem, the ellipses indicate a thought so tantalizing that he dare not even voice it. Finally, however, by the first line of the last stanza he is able to assert, with a weary emphasis and with the characteristic pun, that "The things of the eye are done." Now the luminous figures on the clock face, formerly a symbol of mutability and the persona's terror, are "green ciphers of a new moon," suggesting new life, and the last two lines of the poem set forth the affirmation that he has eked out: "Then morning comes, / saying, 'This was a night.' "

Having wrestled with his angel and gained at least a temporary victory, the poet-speaker can emerge from himself and attempt to deal again with the world at large. Significantly, the following poem in this crucial sequence is entitled "Returning." The poet-speaker is rather befogged and squinty at this point in the volume, as might be expected of a man emerging from the night just described. In "Returning," which might be seen as a revision of "The Exile's Return" in Lord Weary's Castle, he is not the artist-as-hero, but rather a Rip Van Winkle without that character's vigor. The "twenty years' mirage" parallels "the dream-road"; and his reference to "touching bottom," where he found "exhaustion, the light of the world," epitomizes the dark night of the preceding poem. "Exhaustion" is "the light of the world"—an epithet usually used for Christ—simply because if it can be endured it guarantees continuation, at least until it must be endured again. "Myopia: a Night" has provided no answers, but the compass needle no longer points to terror, if only because the vortex has been passed through.

In the middle of "Returning," the persona again reviews his poetic past. The "venerable elm" that "sickens" now, yet had a "former fertility," recalls Lowell's use of the tree and cross symbolism in *Lord Weary's Castle,* and perhaps his whole religious system. The clarity of things in that "hour of credulity / and young summer" would suggest the broader interpretation, and Lowell even quotes the title of the last section of "Between the Porch and the Altar" in the first of these lines:

> and here at the altar of surrender,
> I met you,
> the death of thirst in my brief flesh.

The "you" here is probably Christ; and the fruit of Lowell's conversion to Catholicism, his "first growth," is outlined in the next section, where he claims that what seems to be the Church finally "gave too much shelter." In this context, the last lines of the poem take on a new meaning: "They" are Lowell's early volumes, "dog-eared" now and perhaps baldly naive from his point of view.

The "glazed eye," however, seems also to result from finding his old friends "in business"; and this last phrase in particular, as well as the acknowledgement of his old friends in general, indicates some curiosity about, and contact with, the outside, a concern that grows in the remaining poems. There might be little doubt about the poet-speaker's isolation and fecklessness; but it is doubtful that these characteristics should be allowed to take precedence over his renewed concern. In the following poem, which is a postscript to this central sequence in the way that "Lady Ralegh's Lament" was a preamble, "The Drinker" is still desperate and isolated in his "iron lung" of a room, with its exposed, corroded pipes. Indeed, the drinker might not be wholly sane, and it is understandable that this poem echos several poems in the last part of *Life Studies.* Nevertheless, the observation that "even corroded metal somehow functions" signifies a new attitude. Moreover, "The Drinker" ends with a glimpse of two mounted policemen looking for parking meter violations—a detail that returns us ironically to the opening line—and they are the first solid figures to exist in the present in this volume.

The following six poems also employ special points of view

and an oblique symbolism that enable the persona to prescind from his objects of contemplation without surrendering
a concern with himself. Centered on art and the artist, this
group of poems implicitly opposes the earlier group, stretching from "The Lesson" through "The Public Garden," in
which the turmoil of life threatened to drive the poet-speaker
to despair. In the first two poems in this sequence, Lowell
wants the reader to associate the persona with his subjects,
Nathaniel Hawthorne and Jonathan Edwards. This intention
is indicated in the first poem when a paraphrase of one of the
sentences from "The Customs House" preface to *The Scarlet
Letter*—"I cannot resilver the smudged plate"—is put into the
mouth of the poet-speaker. The same purpose is served in
"Jonathan Edwards in Western Massachusetts" when Edwards's description of himself in a letter to the College of
New Jersey is edited with an eye to selecting details characteristic of the speaker.[20] The details are applicable to Robert
Lowell as well, and thus a chain of identities is forged. Still, it
is salutary to remember that the speaker is the central link,
and that while the lines " 'I am contemptible, / stiff and
dull' " probably represent Lowell's judgment on himself,
they are derived from and attributed to Edwards.[21] Similarly,
in "Hawthorne" the poet-speaker can depict his conjured
subject, as he could not comfortably depict himself, as
"brooding" on

> some stone, some common plant,
> the commonest thing,
> as if it were the clue.
> The disturbed eyes rise,
> furtive, foiled, dissatisfied
> from meditation on the true
> and insignificant.

These carefully measured lines capture the tone and describe the method of much of the rest of *For the Union Dead*.
As the speaker in the Edwards poem says of the Puritan
minister's recusant flock, the poet himself is a man in whom
"Faith is trying to do without / Faith." His only resort, it
would seem, is to meditate upon the commonest things in the

hope that they are true as well as insignificant. Of course this is not to say that Hawthorne and Edwards represent the untroubled, complacent artist. As Lowell says of Hawthorne, in lines that recall "Memories of West Street and Lepke" and therefore emphasize the implicit analogy between Hawthorne and the persona:

> Even this shy distrustful ego
> sometimes walked on top of the blazing roof,
> and felt those flashes
> that char the discharged cells of the brain.

Perhaps the most that the artist can hope for is to come through such shocking and exhausting visions, as the poet himself has done; and perhaps the greatest tribute that he can expect is something like the one paid Hawthorne in Lowell's beautiful lines:

> He shines in the firelight. His hard
> survivor's smile is touched with fire.

The same emphasis on persistence is tersely expressed in the sentence "Hope lives in doubt" in the Edwards poem; and it lies behind those other lines in the same poem:

> You stood on stilts in the air,
> but you fell from your parish.
> "All rising is by a winding stair."

The last line here might also refer obliquely to the progress of Lowell's poet-speaker. In any case, it seems clear that when the poet, addressing the shade of Edwards, says that "We move in different circles," he must have reference to Dantean circles rather than to their methods and beliefs, for the last lines of the poem are spoken by Lowell as much as by his subject.

Like both of these poems, the following four study the processes of meditation and imagination. The "Tenth Muse" is Sloth, that common poetic vice that Lowell here turns against itself by the Yeatsian device of making it the occasion for writing. The lack of a coherent scheme is treated here with

much more levity than it would have been in the earlier parts
of the book: if "even God was born / too late to trust the old
religion," little faith should be demanded of anyone else. The
last lines of the poem—"all those settings out / that never left
the ground, / beginning in wisdom, dying in doubt"—have
no single referent, but they might apply to Lowell's own past,
and this possibility is strengthened by the subject of the following poem.[22]

"The Neo-Classical Urn," the title of which invites an
ironic comparison of Lowell's subject with Keats's, constitutes yet another review of Lowell's earlier work, with *The
Mills of the Kavanaughs* the focal point this time. In stressing
his youthful energy ("I could not rest"), this poem also coun-
terpoints "Tenth Muse." The situations recounted in the
body of the poem, with "the caste stone statue of a nymph"
and the "water bogs" and "painted turtles," reflect those of
"The Mills of the Kavanaughs" and perhaps some of those in
Life Studies. The note that "In that season of joy / my turtle
catch / was thirty-three" would make the earlier poem the
most likely candidate since Lowell was thirty-three when it
was published. In this context, the last lines of the poem are
less obscure:

> Turtles! I rub my skull,
> that turtle shell,
> and breathe their dying smell,
> still watch their crippled last survivors pass,
> and hobble humpbacked through the grizzled grass.

As in "Water" and several of the other poems discussed
above, Lowell's symbols here are ambiguous but decipherable. The turtles seem to represent his poems, and therefore it
is not inappropriate that his balding head itself is compared
to a turtle shell; since a poet is in a sense his poetry, especially
when the poems include as much of his own life as Lowell's
do, it is fitting that one should be unable to tell them apart.
For this reason, the inspired syntax permits the concluding
line, which rewrites Keats's famous line in "The Eve of St.
Agnes," to be descriptive either of the poet ("hobble" can be
parallel to "breathe" and "watch") or of his poems (it can also

be parallel to "pass"). In either case, the reference to the "crippled last survivors" reminds us of the description of Hawthorne and thereby intimates again the progress of the poet-speaker.

The latent autobiography comes closer to the surface of the poetry in "Caligula," perhaps the only poem in the language based on the poet's nickname, as "Cal" Lowell projects on the page a grotesque vision of himself as the mad, murderous Roman emperor. As in "Hawthorne" and "Jonathan Edwards in Western Massachusetts," the format of this poem, with its address to an absent figure who serves to objectify the poet-speaker's self, enables Lowell to continue his subjective scrutiny without lapsing into the solipsism of the earlier poems. Both the emperor's insanity and his penchant for decapitation (which extended even to statues of the Roman gods, whose heads he then replaced with sculpted models of his own, in ironic parallel to Lowell's method here)[23] lead into "The Severed Head," where the poet-speaker is again divided against himself and where the artistic imagination is again the subject.

A dream-vision in *terza rima*, "The Severed Head" is one of those poems in which the details are insistently symbolic yet so enigmatic that few critics have ventured an interpretation of the poem as a whole.[24] Although parts of this poem are esoteric and might remain obscure unless the poet chooses to comment upon them at some future date, the general import of "The Severed Head" is clear enough once its context has been considered. As in the poems that precede it, the subject is the poet-speaker as artist and his relationship to his material; more specifically, this poem resembles "Myopia: a Night" and "The Neo-Classical Urn" in that its structure derives from that of the poet's career. The first section deals in symbolic terms with his former religious attitudes and values, his attraction to and advocacy of the "darker passages" in his "ponderous Bible."[25] This phase of his development seems to him analogous to having been shut up rather like one of Poe's characters in a dark, windowless cell that might have doubled as a tomb. This view of his early career is not just retrospective, for even at that time

                                            What
I imagined was a spider crab, my small
chance of surviving in this room. Its shut
windows had sunken into solid wall.

As long as he was locked inside his beliefs like a crab in its
shell or a prisoner in solitary confinement, sequestered from
the world, the young poet could not survive as an artist.

The escape that he effected is outlined in oblique terms in
the second and third sections, where a dream-figure serves as
both the poet-speaker's tutor and his alter ego. This figure is
limned in such detail that it seems not unlikely that Lowell
has a particular person in mind, but it is not necessary to
believe that this is indeed the case to understand the gist of
these sections of the poem.[26] Clearly, the "man . . . with a
manuscript" and a pen that was fed from his heart and
"dripped / a red ink dribble" of blood represents an intimate,
immediate kind of poet, a poet of feeling rather than of doctrine, one who could not have written *Land of Unlikeness* or
Lord Weary's Castle but who might very well have written *Life
Studies*. A judgment on the two kinds of poetry at first seems
implicit in the description of himself "hunting the desired /
butterfly here and there without success," presumably in
contrast to the man with "a glassy cuff-link with a butterfly /
inside"; but the conclusion of the second section implies that
"raw" poetry is ultimately no less frustrating than the
"cooked" variety.[27] This last theme recurs in the third section, where the "ocean butterflies"—probably literally the
flying gurnards of the Atlantic coastal waters—seem to symbolize the ideal beauty that remains inaccessible to both
figures.

This third section also extends the volume's personal narrative in its last lines:

                               Then I heard
my friend unclasp a rusty pocket-knife.
He cut out squares of paper, made a stack,
and formed the figure of his former wife:
Square head, square feet, square hands, square breasts,
    square back.

These images refer us once more to "The Old Flame," thereby indicating the direction that Lowell's own work had taken after *Life Studies* and bringing this poetic autobiography up to the approximate present. In the concluding seven lines of "The Severed Head," Lowell turns the story of Jael and Sisera (Judg. 5:24 ff.) into a parable that reflects ironically upon the poet-speaker's recusancy. The Biblical allusions outline the plight of a poet who realizes that he can no longer accept the religious tenets upon which much of his poetry has been based but who also knows that he has no adequate substitute for those tenets. In other words, Jael is more or less a projection of his former self, whereas Sisera occupies his present "idolatrous" position.

This sequence of poems from "Hawthorne" through "The Severed Head" corresponds to the series that reaches from "The Lesson" to "The Public Garden"; and if the earlier group is symptomatic of the desperate and increasingly subjective view of the poet-speaker, the later group indicates a troubled but increasingly objective state. This later development is complicated by the fact that the poet-speaker is still his own primary subject, but it is not nullified by any means, since it is partly his ability to see himself from without, to get outside himself, that constitutes his new objectivity. In the earlier poems the topography and situations are projections of his own mind and thought, whereas in these poems his thoughts and views are embodied in dramatic figures.[28] In the earlier sequence, other people, when they enter at all, are "all outline, uniformly gray"; in this sequence, instead of describing vaguely "those before us," the poet-speaker delineates specific historical figures. Just as important as this change is the shift from a focus upon the past to a focus upon the present. That the invocation of historical figures implies an orientation toward the past is no more (if no less) complicating than the superficial paradox of objective concern with the self. Inasmuch as Hawthorne, Edwards, and Caligula represent aspects of himself and inasmuch as the issues which they dramatize are relevant to the present, they are contemporary with the speaker.

Beginning with "Beyond the Alps," which Lowell reprints

here with the restoration of the original third section, the poet-speaker's objective world is enlarged as a sociopolitical concern reenters the volume. Whether fortuitously or not, the restored stanza of "Beyond the Alps" has the effect of linking the poems that center on the artist with those that are socially and politically oriented. Ovid, banished to Tomis on the Black Sea by Augustus Caesar (because of a combination of his amorous verse, his knowledge of Augustus's daughter's liasons, and his anarchistic tendencies), is another of Lowell's "survivors," as the laconic summary of the famous conclusion to the *Metamorphoses* in the last half-line of this stanza indicates. "'Lucan, Tacitus and Juvenal,'" all bitter critics of a decadent empire ruled by psychopaths like Nero and tyrants like Domitian, are spiritual heirs of Ovid and the guiding lights of the political poems that follow—and, incidentally, of many of the poems in *Near the Ocean*.

"July in Washington," instead of celebrating the Fourth, takes over the theme of imperialism latent in the third section of "Beyond the Alps" and unobtrusively elaborates it in contemporary terms. Repeated references to "circles" and the image of "the sulphurous wave" on the Potomac suggest that the American capital is an infernal hub of colonialism whose "stiff spokes" prod at "the sore spots," the underdeveloped and vulnerable nations of the world. The United States seems as incapable of controlling its destiny here as the poet-speaker was of controlling his own destiny earlier; the country's influence expands aimlessly and inexorably, "circle on circle, like rings on a tree."

But the rings in the trunk of a tree tell age as well as growth, and the poet-speaker seems to detect signs of the passing of this era and the introduction of a new one in the oxydizing "green statues" and the "breeding vegetation" that is probably the avant-garde of a second invasion of the Continent. The implication is that the new era will be one in which American civilization will sink back into the wilderness from which it sprang. The reason for this retrogression is suggested by the mocking juxtaposition of "The elect" and "the elected," which points up the great disparity between virtue and political success even as it jeeringly identifies salvation with worldly power. The obsolescence of the concept of heroism implicit in this irony prompts the reference to the men whom the statues are supposed to commemorate: "We cannot name their names, or number their dates." If in "The Mouth of the Hudson" the poet-speaker contradicted Hart Crane's optimistic view of man's ability to transcend the apparent future of the New World, in these lines he declines the role that Yeats arrogated to the poet in "Easter 1916"—that of murmuring the "name upon name" of legendary political heroes. Neither meliorism nor mythology is possible in a world whose leaders are unctuous as otters that "slide and dive and slick back their hair" and rapacious as raccoons that "clean their meat in the creek." Nevertheless, it is possible to face that world squarely and to attempt to survive it, as the persona does in this sequence, rather than to retreat into himself as he had in those earlier poems.

The "South American / liberators" of "July in Washington" are counterpointed in "Buenos Aires" by the "internecine generals" who exploit the "herds" of impoverished farmers and laborers. The military dictators, alternatively "leaden" and like "lumps of dough," seem hardly more human than the "literal commemorative busts" of their predecessors. Futilely arrayed against them are the marble statues of the goddesses, whose hard breasts, the poet-speaker's only source of comfort, are emblematic of the paucity of the milk of human kindness in the country. The goddesses, as well as the setting, link this poem to "Dropping South: Brazil." Here it is the supplanting of *"Yemanjá,"* a sort of South American Aphrodite, that is the poet-speaker's symbol of the death of a way of life in which belief in transcendental beauty and power predominated. "The Latin blonde, / two strips of ribbon" who "ripened in the sun," is a travesty of "the fish-tailed Virgin of the sea."

Yemanjá and the goddesses of the preceding poem are the American versions of the heroes and gods whose passing was lamented in "Florence," and it is even possible that the title of "Dropping South: Brazil" is intended to recall the punning title, "Fall 1961," while the phrase "walking and walking" reminds us of "Back and forth" and "to and fro." The essential difference between these poems and those earlier ones is the recognition of the condition of others, the people who "starved, and struck, and died" and the "frowning, starch-collared crowds." The change is not immediately apparent, but it is significant. A similar parallel, and one which reveals an even more significant change in attitude, obtains between the first four poems in the book and the four that follow "Dropping South: Brazil."

By returning to the locus of family relationships in these four poems, Lowell balances the sequence that began the volume. If in those poems the poet-speaker found himself cut off from his friends and family and less able to deal with the world outside himself as a result, in these poems he discovers new and indurating relationships. As if to emphasize this implicit comparison, "Soft Wood," like "Water" and "The Old Flame," is set in Maine; makes use of the sea, house, and animal symbols; and treats the themes of mutability and cap-tivity. Now, however, there is something "more than water," something more than merely transient experience. Similarly, captivity is no longer the insuperable condition of existence that it seemed when the poet-speaker saw himself as a bait-fish trapped in a weir. Although the speaker is still shut in behind "curtain and screen," rather like the seals in their "barred pond at the zoo," a new point of view provokes his observation that the breeze blowing through the window is "touched with salt and evergreen" suggestive of health and immortality. Indeed, the whole atmosphere of the first three stanzas of this poem, from the wind "blasting an all-white wall whiter" to "the scouring effervescence / of something healing, / the illimitable salt" of the sea, is one of vigorous renewal. The fourth and fifth stanzas, however, constitute a relapse into discouragement and a feeling of futility, as it suddenly occurs to the speaker that "there is no utility or inspiration / in the wind smashing without direction," that "bright and clean" exteriors serve only to conceal the physical or moral debility beneath, and that only "Things last," while their owners never do.

These two points of view are reconciled in the last stanzas of the poem in two different ways. While only "Things last" in more or less original form,

Yet the seal pack will bark past my window
summer after summer.
This is the season
when our friends may and will die daily.
Surely the lives of the old
are briefer than the young.

Each of these sentences is carefully ambiguous enough to
present both the negative and the positive ramifications of a
cyclical view of life. The first two lines stress the permanence
of the species even while hinting at the transience of the
individual; while "Shed skin will never fit another wearer,"
as another line has it, there are always skins to be shed and
there are always other wearers. The following two lines
suggest not only the literal deaths of people whom one
knows, but also the daily death that constitutes life, the
evolution of the individual that recapitulates the evolution of
the species. This second implication is perhaps supported by
latent puns on "may" and "will," which might signify not the
passage from life to death but the transition from one stage of
life to another; and if so, the contrast between two stages of
life would connect this pair of lines with the last pair. In the
first place, these last lines imply that life amounts only to the
time that one has left to live, so that "daily" deaths add up to
"briefer" lives; but in the second place, the very generalization and opposition in the phrases "the old" and "the
young"—as well as in "season" and "daily"—guarantees the
continuity of life on a higher plane.

In this stanza, each agonizing thought entails a consolation; the converse is true of the poem's conclusion: "each
drug that numbs alerts another nerve to pain." But Lowell is
not content to end the poem with a counsel of futility; for his
point is not that this proposition is in fact the case, but rather
that someone *knows* that it is the case. Insofar as it implies
enduring a condition in which every comforting notion about
life entails a painful recognition, this knowledge represents a
more positive response than the claim that all thoughts and
conditions cancel one another out. The distinction is difficult
to keep hold of, but it is crucial, for it makes Harriet Winslow
a true "survivor" and thus distinguishes what she represents

from what the seals symbolize. If the seals are "happy," it is their ignorance that is their bliss; and if they "live as long as the Scholar Gypsy," it is their brute instinct that assures their immortality. "Soft Wood" begins with the seals, but it ends with Harriet Winslow, and the concluding affirmation does not rest on any self-effacing determinism. The poem comes as close to Nietzsche's joyous willing of eternal recurrence as it does to Schopenhauer's disgusted acceptance of the self-preserving instincts of man.

It will not do, then, to attribute to the Lowell of this volume the belief that man is "truly animalistic, and the whole universe—man, animal, and thing—moves relentlessly to the same principle."[29] These comments characterize some of the earlier poems, but they are inapplicable to these concluding poems, a point that increases in importance with the realization that *For the Union Dead* is a narrative in the course of which the narrator seeks an alternative to a pessimistic view of a haphazard universe. As in "Skunk Hour," the response is existential in that it stresses conscious endurance and love, neither of which is at all "animalistic." "Harriet Winslow," says the speaker in this poem, "was more to me than my mother," and thus he asserts his love for her and controverts his earlier acceptance of his isolation from his ancestors.

In the next three poems, the first of which is dedicated to Elizabeth Hardwick Lowell, the poet's second wife, love and reliance upon another are again the themes; and consequently, these poems reverse the implications of "Water" and "The Old Flame." Such themes are least in evidence in "New York 1962: Fragment." The "Soft Wood" of the preceding poem reappears here in "the termites digging in the underpinning," an image the import of which is brought out by the speaker's reference to himself as "a wooden workhorse." Subhuman connotations also radiate from other metaphors in the poem, such as the bizarre comparison of the two lovers lying side by side to a one-celled organism in the process of fission and the description of their breathing as a failing machine "sawing and pumping to the terminal." Such images hardly guarantee that this poem is concerned with love, but there is justification for this idea in the scattered allusions to Donne's "Valediction: Forbidding Mourning." These allusions are perhaps partially ironic, but the insistence upon the concept of the "two" being "one" in actuality seems too strong to be entirely so. Moreover, as Mazzaro has noticed, the description of the two lovers "bed to bed" and yet "one cell" is an inversion of the description of the lovers in "The Old Flame" who were "in one bed and apart";[30] and whereas water was a destructive force in the other poem, it is here symbolic of union.

There may be echoes of Donne's love poetry again in "The Flaw," where several lines seem to allude to "The Extasie," but as Lowell has suggested, the chief debt here is to "Le cimetière marin."[31] Valéry's "défaut" gives Lowell his title, his "derniers dons" is rendered in the singular as "the final gift," the "cris aigus des filles chatouillées" becomes "our eager, sharpened cries," and so on. However, Valéry's speaker's inspired vision—"O puissance salée! / Courons à l'onde en rejaillir vivant!"—has no counterpart in Lowell's more restrained poem. Instead, there is an echo of the key line in "Jonathan Edwards in Western Massachusetts," "Hope lives in doubt," in the couplet: "Hope of the hopeless launched and cast adrift / on the great flaw that gives the final gift." The "great flaw" seems to include the sea through which "A seal swims like a poodle" and the "heat waves" into which the poet-speaker and his lover lean, as into "the sheet / of blinding salt"; it seems to refer, in short, to life, which is taken to be unremittingly painful. The "final gift," however, cannot be reduced to a single meaning, since the nature of this gift is the motivating and unanswered question of the poem.

To put this last point another way, the problem in the poem is a teleological one—what is the relationship between sin or evil and postmortal existence?—and the response is thoroughly agnostic. The opening stanza juxtaposes images of painful and perhaps benumbing life (the seal and the pines) with one of death (the "country graveyard"), and from this juxtaposition issues the question that provides a transition to the second stanza: what does the mote in the poet-speaker's eye (or the flaw on his contact lens) symbolize? Or, literally: what is the nature of the flaw in the I? The "answer" consists of acceptance of the terms that Dostoevsky thought precluded such an answer when he noted that without God all is possible. The potential implications of the flaw that are singled out in the second stanza cover the whole range of possibilities, from "a noose" (damnation or total negation of the soul) through "a question" (uncertainty about the future of the soul) to "grace" (salvation of the soul).[32] A collateral problem is whether there is "free will," which is closely related to the problem of evil, since if there is no freedom of will, then it is difficult to justify divine sanctions. This problem is subordinated, however, with the premise that God's existence itself is not certain and that therefore "all's possible, all's unpredictable." The certainty of physical annihilation, however, is unquestioned, and the third stanza is a vision of the grave that is accompanied by a premonition of the unfettered souls of the lovers cutting "through the boundless wash" that alone rids them of "eye-flaws." The "flash" of vision seems to continue into the fourth stanza, the first lines of which look back at the present as though from the vantage of the future and depict with the melancholy wisdom of one of Dante's souls the vanity of corporeal love. Although the vision fades, the desire for transcendence of the physical self increases in the fifth stanza. The final couplet asserts what was implicit in the statement "all's possible," that the "eye-flaw" is "a questionmark" demanding an answer. But the answer given by the poet is itself a question:

> Dear Figure curving like a questionmark,
> how will you hear my answer in the dark?

The "Dear Figure" of this last couplet seems also to refer to the poet-speaker's wife, who is leaning forward into the "heat waves," and if so, the question that this couplet asks deplores the possibility of separation in death. The same dependence upon her might be implied in the closing lines of the second sonnet in "Night Sweat," where the "Dear Figure" becomes a "Dear Heart." On the other hand, although "my wife" is clearly to be associated with the "lightness" that "alters everything" in the sonnet, there is a syntactical break before the last sentence in the sestet, and it is not certain that "Dear Heart" refers only to her. In fact, the plea for absolution and the epithets "Poor turtle, tortoise," which recall "The Neo-Classical Urn," suggest that the "Heart" is the seat of poetry. In a similar fashion, the "Figure" of the preceding poem might refer to the poetic figure, the "eye-flaw," and thus represent the questions and by extension the poem that is asking them.

It does not seem imperative that either of these options be chosen in either case, especially since it will do no harm to regard the ambiguities as deliberate. What is imperative is the recognition that in these poems the speaker's efforts are not overwhelmed by the conditions of life, but rather bent toward enduring them. Whether it is from his wife or from writing itself or from both that he derives his "utility" and "inspiration," he is undeniably anxious to compose an "answer" and to "clear / the surface of these troubled waters."

The title poem stands at the end of the volume and more or less outside the sequence that precedes it. At the same time, as the most comprehensive expression of the persona's renewed concern with the objective and historical world, "For the Union Dead" provides a marvelous conclusion to the book. Although it must be admitted that the speaker in "For the Union Dead" is apparently incapable of significant action, it does not follow that his attitude is solipsistic. Not only does this poem assume the existence of the objective world, it also insists upon the terrible reality of the malignant forces at work in that world. Furthermore, if the speaker remains ineffectual at the poem's close, he also realizes what kind of character is prerequisite to effective action. This kind of character is manifest in Colonel Robert Shaw, who "cannot bend his back," and not just because he is a bronze statue. His uncompromising nature is to be contrasted with that of the poet-speaker, whose crouching before the television set implies a subservience that the colonel, to whom Lowell is distantly related, could never have countenanced.[33]

Shaw, who is described in lines that echo W. D. Snodgrass's "April Inventory" as he "rejoices in man's lovely, /

peculiar power to choose life and die," is the last of the survivors who populate the last half of this volume.[34] He is the
figure who is comparable in the public realm to Harriet
Winslow in the persona's private life, to Edwards in the religious realm, and to Hawthorne in the literary world. If
Shaw is to be distinguished from these other figures, the
distinction should be grounded in his symbolic ambiguity.
Although he represents those qualities to which men should
aspire, or perhaps precisely because he does represent those
qualities, he also reminds the speaker of man's capacity to
destroy himself. By virtue of the very fact that he embodies
the heroic ideal, the colonel exposes the vitiation of a culture
that cannot understand heroism and therefore resents it:

> Their monument sticks like a fishbone
> in the city's throat.
> Its Colonel is as lean
> as a compass-needle.

Like the statues in "Florence," the monument to Shaw and
his black regiment is a memorial to an anachronistic spirit;
and like that other compass needle in "Lady Ralegh's Lament," this one points to the terror of imminent destruction.

However—and the observation warrants emphasis—the
destruction to which the colonel points is not that of an individual personality, as in the earlier poem, but rather that of a
nation, and by implication that of all nations. In other words,
to view this poem as solipsistic is to invite the problem of
reconciling solipsism and apocalypticism, modes of thought
whose ramifications seem difficult if not impossible to combine. Nor could the problem be obviated by denying that the
poem is apocalyptic, for its recurrent theme is that we are on
the very brink of chaos. When Lowell puts this theme in
terms of the disintegration of the United States, he composes
a future for this country out of its past: "The stone statues of
the abstract Union Soldier / grow slimmer and younger each
year" because the country itself is growing in reverse, approaching a Civil War that it had thought was but a historical
episode. Similarly, an emblem of the triumph over slavery
and over civil war, the "shaking Civil War relief, / propped by

a plank splint against the garage's earthquake," threatens to topple and thereby signifies the possibility that the nation's ideals will collapse and the country itself fall back into its own tumultuous past.

The theme of disintegration is handled in a comparable way when Lowell's subject is not even nominally the United States. The "dark downward and vegetating kingdom / of the fish and reptile" is to the evolution of human consciousness what the Civil War is to the development of "the Union"; and the observation that it seems to have reappeared in the form of the "yellow dinosaur steamshovels" that "cropped up tons of mush and grass / to gouge their underworld garage" bodes as ill for the future of man as the sight of "the drained faces of Negro school-children" that "rise like balloons" on the television screen does for the future of the country. Both man's bestiality and America's slavery have been sublimated, but neither has been eradicated, and each is ultimately a means of self-destruction.

Although the terms in which it is expressed are evolutionary and historical, the vision behind this poem is reminiscent of a younger Lowell, the "consciously Catholic poet" whose chief themes were man's fallen nature and his corrupt sociopolitical structures which continually embroil him in war. So is the ambivalent attitude toward devastation. On the one hand, Lowell deplores the conditions that seem to make it inevitable and cringes at the horror that it must involve; but on the other hand, the conditions themselves are so deplorable that the thought of their destruction, even at the expense of civilization, is not without some appeal.[35] It is this second thought that prompts the poet-speaker's nostalgia for a subhuman world, that motivates his longing "to burst the bubbles" symbolic of the precarious ascendancy of a complacent civilization, and that lends to the phrase "the blessed break" a literal meaning in addition to its ironic one. The competing idea—that another Civil War or World War must be avoided at all costs—gives rise to the speaker's acrimonious reflections on Hiroshima and to his admiration for those men like Colonel Shaw who refuse to tolerate the conditions that lead to war in the first place. These two ideas differ in respect to the final end of humanity, for the one assumes that man's flaws are irremediable while the other presupposes the possibility that man might improve his lot; but they have in common the judgment that evil pervades the most civilized institutions and societies, and this judgment, rather than the intimation of a Second Coming, seems to predominate in the poem's last stanza.

One might argue that Lowell's fundamental position is either one of the two just distinguished, rather than ambivalent; but even if that argument were convincing, it would not affect our thesis about the relationship of this poem to the rest of the volume. Whatever Lowell's conclusions might be regarding the nature and end of man and his institutions, it seems clear that this poem is concerned with these problems, that it is objectively rather than subjectively oriented. Even the title of the poem denominates it an occasional piece, a formal elegy; and the genre, together with the poem's strong moral judgment (conveyed by the pun on "Dead" in the title and the partially ironic quotation from Shaw's monument that prefaces the poem[36]), immediately identifies this as a public statement. The various historical allusions and universal themes touched upon above only justify that identification.

By placing this poem last, immediately after the four poems that involve his family and balance the first four in the book, Lowell suggests that his persona has not only regained the vantage point that he had at the beginning of *For the Union Dead* but has also transcended it. Far from being isolated and solipsistic, as he is in the center of the volume, the persona is engaged by the issues of his time and painfully conscious of the existence of the "outward world," to recall Bly's term; but instead of seeing himself only in the context of his family, as he does at the beginning of the book, he sees himself in relationship to a complex of social and political forces. Having weathered the confrontation with self, Lowell's persona is even more objectively oriented at the end of *For the Union Dead* than at the beginning. The extraordinary title poem is a triumph in more than one way.

The merry-go-round of years has brought them
full circle, for are they not returning to Rome?
—AMY LOWELL, "The Bronze Horses"

O Rome! From all your palms, dominions, bronze
and beauty, what once was firm has fled. What once
was fugitive maintains its permanence.
—"The Ruins of Time, IV"

7

DARK DESIGNS:

Near the Ocean (1967)

At once tall, wide, and thin, and containing twenty
full-page drawings by Sidney Nolan, the hardbound
edition of *Near the Ocean* is rather an anomaly. Like
the renditions of Baudelaire taken from *Imitations* and published as *"The Voyage" and Other Versions of Poems by
Baudelaire*, this volume almost seems intended less for the
bookshelf than for the coffee table. The poet and the pub
lishers have made it easier than they might have, certainly,
to leaf through it, to admire it casually in bits and pieces. The
drawings—accompanied by the lines (excerpted, oddly brok-
en, and printed variously askew) that they illustrate—inter-
rupt the text more often than not, and the poems are laid out
in such a way that there are large margins and great empty
spaces, with a single short stanza sometimes the only intrusion
upon the page. It is not a format calculated to display a subtly
unified set of poems to its advantage, and thus it might
have at least something to do with the reception accorded
Near the Ocean.

With the publication of this volume, at any rate, it becomes
not uncommon for critics to refer to the "fragmented" quality

241

of Lowell's work and to suppose that the flinders and shards are to be justified, if at all, in the same suspect terms that Eliot's early apologists used to justify *The Waste Land*—namely, those of an imitative aesthetic in a chaotic world. As Paul Zweig puts it in his review of this volume:

Lowell, in his brilliant, pained way, sets out to tell it as it is. If the poems are nervous and violent, it is because our own scene is nervous and violent. If the poems are fragmented, it is because our world is stifled and discontinuous. Lowell tells and dramatizes for us what we know. . . .[1]

Hayden Carruth, in the course of one of the finest reviews of one of Lowell's volumes since Jarrell's early ones, has similar if less peremptory criticisms:

He has resolved to accept reality, all reality, and to take its fragments indiscriminately as they come. . . .
. . . We now have poems which are compositions of brilliant minutiae, like mosaics in which the separate tiles are so bright and glittering that we cannot see the design. A mosaic is fine, it is the model *par excellence* for poetry in our time, but if we are to see the pattern, the separate pieces must be clearly and naturally arranged. . . .[2]

Because Carruth does not quite discount the possibility that there is some method to the mélange, his comments are the better guidelines for the reader interested in assessing the extent of fragmentation in this book; for complex though it might be, there is a design in this volume, just as there is in each of Lowell's volumes after *The Mills of the Kavanaughs,* and that design provides for the unity of the most important poems and for the coherence of the title sequence.

There can be little doubt that the reality that is described in *Near the Ocean* seems fragmentary, that Lowell often assumes the role of an archaeologist sifting through the kitchen middens of a culture. The characteristic observation here is of material and ideological deterioration:

O Bible chopped and crucified
in hymns we hear but do not read. . . .
. . . .
No weekends for the gods now. Wars
flicker, earth licks its open sores,

fresh breakage, fresh promotions, chance
assassinations, no advance.
                    ("Waking Early Sunday Morning")

New England, everywhere I look,
old letters crumble from the Book. . . .
                    ("Fourth of July in Maine")

pigeons ganging through
broken windows and cooing
like gangs of children tooting
empty bottles.
                    ("The Opposite House")

The severed radiance filters back,
athirst for nightlife. . . .
. . . .
the downslope of some gritty green,
all access barred with broken glass;
and dehydration browned the grass. . . .
                    ("Near the Ocean")

Nor can it be disputed that the poetry itself is fragmentary
in several respects. The exclamation points, dashes, and ellipses that mark every page testify to the elusive, broken-field
style that Lowell began developing in *Life Studies* and that he
has continued to exploit right through *History* and *The Dolphin*. The first poem opens with an exclamation—"O to break
loose"—that is twice repeated, yet never given an explicit
object. The same poem erupts sporadically in emotional out-
bursts ("anywhere, but somewhere else!") and self-
admonitions ("Stop, back off") with equally vague import.
Other poems include even more, and more obscure, snatches
of internal monologues. A crucial stanza in "Near the Ocean"
begins with these lines:

        Betrayals! Was it the first night?
        They stood against a black and white
        inland New England backdrop.

Neither the specific sort of betrayals, nor the "it," nor even
the "They"—and both of the pronouns recur several times—

is ever identified in this poem, and one is left to deduce
situation and subject as best he can. Disjointed syntax and
discontinuity of image combine to produce the vagaries of
"1958." The last lines of this sonnet are:

> Hammerheaded shark,
> the rainbow salmon of the world—your hand
> a rose . . . And at the Mittersill, you topped
> the ski-run, that white eggshell, your sphere, not land
> or water—no circumference anywhere,
> the center everywhere, I everywhere,
> infinite, fearful . . . standing—you escaped.

Even after one has recognized the allusion to Pascal's description of God ("La sphere dont le centre est partout et la circumference est nulle part") and speculated about the traditional religious symbols (the "rainbow" and the "rose"), the
subject of this poem does indeed escape. Although these
lines from "Central Park" are more comprehensible in context, they also exemplify a lack of organization that is at least
superficial:

> Scurrying from the mouth of night,
> a single, fluttery, paper kite
> grazed Cleopatra's Needle, and sailed
> where the light of sun had failed.
> Then night, the night—the jungle hour,
> the rich in his slit-windowed tower . . .
> Old Pharaohs starving in your foxholes,
> with painted banquets on the walls. . . .

The poems in *Near the Ocean* are also apt to appear ran-
domly or carelessly grouped. Even in the title sequence, the
common denominator is not immediately apparent. Although this sequence begins and ends with poems in tetrameter couplets, it includes one poem that is much more
loosely rhymed ("Central Park") and another that is almost
without rhyme and metre ("The Opposite House"). There are
comparable discrepancies in perspective and subject: the
esoteric reverie about adultery in "Near the Ocean," the title
poem of the title sequence, seems virtually unrelated either to

the candid judgments on contemporary society in "Waking Early Sunday Morning" or to the surrealistic description of the scene at the "abandoned police stable" in "The Opposite House." The book itself might at first appear a potpourri of those poems that Lowell had on hand when it came time to publish again. Carruth, at any rate, is referring to the volume as well as to its constituent poems when he says that Lowell's work is fragmentary, linear, and open-ended; and it must be admitted that the two-part structure—the sequence of five original poems at the beginning and the section of six imitations at the end—seems at first a gross imitation of the subtle structures of preceding volumes and that the two short poems placed between these two sections seem unassimilated elements. Indeed, in their lack of relationship to one another or to the two main sections, these poems are presumably prime examples of the flotsam that Lowell seems to have collected near the ocean.

As the passages quoted above will have suggested, however, there seems to be at least one area in which this poetry is not random and fragmentary. While lines and stanzas sometimes disintegrated in *For the Union Dead*, and while Lowell himself will say that the verse in *Notebook 1967–68* occasionally "corrupts into prose," the prosody in *Near the Ocean* is on the whole more rigorous than that in any volume since *The Mills of the Kavanaughs*. The combination of the apparently fragmentary and the obviously formal elements in this book is bound to be provocative, as Carruth's speculations testify. At one point in his review, Carruth raises the crucial issue when he asks whether the iambs and the rhymes might not represent Lowell's one attempt "to give greater objectivity to the random, fragmentary materials of his autobiography by reintroducing elements of fixative convention."[3] This comment is actually twofold: in the first place, it springs from the valuable insight that there is a conscious struggle going on in these poems between the desire to report the flux of experience and the wish to impose a form upon it; and in the second place, it leads to the conclusion that since conventional prosody is the only framework that Lowell imposes consistently on his mass of heterogeneous data, form is bound to lose the struggle. In fact, Carruth ends by viewing this single impulse to form as inimical to itself, for he maintains that Lowell's return to formalism instigates a concentration upon "the verbal surface" of the poetry and therefore encourages its epigrammatic disparateness.

If one returns to Carruth's original insight that there is a struggle between form and flux in these poems and then assumes that the rigorous prosody is merely indicative of the claims of form rather than exhaustive of them, a different conclusion can be reached. To anticipate the argument, Lowell's verse forms are but the smallest or the innermost of an arrangement of increasingly inclusive forms in *Near the Ocean*. These successive frameworks enclose or complement one another, or do both, until the outline of the last is identical with the structure of the volume. If in the opening poem individual images are often formulated by couplets in virtual epigrams, these couplets are disposed in eight-line stanzas that are almost invariably unified by theme; and these fourteen stanzas are components of a structure that is unobtrusive and yet so definite that hardly a stanza could be omitted or displaced. Moreover, the relationship between the first of these stanzas and the structure of "Waking Early Sunday Morning" is a microcosm of the relationship between this poem and the title sequence, for both the poem and the sequence are chronologically ordered. The structure of this sequence, in turn, adumbrates the organization of the imitations in the second half of the book, since the latter comprises a series of successive views of Rome that parallel the opening poems on America. Finally, in addition to balancing the title sequence, the section of imitations combines with it to give the book a structure that is a self-enclosed whole rather than a juxtaposition of two open-ended sequences. Although each group of poems is chronologically arranged (with one minor exception), both the original composition and the subject of the second group antedate those of the first one, so that over the course of the book the implied linear movement into the future is converted into a circular movement into the past.

The nature of the book's structure—which will be detailed soon—has two important implications. In the first place, the transformation of a linear, temporal progression into a circular, cyclical form implies a view of reality very different from that usually assumed to characterize this book. Just as a linear and open-ended structure is a projection of a formless process, so a circular and closed structure is a metaphor for form and permanence. Lowell's conversion of the one structure into the other implies a complicated view of the world as a process that is part of a coherent (which is not to say pleasant) whole. If the aesthetic is imitative, in other words, the world it imitates is hardly chaotic. But perhaps the best way to regard the fusion of process and order in this book is simply as a transformation for which every artist strives, the transformation of the temporal and the empirical into the eternal and the archetypal. Regardless of the nature of the world that produced it, the book strives both to incorporate and to transcend that world. Lowell's circularizing of a linear movement is an attempt, in his Quevedo's words, to make what once was fugitive maintain its permanence.[4]

In the second place, the fusion of process (temporal progression) and order (circular form) at the level of the structure of the book suggests that there will be an integral relationship between the two at other levels. In other words, if one should not expect the unorganized poetry that Zweig and Carruth describe, neither should one expect the rigidly organized poetry that the preceding summary of the frameworks in this volume might seem to entail. Thus, in the title sequence, which opens the volume, the basic form is the tetrameter couplet; but as soon as that statement is made, it has to be qualified, for the challenge to form is evident even at this level. Many of Lowell's couplets, for example, are imperfect rhymes. Sometimes the imperfection is a matter of careful calculation, as in these lines on the frame house:

> the Americas'
> best artifact produced en masse.

Even as this rhyme reproduces Whitman's equation, its imperfection mocks that equation; it is as though the discrepancy between the hard and the soft *s* were to stand for that between this culture and the one that is implied. Frequently, however, the rhymes seem pointlessly imperfect, and the couplet loses some of its rigidity as a result. A more obvious infringement upon the couplet is the occasional appearance of alternating rhyme or, as at the end of the first poem, enveloping rhyme.

Similarly, although more obviously, Lowell gives up the eight-line stanza itself in the third and fourth poems of the title sequence. This departure is indicative of the complexity of the relationship between form and flux in this book, for it becomes the middle of an enveloping form itself, since the "normal" stanza predominates in the first two and the last poems. In what might be considered a refinement of this method of making departure from form a part of form, the central poem in the sequence, "The Opposite House," is the only one written in lines loose enough to remind one of *For the Union Dead*. There is an analogy to the positioning of this poem in that of the two poems that follow the title sequence, for they interpose between the two main sections of the volume. A part of neither the opening sequence nor the sequence of imitations, "For Theodore Roethke" and "1958" can be taken together either as a disruption of the structure of the book or as a sort of buffer between its two halves. Viewed apart from the rest of the book, the relationship between these two poems suggests the battle going on elsewhere, for the first one comprises quatrains utilizing delayed near-rhymes and a free metric, while the form of the second is close to that of a Petrarchan sonnet.

This form is perhaps not unrelated to the positioning of "1958," since one subject that binds together the imitations that follow it is that of Rome; and in the first of these imitations, Lowell uses more dignified and less informal verse forms than in the title sequence. Three of the Latin poems are done into blank verse, and the version of Canto XV of the *Inferno* is written in a fine approximation of *terza rima* that rivals in flexibility the comparable attempt in the "dead master" episode of "Little Gidding." Although "Brunetto Latini" is not divided into stanzas and although there are no interlocking rhymes, the first and third of every three pentameter lines rhyme roundly but unobtrusively. Finally, the four sonnets based on Spanish originals, which Lowell admits are the

most freely adapted of these imitations, also use comparatively free forms; written in a flexible iambic pentameter, they
are more or less loosely rhymed, with a few identical and
many more approximate rhymes.

At the same time that they prove Lowell capable of some
prosodic finesse, then, these verse forms and their juxtaposi-
tions witness the ubiquity of the struggle between flux and
form. Or perhaps it is more accurate to say that they show
that the struggle creates its own form. In some sense, of
course, this is true of any art work that does not slavishly
follow a model, and Lowell's volume (and his work as a
whole) is distinguished by the consistency and the explicit-
ness with which he makes the point. The creation of form
(permanence) by the struggle (the fugitive process) is the
point, as it were, at which the structure and the theme of *Near
the Ocean* intersect.

Lowell's theme—the struggle between flux and form,
transience and permanence—is announced in the first stanza
of the first poem, "Waking Early Sunday Morning":

> O to break loose, like the chinook
> salmon jumping and falling back,
> nosing up to the impossible
> stone and bone-crushing waterfall—
> raw-jawed, weak-fleshed there, stopped by ten
> steps of the roaring ladder, and then
> to clear the top on the last try,
> alive enough to spawn and die.

This stanza is surely evidence of Richard Howard's observation that the opening poem is a "masterpiece of prosody."[5]
Since the four couplets constitute one sentence, the motivating tension and the projected resolution of that tension—the
desire to "break loose" in the first line and the thought of
dying in the last—are as much of a piece in syntax as in the
metaphorical action of the salmon; and the dangling of the
adjectives—"chinook," "impossible," "ten"—at the ends of
the lines imposes upon the reading voice a certain strain that
produces an aural analogue to the salmon's struggle. The

basis of the success of this stanza, however, is the tension between the speaker's desire and the metrical scheme. One cannot imagine either apart from the other, for the latter is what provokes the former. For all poetic purposes, in other words, the tetrameter couplets constitute the straitening conditions from which the speaker would escape, and the off-rhymes, the suspended adjectives, the spondees, and the enjambed lines bear witness to the attempt. To put it the other way around: this stanza is not *in* tetrameter couplets; it *creates* those couplets. It is as though no one had ever had the idea before, as though the poet had to fight every inch or rather every foot of the way. The result is a stanza in which form and process are interdependent, in which the process is eternally formalized. Perhaps nowhere else in *Near the Ocean* does Lowell so successfully embody simultaneously the limitations imposed upon human experience by temporal forms, and the reshaping of those limitations by poetic forms. This stanza does in small what the structure of the book intends as a whole.

The struggle to "break loose" is one with which we should be familiar by now, for we have encountered it in a number of Lowell's finest poems. In "Falling Asleep over the Aeneid" it took the form of the advice given Aeneas, " 'Try to die . . . To die is life' "; in "Skunk Hour" it appeared as the oblique death wish in the lines "I hear / my ill-spirit sob in each blood cell, / as if my hand were at its throat"; and in "Going to and fro" it received indirect expression in the incomplete thought "If you could get loose / from the earth by counting / your steps to the noose. . . ." In "Pigeons," the imitation of Rilke that closes *Imitations*, the speaker tells himself to "Think of Leonidas perhaps and the hoplites, / glittering with liberation" as they "moved into position to die." One of Lowell's most dramatic expressions of the allure of such liberation can be found in his foreword to Sylvia Plath's *Ariel*, published in 1966, three years after she had committed suicide and one year before the publication of *Near the Ocean:*

There is a peculiar, haunting challenge to these poems. Probably many, after reading *Ariel*, will recoil from their first overawed shock, and painfully wonder why so much of it leaves them feeling empty, evasive and inarticulate. In her lines, I often hear the serpent whisper, "Come, if only you had the courage, you too could have my rightness, audacity and ease of inspiration." But most of us will turn back.[6]

"But most of us will turn back"—and the second stanza of "Waking Early Sunday Morning" does just that, as the speaker warns himself to "Stop, back off" and then proceeds to a complicated statement of the consequences of observing the warning:

> now my body wakes
> to feel the unpolluted joy
> and criminal leisure of a boy—
> no rainbow smashing a dry fly
> in the white run is free as I. . . .

What the speaker backs off from is death, and what he retreats to is life; for if to "break loose" is synonymous with "to die" in the opening stanza, then to "back off" means to accept life in this stanza. The decision, however, is not an entirely joyful one. The waking of the "body" in these lines perfectly complements the dreaming of the mind (Yeats would have called it "Soul") in the earlier passage; and just as that dream is of an escape, so this event turns out to be one of confinement. Although the speaker is proclaiming his freedom here, the proclamation is ironic and the images undercut themselves: a leisure that is "criminal," if indeed the idea is not self-contradictory, is one that is subject to revocation at any moment, and to be more free than a hooked fish is not necessarily to be free at all. The rejection of the example of the heroic but suicidal salmon is thus tantamount to the acceptance of the struggle, the conditions of life, the very conditions from which the speaker would "break loose" in the opening lines.

The decision parallels Yeats's in his "Dialogue of Self and Soul"—not that one must go so far afield to find an analogue. Lowell's Aeneas could not die; the speaker in "Skunk Hour" in the end finds himself breathing "the rich air"; the persona in *For the Union Dead* rejects suicide; and in "Pigeons":

the ball thrown almost out of bounds
stings the hand with the momentum of its drop—
body and gravity,
miraculously multiplied by its mania to return.

The return in "Pigeons" is to the temporal world, the world
that remains undominated by the cycle of rot and renewal
simply because of man's willing of that cycle. In that poem
we are told that "only by suffering the rat-race in the arena /
can the heart learn to beat." That is the implication too of the
whole of this volume. At the end of "Brunetto Latini" in the
sequence of imitations there is this description of Dante's
friend, the poet, who is condemned to remain in hell:

> Then he turned back, and he seemed one of those
> who run for the green cloth through the green field
> at Verona . . . and seemed more like the one
> who wins the roll of cloth than those who lose.

Ser Brunetto accepts his lot, and in doing so triumphs over it.
If it were the temporal world instead of hell to which he were
turning back—and the distinction is never easy to make in
Lowell's work—he would resemble Colonel Shaw, who "rejoices in man's lovely, / peculiar power to choose life and
die." However small it might appear to him sometimes, the
difference between choosing death and choosing life and
dying is crucial to Lowell, as the structure of this book—like
those of *Imitations* and *Notebook 1967–68*—attests.

The difference is a matter of time. Its last lines, which expose this difference, constitute the affirmation toward which
Near the Ocean points:

> The hours will hardly pardon us their loss,
> those brilliant hours that wore away our days,
> our days that ate into eternity.

> ("The Ruins of Time, IV")

Although there is a characteristic ambivalence here (especially in the first line, where the refusal to grant a pardon
amounts to a fatal decree that derives from jealousy), the

emphasis is on the brilliance that time does after all permit, and the concluding line even seems to attribute to temporal action some efficacy. Even as time is the evil, it is the ground of significant human achievement. These lines do not quite aver, with Eliot, that only through time, time is conquered, but other passages at the end of *Near the Ocean* do.

Here, at the beginning of the volume, the subject is the ravages of time rather than the triumph over it, so it makes an ironic sense that the original poems, far from proceeding "by sudden unaccountable shifts,"[7] are rigorously organized according to chronology. In "Waking Early Sunday Morning" the progression is from predawn darkness, through daybreak and the beginning of activity at the docks, and through the beginning and end of a church service, to the "Sabbath noon" at the conclusion. Concommitant with this progression, there is a gradual widening of scope in the first poem. At the outset, the speaker's own existential predicament is the focal point, but with the third stanza the condition of the world about the speaker enters the poem, and from this point on the private and public concerns are interwoven. Toward the end of the poem, Lowell extrapolates from personal and American history a view of the contemporary world and its apparent fate. Like the poem's chronological progression, which is the first stage in a scheme that continues throughout, its widening of scope anticipates a development within the book as a whole; for while the first sequence concerns itself chiefly with the speaker as artist and the deficiencies of contemporary America, the imitations turn to the power of poetry in general and the shape of world history.

That the structures that have been outlined in "Waking Early Sunday Morning" have not received much attention is probably owing in part to the compression characteristic of its imagery. Frequently a single passage, sometimes just a phrase, has both a personal and a public dimension and at the same time marks a stage in the chronological progression, and the various functions tend to obscure one another. This is perhaps the case in the third stanza, where Lowell turns back almost specifically to "the rat-race in the arena" or to Yeats's "blind man's ditch":

Vermin run for their unstopped holes;
in some dark nook a fieldmouse rolls
a marble, hours on end, then stops;
a termite in the woodwork sleeps—
listen, the creatures of the night
obsessive, casual, sure of foot,
go on grinding, while the sun's
daily remorseful blackout dawns.

This passage not only moves the meditation from early morning to daybreak but also characterizes the speaker's world in
general terms and relates him specifically to that world. Like
"Skunk Hour," it presents an existentialist's dark night of the
soul, in which the world seems to be characterized by sense-
less, Sisyphean activities, affected by unseen but certain de-
bilities, and inhabited by creatures that are either despicably
timorous or dreadfully brutal. Lowell probably has himself in
mind at the end of the stanza. Having caricatured himself as a
"dragon" a few lines above, he implicitly views himself here
as one of the "creatures of the night"—the human race,
which Aeschylus called with more literalness and tolerance
"creatures of the day"—indulging his own obsessions, grinding out his verse, monotonously sure of his metre and
movement.[8]

At this juncture, the limitation felt by the speaker is extended to the natural world; his inability to "break loose" is
seen as an instance of the subjugation of all living things to
natural law. Lowell's theme is moving outward in a widening
orbit, and it continues to do so in the following stanza,
where, in the image of the "Fierce, fireless mind, running
downhill," the suppression of a referent produces an unobtrusive equation of the dying sun and the man disgusted with
his own inevitable expiration. This evocation of the sun
seems incongruous at first, perhaps, since it is dawn; but the
fact that the speaker can see the unimaginably distant but
nonetheless inevitable decline of the sun in its rising (just as
he can see at its beginning this volume's end, where "each
ascending sun / dives like a cooling meteorite to its fall") is
itself indicative of the extent to which he has moved beyond

the immediate moment and the consideration of himself. In just over three stanzas, Lowell has amplified his theme of personal frustration into one that could truly be termed "cosmic pessimism."

This line is, however, one of the instances in which a detail anticipates the development of the poem; indeed, it is not fully comprehensible until that development has taken place and is probably not fully appreciated until it has recurred in its other forms in the other poems in the book. The mainstream in this poem moves more slowly and inexorably toward a cosmic view, as Lowell goes on subtly but precisely telling the time and simultaneously extending his theme. If the third stanza is ostensibly concerned with the animal world, the fourth is devoted mostly to the world of commerce. "Business," in a passage that reverses the upward struggle of the salmon and travesties a psalm, "goes down to the sea in ships."[9] It is "in eclipse" not only in the ironic sense that it is poor, as the stereotypical businessman will claim at any time of the year, but also in the sense that it is still partly dark outside, and in the sense that the activity is sinful because it is taking place on Sunday. After a single introspective stanza (the fifth), which suspends the general movement of the poem, the speaker hears the call to the Protestant service, the "new electric bells" that incongruously chime "'Faith of our fathers'" and thus—like the pope's "electric razor" in "Beyond the Alps"—suggest both religion's divorce from its roots and its affinity with commerce.

The stanzas centered on religion are especially remarkable for their compression. On the one hand, in what is perhaps the most surprisingly managed section of the poem, Lowell again integrates the private and the public spheres:

> No, put old clothes on, and explore
> the corners of the woodshed for
> its dregs and dreck: tools with no handle,
> ten candle-ends not worth a candle,
> old lumber banished from the Temple,
> damned by Paul's precept and example,

cast from the kingdom, banned in Israel,
the wordless sign, the tinkling cymbal.

The past that he explores in vain is both the past of Western religion and his personal past. The first word is a repudiation of the Protestant heritage that he has previously described, some of the "old clothes" are those he wore when he was a Catholic and writing his earlier poetry, and the "woodshed" is a variation on the house symbol that recurs throughout his work and often, as here, represents that work and the traditions that it incorporates. The "dregs and dreck" that he finds in his first volumes or in his old beliefs or in the Old Testament are exemplified in the following lines, which might allude to such poems as "Colloquy in Black Rock," where Lowell also draws upon I Cor. 13, and "Where the Rainbow Ends," where Paul's parable of the olive tree in Rom. 11:17 figures prominently.[10] The personal and the public concerns are still associated, although more loosely, in the following stanza's description of the church's spire and flagpole that stick out

above the fog,
like old white china doorknobs, sad,
slight, useless things to calm the mad.

As it does continually in *Notebook 1967–68*, the fog on the town signifies the muzzy appearance of things to a speaker who considers himself befuddled; and the last words remind us of Lowell's confinements in McLean's at the same time that they suggest that in this world madness might be a common, rather than an aberrant, condition.[11]

If a consideration of religion is the vehicle for a review of the present state of his society and for a summary of the poet's own past, it is also a means of exploring the entire history of Western civilization in the climactic tenth stanza:

Hammering military splendor,
top-heavy Goliath in full armor—
little redemption in the mass
liquidations of their brass,
elephant and phalanx moving

> with the times and still improving,
> when that kingdom hit the crash:
> a million foreskins stacked like trash. . . .

This is the complete stanza, a good example of what critics mean by the fragmentary quality of this poetry. This "sentence" lacks not only a main verb but also any apparent link with the preceding stanza, so that even the subject is not immediately clear. Both the ambiguity and the solecism, however, are functional. Lowell is presenting an image of all of history as a "darkling plain" that is "swept with confused alarms of struggle and flight," and therefore it is suitable that the participants not be immediately identifiable. Identities are ascertainable upon inspection—the Philistines, the Catholics, the Carthaginians and the Romans, the Americans, and the Nazis and the Jews—but these are only representative groups anyway, for the point is precisely that history is a succession of victors become victims soon forgotten. Given such a continuously destructive process, the participle is more appropriate than the verb. The absence of a subject-verb construction, together with the earlier and later references to the poet's craft, also permits Lowell to criticize and parody his own poems, some of which he has described as being "like prehistoric monsters dragged down into the bog and death by their ponderous armor."[12]

Lowell's rhythms in this stanza imitate the hammering, brassy quality of a hymn being sung in the church, so that the chronological scheme is extended; and it is continued through the next stanza, where "Sing softer!" describes or anticipates the course of the hymn. This phrase provides another example of the condensation in this poem, for it constitutes the poet-speaker's plea for a period of peace, as well as advice to himself to initiate "a new / diminuendo." Accordingly, the following lines, in sharp contrast to the preceding approximation of "Onward Christian Soldiers," sound as much like Eliot in a meditative mood as tetrameter couplets can:

> no true
> tenderness, only restlessness,

excess, the hunger for success,
sanity of self-deception
fixed and kicked by reckless caution. . . .[13]

With the casual reference to "the bells" at the end of this stanza, Lowell indicates that, in the words of "Falling Asleep over the Aeneid," "Church is over."[14]

Randall Jarrell defined the theme of that earlier poem as "the terrible continuity of the world,"[15] and the same phrase might summarize the last stanzas of this one. By the next to the last of these, the perspective has been slightly altered again, so that religion, Western history, and contemporary politics all come into focus:

No weekends for the gods now. Wars
flicker, earth licks its open sores,
fresh breakage, fresh promotions, chance
assassinations, no advance.

The first sentence is appropriate because the situation is a Sunday that everywhere witnesses virulent corruption instead of peaceful worship, and the last lines guarantee that the future will be no different from the present than the present is from the past or Sunday is from the weekdays. The poem's concluding lines reiterate the familiar theme, but with an unexpected and significant addition:

peace to our children when they fall
in small war on the heels of small
war—until the end of time
to police the earth, a ghost
orbiting forever lost
in our monotonous sublime.

A parody of the benediction at the end of the church service, this passage is a comprehensive summary of those forces that prohibit radical freedom. It is typical of Lowell that the comprehensiveness is a result of several deliberate ambiguities, the most notable of which derive from the indefinite referent of the phrases following the dash. The grammatical uncertainty as to whether it is the "children" or the "small / war" that must "police the earth" produces an equation of the two possibilities; and while the future of man is thus identified with the future of war, the continuous police actions are identified with the orbiting of the sun by the earth. The necessity operative in human history, it is implied, is comparable to the necessity that controls the movements in the cosmos; individuals, nations, and planets are equally subject to antecedent causes that bring about their destruction. The "terrible continuity of the world" can thus be visualized either as concentric circles of oppressive forces or as an infinitely extensible line of catastrophic events. What happens in the poem, in effect, is that these spatial metaphors take the structural forms of a gradual widening of scope and an inexorable progression in time.

While it is true that this poem is "linear" and "open-ended,"[16] then, it is also true that it has a definite structure that embodies its theme. So far, however, that theme has been only partially stated, for according to the poem's last words—the unexpected addition noted above—the continuity of the world is "sublime" as well as terrible. Nor is that term as facetious as it might seem at first, for it is echoed without a hint of irony in later poems, including "The Ruins of Time," quoted earlier. Of course it is no more novel than it is fundamentally contradictory to claim that the world is filled with both "greatness and horror"—to borrow Lowell's phrase (in his prefatory note) for Rome—although that claim can be justification for accepting the conditions of life, as the speaker does in the opening stanzas. In the end, however, the lesson of Lowell's antisermon is not simply that one must accept the suffering and the horror along with the beauty and the greatness, but rather that the two are inextricable. Transposed into aesthetic terms, the paradox is that permanence is created only through transience. Lowell's chief means of embodying these paradoxes are two: to give time a structure, as he does over the course of this book as a whole by making its linear progression circular, and to use the linear progression of time itself as a structural framework, as he does in this first poem.

Besides having a structure of its own, this poem is a part of a larger scheme. The second poem, "Fourth of July in

Maine," complements the movement from morning to noon
in the first as it moves from "High noon" to evening; "The
Opposite House" is a meditation at night; "Central Park," as
though to balance "Fourth of July in Maine" even as it continues the general progression, opens with some unspecified
time in the day and ends with the beginning of another night;
and "Near the Ocean," the concluding poem in this sequence, is the second entirely nocturnal poem, where we
meet with "the creatures of the night" just glimpsed in "Waking Early Sunday Morning." The dominant setting in these
poems, it will be noticed, is night, just as the dominant mood
is a dark one. One cannot help thinking of a passage in
"Fourth of July in Maine":

> New England, everywhere I look,
> old letters crumble from the Book,
> China trade rubble, one more line
> unravelling from the dark design
> spun by God and Cotton Mather. . . .

The poet too is spinning a "dark design"; indeed, the ruin he
sees about him is part and parcel *of* that design, which ultimately involves not only this sequence and this book but all
of Lowell's poetry. What Lowell says of God and Cotton
Mather one would say of Lowell.

As one section of the whole design, the title sequence of
Near the Ocean shares structural features with most of the
volumes previously examined, and the most important of
these is probably the motif. The first two lines in "Fourth of
July in Maine," for instance, end with "Independence" and
"innocence," and the rhyme yokes those two qualities whose
loss is again their real common denominator and the subject
of the poem. A potentially positive aspect of the fall from
freedom and innocence, intimated in the last word of the first
poem ("sublime"), appears here in conjunction with the
house symbol, which is again associated with tradition and
poetry:

> This white Colonial frame house,
> willed downward, Dear, from you to us,

> still matters—the Americas'
> best artifact produced en masse.
> The founders' faith was in decay,
> and yet their building seems to say:
> "Every time I take a breath,
> my God you are the air I breathe."

In the fifth line Lowell says both that the religious faith of his ancestors was decaying when the Winslow house was built and that they believed in decay, the transience of all things;[17] and yet the house not only stands but also seems to stand for, to express a belief in, an immanent deity. Presumably both the lapse from faith and the faith itself, as well as the belief in mutability and the belief in at least some sort of permanence, are also strains in the poet's heritage. In other words, his own creation or "building" seems to embody exactly what the "frame house"—an "artifact" itself embodies: an expression of faith in decay that itself endures.

The idea that the poet's dedication to his task is one meaningful response to the flux of history becomes crucial in the last section of *Near the Ocean*. This early in the volume, there are few such positive passages, and this one obviously contains its own "Blue twinges of mortality." The house has been "willed downward" not only in the sense that it has been left to another generation but also in the sense that it has fallen into less capable hands. Like the tradition that it represents here, the house has deteriorated. Lowell formulates the decline of the House of Winslow, dealt with earlier in "Soft Wood," in these lines later in the poem:

> Your house, still outwardly in form
> lasts, though no emissary come
> to watch the garden running down,
> or photograph the propped-up barn.

Toward the end of this poem, as in its predecessor, Lowell's theme expands to encompass the history of the world, but the house is never abandoned. In a passage that echos the bitter pronouncement in "Eye and Tooth" that "Even new life is fuel," Lowell writes:

> And here in your converted barn,
> we burn our hands a moment, borne
> by energies that never tire
> of piling fuel on the fire. . . .[18]

The "energies" are of course those of the life-force, but the
latter is ultimately indistinguishable from the fire, the death-
force, as the concluding stanza makes clear:

> We watch the logs fall. Fire once gone,
> we're done for. . . .
> . . . .
> Great ash and sun of freedom, give
> us this day the warmth to live,
> and face the household fire. We turn
> our backs, and feel the whiskey burn.

The parody of the Lord's Prayer underscores the irony of the
celebration of Independence Day. The speaker and his family
are dependent for their lives upon the very forces that will
destroy them. The sun is this poem's equivalent of the "simmer of rot and renewal" in *For the Union Dead*, and it has its
mirror image in "the household fire" that also eventually
"cinders like the soul."

Lowell's motif recurs in "The Opposite House," the least
ambitious poem in his title sequence. Both the symbolic
house and the literal situation are ambiguous; and although it
has been suggested that the "abandoned police stable" is on
fire, it seems more likely that some gruesome crime, probably
murder, has just been committed in a slum, probably Puerto
Rican, and that the speaker is watching the police try to con-
duct an investigation and control the crowd that has
gathered. It would be ironically appropriate that the crime
was committed on grounds belonging to the police depart-
ment, since the common denominator of lawlessness and
oppressive authority is violence. ("A violent order is disorder," Stevens says in "Connoisseur of Chaos.") That the
police are oppressive is surely the point of the pun on
"crooked" and the incongruous references to the rosary in
these lines:

> A stringy policeman is crooked
> in the doorway, one hand on his revolver.
> He counts his bullets like beads.

The house seems to be "opposite," then, both in the sense that it is *en face* and in the sense that it is the symbolic opposite of Harriet Winslow's "converted barn." Instead of guinea pigs, "little pacific things," this old stable once housed horses that are now used in conjunction with an "armed car, / plodding slower than a turtle" to force the crowd to the curb.

Incomplete though it is, this third poem in the sequence succeeds in becoming more than a fragment simply "luminous / with heraldry and murder" itself partly because it transcends the specific occasion, because the observation has been converted into a symbol that takes its place in the constellation of this sequence. When Lowell says, rather strangely, that the stable is "like some firework to be fired / at the end of the garden party," he recalls the images of "the household fire" in "Fourth of July in Maine" and restates in a condensed form a view characteristically colored by religious symbolism.[19]

Both the equation of the lawless and the authoritarian and that of the existential present and the eschatological future reappear in "Central Park," which ends with a different sort of plea from "Fourth of July in Maine":

> Old Pharaohs starving in your foxholes,
> . . . .
> all your plunder and gold leaf
> only served to draw the thief . . .
>
> We beg delinquents for our life.
> Behind each bush, perhaps a knife;
> each landscaped crag, each flowering shrub,
> hides a policeman with a club.

In working backward from the omnipresent "policeman" through the "delinquents" to the "thief" who is both the Egyptian grave robber and the Biblical "thief in the night," one can trace Lowell's metaphoric connections: perverted authority is as evil as the forces authority was established to control, the forces that direct our lives are therefore compounded instead of reduced, and consequently our lives consist of continual infringements on our freedom, with death being the infringement to end all others.

Another way to put the same ideas is to say that life, the only opportunity for freedom, is an incarceration and therefore a death. This is the way that Lowell put them as early and as late as "In the Cage," which first appeared in *Lord Weary's Castle* and was to be reprinted in *Notebook 1967–68* and its descendants, and he uses virtually the same metaphor in these lines on a lion in the Central Park Zoo:

> Drugged and humbled by the smell
> of zoo-straw mixed with animal,
> the lion prowled his slummy cell,
> serving his life-term in jail—
> glaring, grinding, on his heel,
> with tingling step and testicle. . . .

Since the speaker, like his precursor in "Skunk Hour," is also on the prowl, "gasping at game-scents like a dog" and half-enviously, half-cynically spying on the lovers, the lion is a rather obvious projection of himself. Just as in the opening poem of this sequence, he is seeking a means to "break loose"; but the "single, fluttery, paper kite" alone escapes the earth (only to go "where the light of the sun had failed"), while he, in effect "a snagged balloon," remains.

The "life-term" is a universal sentence, as is indicated not only by the pun on that phrase but also by the descriptions of "the lovers" and "the rich." The "anatomy" of each of the lovers is "trapped" by life as well as by another lover, and the ironic allusion to the twenty-third Psalm in these lines is proof that none of them is better off than the speaker:

> All wished to leave this drying crust,
> borne on the delicate wings of lust
> like bees, and cast their fertile drop
> into the overwhelming cup.

The "drying crust" seems to be at once the body, the park,

and the earth, while the "overwhelming cup" is death, the All, the Ocean of the book's title. [20] As far as anyone gets from the "drying crust," however, is the "dripping rock" of the third strophe, and behind it there is a deserted kitten, whose "deprived, weak, ignorant and blind" condition is a pathetic exaggeration of the "fear and poverty" that stigmatizes each of the lovers. The "poverty" is more spiritual than economical, for later comes "the night—the jungle hour, / the rich in his slit-windowed tower. . . ." Because of the insinuation that he shares the lion's fate, the rich man might as well be confined in an oubliette or in the Tower of London, awaiting execution.

Both the "tower" and the "cell" are variations on the house symbol, which takes a new form in the opening lines of the title poem of the sequence, "Near the Ocean":

> The house is filled. The last heartthrob
> thrills through her flesh. The hero stands,
> stunned by the applauding hands,
> and lifts her head to please the mob . . .
> No, young and starry-eyed, the brother
> and sister wait before their mother,
> old iron-bruises, powder. . . .

In these extremely difficult lines, "The house" is apparently a theater in which Lowell imagines, first, some unknown play involving Perseus and Medusa and, second, a scene out of the *Oresteia*. This reading seems more reasonable as soon as we realize that the "E. H. L." to whom the poem is dedicated is the poet's second wife, Elizabeth Hardwick Lowell, who, among other pursuits, writes criticism of drama.

This realization, however, entails other, but unavoidable, difficulties, which begin with the pronoun "her" as it is used in the second and fourth lines. The first of these might conceivably refer to the speaker's wife as she watches the climax of a play, but the second would not seem to be at all applicable, and therefore one tends to think that the referent of both pronouns is Medusa (or Clytemnestra). One tends to think so, at least, until the last lines of this poem addressed to the poet's wife:

A hand, your hand then! I'm afraid
to touch the crisp hair on your head—
Monster loved for what you are,
till time, that buries us, lay bare.

Whatever suspicions one had at first that Lowell was making
a composite of Medusa, Clytemnestra, and Ms. Hardwick
cannot be allayed by talk of the obscure or the outré in view
of these lines. The penultimate unequivocally addresses the
poet's second wife as a sort of "Terrible Mother."[21]

What sense can be made, then, of that initial stanza? Some
light can be shed on it by remembering that Lowell's indirect
subject is frequently his own work, that the "house" often
symbolizes that work, and that "Near the Ocean" is the fifth
act in the title production. The first four lines of that stanza
seem to caricature a potential version of this last poem itself,
for here, perhaps thinking in the same vein as he was earlier
when he described himself as hungry for success, Lowell
does in effect hold his wife up to public scrutiny. In the following lines, however, Lowell "rejects" this version of the
poem and offers a second model in terms of which the
speaker is comparable to Orestes and his wife to Clytemnestra and, in order to stress her ambiguous nature, to Elect-
ra. This myth will not do either, however, since Orestes did
kill his mother, and at the same time that he hints that
Orestes' punishment is his ("his treadmill heart will never
rest"), Lowell fades out into ellipses in the second stanza and
leaves the impression that he is revising his second model.
The last "revision" is effected in the lines from the final stanza, quoted above, in which Lowell-Orestes-Perseus accepts
Hardwick-Clytemnestra-Medusa for what she cannot but be.

Within these boundaries, the poem endeavors to modulate
the classical past, with its "radiance" and its heroes, into the
present, with its "neon light" and its drunks, with "Betrayals" as the constant factors and some small consolation as the
object. At times, it seems that Lowell will be successful, as in
the second stanza, where "The severed radiance filters back, /
athirst for nightlife." The light and dark imagery and the
implicit use of the theatrical situation blend past and present

here, where the "severed radiance" is that of the classical world, revived on the stage (presumably in a production of Aeschylus), and where the "nightlife" is in the theater or in the more sordid settings presented in later stanzas. Again, in the oblique description of the first of what seem to be adulteries:

> Betrayals! Was it the first night?
> They stood against a black and white
> inland New England backdrop. No dogs
> there, horse or hunter, only frogs
> chirring from the dark trees and swamps.
> Elms watching like extinguished lamps.

By moving the presumably autobiographical events onto a stage, the imagery connects them and those of mythology and keeps the lines from being simply confessional. Lowell associates present and past directly but effectively in another couplet: "Sand built the lost Atlantis . . . sand, / Atlantic ocean, condoms, sand." The identical rhyme and the repetition of other words epitomize the redundance of history's conjunction of the ugly and the sublime.

On the whole, however, the four personal vignettes stand apart from the visionary and symbolistic sections of the poem, and consequently the present does not seem as continuous with the past as it is in the first poems in the sequence. In fact, Lowell seems to posit a disjunction of the two in the first lines of the last stanza:

> Sleep, sleep. The ocean, grinding stones,
> can only speak the present tense;
> nothing will age, nothing will last,
> or take corruption from the past.

His point, however, is that the ocean *always* speaks the present tense, that erosion and destruction are themselves continuous, that "life is much the same."

This is also one theme in the imitations that Lowell includes in *Near the Ocean*. Even as the first of them, entitled "Spring" and based on Horace, signifies a new beginning, mutability is its central theme.[22] Lowell goes out of his way to heighten the *carpe diem* element in this poem and to lend the description of spring a violence that seems to foretell its own passing. Instead of Horace's "caput impedire" ("to garland our heads"), for example, he has "to tear the blossoms from the bough"; and where Horace's sacrifice takes place "in umbrosis" ("in shady woods"), Lowell's occurs in "the green and bursting woods." In the last lines, Lowell virtually parts with his original in order to particularize and therefore to emphasize the theme of loss:

> Sestius, soon, soon, you will not rush to beat
> the dice and win the lordship of the feast,
> or tremble for the night's fatiguing joys,
> sleepless for this child, then for that one—boys
> soon lost to man, soon lost to girls in heat.

The third and fourth lines are Lowell's own additions, as are the urgent repetitions in the first and the last.

The alterations of the Latin are fewer and less radical in "Serving under Brutus," but even the least noticeable changes accentuate the theme of transience. Where the Latin is merely "ciboria" ("goblets" or "cups"), Lowell has "frail goblets," and where in the following line the original is simply "conchis," the translation is "fragile shells." These details, no less than the background of the defeat at Philippi against which this poem is set, anticipate the end of the feast at its very beginning. The ironic juxtaposition of temporary joy and imminent destruction informs both detail and structure in "Cleopatra," the last poem derived from Horace. In at least two places, Lowell revises his original to condense the opposites of life and death into a phrase, as though to exemplify their intimacy. Horace wrote:

> dum Capitolio
> regina dementes ruinas,
> funus et imperio parabat
>
> (against the Capital
> a demented queen was plotting ruin
> and destruction of the Empire. . . .)

Lowell compresses the idea, writing that Cleopatra "plotted /

to enthrone her ruin in the Capitol," and thereby implies that kingdom and ruin go hand in hand. Near the end of the poem, Horace describes Cleopatra as

> fortis et asperas
> tractare serpentes, ut atrum
> corpore combiberet venenum,
>
> deliberata morte ferocior. . . .

Lowell's beautifully succinct description is:

> Then bolder, more ferocious,
> death slipping through your fingers. . . .

Because that participial phrase is commonly used in connection with the loss of the most desired things in life, Lowell's use of "death" as subject implicitly identifies life, transience, and death; and at the same time, it perhaps suggests that Cleopatra's death itself was lost in the immortal manner in which she met it.

The structure of this poem also embodies the theme of transience. Lowell's imitation opens with sharp, staccato rhythms perfectly suited to the bacchanalian celebration after the defeat of Antony and Cleopatra:

> Now's the time to drink,
> to beat the earth in rhythm,
> toss flowers on the couches of the gods,
> Friends!

Then it moves into the past, recounts Cleopatra's capture in a section that shows Lowell to be highly skilled in the use of such rhetorical devices as traductio and anaphora, and concludes in a grand meditative manner that testifies to the queen's regality and constitutes a miniature elegy. That this movement from victorious celebration to dignified defeat summarizes, not the necessary course of life and empire, but the best possible course, is one implication of Juvenal's *Tenth Satire*, which Lowell translates under the same title that Dr. Johnson used.

"The Vanity of Human Wishes," the title of which represents the ironic response to the expressed desire to "break loose" from the imprisoning conditions of life, both extends the main concern of *Near the Ocean* and provides one reason for the special structure of this volume. In his introductory note, Lowell says disingenuously that "how one jumps from Rome to the America of my own poems is something of a mystery to me"; but the implication of the volume's structure is surely that Lowell sees America's future in the past, in the fall of Rome, just as Juvenal saw the future of Rome in the past. Simple apposition of sections on America and Rome would doubtless be sufficient to suggest this analogy, but Lowell's arrangement of his poems is designed to establish the connection firmly. For one thing, the imitations, united by the theme of "the greatness and horror" of the empire and focused on the destruction of the empire, follow the originals, and spatial succession in a book naturally suggests chronological succession. For another, within the section of imitations the poems are ordered chronologically, with the exception that Quevedo (1530–1645) precedes Góngora (1561–1627), so that in the sequence of authors there is implicit the passage of eras. In short, whether one views the volume in two parts and finds a single *de casibus* structure or examines the last half and discovers a succession of civilizations, he will see exactly how Lowell "jumps" from America to Rome.

After the imitation of Juvenal, another element enters into the organization of these poems, and to neglect mention of it would be to distort Lowell's view of things as implied by this book. This new element is perhaps suggested just by the canto that Lowell chooses to translate from the *Inferno*, for he turns from the comprehensive historical perspective of Juvenal to Dante's sympathetic portrait of a single poet, Brunetto Latini, as though to intimate that the poet can successfully challenge the process that eradicates civilizations. Ser Brunetto's last words, and the commentary on them, constitute the volume's most explicit statement yet of the potential to endure of any human production:

> "Give
> me no pity. Read my *Tesoro*. In

my book, my treasure, I am still alive."
Then he turned back and he seemed one of those
who run for the green cloth through the green field
at Verona . . . and seemed more like the one
who wins the roll of cloth than those who lose.

If it is accidental that this last line's denial that Ser Brunetto
has lost seems a counterweight to the last line of "Spring"
with its redoubled loss, the accident is nevertheless indicative
of the affirmation eked out at the end of *Near the Ocean*. Less
explicitly, the claim about the durability of the word is made
in the triplet that concludes the second imitation of Quevedo:

O Rome! From all your palms, dominions, bronze
and beauty, what was firm has fled. What once
was fugitive maintains its permanence.

The first of the Góngora imitations is much more straightforward:

This vault
seals up the earth of those who never felt
the earth's oppression. Whose? If you would know,
stand back and study this inscription. Words
give marble meaning and a voice to bronze.

This "vault" might as well be the one that holds the "treasure" that Ser Brunetto mentions, for it is also the book that
bears the poet's "inscription" and that Lowell identifies in his
next volume with his "coffin." In other words, because the
poet's life ("What once / was fugitive") is his poetry (which
"maintains its permanence"), in living he is making the one
monument that just might stand up under the erosion of
time, the terrible redundance of the Ocean's waves.

Another image that signifies the transition from Ser
Brunetto's *Tesoro* to Lowell's next work occurs, characteristically, in the final poem in this volume:

The whistling arrow flies less eagerly,
and bites the bull's-eye less ferociously;
the Roman chariot grinds less hurriedly
the arena's docile sand, and rounds the goal. . . .

The race in this loose translation of Góngora looks back to the race that Dante's figure ran.[23] Indeed, these lines look back much farther than that, through "the rat-race in the arena" in the last poem in *Imitations* and the "arena" in which Santayana died wielding his "red crayon" in *Life Studies* to the "red arrow on this graph / Of Revelations" in the last poem in *Lord Weary's Castle*. By virtue of the reference to rounding the goal, they look forward to the *Notebooks* and *History*, where "the round" is a crucial symbol. There is of course no determining how much farther into the future these lines look, but the reference to failing energy has to be regarded as a conventional, rather than a candid, confession. Lowell's *Notebooks* and *History* evince more expense of energy than the complete works of many poets. And that is only partly because, in a sense that is not simply symbolic, each of them, but especially *History*, is a complete works.

und ein Gesetz ist
Dass alles hineingeht, Schlangen gleich,
Prophetisch, träumend auf
Den Hügeln des Himmels.
—HÖLDERLIN, "Erntezeit"

an arabesque, imperfect and alive,
a hundred hues of green, the darkest shades
short of black, the palest leaf-backs far from white. . . .
—"Stalin"

8

IN THE ROUND:

The *Notebooks* (1969, 1970)

y now it is clear that one of the distinctive features of Lowell's work ever since his first volume has been its tendency to press against the boundaries of the poem, to expand into the space beyond the lyric. As the preceding chapters have indicated, this expansion has made the individual poems increasingly vulnerable to the charges of incompleteness and fragmentation. Perhaps one of the reasons that these criticisms have been advanced is that the creation of the larger frameworks is not as immediately apparent as the loosening of the organization of the poems; or perhaps it is that, in spite of the larger schemes, the poems have seemed sufficiently discrete to warrant tighter structures, although little enough attention has been given to the organizations of the sequences and volumes. In either case, with the publication of *Notebook 1967–68*, Lowell's scope has enlarged to the extent that the old criticisms hardly seem pertinent. As in the cases of its successors, *Notebook* and *History*, judgments on the poems included in this volume are almost irrelevant to an evaluation of the book precisely because they are only parts of a whole and so clearly subordinate to that whole that if it did not suggest indifference to art, the term *entries* might be preferable to *poems*.

The terminological problem is even evident in Lowell's "Afterthought" in *Notebook 1967–68*, which is of course the place to begin a discussion of this book.[1] In a trenchant introductory paragraph, Lowell writes as follows:

NOTEBOOK 1967–68: as my title intends, the *poems* in this book are written as *one poem*, jagged in pattern, but not a conglomeration or sequence of related material. It is not a chronicle or almanac; many events turn up, many others of equal or greater reality do not. This is not my diary, my confession, not a puritan's too literal pornographic honesty, glad to share private embarrassment, and triumph. The time is a summer, an autumn, a winter, a spring, another summer; here *the poem* ends, except for turned-back bits of fall and winter 1968. I have flashbacks to what I remember, and notes on old history. My plot rolls with the seasons. The *separate poems and sections* are opportunist and inspired by impulse. Accident threw up the subjects, and the plot swallowed them—famished for human chances. [Italics added.][2]

The equivocation on "poem" reveals at once the distinction between this volume and several of the others discussed above. Like all of Lowell's books from *Life Studies* on, *Notebook 1967–68* is an organized whole; but unlike the other books, this one is enough of a piece to be called a single poem. While this identification of book and poem is the nearly predictable culmination of the experiments with larger structures, it raises in the most uncompromising form the problem of how to understand and evaluate what Lowell unhelpfully refers to as his "separate poems and sections."

It is clear, however, that there are at least three levels on which this book might be discussed: that of the individual "poems," of which there are 279; that of the "sections," which range from one to seventeen poems in length and which total fifty-eight if each capitalized title in the table of contents denominates a section; and that of the "one poem, jagged in pattern." One reason that Lowell finds it necessary or convenient to refer to "separate poems" is obvious at a glance: all of them are fourteen lines long and all but a few are in blank verse. In spite of his prohibition of the term "sequence," it is difficult not to think that Lowell is writing in the shade of the venerable tradition that originated in English with the Elizabethans; and his comment a few paragraphs later that he fears that he has "failed to avoid the themes and the gigantism of the sonnet"[3] can only justify those thoughts. Nevertheless, there is little attempt on his part to adopt or discover a consistent syntactical or thematic structure within the fourteen-line blank verse format, and therefore there is little practical advantage in regarding his form as a variation on the sonnet.

The one qualification to the statement that the poems do not have a consistent formula is that they frequently build toward a one-line or two-line conclusion. Sometimes the concluding lines are the emotional climax of a poem, as in two of the poems in "Through the Night":

> She rides the hood and snuffs the smog of twilight:
> "I want to live," she screams, "where I can see."

> before he sprang, his sword
> unable to encircle the circle of his killers.

Sometimes the conclusion is also an epitome, as in the first poem in "Randall Jarrell: 1914–1965," where Lowell returns to the theme of "The Lesson" and other poems in *For the Union Dead:*

> Randall, the same fall splinters on the windshield,
> the same apples wizen on the whiplash bough.

The other uses to which Lowell puts this concluding unit are admirably various. He often fixes some recollected snatch of conversation with it, as when he quotes John Crowe Ransom on the "primitive African" nations ("Munich 1938"):

> John saying, "Well, they may not have been good neighbors, but they never troubled the rest of the world."

Or Ford Madox Ford on Robert Lowell:

> "If he fails as a writer," Ford wrote my father, "at least he'll be Ambassador to England, or President of Harvard."

Or William Carlos Williams on himself:

> And saying, "I am sixty-seven, and more
> attractive to girls than when I was seventeen."

Lowell also takes advantage of his last lines to exercise his epigrammatic talent:

> Old age is all right, but it has no future.

> this the sum of the world's scattered elements—
> fame, a bouquet in the niche of forgetfulness!

> This whirlwind, this delirium of Eros—
> winds fed the fire, a wind can blow it out.

> It's not the crowds, but crowding kills the soul.

As several of these examples suggest, the concluding lines are frequently in a regular iambic pentameter, but Lowell also saves some of his finest metrical improvisations for the last. "Alba," for instance, concludes on three monosyllables whose successive stresses drive the point home in a manner reminiscent of Keats's refrain in "La Belle Dame sans Merci":

> Nothing more established, pure and lonely,
> than the early Sunday morning in New York—
> the sun on high burning, and most cars dead.

In one of the poems in the "Long Summer" section, the last line swirls by like a river with a fast current:

> Who can help us from our nothing to the all,
> we aging downstream faster than a scepter can check?

Both of these quotations also exemplify the tendency of Lowell's conclusions to be slightly flat; and this flatness is the appropriate punctuation, one imagines, in a world as discordant as Lowell's. "End of the Saga" concludes:

> The king is laughing, all his men are killed,
> he is shaken by the news, as well he might be.

In short, one comes to look forward to the ends of these poems in the way that one anticipates the conclusions of sonnets by Sidney or Shakespeare; but partly because Lowell does not avail himself of the framework of rhyme, he has no means of deploying image or argument that is analogous to those of the English poets.[4] In only a few poems, such as this second one in "Randall Jarrell: 1914–1965," does Lowell's structure (which is not to say form) resemble those of more traditional sonnets:

> Grizzling up the embers of our onetime life,
> our first intoxicating disenchantments,
> dipping our hands once, twice, in the same river,
> entrained for college on the Ohio local;
> the scene shifts, middle distance, back and foreground,
> things changing position like chessmen on a wheel,
> drawn by a water buffalo, perhaps
> blue with true space before the dawn of days—
> then the night of the caged squirrel on its wheel:
> lights, eyes, peering at you from the overpass;
> black-gloved, black-coated, you plod out stubbornly,
> as if asleep, Child Randall, as if in chainstep,
> meeting the cars, and approving; with harsh
> luminosity grasping at the blank coin of the tunnel.

Behind these lines, brought into sharper focus by the syntactical units, there is the ghost of a structure consisting of three quatrains and a couplet. The first four lines deal with the youth of Jarrell and Lowell at Kenyon College; the next four concern the passing of time and perhaps the approach of middle age; the next four and a part of the fifth bring the time and the poem up to the night of Jarrell's death, which might also be a dark night of the soul, as both the image of "the caged squirrel" and the possibility that Jarrell was a suicide suggest; and the last line and a fraction, remarkable for the chiaroscuro that suppresses any direct reference to impact or noise, convert the poet's last second into a universal emblem of death.

While its approximation of the structure of a Shakespearean sonnet is not characteristic, other features of this poem are.[5] The elliptical and even ungrammatical syntax, sometimes much more frustrating than here, is one of the stylistic traits of these poems that suggest their affinity with those in *Near the Ocean* and seem to have rather dark philosophical implications. If an orderly syntax is indeed a projection of a view of the universe as a harmonious whole, a tortuous, fragmented syntax suggests the opposite, and in his most recent books Lowell seems almost to have developed a prejudice against the complete sentence. In at least this case, however, the syntax seems adapted to the particulars under consideration, and those particulars point not so much to a chaotic universe as to a deterministic one. The poem is technically all one sentence, so that Jarrell's death is linked directly with his youth, "as if in chainstep," even though thirty years of his life and several lines of this poem separate the two. The repeated participial phrases accent the theme of transience, a theme that receives ironic expression in the allusion to Heraclitus, who said that one cannot step twice in the same river. To abridge the points, the continuity of life is to be found in loss. Things are always "changing position" and actions are therefore ultimately as indistinguishable and as futile as those of a "caged squirrel" on a treadmill. Both the chessmen on their wheel and the squirrel on its wheel suggest the control of life by antecedent causes and the consequent pointlessness of it all; "the scene shifts" and the end of the shifting is certain.

That last quotation is one of only two main clauses in the poem, though, and if we hold that Lowell's syntax is significant here, it should be noted that the other clause is "you plod out stubbornly." If the inexorable shifting of scenes is that over which man has no control, the stubborn plodding testifies to his volition, and the poem appears less strictly deterministic than it might have at first glance. Moreover, Jarrell is characterized not only as stubborn but also as "approving" of his death and perhaps of the whole chain of events leading to it. At the end of the poem, at the end of his life, Jarrell is envisioned in a "harsh / luminosity" that is probably more than the glare of the oncoming headlights that struck him down; and since "the blank coin" suggests a planchet, a disk that has yet to be stamped as a coin, the connotations of a beginning attach even to this end. In other words, this conclusion is ambiguous enough not to contradict Lowell's description of himself in "My Death" as "lacking half-way to atheist" or his adaptation of the Nietzschean doctrine of "eternal return" in "Obit."

Jarrell is one of a host of writers who turn up in *Notebook 1967-68*—there is one sequence called "Writers"—and that feature signifies the growing importance of poetry as a subject matter for Lowell. It is the explicit subject of "We Do What We Are," a shorter, more compact, and denser sequence than several in this volume, in which the fact of transience, the possibility of permanence, and the necessity of plodding stubbornly out are again the main concerns. It is probably not accidental that the title of this sequence is rather Stevensian, because its themes and techniques often recall Stevens, too. From its title through the quotation of Valéry and the approval of the mutable nature of things to the imagery and the complex of puns in the last lines, "The Nihilist as Hero" is especially reminiscent of the other American poet. Lowell gives a couple of unexpected twists to the words of Valéry, which he quotes as:

> "All our French poets can turn an inspired line,
> but which has written six passable in sequence?"

Lowell assails this rhetorical question, one of the least encouraging expressions of the poetics founded on *le mot juste*, in no uncertain terms:

> That was a happy day for Satan . . .
> One wants words meat-hooked from the living steer—
> but the cold flame of tinfoil licks the metal log,
> it's the beautifully unchanging fire of childhood;
> it betrays monotony of vision.

It was a happy day for Satan presumably because Valéry's comment implies the virtual impossibility of perfection, on the one hand, and the necessity of writing very little in the search for perfection on the other.[6] While Lowell is willing to admit the ineluctability of the vision of the perfect poem that one has in youth, he maintains too that the poet should seek, not the cold inevitability of *le mot juste*, but rather the vital and possibly violent and repulsive language of life. Against Valéry's demand for finer art, Lowell sets his demand for more evidence of life. The very image of "words meat-hooked from the living steer" has at once a repugnant power and a certain imprecision that exemplify his desideratum; and the following lines, so difficult to relate directly to those that precede and follow, seem to flaunt their intransigency in the face of the phrase " 'six passable in sequence.' "

The justification for Lowell's insistence that poetry must accommodate the rawness of experience is suggested in the following lines:

> Life by definition must breed on change,
> each season we scrap old cars and wars and women.

Unless one takes them as a superficial aphorism, those lines are difficult, but they involve an identification of life and poetry that is in effect a rationale for the volume. If change is the essence of life, and if life is what one wants in poetry, poetry must somehow embody mutability. At this point in the poem, although it is not yet obvious, Lowell is anticipating his quibble on Valéry's " 'passable,' " which for the French poet was an understatement for something like "flawless" and for Lowell is also synonymous with "transient." Because the transient is imperfect, it is desirable that one's poems be flawed, that the poet be willing to "scrap" them; and it is desirable because imperfection, unlike the "cold flame" of the vision of the perfect poem, is reproductive. Nevertheless, the next lines suggest that Lowell is unwilling to view the opposing terms that he has established as irreconcilable:

> But sometimes when I am ill or delicate,
> the pinched flame of my match turns living green,
> the cornstalk in green tails and seeded tassel. . . .

These lines bring together images that have been opposed before: the "flame" that was "cold" becomes a "living green," a green like that of the mature corn that reproduces itself. Whether these lines succeed in exemplifying a union of the imperfect, fertile life and the vision of perfection is a matter that must probably be left to individual judgment, but that such a union is their subject seems clear enough. As usual, Lowell is not content to choose when the road divides before him; he is determined somehow to take both branches at once. The same determination informs the concluding lines of the poem:

Only a nihilist desires the world
to be as it is, or much more passable.[7]

"More passable" here means either "more changeable," on the assumption that change is the staple of life, or "more perfect," on Valéry's assumption that one must aim for impeccable poetry, or both; and the conjunction "or" indicates either apposition, in that the world is "more passable," or more quickly lost, than Valéry seemed to realize, or opposition, in that the world could be much more perfect than it is, or both. On the basis of the first meaning of each term, the nihilist is a "Hero" because he desires the very metamorphosis of things that reduces him and his works to nothing. He is heroic on the basis of the second meanings because he wants the impossible substitution of perfection for imperfection. Perhaps in the final analysis he is the hero because he can desire apparently contradictory conditions and even assert—as Lowell does here—their coexistence.

"The Nihilist as Hero," like many of these poems, retains certain crucial ambiguities even after close analysis. As this poem attests, the reader's difficulties are due not only to elliptical syntax, and not only to the attempt to encompass contradictory ideas in a small space, but also to the tangential relationship among successive thoughts. Instead of going at his subjects systematically or organizing their parts so that they seem to have been approached systematically, Lowell often gives his tangents their heads and seems to create his subjects as he goes along, much as one might expect, in fact, in a notebook.[8] This tendency to indulge seemingly peripheral concerns, to circle the chief concern, is probably most troublesome within individual poems, but it is primarily characteristic of the sequences. Even in a sequence as brief and apparently restricted in scope as "We Do What We Are," it is not always easy to imagine the means by which Lowell got or would have us get from one poem to another.

"Grave Guild" seems most closely related to the foregoing

poem by virtue of the *sic transit* theme, suggested here by the
gathering at a reading of a group of poets who are "out of
style" and formulated in the phrase "Six hands on the dusty
bust of the microphone." At the same time, the last lines of
this poem, which are obviously the most important, do not
seem to have any direct bearing on the preceding poem:

> "Read us your great collage, or something old,
> since nothing dead is alien to our tongue."
> O Weathercock made to face both ways! I read;
> by some oversight not a word is I—
> two O's for eyes in an O for the face of an I. . . .

Again there are certain obstinate problems—it is unclear, for
example, whether the penultimate line means that Lowell
read the work of someone else, or that he read his own work
and substituted the third-person for the first-person pronouns, or that his own poetry did not seem to be his, although the latter seems most likely—but the general import is
decipherable and amounts to an equation of "O" and "I." If
the "'great collage'" is this book and if "'something old'"
refers to Lowell's earlier work, then "both ways" would seem
to be the past and the future, and the "O" would seem to be
the poet's image for the eternal vacancy of the present, a
placeholder between dead past and feared future. Combined
with the reference to the "Weathercock," the "O's" might
also suggest a spiritual vertigo produced by concentration
upon past and future, future and past. If that interpretation
seems needlessly elaborate, one can read the last lines simply
as an expression of the feeling of the effacement of the individual by eternity and infinity. In any event, Lowell is certainly indicating that the self might be a negligible entity; but
except for the continuation of the general theme of mutability, this poem still does not appear closely related to the first
one.

   Some more light can be shed on both the "O" symbol and
the connection between these two poems by the third, "Reading Myself," which quite naturally follows the description of
the poetry reading.[9] The first few lines of this poem develop
the flame motif initiated in "The Nihilist as Hero" and thus

exemplify one rather ordinary means by which Lowell links poems within his sequences; but the last lines, which are in effect if not in intent a triumphant response to Valéry's challenge, are by far the most interesting in the poem and among the finest in the volume:

> No honeycomb is built without a bee
> adding circle to circle, cell to cell,
> the wax and honey of a mausoleum—
> this round dome proves its maker is alive,
> the corpse of such insect lives preserved in honey,
> prays that the perishable work live long
> enough for the sweet-tooth bear to desecrate—
> this open book . . . my open coffin.

In view of the circles in this delineation of Lowell's own work, the "O's" of "Grave Guild" might be the same poetic elements—paradoxes or poems or, better, both; and Lowell would then see them instead of "eyes" or "I's" in the mirror of his work because he is his poetry. If the idea that "We Do What We *Are*" implies a basis for the rejection of Valéry's temptation to seek perfection, the notion that "We *Do* What We Are" allows a belief in the insignificance of the self that at least permits some recompense. Moreover, the first two poems in this sequence, both of them circular, although in different senses, can now be viewed as parts of a whole, not necessarily intimately related, but rather adjacent cells in a honeycomblike structure that is immediately this book, eventually the oeuvre—and one remembers that the emblem of St. Bernard of Clairvaux is a beehive—and at every point the man himself.

To understand the variegated, honeycombed whole that its author claims *Notebook 1967–68* is, one need only move in his circles. In the paragraph quoted earlier, Lowell provides us with a rough sketch of this book's circular organization; the structure that he outlines bears a family resemblance to those of *Lord Weary's Castle*, *Imitations*, and *For the Union Dead* in that all of these volumes end very near where they begin. *Notebook 1967–68* recalls *Imitations* in particular because here again Lowell not only describes a circle but makes the end

and the beginning overlap. This volume begins in one summer and then ends in the next, so that the cycle is not only
completed once but begun again, exactly as in the imitation of
Pasternak called "The Seasons," except that the latter poem
begins and ends with spring. Moreover, as in *Imitations* and
"The Seasons," the beginning again at the end of this volume
implies an affirmation and even a transcendence of the cyclical natural process. It might be misleading to insist too much
upon this last point, however, because Lowell, no more a
meliorist now than ever before, returns so often to the repeti-
tive aspect of the cycle of life.

Among the many recurrent images in this book, probably
no other appears as often as the circle, which is thus (as in
Lord Weary's Castle) a crucial thematic motif as well as the
shape that the poems take collectively.[10] Frequently, the circle connotes useless repetition or redundancy, as in the
image of the squirrel on a treadmill in the elegy for Jarrell and
as in this image at the beginning of the "Long Summer"
sequence:

> At dawn, the crisp goodbye of friends; at night,
> enemies reunited, who tread, unmoving,
> like circus poodles dancing on a ball. . . .

With the juxtaposition of these two images of animals performing pointless activities, we get a glimpse of Lowell's tendency in this book to repeat certain associations. Mutability
often calls to his mind another image complex involving the
circle and including the moon and a saw. Here, for example,
are the opening and closing lines of "Nature":

> The circular moon saw-wheels up the oak-grove;
> ....
> His drawing wears; the hand decayed. A hand does—
> we can have faith, at least, the hand decayed.

The last two lines, yet another instance of Lowell's ending
slightly flat, expound the theme that is implicit in the first.
Lowell's verdict on the technocracy whose growth is its own
death is presented in related images in "The Spock etc.
Sentences":

All night we slept to the sawing of immense
machines constructing: saws in circles slicing
white crescents, shafts and blocks, as if the scheming
intellectuals had rebuilt Tyre and Sidon *ab ovo*. . . .

The endless and mechanical monotony of the cosmos, which
contrasts ironically with the transience of man's mechanisms,
gives rise to this image near the end of the book:

no earthly ripple disturbs the ballbearing
utility of the bald and nearest planet. . . .

Lowell often suggests both the visual and the emotional
equivalents of monotonous continuity in the ambivalent
word "round," as in the second poem in "Sleep," where the
hint of the boxing metaphor and the internal rhymes give the
word even greater resonance:

I get to know myself, old bluff and bruiser,
who cannot stand up to the final round. . . .
To enjoy the avarice of loneliness,
sleep the hour hand round the clock, stay home,
lie like a hound, on bounds for chasing a hound. . . .

References of one sort or another to Blake's "same dull
round" of existence are so abundant that one almost imagines
that Lowell intends to make the quotidian the defining feature of reality in "Close the Book":

The book is finished and the air is lighter.
I can recognize people in the room;
I touch your pictures, find you in the round.

The pictures are also to be found "in the round," however,
because the book has made them lifelike, because the book is
actually a single polyphonic poem, and of course because its
structure is circular. In fact, Lowell repeats his round motif in
such a way as to highlight that circular structure and also to
qualify its implications significantly. The dense and beautiful
opening lines of the last sequence, "Half a Century Gone,"
constitute a small fantasia on the motif that is introduced in
the first sequence. "Half a Century Gone" begins:

We can go on, if free to leave the earth;
our blood, too high, resumes the mortal coil,
hoping past hope to round the earth of Greenbeard,
our springtide's circlet of the fickle laurel,
a funeral wreath from the Despotic Gangster.

Especially in the last lines, the circle is again associated with
futility and mortality, as the symbol of poetic excellence turns
into a funeral wreath and a god once conceived of in terms of
fairy tales and fertility rites becomes a mafioso paying ironic
tribute to his victims. But the air—in both the musical and the
atmospheric sense—is lighter throughout this passage, and
particularly in the first lines the circle image has a new force
and form. There Lowell seems to be alluding obliquely to the
possibility of an existence that succeeds and transcends this
earthly one, and his corresponding image, drawn from *Hamlet*, is that of the "mortal coil." The phrase "hoping past
hope" sounds rather like a line in "Jonathan Edwards in
Western Massachusetts"—"Hope lives in doubt"—and it is
provocative to recall that the earlier poem is one of several in
For the Union Dead to use the circle image extensively.[11] The
key image in that poem is " 'All rising is by a winding stair,' "
and the "mortal coil" might carry much the same connotation. This possibility is strengthened by recollection of other
appearances of the image of the spiral in this book, as in "In
Sickness," where Lowell says "I climb the spiral steps to my
own music." Associated images are numerous. In the poem
immediately preceding "Half a Century Gone," for instance,
he speaks (humorously though not unambiguously) of the
"passage from lower to upper middle age"; it is as though his
"Hell," which begins significantly with the words "Circles of
Dante," had given way to a purgatory with a winding road
leading upward. Again, late in the book, he remembers the
"dead sounds ascending" from the "fertile stench" of the
street.
    The point is that in the final analysis the simple circle is not
always the geometrical form most compatible with Lowell's
view of life, although it can and does stand for a large part of
that view. Inasmuch as Lowell is intensely, morosely aware of

the cycle of "rot and renewal" in the actual world, the circle serves his purposes; but inasmuch as he thinks that cycle can be transcended or overcome, inasmuch as he hopes beyond hope, the circle sometimes proves inadequate. In short, the figure of the circle cannot readily accommodate the vertical thrust of Lowell's beliefs, and therefore it is easy to understand why the "spiral steps," the "mortal coil," and comparable images occupy salient positions in his poetry.

It should not be concluded, however, that the image of the spiral is always employed after Lowell has calculated that the circle is ultimately insufficient, much less that the spiral is the sole image that can approximate his view. There is only something analogous to the use of the spiral at the end of "My Heavenly Shiner":

> The fish, the shimmering fish, they go in circles,
> not one of them will make it to the Pole—
> this isn't the point though, this is not the point;
> think of it going on without a life
> in you, God knows, I've had the earthly life—
> we were kind of religious, we thought in images.

This passage, one of the few instances in which Lowell's model could have been the two tercets of a sestet, moves from the contemplation of the pointless circular movement of mundane existence to the thought of God and religion and therewith epitomizes Lowell's peculiar combination of cyclical determinism and transcendentalism. The implications of the last three lines seem to be that "going on without a life" is virtually unthinkable, that the speaker has already "had the *earthly* life," and that therefore the religious inclinations of his youth might have some teleological as well as aesthetic justification. The hopeful syllogism is barely discernible in the midst of a more desperate rationality, but barely discernible nevertheless.

The real point of this passage is of course the *going* in circles, the living, the conversion by sheer persistence of the same dull round into an action that is its own point. This is the myth of Sisyphus according to Camus, and it is Jarrell's stubborn plodding out according to Lowell, and it is the

closest atheistic approximation of the shady transcendentalism mentioned above. If the two views are not perfect
equivalents, it must be remembered, first, that consistency is
not necessarily Lowell's primary concern and, second, that
he describes himself as "lacking half-way to atheist." In any
case, this transformation of meaningless repetition into
meaning through repetition is as prominent a theme in
Notebook 1967–68 as in *Imitations,* and by a truly circuitous
route this point brings this discussion back to the circular
structure of this book.

It was pointed out earlier that the round motif that is elaborated in the last sequence occurs first in the initial sequence,
indeed in the first poem, which because of its importance can
be quoted entire:

Half a year, then a year and a half, then
ten and a half—the pathos of a child's fractions, turning up each summer. God a seaslug, God a queen
with forty servants, God . . . she gave up—things whirl
in the chainsaw bite of whatever squares
the universe by name and number. For
the hundredth time, I slice through fog, and round
the village with my headlights on the ground,
as if I were the first philosopher,
as if I were trying to pick up a car
key . . . It can't be here, and so it must be there
behind the next crook in the road or growth
of fog—there blinded by our feeble beams,
a face, clock-white, still friendly to the earth.

The crux of this poem—the recurrent search for the "key"—is
yet another analogue for Jarrell's plodding out; the going
round the village is comparable to the fish going round in
circles; and finding the key would be tantamount to rounding
"the earth of Greenbeard."[12] God is as undiscoverable as the
key, and they are in effect synonymous. They are both undiscoverable, that is, unless the very act of searching constitutes
the only discovery, a possibility that is suggested by another
of the subtle equations set up in this poem. "Whatever
squares / the universe by name and number" is surely God;
but it is just as certainly the poet, whose task is precisely one

of names and "numbers." Moreover, the phrase "round / the village" might be parallel in sense as well as in the disposition of its elements to the phrase "squares / the universe." The identification of the creation of the gods and the creations of the poet is as old as the Greek verb that gives us the word *poetry* and means "to make," and this version of it is remarkable only for its literalness and delicacy. The same identification is made later in less detail in a line already quoted: "I climb the spiral steps to my own music."[13]

The circular movement in this first poem in "Harriet" is thus an element in the structure of the book, an adumbration of that structure, and a statement of its methods, which Lowell calls, in the title of an early sequence, "Searchings."[14] In fact, this whole introductory sequence is closely related to the body of the poems and especially to the concluding sequence. It will already have been noticed that the image complex of circle, saw, and moon appears in this poem; and one does not have to read far to see that the "fog" is another of Lowell's main motifs. In "Long Summer" it recurs as "the inarticulate mist" and "The vaporish closeness of this two-month fog," in "Through the Night" as "the smog of twilight" that keeps the figurine on the car's hood (the muse?) from seeing, in "Night Worms" (retitled "Trunks" in *Notebook*) as a "fog of Mace" that makes the police weep for a change, in "Nature" as "strings of fog" and "smoke-dust," and so on. It seems usually to be associated with the poet's imagined incoherence or inaudibility, as in the third poem in "Harriet," where the gulls ironically mirror the speaker:

> Squalls of the seagulls' exaggerated outcry,
> dimmed out by fog. . . .

Lowell discovers another momentary image of himself in the "repeating fly" of the second poem that is both "one of the mighty" and "one of the helpless." The fly is ambiguous, however, and might also be thought of as one of these poems, or one of the insights giving rise to a poem:

> It
> bumbles and bumps its brow on this and that,
> making a short, unhealthy life the shorter.

> I kill it, and another instant's added
> to the horrifying mortmain of
> ephemera: keys, drift, sea-urchin shells,
> packratted off with joy, the dead fly swept
> under the carpet, wrinkling to fulfillment.

In the last lines here Lowell must have his own book, his huge collection of *objets trouvés,* in mind. It is the organization of this potpourri that he is thinking of in the first lines of the fourth poem of this sequence:

> To summer on skidding summer, the rude spring rain
> hurries the ambitious, flowers and youth. . . .

As he points out in the "Afterthought," the book too moves from summer to summer. Moreover, there is every reason to consider Lowell among those who are hurried by "the rude spring rain." Later, in the second poem in "School," he puts in Randall Jarrell's mouth a statement of his "ambitious" nature and an image that suggests the more positive side of the view of life as a treadmill.[15] The ghost of Jarrell speaks to the shade of Lowell:

>   "What kept you so long,
>   racing your cooling grindstone to ambition?
>   Surely this life was fast enough . . . But tell me,
>   Cal, why did we live? Why do we die?"

If Lowell counts himself among "the ambitious," he also suggests, in the very first lines of the first poem, that he shares his child's "youth." He explains these lines in his "Afterthought":

My opening lines are as hermetic as any in the book. The "fractions" mean that my daughter, born in January, is each July, a precision important to a child, something and a half years old. The "Seaslug etc." are her declining conceptions of God.

The observation about children is a charming and accurate one, but that will not keep us from seeing that the book's opening lines pertain to Lowell as well as to his daughter. They share, in addition to the "declining conceptions of God" (or the *declension* of "God"), an anxiety about fractions that turn up "each summer." As Lowell himself points out, the summers that are such important markers to Harriet are the boundaries of her father's *Notebook 1967–68,* and the "half a year" that has just passed at the beginning of the book is a microcosmic version of the "Half a Century Gone" at the end. It is thus his "youth" as well as his "ambitious" nature to which he refers specifically in "Harriet, 4." As for the middle term in that poem's second line—"flowers"—the last lines of "Harriet, 4" refer to "beautiful petals" which seem to be his poems as well as the beautiful moments of life.

A brief comparison of the last lines in this sequence and the last lines of poetry in the book can elucidate the meaning of the relationship between the poet and his daughter. Not surprisingly, both the "Harriet" sequence and "Obit" end with questions. The first of these, nominally addressed to Harriet, is:

> beautiful petals, what shall I hope for,
> knowing one choice not two is all you're given,
> health beyond the measure, dangerous
> to yourself, more dangerous to others?

The passage from "Obit" goes:

> I'm for and with myself in my otherness,
> in the eternal return of earth's fairer children,
> the lily, the rose, the sun on dusk and brick,
> the loved, the lover, and their fear of life,
> their unconquered flux, insensate oneness, their painful "it
>   was . . ."
> After loving you so much, can I forget
> you for eternity, and have no other choice?

The second question answers the first: what will be hoped for is a "return" in one form or another, a return that would make possible, after all, another choice. The closing passage is more affirmative than that sentence might suggest, however, for the question wants to be rhetorical; the implication is that there must be some "other choice" than to forget the all-inclusive "you" that the poet has known. Lowell is not specific about the alternative to death, although he alludes to

Nietzsche's doctrine of "the eternal return," or rather to Herbert Marcuse's summary of that doctrine;[16] but it is clear that Harriet, one of "earth's fairer children," is at least symbolic of his return. *Notebook 1967–68* itself is at least symbolic of the whole process of "the eternal return," for this poem takes us back to the opening sequence. The endless repetition, the stubborn plodding out that is the poet's modus operandi, thus reflects the ultimate nature of things, and both are epitomized in the circular structure of the book, which is implicit in the first sequence.

If that last comment sounds at all familiar, it is because it has been made in regard to others of Lowell's volumes and developed in some detail in the discussion of *Lord Weary's Castle*. Mention is made of these facts so that the extraordinary continuity of Lowell's poetics can be emphasized. If it would not be fair to label his method at this juncture neo-symbolist, it is only fair to recognize that his roots are in that tradition. At the same time, as was suggested early in this study, neo-symbolism was not Lowell's only poetic source; indeed, the reason that the discussion thus far in this chapter has been able to move quickly from passage to passage is that an understanding of Lowell's means of developing personal symbols in the course of his work, a procedure more closely related to Yeats's poetry than to Tate's, can now be taken for granted. Perhaps it would be negligent, however, not to outline the circular structure of *Notebook 1967–68* more definitely, although that project is also facilitated by recollection of Lowell's earlier volumes.

There are five main divisions here, one for each of the successive seasons that Lowell mentions in the "Afterthought." Any attempt to demarcate them exactly would be pointless and probably futile, but their approximate limits can be indicated by reference to the titles of several of Lowell's "sections." The first of the five parts might be said to begin with "Long Summer," the second with "October and November," the central one with "Blizzard in Cambridge," the fourth with "April 8, 1968," and the fifth with "To Summer." On the basis of previous volumes, one would expect these poems to have a determinable center; and although it is clever rather than dramatic, there is one here. Doubtless anticipating such a search, Lowell has conveniently and wittily entitled the poem at the middle of the volume "The Golden Middle," which in this case carries the sardonic meaning of "luxuriant middle age."[17] There is, however, no single poem at the thematic center of the book; that center, instead, comprises several poems stretching from the dead of winter through "My Death" and "February and March" to the beginning of spring. The poet's life, in short, is mirrored in the seasons, and the year's simultaneous death and rejuvenation are also his—at least partly because his daughter's birthday is in January.

If the structure of *Notebook 1967–68* embodies the theme of the "eternal return," it also makes concessions to the "unconquered flux" of experience. At the same time that Lowell arranges his poem in an order, he partially erases the boundaries that he has established. Flashbacks to times of year other than that of the present sporadically disrupt the seasonal progression, as in the memory of May in "Midwinter" and the recollection of November in "The Races" of August; and geographical shifts sometimes obscure the season, as when the "Mexico" sequence with its sun and scarlet blossoms appears between the "Christmas and New Year" and "Midwinter" sequences. Again, a prologue and an epilogue infringe upon the circular structure, for although "Harriet" is set in June and "Half a Century Gone" in a "summer's landscape," these sequences are more comprehensive than most of the others and their chief importance is as summaries of the themes and implications of the book's organization. Lowell indicates this in the earlier instance by entitling the second sequence "Long Summer" and in the later one by placing "Close the Book" immediately before and "Obit" immediately after. And then there is even the "Afterthought" to stress the linear progression of daily life at the expense of the circular organization of the poems.

Since the "Afterthought" is in prose, it has the further function of blurring the boundaries between the book and the world, of suggesting the continuity of this poetry and the poet's life that is implicit in the very title. This is the fourth

level on which this book might be discussed: as a symbol of
the intersection of the poet's ordinary life and his poetry. The
volume's structure is of course borrowed from nature—in
both, season follows season in a predetermined order, while
events within that general order are multifarious and apparently capricious—and many of its techniques are naturalis-
tic. The flashbacks, the elliptical language, and the mélange
of speculation and fact all imitate the peregrinations of any
inquiring mind as they would be set down in a notebook. The
prose into which the poetry sometimes "corrupts," to use
Lowell's term, is also a means of breaking down the distinction between experience formulated and experience in flux.
At times, Lowell's poetry is no more verse than Pound's is in
the most boring sections of the *Cantos*, several of which could
have inspired the beginning of "Caracas":

Through another of our cities without a center, as hideous
as Los Angeles, and with as many cars
per head, and past the 20-foot neon sign
for *Coppertone* on a church, past the population
earning $700 per capita
in jerry skyscraper living-slabs, and on to the White House
of El Presidente Leoni, his small men with 18-
inch repeating pistols, firing 45 bullets a minute. . . .

The poem gains rhythm toward the end, and its last two
lines, which seem to echo "Children of Light" in *Lord Weary's
Castle*, exhibit Lowell's ability to clinch a poem in the old,
rhetorical manner when the occasion arises:

   This house, this pioneer democracy, built
   on foundations, not of rock, but blood as hard as rock.

But this very fluctuation in manner is itself characteristic of a
notebook. Lowell indicates his awareness of the unevenness
of many of these poems—an unevenness analogous to the
"jagged pattern" of the whole book—when he contrasts himself with Mary McCarthy:

   I slip from wonder into bluster; you align
   your lines more freely, ninety percent on target—
   we can only meet in the bare air.

He comments on and exemplifies the same feature in "Harvard, 2":

> My mind can't hold the focus for a minute.
> A sentence? A paragraph? The best tale
> stales to homework. Flash-visions; as if I saw
> the dark of the moon on the white of my eye;
> and now, her Absent-present. . . .

Those last lines are representative of another stylistic trait that seems closely related to the intentional artlessness of this book. In the "Afterthought" Lowell says:

> I lean heavily to the rational, but am devoted to surrealism. . . .
> Surrealism can degenerate into meaningless clinical hallucinations,
> or worse into rhetorical machinery, yet it is a natural way to write
> our fictions.[18]

These comments, and the last clause in particular, seem to be based on the notion that surrealism affords means of getting the capricious, the irrational, and the immediate across the moat and into the bastion of art. Although Lowell's indulgence of his "Flash-visions" results in some virtually impenetrable lines, these surrealistic touches are certainly more "natural" than some of his other attempts at artlessness, such as the acknowledgement of contemporary slang in "Alcohol, 3," which begins: "Nature might do her thing for us; so they swore." He is usually better with the age-old slang, as in "The Going Generation":

> hear the swallow's coloratura cheep and cluck,
> shrilling underneath its racket, *fuck*. . . .

It is not simply the dialectic of life and art with which Lowell is concerned, however; he is also and primarily concerned with the relationship between his work and his life. *Notebook 1967–68* says more clearly than any preceding volume that Lowell has set himself the task of creating—or revealing—the unity of the flux of his experiences and the form of his poetry as a whole. If it is uncertain whether creation or revelation better describes the process, the uncertainty itself is indicative of the extent to which the task has progressed. Lowell has so conjoined his life and his poetry that it is difficult to tell where the shape of the experiences comes from. Hayden Carruth made a similar point several years ago, and his comments can be extended to include *Notebook 1967–68* and its descendants:

Whatever the rationale, or whether or not there is any rationale, we cannot read Lowell's autobiographical writing, from *Life Studies* to *Near the Ocean*, without seeing that we are in touch with a writer who is in fact making his life as he goes along. . . . He has resolved to accept reality, all reality, and to take its fragments indiscriminately as they come, forging from them this indissoluble locus of metaphoric connections that is known as Robert Lowell.[19]

Carruth's phrase "making his life as he goes along" applies even better to *Notebook 1967–68* than to *Near the Ocean*, and it applies to a greater extent to *Notebook*, the revised and enlarged edition of *Notebook 1967–68* which Lowell published in 1970. At the same time, if "making" has much force in Carruth's remarks, his comments seem to harbor a contradiction, for to redact "fragments indiscriminately" would not seem to involve "making" or the "forging . . . of metaphoric connections."

The contradiction is of course Lowell's before it is Carruth's, for even though his recent works have discernible structures, those structures are tentative and continually imperiled by the journalistic bias. This bias is more evident in *Notebook* than in its predecessor. In his note to the new edition, Lowell tells us that "about a hundred of the old poems have been changed, some noticeably. More than ninety new poems have been added. These have not been placed as a single section or epilogue. They were scattered where they caught, intended to fulflesh my poem, not sprawl into a chronicle." The new poems, in other words, attempt to do justice to the year that still provides the volume with a circular structure. Now 372, the poems just outnumber the days in a year, and the volume comes closer to approximating the variegated rush of events, reflections, and anticipations that constitute the period of time that it covers. Inasmuch as it does so, however, *Notebook* begins to turn back into the welter of experience the poems it has extracted from it. The basic structure of the book as outlined earlier in this chapter is unaltered in the enlarged edition, but the poem is so "fulfleshed" that the skeletal framework, never very strong, can give it little shape. Because the new poems are in the same rather arbitrary form and the same frequently obscure style as the original poems, very few of which have been altered in the direction of clarity, the *Notebook* cannot avoid—indeed, seems not to want to avoid—giving the impression that it gives asylum to random fragments. The balance seems to have been tipped in favor of the journalistic rather than the formalistic impulse.

But Lowell was not through with his *Notebook* in 1970. In fact, he has clung to it with a tenacity perhaps illuminated by "My Death, 1":

> Reading this book to four or five at night
> at Cuernavaca, till the lines glowered and glowed,
> and my friend, Monsignior Illich, ascetic donkey,
> braying, "Will you die, when the book is done?"
> It stopped my heart, and not my mouth. I said,
> "I have begun to wonder."

How does one end a book that he has come to identify so closely with his life? The poem in *Notebook* called "Close the Book" is followed by an epilogue because the "book" must remain open. Similarly, "Obit" is not an obituary at all, but a celebration of the "eternal return," which summarizes the poet's method, and therefore his life. In *History* and its companion volumes, Lowell returns to the "open book" that is increasingly his life.

Baudelaire, for example, planned *Les Fleurs du Mal* not as a mere collection, but as a book. But one does not plan such a book as one might plan a novel: the planning begins with the planning of one's life. Such a book should, in theory, explore as wide a range of experience as possible. This calls for a knowledge of the history of literature and ideas, for a knowledge of one's own period, for a grasp of the relationship between ideas and action on the one hand and ideas and style on the other. It calls for a command of the minutiae of style. And it calls for both patience and genius. The actual writing of such a book will be important, but most of the work will be in the preparation.

—IVOR WINTERS, *The Function of Criticism*

Now while the common multitude strips bare,
feels pleasure's cat o'nine tails on its back,
accumulating remorse at the great bazaar—
give me your hand, my Sorrow. Let's stand back,
back from these people. Look, the defunct years, dressed
in period costume crowd the balconies of the sky.

—"Baudelaire 2. Recollection"

9

HISTORY REPEATING ITSELF:
History and Company (1973)

S o, almost from the beginning, he has sought to fulfill an epic ambition with essentially lyric means. At least since *Life Studies*—and the germ of the method was there in *Lord Weary's Castle*—his volumes have comprised poems so intricately interrelated that, however strong or weak in their own right, they gain from context. Gradually, he has implicitly enlarged his context until it has come to include the volumes themselves. If the earth attracts the apple, it must affect the moon. The more we discover about this evolving system, the more its center and source seems an incandescent, tumultuous, raw energy, the most notable recent product of which is a huge body of work called *History*, which is also a kind of microcosm of the whole. It is accompanied by *For Lizzie and Harriet*, a smaller volume that in a different form was part of *History's* preceding stage, *Notebook*, and has now organized itself into a related but independent thing, an orbiting relict, and by *The Dolphin*, a second satellite, balancing the pull of *For Lizzie and Harriet* and composed of the same formal elements (blank verse in fourteen-line sections).

Unlike *Notebook*, *History* is a radical revision of the structure Lowell has been at work upon since 1967. It includes 368 poems, most of which have been taken, often by way of heavy revision, from *Notebook*, and about eighty of which are new.[1] What makes *History* fundamentally different from its predecessors, however, is not the sum of its new parts, but rather the new orientation and the dependent ordonnance of all of its parts. Instead of reflecting the rotation of the seasons, it traces, in a chronological order, the revolutions of cultures.

The immediate origin of *History's* structure was there in *Notebook*, buried in the midst of the other subsequences, in a twenty-two poem section called "The Powerful," which was itself an amplification and revision of "Power" in *Notebook 1967–68;* but it can be traced back through the chronological progressions in *Near the Ocean* and *Imitations* and through the thematic implications of such historical pieces as "For the Union Dead," "Beyond the Alps," and "Falling Asleep over the Aeneid" to "On the Eve of the Feast of the Immaculate Conception 1942." This book implies such a clear example of Lowell's modus operandi, of "this way that generates itself, leads itself on, and returns into itself," that Randall Jarrell's observations more than two decades ago are perhaps the most appropriate gloss on Lowell's latest work:

Mr. Lowell has a completely unscientific but thoroughly historical mind. It is literary and traditional as well; he can use the past so effectively because he thinks so much as it did. He seems condemned both to read history and to repeat it.[2]

Now that is an instance of poet as seer. In this volume's

revision of one of the poems dedicated to Jarrell, Lowell
writes:

Thirty years ago,
as students waiting for Europe and spring term to end—
we saw below us, golden, small, stockstill,
the college polo field, cornfields, the feudal airdrome,
the McKinley Trust; behind, above us, the tower,
the dorms, the fieldhouse, the Bishop's palace and chapel—
Randall, the scene still plunges at the windshield,
apples redden to ripeness on the whiplash bough.

Even when Lowell focuses on his own past ("Thirty years
ago"—although from the detail one might think it were the
present), he sees through it into the distant past ("the feudal
airdrome"); the scenes that still plunge at his windshield are
from times gone by, whether decades or centuries ago, and
nothing is more natural than for him to marshall the elements
of his longest poem in a chronological narrative. He has this
new scheme in mind when he says in his prefatory note: "I
have plotted. My old title, Notebook, was more accurate than I
wished, i.e. the composition was jumbled. I hope that this
jumble or jungle has been cleared—that I have cut the waste
marble from the figure." Whether the decision to resculpt the
figure came before or after the decision to excise the sixty-
seven poems that now constitute For Lizzie and Harriet is a
matter of conjecture, but it is clear that without these poems
(which include most of the poems in the groups entitled
"Summer," "Circles," and "Late Summer") the seasonal
structure that informed the Notebook would be enfeebled. If
the latter decision was made first, it was a happy one, for the
organization of History is stronger and more functional than
that of Notebook or even that of the sparer Notebook 1967–68.

Beginning with "History," "Man and Woman," "Bird?,"
"Dawn," "In Genesis," "Our Fathers," and other pointedly
entitled poems, the book moves through sections called, for
example, "Israel," "Rome," "Bosworth Field," and "Versailles," eventually into the twentieth century, and thence
into autobiography. In order to create this structure, Lowell
had not only to resort to a number of ingenious devices, in-

cluding recasting lyrics as dramatic monologues and entitling poems on the basis of passing references, but also to undertake a tremendous amount of labor. The book is a re-vision, and not one of the longer sequences in *Notebook* has been preserved in anything like its original form. The cards have been gathered up, freshly marked, shuffled, and dealt out again. It is indicative of the difference of the new pattern that one of the poems in the second sequence of *Notebook* appears here, under the title "Ice," near the end, while a poem from one of the last sequences in *Notebook* turns up here near the beginning with a title, "In Genesis," that is almost opposite its original one, "Closing 2. Out of the Picture."

In view of the connections between Lowell's beginnings and his ends, of course, those displacements might not be surprising. More interesting and instructive is the difference between the opening lines of "Closing 2" and "In Genesis":

Tank. A camel blotting up the water.
God with whom nothing is voulu or design.
The lay-off . . . the Sun-day now all seven, a trek
for the great image held behind Blue Hill,
the flower of Eden unchanged, since spoiled,
the girl holding the sunset apple, lifeclass unchanged . . .
white as a white cake of coap in the dingy bathlight.
Things have been felt before, before today. . . .

                                                    (Notebook)

Blank. A camel blotting up the water.
God with whom nothing is design or intention.
In the Beginning, the Sabbath could last a week,
God grumbling secrecies behind Blue Hill. . . .
The serpent walked on foot like us in Eden;
glorified by the perfect Northern exposure,
Eve and Adam knew their nakedness,
a discovery to be repeated many times. . . .

                                                    (History)

The later version, with its "grumbling" God, its animated serpent, Eve and Adam, and its sharper focus, dramatizes a situation that exists tentatively and only by virtue of allusion in the earlier version, where it is difficult even to locate the action temporally. At the same time, the revision is disembarrassed of the dubious wordplay of the original ("Sun-day," with its decrepit pun, and "lay-off," with its uncertain one). If the dramatic and comparatively straightforward qualities of the revised lines are not unrelated to one another, neither are they unrelated to the structure of the book; for just as the vividness of the concrete situation encourages the poet to dispense with cleverness, so the book's structure provides him with the situation. This poem knows its place in *History*. One might attribute the emendation of the first word to the advantage of a mind trained on rhyme rather than to structural considerations, but the difference is at least suggestive of the felicities of the chronological organization.

The dramatic quality makes itself felt more strongly elsewhere in *History*, as poems whose speakers were formerly mysterious personalities with bizarre tastes or extravagant extensions of the poet himself are now assigned to figures whom they plausibly if sometimes eccentrically interpret. *Notebook*'s "Europa," an enigmatic poem in the first person in which the poet seems to view his lovemaking (whether immodestly or ironically is hard to say) in terms of Jupiter's rape of Europa, becomes an address by Antony to Cleopatra. "Solomon's Wisdom," formerly "The Book of Wisdom," in which the first line was "Can I go on loving anyone at fifty?" is now a dramatic monologue beginning "'Can I go on keeping a hundred wives at fifty? . . .'" Similarly, "Another Friend," a poem addressed in *Notebook* to a ghostly female friend that risks the ludicrous ("I didn't want you to be warmed by walking, / each drop of perspiration on your face, / an admirer's eye"), is transformed into "Cassandra 2," which is, however paradoxically, a more credible and a more moving monologue; while "For Gallantry" loses much if not all of its obscurity when it is translated into "Cassandra 1" (although the idea that Paris slew Polyxena seems original with Lowell).

This translation of the personal lyric into the dramatic monologue—which one suspected in poems as early as "The Death of the Sheriff" and even "Her Dead Brother"—seems to have a function beyond dramatizing and facilitating the chronological structure, however. Some light can be shed on this function by another kind of translation in *History*. The earliest examples of this second, more ordinary kind of translation are the poems immediately preceding the two given to Cassandra, "Helen" and "Achilles to the Dying Lykaon," which are of course new versions of two of the *Imitations*. In their original context, it will be recalled, both of these poems (like Leopardi's "Infinite," which turns up in a nicely cadenced version here, and like a number of other imitations revised for *History*) seemed to illuminate, from admittedly different angles, the persona's own experience. Here, where they are surrounded by poems for which there is textual evidence that the poet is refracting personal experience through the prism of his *dramatis personae*, they must be thought to serve the same purpose. In other words, the two kinds of translation—which term Renato Poggioli conveniently defines as "the conjuration, through another spirit, of one's own self"—point to the same end: the fusion of the poet and his subjects.[3]

In some instances, this union is explicit; and in others it is virtually so, as in the closing lines of "In Genesis":

Orpheus in Genesis
hacked words from brute sound, and taught men English,
plucked all the flowers, deflowered all the girls
with the overemphasis of a father.
He used too many words, his sons killed him,
dancing with grateful gaiety round the cookout.

Recalling—or, in the case of *History*, anticipating—"The Nihilist as Hero," its "words meat-hooked from the living steer" (as well as the first poem "For John Berryman," also reprinted with revisions in this volume, in which Lowell says "John, we used the language as if we made it"), "In Genesis" describes by overstatement ("hacked words from brute sound") and by irony ("used too many words") the author of *History*. Similarly, the reader familiar with Lowell will recognize in the sketch of "The Poet," which appears here for the first time, features that he associates with the author of *For the Union Dead*: "Hardy, home from cycling, / was glad to climb unnoticed to his study / by a circling outside staircase, his own design." If those lines conjure anyone more than Thomas Hardy, it is surely Robert Lowell (perhaps in the guise of Jonathan Edwards). The title of "Rilke Self-Portrait" suggests a like intent, and the last lines of the poem bear out the suggestion:

> As a thing that hangs together, the picture fails;
> nothing is worked through yet or alive,
> carried to enduring culmination—
> as if hidden in accidents and stray things,
> something unassailable were planned.

If it is just as much the young Rilke as "the picture" that is being described, it is just as much Lowell's self-portrait in *History* as Rilke's that is the subject. One does not have to go to the opening words of *The Dolphin*—where Lowell defines his aims as "Any clear thing that blinds us with surprise / . . . wandering silences and bright trouvailles"—to discover the relevance of those "accidents and stray things."

Having such apparent conjurations of the poet's self in mind is an advantage when one encounters poems like the two on Hannibal. The first of these—a new and unacknowledged translation of José-Maria de Heredia's "La Trebbia" that not only evokes but also measures up to Yeats's miniatures in "The Long-Legged Fly"—provides a stunning example of history dramatized:

> A gloomy flamboyance reddens the dull sky,
> Gallic villages smoulder on the horizon.
> Far off, the hysterical squeal of an elephant. . . .
> Down there, below a bridge, his back on the arch,
> Hannibal listens, thoughtful, glorying,
> to the dead tramp of the advancing Roman legions.[4]

Such a scene is almost too pure, too finely focused and objective, and too close to Heredia's original for one to imagine that Lowell has any ulterior purpose. Perhaps that is the case; perhaps the first person could not have been further from the poet's mind when he translated this passage. And yet is not the success of Yeats's portrait of, say, Michaelangelo owing in large part, if not to an attempt to mirror himself, to the coincidence of the movements of the poet's and the artist's minds and hands? And is there not a comparable coincidence implied in this passage? To think as the past thought is partly to be of the past; and if to rethink Baudelaire is to become that poet's brother, to put oneself so completely in Hannibal's situation is to be his *semblable*. One might even see *History* as a prodigious amplification of the strategy behind "The Long-Legged Fly"—or, more simply, as a broader application of the method of *Imitations,* the narrower application of which this poem also exemplifies.

The second poem on Hannibal, a condensation of a passage in *Near the Ocean*'s Juvenal, includes these lines:

Throw Hannibal on the scales, how many pounds
does the First Captain come to? . . .
. . . .
He scaled the Pyrenees, the snow, the Alps—
nature blocked his road, he derricked mountains. . . .
. . . .
What a face for a painter; look, he's a one-eye.
The glory? He's defeated like the rest,
serves some small tyrant farting off drunken meals . . .
and dies by taking poison. . . . Go, Madman, cross
the Alps, the Tiber—be a purple patch
for schoolboys, and their theme for declamation.

In his moving of mountains Hannibal is a version of "The Nihilist as Hero," whose duty is said in *History* to be that of "gazing the impassable summit to ruin"; while in his defeat, and in his being parsed and parceled out by and to schoolboys, he is a descendant of Orpheus, who in Lowell's telling of the myth used too many words and was eaten by his sons. One does not have to think that Lowell has a kind of academic omophagy in mind to see the parallel. "In Genesis" and the two complementary Hannibal poems embody examples of what Lowell calls in the last poem in *History* "These conquered kings," the great who have invariably fallen, and thus they afford on the one hand a microcosm of the fate of nations and on the other a magnifying mirror of the fate of

the poet. Even if one does not hear any echoes of Lowell's
previous work in the references in "Hannibal 2" to the Alps
and the blocked road, it seems clear that the distance between
Hannibal and Orpheus is no greater than that between Orpheus and Lowell and that neither is harder to bridge than
the distance between the *Notebooks* and *History*. The title of
the latter is one of the first cantilevers, for it must also mean
"his story," which meaning throws a special light on the first
line in the volume: "History has to live with what was here."

Once the principle of the pun has been grasped—and it is
the function of the chronological structure, telescoping history into autobiography, to make us grasp it—this volume
coheres more with every reading. It is as though Lowell had
revised the *Notebook* in the same light that enabled Robert
Penn Warren to say in his preface to *Brother to Dragons,* which
Lowell reviewed twenty years earlier, that "if poetry is the
little myth we make, history is the big myth we live, and in
our living constantly remake." In this remaking of the fusion
of history, myth, and the poet's life, it is not only Orpheus
and Rilke and Berryman who reflect aspects of the poet, but
also Cato the Elder, Antony, Solomon, Alexander, and even
Attila, Tamerlane, and Stalin. "Le Vieux Caton," as he was
called in *Notebook,* puts in an admonitory appearance toward
the beginning of *History,* where it is his purpose to inform the
poet and the reader that "a blindman looking for gold / in a
heap of dust must take the dust with the gold," for "Rome,
if built at all, must be built in a day." Building the Rome of his
day, in the same sense that Juvenal built the Rome of his own
(which is also, *therefore,* the Rome of ours), Lowell has determined to take the dust with the gold. "I give you what you
have already," Juvenal says yet again in this revised excerpt
("Juvenal's Prayer") from the imitation in *Near the Ocean,* and
with those very words Lowell offers the same. Consequently,
the reader finds himself in the position of "the reviewer"
mentioned in *The Dolphin,* who was "sent by God to humble
me / ransacking my bags of dust for silver spoons."

The imagery of dust, draff, kitchen middens, and various
wreckage is one of Lowell's primary means of figuring with a
bitter irony the contents of both history and *History,* of merg-

ing his work and its subject. In "For John Berryman 1," where the characteristic relationship between poet and subject is itself the subject ("I feel I know what you have worked through, you / know what I have worked through—we are words"), the constituents of the literary plot are flung up by the "out-tide": "rivers, linguini, / beercans, mussels, bloodstreams." In a passage that is even more reminiscent of the later Roethke:

> Whatever we cast out
> takes root—weeds shoot up to litter overnight,
> sticks of dead rotten wood in drifts, the fish
> with a missing eye, or heel-print on the belly,
> or a gash in the back from a stray hook. . . .
>
> ("1930's 7")

If "we are words," and if the words catalog such refuse, the awesome self-portrait in "1930's 5," which rather recalls Michaelangelo's portrait of himself as a flayed skin in the Sistine Chapel's *Last Judgment*, seems to follow:

> I hear the moon
> simmer the mildew on a pile of shells,
> the fruits of my banquet . . . a boiled lobster,
> red shell and hollow foreclaw, cracked, sucked dry,
> flung on the ash-heap of a soggy carton—
> it eyes me, two pinhead, burnt-out popping eyes.

This is an application with a vengeance of Lowell's Quevedo's dictum: "Whatever once / was fugitive maintains its permanence."

In a revised form, that poem from *Near the Ocean* returns here, just before "Attila, Hitler," where the two figures named in the title are sublated in the "barbarian" of the concluding lines:

> a barbarian wondering why the old world collapsed,
> who also left his festering fume of refuse,
> old tins, dead vermin, ashes, eggshells, youth?

Earlier in the poem Lowell has pictured Attila, "mounted on raw meat and greens," as a "nomad stay-at-home"; and if the

"raw meat" recalls the words "meat-hooked from the living
steer," the "nomad stay-at-home" must seem an apt description of the Lowell of *History*. Although he quotes Hitler to the
effect (particularly ironic if one has in mind Cavafy's famous
"Expecting the Barbarians") that "'We *are* the barbarians,'"
he has a particular contemporary barbarian in mind in these
last lines. From one point of view, *History* is precisely a "fes-
tering fume of refuse" in which we find the shell of the
speaker's youth.

In which youth we find, or rather have found, an incident
that led Lowell in *Life Studies* to see himself and his fellow
poet or double Delmore Schwartz, who also reappears in this
volume, as created in the images of Coleridge and Stalin. In
History's "Coleridge," the romantic poet, one of a number of
dialecticians who turn up in the book, shares with the
speaker a need for "the one friend" and a certain "power
without strength"; and in its "Coleridge and Richard II," he
is characterized by a "constant overflow of imagination /
proportioned to his dwindling will to act." Further described
as "the one poet who blamed his failure on himself," Coleridge looks back to Alexander, who "of all the kings of old /
. . . had the greatness of heart to repent," and no doubt
glances forward as well to the last of the writers listed in
"Last Night":

> Ah the swift vanishing of my older
> generation—the deaths, suicide, madness
> of Roethke, Berryman, Jarrell and Lowell,
> "the last the most discouraging of all
> surviving to dissipate *Lord Weary's Castle*
> and nine subsequent useful poems
> in the seedy grandiloquence of *Notebook*."

As for Stalin, "What raised him," according to this recusant
Puritan and converted Catholic turned agnostic, "was an unusual lust to break the icon, / joke cruelly, seriously, and be
himself."

Being himself for Robert Lowell entails not only making
such serious jokes as those in "Stalin" and "Last Night" but
also being these others. Perhaps some of his protean changes

still surprise, but this is after all the author of "Falling Asleep over the Aeneid," and "Caligula," and the third stanza in *For the Union Dead*'s "Beyond the Alps," which gives rise to "Ovid and Caesar's Daughter":

> I was a modern. In the Emperor's eye,
> a tomcat with the number of the Beast—
> . . . .
> Thieves pick gold
> from the fine print and volume of the Colossus.
> Because I loved and wrote too profligately,
> Imperial Tiber, O my yellow Wolf,
> black earth by the Black Roman Sea, I lie
> libelled with the boy-crazy daughter of
>
> Caesar Augustus who will never die.

Just as the fifth quoted line turns us back to "In Genesis" and the preceding two lines remind us of the relevance of Cato the Elder's dictum in regard to Lowell's own huge volume, so the first sentence, with its jarring combination of verb and object, points us forward to the remarkably powerful "Timur Old":

> To wake some midnight, on that instant senile,
> clasping clay knees . . . in this unwarlike posture
> meet your grandsons, a sheeted, shivering mound,
> pressed racecar hideously scared, agog with headlight—
> Timur . . . his pyramid half a million heads,
> one skull and then one brick and then one skull,
> live art that makes the Arc de Triomphe pale.
> Even a modernist must be new at times,
> not a parasite on his own tradition,
> its too healthy sleep that foreshadows death.
> A thing well done, even a pile of heads
> modestly planned to wilt before the builder,
> is art, if art is anything won from nature. . . .

As the characteristic dialectic moves from Lowell to Tamerlane to the ambiguous "modernist," a rather shocking vision unfolds. Not only is this volume of "live art" and "words

meat-hooked from the living steer" a kind of "Colossus" and
a kind of "mausoleum" (or beehive tomb), it is also a kind of
"pyramid" (itself a type of mausoleum). The first "skull" is
put in place in the last lines of "History," the first poem; and
numerous "heads," among which there is that of Timur himself, follow. Since for Lowell, as for the Emerson of "On
History," "history is the essence of innumerable biogra-
phies"; and since for him, as for the Stevens of *Adagia*, "all
history is modern history"; and since for him, as for the Snodgrass of "A Visitation," "There's something beats the same in
opposed hearts"—for these reasons it is quite consistent for
Lowell to see himself in the image of the Tartar conqueror,
just as he sees himself in the figures of the Mongol and the
Russian and the German rulers. In "The Worst Sinner,
Jonathan Edwards' God," Lowell, reverting to one of his earlier
alter egos, writes:

> But Jonathan Edwards prayed to think himself
> worse than any man that ever breathed;
> he was a good man, and he prayed with reason—
> which of us hasn't thought his same thought worse?

As he puts that "same thought" in broader terms in
"Bishop Berkeley," after several lines on the philosopher's
"solipsism" (which was "nihilism" in *Notebook*):

> In Mexico, I too caused my private earthquake,
> and made the earth tremble in the soles of my feet;
> a local insurrection of my blood,
> its river system saying: I am I,
> I am Whitman, I am Berkeley, all men. . . .

It is that identification precisely which the many historical
portraits intimate, which all of the motifs weave, which the
chronological structure channels. It is the heart of the ultimate unity of *History*, as surely as it is the cause of the sometimes desultory movement and as surely as it is the basis for
Lowell's latest revision of this strange new "Song of Myself."
It is as though Lowell had not clearly seen until after *Notebook* was published that its strategy and philosophy were
really those of *Imitations* writ large.

Indeed, the relationship between Lowell's earlier volumes and this one is one of the most intriguing aspects of *History* on several counts. For one thing, even as *History* contains, and is to some extent informed by, poems from all of Lowell's previous volumes (except *Land of Unlikeness*, much of which was included in *Lord Weary's Castle*), it also helps us to interpret those volumes. For example: the use of Coleridge in *Life Studies* helps us to realize the use of Stalin in *History*, which in turn enables us to see that he was used in a similar fashion in *Life Studies*, which insight seems to be confirmed by the information provided in this volume ("Mother, 1972") that Lowell's mother died of a cerebral hemorrhage, for in the earlier book Lowell continually regards himself as heir to the family frailties and reminds us that Stalin died of a cerebral hemorrhage. Again, the little blue anchor that the boy in *Life Studies* kept picking at on his sailor blouse, which was tentatively equated in the fifth chapter with the stain upon, or imperfection of, human existence, from which the boy wished to escape, can be more certainly glossed in view of these lines in *History*'s "Flaw," which look back as well to "The Flaw" in *For the Union Dead:*

> My old eye-flaw sprouting bits and strings,
> gliding like dragon-kites in the Midwestern sky—
> . . . .
> I look through the window at unbroken white cloud,
> and see in it my many flaws are one,
> . . . .
> God is design, even our ugliness
> is the goodness of his will. It gives me warning,
> the first scrape of the Thunderer's fingernail. . . .

In addition to information about details such as these, *History* provides us with terms with which we can more comfortably interpret some of Lowell's earlier work. One of this volume's new poems, "Last Things, Black Pines at 4 a.m.," states explicitly an idea the ramifications of which have been encountered several times in earlier volumes:

> for imperfection is the language of art.
> Even the best writer in his best lines

is incurably imperfect, crying for truth, knowledge,
honesty, inspiration he cannot have—
after a show of effort, Valéry
and Trollope the huntsman are happy to drop out.

The principle laid down in the first quoted line—which Lowell purports to derive from Van Gogh, another of the poet's
alter egos—is closely related not only to the structure of *Imitations* but also to the very concept of *imitation*, which term
itself, unlike the less humble *translation*, acknowledges the
necessity of approximation. Again, in retrospect, one element
in the attitude toward God in Lowell's first three volumes is
illuminated by such lines as these:

Was the snake in the garden, an agent provocateur?
Is the Lord increased by desolation?

("Our Fathers")

Students return to Othello and Macbeth,
Shakespeare's insomniac self and murderer,
his visionary captain trapped in scandal
by Shiva, the killer and a third of God.

("Thoreau 1")

The first passage is connected as closely with the Ophitic
strains in "The Mills of the Kavanaughs" and "Mother Marie
Therese" as with the vengeful God motif in this volume,
while the second passage helps to gloss the end of "At the
Altar" at the same time that it provides an analogue to the
relationship between Lowell and many of his protagonists
here. Why, this very feature of his poetry, this self-imitation
("'You didn't write, you *rewrote*,'" Jarrell says in this volume), seems ironically to emphasize what is perhaps Lowell's
single most characteristic stance, a die-hard antimeliorism,
set forth no less in *History*'s "Window Ledge 2. Gramsci in
Prison" ("I saw the world is the same as it has been") than in
"The Death of the Sheriff" ("Nothing underneath the sun /
Has bettered, Uncle, since the scaffolds flamed / On butch-
ered Troy"). If history repeats itself, so does the story of this
chronic chronicler.

It is the extent to which Lowell repeats himself, the inclusion here of a number of "new" poems drawn from volumes earlier than the *Notebooks*, that is perhaps the most interesting element in the relationship between *History* and its predecessors. In many cases—such as "Nunc est bibendum, Cleopatra's Death," a brutal abridgment of "Cleopatra" in *Near the Ocean;* and the two poems called "The Wife of Henri Quatre," which mercilessly divide between them the substance of "The Banker's Daughter" in *Life Studies;* and "Achilles to the Dying Lykaon," a vestige of the first of the *Imitations*—it cannot have been a desire to improve them that induced Lowell to plagiarize the earlier poems. In fact, since many of them are not in a conventional sense revisions, it is difficult to see how the new poems could ever replace the originals; and surely, when and if Lowell comes to collect his work, we will find "Cleopatra" and the others there in (more or less) their original forms.

Yet in a certain sense this volume *is* a collected poems, or a selected poems, and that is the chief reason for the number of pieces lifted from the earlier books. In other words, in addition to being the major work of Lowell's career to date, *History* is a synecdoche for the career, a means of mediating between "Reading Myself" and the virtually unmanageable palimpseste of the work as a whole. What Lowell's work is to history, that is, *History* is to Lowell's work—which is almost to say his life. In some sense, what has been, or so the implication of both the new poems and the autobiography is, is here. It is a grand, literally a monumental conception, a concrete analogue to the "mausoleum" of "Reading Myself" or to the "rough / Cathedral" of "The Exile's Return" in *Lord Weary's Castle*.

At the same time that *History* recounts the rise and fall of "these conquered kings" and cultures, then, it represents, presents again in small, Lowell's attempt, analogous to that of his Duc de Guise, another of the poet's guises, "to encircle the circle of his killers," to encompass the cultural and diurnal changes that attest the triumph of time. Indicative of this attempt is the secondary or latent structure of *History*, a structure not so much left over from the *Notebooks* as reminiscent of them, that both opposes the implications of the chronological arrangement and enlarges a metaphor for them. In spite of the linear chronological scheme—but equally importantly, because of it, since it is what literally delineates, as nothing in the *Notebooks* did, the relationship between historical past and present and thereby allows them to be joined—*History* has a circular form. That form is to be expected partly because for Lowell every discovery is "a discovery to be repeated many times," or because the past continually recurs, and partly because for him past and present form one whole— which is no doubt one reason that the simple chronological structure was so long in coming. At bottom, the world of *History* is as timeless as that of the *Cantos*, the work of another poet who made a pact with Whitman, although Lowell's is hardly as extensive or eloquent a book as Pound's. What *History* has in lieu of extensiveness and eloquence is a certain rigor—a poor enough substitute, perhaps, but one which might keep it from being lost, as Lowell speculates in "Cicero, the Sacrificial Killing" the *Cantos* might be lost, "in the rockslide of history" (an image probably drawn, ironically enough, from the end of *Canto III*). Lowell's mainstay against the rockslide of history—which is admittedly not as useful against the flash floods of contemporary events—is the chronology; but *History* also circumscribes the revolutions it describes.[5]

The contemporaneity of history and a subtle version of the metaphoric circle both appear in the new opening poem's closing lines, which are as "radiant with terror" as anything in Lowell's work:

> As in our Bibles, white-faced, predatory,
> the beautiful, mist-drunken hunter's moon ascends—
> a child could give it a face: two holes, two holes,
> my eyes, my mouth, between them a skull's no-nose—
> O there's a terrifying innocence in my face
> drenched with the silver salvage of the mornfrost.

Jarrell, echoing Eliot on Webster, said that Lowell saw the skull of history beneath the skin of the present.[6] Here, that skull is also God's (there is an outrageous pun, latensified by the reference to the child, on "no-nose," and in "For Robert

Kennedy 2" Lowell says bluntly, "God hunts us"), which is to say not so much that God is dead as that Death is God and that man is made and unmade in that image. The "O" made by the full moon signifies the whole (the hole) of it, the beginning of history and the end.

It is but the beginning of *History*, however, and the moon-circle motif returns in the second poem, "Man and Woman," also first published in this volume, initially in a reference to sheep "galloping in moon-blind wheels" and then in its last lines:

> Galileo, his great glass eye
> admiring the spots on the erroneous moon. . . .
> I watch this night out grateful to be alone
> with my wife—your slow pulse, my outrageous eye.

Seeing as far as man could clearly see, Galileo, like the speaker in the first poem, finds not God but a reflection of himself and "his great glass eye." What the holes are to the face in the first poem (and what the eye-flaw is to the "unbroken white cloud" in "Flaw," yet another poem in which God hunts man) the spots on the moon are to this one: the imperfection that is the first manifestation of mortality (or "the first scrape of the Thunderer's fingernail"). There is a "crack in everything God made" Lowell says in "Lévi-Strauss in London," and it is through that crack, that flaw or error, that death rushes in.

All such echoes, of which there are a great many, help to keep the poem—that is, *History*—going in circles; or to alter the metaphor, perhaps ironically, to another Lowell is fond of, *History* sometimes recalls the logically circular God of Pascal and Augustine, whose center is everywhere and whose circumference is nowhere. Nevertheless, by returning toward the end of the volume to motifs prominent in its beginning, Lowell gives the impression of an aesthetic circumference. In "Gods of the Family" (*Notebook*'s "High Blood"), the poet tells us:

> I feel familiar cycles of pain in my back,
> reticulations of the spawning cell,

> intimations of our family cancer—
> Grandmother's amnesia, Grandfather's cancered face
> wincing at my adolescent spots. . . .

With the reappearance of the "spots," which are so closely associated with death, the reader can say with Lowell, if with less literalness, that this is a familiar cycle indeed.

The cycle is emphasized as well in "Ice," a poem moved from the beginning of *Notebook* to the penultimate position in *History*, where it can help to take us full circle back to "History":

> the naught is no longer asset or disadvantage,
> our life too long for comfort and too brief
> for perfection—Cro-Magnon, dinosaur . . .
> the neverness of meeting nightly like surgeons'
> apprentices studying their own skeletons,
> old friends and mammoth flesh preserved in ice.

Just such an apprentice was the poet at the beginning of *History*, in a poem preceding by just a few those that focused on prehistorical beings, when he found himself studying his own skull in the figure of the moon. The circular face of that first poem reappears here as the "naught" that is the sum of both life and death; and one can imagine it also among the "ciphers" that appear in the early night sky in "End of a Year," once the last poem in "The Powerful" and now the last in *History*:

A year runs out in the movies, must be written
in bad, straightforward, unscanning sentences—
stamped, trampled, branded on backs of carbons,
lines, words, letters nailed to letters, words, lines—
the typescript looks like a rosetta stone. . . .
One more annus mirabilis, its hero *hero demens*,
ill-starred of men and crossed by his fixed stars,
running his ship past sound-spar on the rocks. . . .
The slush-ice on the east bank of the Hudson is rose heather
in the New Year sunset;
bright sky, bright sky, carbon scarred with ciphers.

The first lines of that last quotation, with their sarcastic glance at the journalistic poet whose work is not as well written as good prose, are at least as easily invoked in the case of one of the companion volumes to *History* as in the case of *History* itself. *For Lizzie and Harriet*, to be sure, contains some of Lowell's very best work in this "sonnet" form, and several of its finest poems have been discussed in the chapter on *Notebook*. Moreover, since the poems in this volume once lent *Notebook* much of its seasonal structure, the sequence is just as tightly (or loosely) and certainly more cleanly organized than the larger volume itself was. By virtue of the same thinness of material, however, more is asked of the plot and the "characters" in this sequence; and, strangely enough in view of Lowell's skill at vitalizing figures as seemingly remote from him as Hannibal and Cleopatra, Lizzie (his second wife, Elizabeth Hardwick) and Harriet (his and Hardwick's daughter) and the situation (the last year of his marriage, fraught with affairs and estrangements) lack substance and clear delineation. The volume is also peopled with ghosts of figures addressed in the second person and skeletons in the closet whom Lowell declines to flesh out. Most of this was excusable, if not necessarily more understandable, in *Notebook*, where there was always something else going on in the background either to illuminate indirectly or to dominate the obscure proceedings in the foreground. Here, where the family is the sole focal point, the absence of plotting and characterization raises questions, unanswerable on the basis of the text, that are so comparatively unimportant and uninteresting (who *is* this woman, approximately? what is Lowell *doing* in Mexico?) that one cannot but wonder why they were not anticipated.

The missing factor in *For Lizzie and Harriet*, that is, is something comparable to the prototypical and historical framework that informs *History*, the archetypal experiences that shape *For the Union Dead* and *Imitations*, and the religio-mythological scheme that structures "The Mills of the Kavanaughs": something that molds what he calls in one poem here "the horrifying mortmain of / ephemera." *The*

Dolphin confirms one's impression that Lowell's idea of the legitimate context of his poems has expanded to include events in (not, from our point of view, to be confused with poems about) his private life. A kind of sequel to *For Lizzie and Harriet*, this sequence deals with the breakup of the poet's second marriage and his embarkation upon a love affair with a British lady, Caroline, with whom he has had a child (Robert Sheridan Lowell) and who might or might not have become his third wife by the end of the volume. That this item is hardly determinable on the basis of the text as it stands—even though the question of whether they should marry is one of the main issues in the volume—indicates the odd reticence that afflicts both of these shorter books.[7] It is all the stranger in *The Dolphin*, for this sequence is full of documentation: quotations, probably doctored, from Elizabeth Hardwick's personal letters to him, transcriptions of telephone calls, excerpts from conversations, and so on. The effect is very like that of a diary, which must be expected to neglect plot in favor of raw data and to make fleeting allusions to events known in detail by the writer. For the ordinary diarist, the plot is lived through, and his jottings are primarily accessories to help him do the living. If one is interested in *his* writing, it is because one is interested in his life.

It sometimes seems that style is a luxury for the author of *The Dolphin*, too. The visceral stream of consciousness that Lowell has been developing ever since *Near the Ocean* takes its most extreme form in this volume: ellipsis after ellipsis, non sequiturs and metastases, fragmented sentences, and all manner of mannerisms that contribute to a quirky opacity partly pithy and partly platitudinous, partly genuine and partly brummagem. Passages from the opening and the concluding poems brilliantly exemplify both the aim and the result:

> Any clear thing that blinds us with surprise,
> your wandering silences and bright trouvailles,
> dolphin let loose to catch the flashing fish. . . .
>
> ("Fishnet")

My Dolphin, you only guide me by surprise,
forgetful as Racine, the man of craft,
drawn through his maze of iron composition
by the incomparable wandering voice of Phèdre.

("Dolphin")

But if Lowell pays a certain price for the fresh meat in the
Notebooks and *History*, he does not get the flashing fish cheap
in *The Dolphin*. There are some real gaffes (in "Morning Blue"
life is said to be "withdrawn like a bad lead in poker"); the
grammar is frequently awry (in "Angling" his lover's
"eyelashes are always blacked, / each hair colored and quick-
ened like tying a fly"); and the sequence as a whole carries
to a disturbing extreme a tendency evident in the poet's
manner "On the End of the Phone": "My sidestepping and
obliquities, unable / to take the obvious truth on any subject."[8]

At the same time, Lowell gives to his sidestepping and
obliquities, to the wandering course of his dolphin, a certain
shape. As the quotations from the first and last poems will
suggest but certainly not prove, that shape is from one point
of view a familiar one. As we know from others of Lowell's
volumes, a circular structure is often accompanied by
another, which can be figured as an inverted equilateral
triangle whose low point comes at the center of the work, and
so it is in *The Dolphin*. Frank Parker's drawing on the title
page of the volume combines these two geometric figures, for
it pictures in the shape of an inverted cone a female figure
who seems just to have dived into a body of water. The tip of
the cone, at the bottom of the drawing, coincides with her
head, while its base, at the top of the drawing, is formed by
the annulose ripples made by the plunge and its sides by the
water itself, through which we see the figure.

Something about the graceful position—one wants to say
the stance—of the figure makes one invert Parker's drawing,
and when this is done she seems more a dancer or perhaps
someone emerging from the water than someone diving. A
glance at the organization of the poems immediately confirms
the artist's implicit interpretation. There are thirty-three

groups here, the seventeenth of which is a three-poem sequence entitled "Doubt," whose the central poem, called
"Pointing the Horns of the Dilemma," defines its subject as a
"water-torture of vacillation." Now the horns of the dilemma
responsible for the abulia and vacillation that are the blurred
focuses of this group are of course Lizzie and Caroline; and in
the last half of the book the issue is resolved in favor of the
latter. In "Closed Sky," the first poem after this central sequence, Lowell notes, as though the decision had been made,
that "we use identical instruments / for putting up a house
and pulling down." If the emphasis is upon the "pulling
down" in the first half of this volume, it is upon the "putting
up" in the second half. That is what makes Parker make us
want to invert his title page.

The main theme as well as the structure of the volume is
the product of the movement of this ambiguous female; she is
the generatrix of the oddly convoluted figure that *The Dolphin*
is. Several pages before "Doubt" there occurs a group of
poems called "Mermaid"—and several pages after the central
sequence, almost predictably, there is a poem called "Mermaid Emerging." The group called "Mermaid" limns its main
figure as a kind of Lorelei, a variation on the theme of the
monstrous female that haunts Lowell's poems from "Between the Porch and the Altar" through "Near the Ocean"
to this volume. "None swims with her and breathes the air,"
we discover; and then, in a passage with a prominent pun:

> A mermaid flattens soles and picks a trout,
> knife and fork in chainsong at the spine,
> weeps white rum undetectable from tears.
> She kills more bottles than the ocean sinks,
> and serves her winded lovers' bones in brine,
> nibbled at recess in the marathon.

"Baudelaire feared women," the second poem in the group
begins, and the third vindicates such a fear by interpreting
the "you"—just as surely Caroline as the mermaid and the
figure on the title page—in terms reminiscent of the devastat-
ingly aloof Beloved of courtly love literature. The fourth
poem begins by comparing the mermaid-lover to a "baby
killer whale"; and the fifth concludes:

> I lack manhood to finish the fishing trip.
> Glad to escape beguilement and the storm,
> I thank the ocean that hides the fearful mermaid—
> like God, I almost doubt if you exist.

By the time we have gone beyond "Doubt" and reached "Mermaid Emerging," however, the beloved has reappeared, but as a savior rather than a threat:

> "I am a woman or I am a dolphin,
> the only animal man really loves,
> I spout the smarting waters of joy in your face—
> rough weather fish, who cuts your nets and chains."

Most of this is clear enough: the transformation of the killer whale into the beneficent dolphin accompanies the change from a precarious liaison to a solid relationship and the change from the agonizing destruction of the marriage to the establishment of the new household. In the last poem, Arion-Lowell addresses his dolphin thus:

> When I was troubled in mind, you made for my body
> caught in its hangman's-knot of sinking lines,
> the glassy bowing and scraping of my will. . . .

The telling complications arise when we realize, say—for a comparable realization could come at any point in the book— in what an odd way the last two quoted poems look back to "Fishnet," the first lines of which were quoted earlier. Here are the opening poem's concluding lines, which seem to echo the last lines of the first section of Eliot's "Dry Salvages":

> The line must terminate.
> Yet my heart rises, I know I've gladdened a lifetime
> knotting, undoing a fishnet of tarred rope;
> the net will hang on the wall when the fish are eaten,
> nailed like illegible bronze on the futureless future.

As we begin to see how these poems tie into one another, a host of other surprising connections appear. It is the poet who is in dire straits in the middle of the volume, but it is the mermaid who emerges later. The mermaid, in turn, is both the dolphin let loose "to catch the flashing fish" of poetry and one of the fish who is caught; she is comparable to the bronzed net that is the poet's salvation, and she cuts the net that threatens to drag him to his death. And the poet, caught and then freed (or is it vice versa?) like "the glass torpedo of a big fish" in "Lost Fish," sometimes seems himself to be the dolphin.

The analogies, as intricately woven as any since *The Mills of the Kavanaughs,* are arresting, and what they finally add up to is a startlingly insistent identification of the poet's life with his work. They constitute, that is, a network, or a net work, of which the reticulations and decussations are reality (people and events in the poet's life) and fiction (figures in his poetry)—although certainly not respectively, for that would be to separate them. Indeed, upon close examination Lowell's reality and fiction turn out to be as bound together as the fibers that make up the strands of one line in the net. If the dolphin is both mistress and muse, the net is at once life and art. Lowell speaks in several poems here of plotting his life ("Dolphin," "Exorcism 2") and of living out a plot ("Plotted," "Artist's Model 3"), and the terms seem to be interchangeable. Hence, perhaps, the inclusion in this volume—as in *For Lizzie and Harriet* and, to a lesser extent, *History*—of all of the adventitious and ephemeral material. Once life and fiction are so fused and confused, the details of the former are likely to be viewed as elements in the structure of the latter. At this juncture, what is already a major accomplishment imperils its future.

To no little extent, then, Lowell seems already to have achieved what he once admired in the work of Eliot. Not only have all his poems become one poem—both in the broad sense that they make up a context that serves a maieutic purpose for any one of them and in the narrower sense that they have all in effect contributed to *History*—but his one poem has increasingly become his life. The latest books point the difficulty: the achievement groans under its own weight. Precisely because his career has developed in a manner comparable to that of one of his poems or one of his volumes, each new work labors directly under the burden of the past.

How almost inconceivably difficult it must have been to re-
shape this burden as it appeared in *Notebook* into *History*. Nor
does it seem—not that there is any indication that he would
prefer to be able to do so—that there is any easy way for
Lowell to retrench at this point. Given the vast echo chamber
that he has constructed, every word that he utters must re-
verberate on and on for him, and consequently it is no wonder that he sometimes sounds as though he were sealed off
from common experience by his ordinary personal experience. He has used virtually all the available material in weav-
ing the net in which he is enmeshed; and yet he is convinced,
this unlikely Penelope of the littoral, that it is his obligation to
go on knotting and undoing the tarred rope.

Even as he sets down that image at the beginning of *The
Dolphin* of the "illegible bronze" fishnet (or "eelnet" as he has
it in that volume's last poem), he ties another knot. The intersecting line in this case extends from *History*, from the poem
entitled "Marlowe," where the playwright is made to say,
"'my plays are stamped in bronze, my life in tabloid.'" In his
latest work, Lowell is concerned to surmount the distinction.
The question, or one question, is whether the network can
support the weight of all of the seemingly inconsequential
details caught in and encrusting its ever-denser weave. In
"For John Berryman 2," a new poem that comes near the end
of *History*, Lowell writes:

> *When will I see you,*
> *John?* You flash back brightly to my mind,
> a net too grandly woven to catch the fry.

There is perhaps a wistful note, a self-critical comparison
implicit in that last line.

In any case, the position that Lowell has recently put himself in must sometimes call to his mind the remarks of his
mentor, Allen Tate, in "What Is a Traditional Society?":

First there is the religious imagination, which can mythologize indiscriminately. . . . Second there is the historical imagination,
which is the religious imagination *manqué*—an exercise of the
myth-making propensity of man within the restricted realm of the
historical event. Men see themselves in the stern light of Cato, but

they can no longer see themselves under the control of a tutelary diety.

The third stage is the complete triumph of positivism. . . . Under positivism we get just plain everyday history.[9]

Is Lowell so much the poet of our time that we can see the threat of a parallel in the course of his work? Perhaps. But then we were asking comparable questions before we had had a chance to accustom ourselves to *Life Studies*. It was in that volume that we had our first taste since *Lord Weary's Castle* of Lowell's Dante, a section of the *Inferno* that he was to render at length in *Near the Ocean* and then adapt for *Notebook*, before redoing it once more for *History*. I quote the latest version:

> A man running for his life will never tire:
> his Ser Brunetto ran through hell like one
> who ran for the green cloth through the green fields
> at Verona, looking more like one
> who won the roll of cloth, than those who lost. . . .

APPENDIX:
The "New" Poems in *History*

What follows is the result of the kind of work that one almost wishes he could delegate to a computer. One cannot do so, however, even if one would, because determining which poems in *History* previously appeared in *Notebook* is not a simple matter of matching opening lines or even central images or arguments. Lowell says that many of the poems brought over from *Notebook*—which are of course in nothing like their original order—have been "heavily revised," but he does not indicate where heavy revision ends and new work begins. Is a poem that has three lines from an earlier poem a revision or a fresh composition? What of the poem with only one old line? I am inclined to regard the latter case, at least, as a new poem, and so I have included an example below ("Sheik Without Six Wives in London"); but it is possible, since Lowell refers to "about 80" new poems, whereas I count eighty-five (if I include poems adapted or appropriated from volumes earlier than the *Notebooks*), that for him a revised poem is one that incorporates any element from *Notebook*, and I have probably inadvertently listed others that do so. At least the lists will provide a point of departure for other scholars and critics.

NOTES

INTRODUCTION: PROSPECTS

1. Lowell's account of his visit to Frost, during which they also discussed Keats's *Hyperion* and perhaps Milton's appeal to Lowell, is in "The Art of Poetry III: An Interview [with Frederick Seidel]," *The Paris Review*, no. 25 (Winter-Spring 1961), p. 82.

2. Ibid., p. 92. Lowell had in mind Eliot's comments on Shakespeare in "John Ford" (1932), in *Selected Essays* (London: Faber & Faber, 1951), pp. 193-204. Eliot argues that "what is 'the whole man' is not simply his greatest or maturest achievement, but the whole pattern formed by the sequence of plays; so that we may say confidently that the full meaning of any one of his plays is not in itself alone, but in that play in the order in which it was written, in its relation to all of Shakespeare's other plays, earlier and later: we must know all of Shakespeare's work in order to know any of it"; and that "the whole of Shakespeare's work is *one* poem, and it is the poetry of it in this sense, not the poetry of isolated lines and passages or the poetry of the single figures which he created, that matters most." For his extension of the argument, see "What Is Minor Poetry?" (1944), in *On Poetry and Poets* (1956; rpt. New York: Noonday, 1961).

3. S. T. Coleridge, *Unpublished Letters*, ed. E. L. Griggs (London: Constable, 1932), I, 256; quoted in Charles Feidelson, Jr., *Symbolism and American Literature* (Chicago and London: University of Chicago Press, 1953), p. 75. Chapter two below owes a great deal to Feidelson's book. See also M. II. Abrams's remarks on "Coleridge and the Aesthetics of Organicism," in *The Mirror and the Lamp: Romantic Theory and the Critical Tradition* (New York: Oxford University Press, 1953).

4. See esp. Hugh B. Staples, *Robert Lowell: The First Twenty Years* (New York: Farrar, Straus, 1962), pp. 38-39; and M. L. Rosenthal, *The New Poets* (New York: Oxford University Press, Galaxy, 1967), p. 71.

5. Irvin Ehrenpreis, "The Age of Lowell," in *American Poetry*, Stratford-on-Avon Series, 7, ed. Irvin Ehrenpreis (New York: St. Martin's Press, 1965), pp. 69-72.

6. "And Others," in *Form and Value in Modern Poetry* (New York: Doubleday Anchor, 1957), pp. 336-337.

7. Quoted in Stanley Kunitz, "Telling the Time," *Salmagundi*, 1, 4 (1966–67), 22.

8. *The Poetic Image* (London: Jonathan Cape, 1947), p. 50. Like Sypher's book, cited below, Day-Lewis's has been a valuable but general reference.

9. "The Added Artificer," in *On Translation*, ed. Reuben Brower (1959; rpt. New York: Oxford University Press, Galaxy, 1966), p. 139.

10. *Loss of the Self in Modern Literature and Art* (New York: Random House, 1962), pp. 58–59. The dates of the two publications together with the similarity of the imagery make it seem that Lowell may have read Sypher's account.

11. "A Meaning of Robert Lowell," in *The American Literary Anthology 2*, ed. George Plimpton, et al. (New York: Random House, 1969), p. 72.

12. "*Ekphrasis* and the Still Movement of Poetry; or, *Laokoön* Revisited," in *Perspectives on Poetry*, ed. James L. Calderwood and Harold Toliver (New York: Oxford University Press, Galaxy, 1968), p. 324.

13. Lowell, "The Art of Poetry III," p. 72.

1: THE WORD IN THE GARDEN

1. Eleven of the twenty-one poems appear, with revisions ranging from minor emendations to complete overhauls, in *Lord Weary's Castle*. These eleven are "The Park Street Cemetery" ("At the Indian Killer's Grave," which also incorporates the last lines of "Cistercians in Germany"); "In Memory of Arthur Winslow"; "Salem"; "Concord"; "Napoleon Crosses the Beresina"; "The Slough of Despond" (in *Land of Unlikeness*, the first poem in "Scenes from the Historic Comedy"); "Dea Roma"; "The Crucifix"; "Christmas Eve in the Time of War" ("Christmas Eve under Hooker's Statue"); "The Drunken Fisherman"; and "Children of Light."

2. Beginning with *Lord Weary's Castle*, Lowell's chief title-page illustrator has been his friend Frank Parker. Parker's drawings, almost always significant, will be commented upon from time to time in the course of this book.

3. The source of the epigraph is given in Hugh B. Staples, *Robert Lowell: The First Twenty Years* (New York: Farrar, Straus, 1962), p. 22.

4. "Notes on Seven Poets," in *Form and Value in Modern Poetry* (New York: Doubleday Anchor, 1957), p. 335.

5. Lowell's true affinity with Baudelaire, testified to by the number of "imitations" that he has done of that poet, is touched upon by D. S. Carne-Ross, "The Two Voices of Translation," in *Robert Lowell: A Collection of Critical Essays*, ed. Thomas Parkinson (Englewood Cliffs, N.J. Prentice-Hall, 1968), pp. 160–164.

6. "Consciously," Tate's adjective in his introduction, is particularly interesting in view of Lowell's later heretical views and eventual apostasy. Was Tate belaboring the obvious, or was he perhaps suggesting that Lowell's Catholicism had its strategic aspect? "The Symbolic Imagination" (1951) is reprinted in Tate's *Essays of Four Decades* (1968; rpt. New York: William Morrow, Apollo, 1970), pp. 424–446. "The Angelic Imagination" (1951) is the title of the preceding essay.

7. "The Symbolic Imagination," p. 430.

8. For Lowell's trial and sentencing see John McCormick, "Falling Asleep over Grillparzer: An Interview with Robert Lowell," *Poetry*, 81 (January 1953), 271. See also Phillip Cooper, *The Autobiographical Myth of Robert Lowell* (Chapel Hill: University of North Carolina Press, 1970), pp. 13–28.

9. My point should not be confused with that of John Bayley, "Robert Lowell: The Poetry of Cancellation," in *Robert Lowell: A Portrait of the Artist in His Time*, ed. Michael London and Robert Boyers (New York: David Lewis, 1968), pp. 187–198. Bayley's purely pejorative term, "a poetry that is purely verbal," is borrowed from T. S. Eliot and applied to a body of work that, he says, provides no "world which our own consciousness can inhabit and find out more about each time the poetry is re-read."

10. Cf., however, Lowell's more recent comment that the idioms in his poetry usually "come later [in the course of composition] because they don't prove much in themselves and they often replace something that's more formal and worked up." "The Art of Poetry III: An Interview [with Frederick Seidel]," *The Paris Review*, no. 25 (Winter-Spring 1961), p. 73.

11. "Tension in Poetry," in *Essays*, pp. 56–71.

12. See W. H. Auden, *The Dyer's Hand* (New York: Random House, 1962), p. 40; and Lowell, "The Verses of Thomas Merton," *Commonweal*, 22 June 1945, pp. 240–242.

13. "Thomas, Bishop, and Williams," *Sewanee Review*, 55 (Summer 1947), 493.

14. Charles Feidelson, Jr., *Symbolism and American Literature* (Chicago and London: University of Chicago Press, Phoenix, 1953), p. 71.

15. Blackmur, "Notes," p. 334.

16. "Playing Ball with the Critic" in *Notebook 1967–68*, in which Lowell quotes from the review cited above. The quote from Blackmur is recast in Lowell's own words in the version of the poem that appears in *History*.

17. For another view of these lines, see Marjorie Perloff, *The Poetic Art of Robert Lowell* (Ithaca, N. Y., and London: Cornell University Press, 1973), pp. 133–135. Perloff argues that since the whole sentence is "You ponder why the coxes' squeakings dwarf / The *resurrexit Dominus* of all the bells," the lines imply that "Arthur Winslow did not have faith in Christ." But I see no reason to suppose that the *resurrexit* is diminished only for the ears of Arthur Winslow.

18. John Frederick Nims, "Two Catholic Poets," *Poetry*, 65 (February 1945), 267–268; and Randall Jarrell, "From the Kingdom of Necessity," in *Poetry and the Age* (1953; rpt. New York: Random House, Vintage, 1959), p. 192.

19. Feidelson, *Symbolism and American Literature*, p. 33. The remark is made in regard to Melville's ocean in *Moby Dick*, but it is quite appropriate to Lowell's "wide waters."

20. There are of course three other poems in the sequence, but "Death from Cancer" is nonetheless an entity. Perloff, *Poetic Art*, p. 135, indicates its integrity even as she suggests that it has shortcomings when she says, "The poem never comes to terms with these questions; the salvation theme is abruptly dropped" in the sequence. The questions to which she refers are these: since "Arthur Winslow did not have faith in Christ," "how then can he cross the 'wide waters' of the Acheron to heaven? And how does the speaker *know* with such assurance what Arthur's fate will be?" My point is precisely that he does *not* know what Arthur's fate will be. Consequently, there is no theme of certain salvation to be dropped in the remaining poems. This poem stands apart from the others, but the source of its integrity is its structure, not its theme.

21. See Staples, *The First Twenty Years*, p. 15 and p. 32; Irvin Ehrenpreis, "The Age of Lowell," in *American Poetry*, Stratford-on-Avon Series, 7, ed.

Irvin Ehrenpreis (New York: St. Martin's Press, 1965), p. 74; and Cooper, *Autobiographical Myth*, p. 51.

22. Tate's comment in the introduction is accepted by many of Lowell's critics.

23. As Staples notes in his "Appendix II," this poem was published in *Chimera*, 1 (Spring 1943), 20, and revised for publication in this first volume. Nevertheless, it seems sufficiently different from any other poem in *Land of Unlikeness* to warrant this conjecture.

2: A DIALECTICAL SYMBOLISM

1. R. P. Blackmur, "Notes on Seven Poets," in *Form and Value in Modern Poetry* (New York: Doubleday Anchor, 1957), pp. 324–325; Randall Jarrell, "From the Kingdom of Necessity," in *Poetry and the Age* (1953; rpt. New York: Random House, Vintage, 1959), pp. 188–199.

2. The quoted phrase is Thom Gunn's, in "Excellence and Variety," *Yale Review*, 44 (Winter 1960), 304.

3. Lowell comments briefly on the Elizabethans and Metaphysicals in "The Art of Poetry III: An Interview [with Frederick Seidel]," *The Paris Review*, no. 25 (Winter-Spring 1961), pp. 79–80.

4. Tate uses the former term in reference to Crane and others in "Hart Crane," in *Essays of Four Decades* (1968; rpt. New York: William Morrow, Apollo, 1970), p. 310. It seems more specific than "post-symbolist" or "symbolistic." The influence upon Lowell of New Criticism, about which he has never been reticent, is summarized in general terms in Phillip Cooper, *The Autobiographical Myth of Robert Lowell* (Chapel Hill: University of North Carolina Press, 1970), pp. 29–37. Some of Lowell's most interesting remarks on the subject are to be found in "Robert Lowell in Conversation with A. Alvarez," *The Observer*, 21 July 1963; rpt. in part in *The Review*, no. 8 (August 1963) pp. 36–40. In *History*, glossing a photograph of himself at an early age, he writes: "I lean against the tree, and sharpen bromides / to serve our great taskmaster, the New Critic, / who loved the writing better than we ourselves."

5. "Thomas, Bishop, and Williams," *Sewanee Review*, 55 (Summer 1947), 493.

6. "The Art of Poetry III," p. 62.

7. Ibid., p. 89. Cf. Tate, "The Angelic Imagination," in *Essays*, p. 406, and "Hart Crane," in *Essays*.

8. "From Mr. Crane to the Editor [Harriet Monroe]," in *Modern Poets on Modern Poetry*, ed. James Scully (London and Glasgow: Collins, The Fontana Library, 1966), p. 168.

9. "General Aims and Theories," rpt. in *Modern Poets*, p. 165.

10. Letter to Henry Treece, quoted in Treece, *Dylan Thomas: Dog Among the Fairies*, rev. ed. (London: E. Benn, 1957), p. 25.

11. William Empson, *Seven Types of Ambiguity*, 2d ed. (New York: Meridian, 1955), p. 265.

12. For key discussions of these terms, see esp. Charles Feidelson, Jr., *Symbolism and American Literature* (Chicago and London: University of Chicago Press, Phoenix, 1953), pp. 54–65; John Dewey, *Art as Experience* (New York: Minton, 1934); C. Day-Lewis, *The Poetic Image* (London: Jonathan Cape, 1947), esp. pp. 117–119; Susanne K. Langer, *Feeling and Form* (New

York: Charles Scribner's Sons, 1953); Lawrence S. Dembo, *Conceptions of Reality in Modern Poetry* (Berkeley and Los Angeles: University of California Press, 1966). An important related discussion upon which I have drawn is Günther Müller's "Morphological Poetics," in *Reflections on Art*, ed. Susanne K. Langer (1958; rpt. New York: Oxford University Press, Galaxy, 1961), pp. 202–228.

13. Tate, "The Symbolic Imagination," in *Essays*, p. 432.

14. *First Truths*, rpt. in *From Descartes to Locke*, trans. and ed. T. V. Smith and Marjorie Greene (1940; rpt. Chicago and London: University of Chicago Press, Phoenix, 1966), p. 300.

15. *Hegel: Texts and Commentary*, trans. and ed. Walter Kaufmann (1965; rpt. New York: Doubleday Anchor, 1966), pp. 98 and 31, n. 8, where Kaufmann also points out the connection between Hegel's principle and Nietzsche's subtitle that I have adapted above. Lowell, in reviewing Wallace Stevens's *Transport to Summer* in "Imagination and Reality," *The Nation*, 5 April 1947, p. 400, says that "directly or indirectly much of Stevens' thought is derived from the dialectical idealism of Hegel." If one substitutes "method" for "thought," this statement applies to Lowell. References to other dialecticians—ranging from Plato through Abelard and Coleridge to Marcuse—are scattered throughout Lowell's *Notebooks* and *History*.

16. Hegel's statements might also be compared with those of the "Projectivist" poets. Cf., e.g., Charles Olson, "Projective Verse," in *Modern Poets*, esp. pp. 272–275.

17. The quoted sentence is R. P. Blackmur's in "The Craft of Herman Melville: A Putative Statement," in *The Lion and the Honeycomb* (New York: Harcourt Brace, Harvest, 1955), p. 138, but it summarizes succinctly the point.

18. In *The Language of Poetry*, ed. Allen Tate (Princeton, N.J.: University of Princeton Press, 1942), p. 74.

19. "Letter to the Editor," in *Modern Poets*, p. 168; Treece, *Dylan Thomas*, p. 25.

20. On the concept of "function," see Langer, *Feeling and Form*, esp. pp. 88 ff.; and Feidelson, *Symbolism and American Literature*, p. 56.

21. The quoted phrase is from Feidelson, *Symbolism and American Literature*, p. 61. Here, as through most of his book, and as in the cases of some of the other preceding quotations, the subject is literary structure in general. The distinction between general and particular aesthetic theory, however, is a difficult one to make. Shelley in his *Defense of Poetry* is articulating not Romantic theory but general principles; Boileau in his *L'Art poétique*, not Gallic neoclassicism but poetics. The distinction seems to be blurred in most major writings on the subject. Be that as it may, the foregoing discussion rests not upon the premise that the writers quoted were consciously defining the aesthetics of a period but upon the premise that certain ideas were in fact current during that period. I have read too late for it to influence this discussion Hugh Kenner's masterful analysis of the concept of "patterned energy" or "patterned process" in *The Pound Era* (Berkeley, Los Angeles, and London: University of California Press, 1971). What I refer to as neo-symbolism, however, he might well regard as a legacy of Vorticism. I quote from p. 159:

"Then late in 1913, through the Fenollosa mss., China itself appeared to be declaring the needful truth to liberate Imagism, the truth that words pattern process, and that Nature, from which language comes, is patterned process. 'The forces which produce the branch-angles of an oak lay potent in the acorn,' wrote Fenollosa; and again, 'The development of the normal transitive sentence rests upon the fact that one action in nature promotes another; thus the agent and object are secretly verbs.' And what does the Chinese writer set on his page? Why, a picture of the active thing."

22. *Hegel: Texts and Commentary*, p. 30.

23. Jarrell, "Kingdom of Necessity," p. 198. The other three: "Colloquy in Black Rock," the first part of "The Death of the Sheriff," and "Where the Rainbow Ends." Jerome Mazzaro, *The Poetic Themes of Robert Lowell* (Ann Arbor: University of Michigan Press, 1965), pp. 63–65, has a brief discussion from another point of view.

24. A remarkably similar structure is to be found in "During Fever" *(Life Studies)*. "Mother and Son," by the way, is also the title of a poem by Allen Tate in *The Swimmers and Other Selected Poems* (New York: Charles Scribner's Sons, 1970), pp. 53–54. Written before Lowell's poem, Tate's is also concerned with the inevitably hostile relationship of mother and son and with original sin.

25. *Anatomy of Criticism: Four Essays* (1957; rpt. New York: Atheneum, 1966), p. 322.

26. See chapter four, n. 14, for comments on a passage in which Lowell's punning description of a rebirth is more obvious but at least as outrageous.

27. E.g., "The Death of the Sheriff" and "In the Attic."

28. Cf. *Paradise Lost*, X, 511–521.

29. Hugh B. Staples, *Robert Lowell: The First Twenty Years* (New York: Farrar, Straus, 1962), pp. 87–88 gives the Biblical source of the title and other background information. Other relevant passages in Joel, it might be added, are 2:28 ("and your sons and daughters shall prophesy, . . . your young men shall see visions") and 3:10 ("Beat your ploughshares into swords"). Lowell's title must also allude to the identically entitled short story by Jean Stafford, his first wife, to whom *Lord Weary's Castle* is dedicated, which is included in the collection *Children Are Bored on Sunday* in *The Interior Castle* (New York: Harcourt Brace, 1953), pp. 144–155. Stafford's story, details of which recall "Katherine's Dream," was first published in *Harper's*, 190 (June 1945), 654–657. If there is a relationship between the title of another Stafford story in this collection, "The Interior Castle," itself derived from St. Teresa's work, and the title of Lowell's second volume, it is not immediately apparent; it might be pointed out, however, that the heroine of the story, but not her driver, survives an accident in a taxicab.

30. Lowell's comment is in "The Art of Poetry III," p. 76.

31. "Thomas, Bishop, and Williams," 494.

32. See Joel 3:12 and *Smith's Bible Dictionary*, ed. William Smith (New York: Pyramid, 1967), under "Jehoshaphat."

33. Jarrell, "Kingdom of Necessity," p. 196. In fact, Jarrell remarks on the "extraordinary degree" to which Lowell's details keep their particularity even as they function symbolically. Earlier in his essay, however, he has commented on the "magically and professionally illusionary quality" of these details and on the excessive "rhetorical description" of "The Quaker Graveyard in Nantucket."

34. For analyses of the poem see Staples, *The First Twenty Years*, pp. 45–52; Mazzaro, *Poetic Themes*, pp. 37–43; Patrick Cosgrave, *The Public Poetry of Robert Lowell* (New York: Taplinger, 1972), pp. 89–105; Richard J. Fein, *Robert Lowell* (New York: Twayne, 1970), pp. 29–30.

35. Fein, *Robert Lowell*, p. 30.

36. "Preface to *Roderick Hudson*," in *The Art of the Novel* (1934; rpt. New York and London: Charles Scribner's Sons, 1962), p. 5.

37. T. H. Jones, "The Poetry of Robert Lowell," *The Month*, N.S. 9 (1953), 137.

38. W. B. Yeats, *A Vision*, rev. ed. (1956; rpt. New York: Macmillan, 1961), p. 8. In the following discussion, I do not mean to imply that Yeats's poetry cannot be properly understood without reference to *A Vision*. His comment in the introduction that Blake "remains almost unintelligible because he never drew" a diagram of his own system could not be echoed in the case of Yeats even in the absence of *A Vision*, partly because his poetic contexts, like Lowell's, define his "metaphors" even as they transmute them. To recognize the integrity of Yeats's poetry, however, is not to deny the importance of "those hard symbolic bones under the skin," as he calls them.

39. "The Art of Poetry III," p. 85.

40. *A Vision*, pp. 24–25.

41. "The Art of Poetry III," pp. 75–76.

42. Lowell's spelling, "Lambkin," and its ramifications are discussed by Cooper, *Autobiographical Myth*, pp. 53–54.

43. For an interpretation of several aspects of the castle symbol, see John Berryman, "Lowell, Thomas & Co.," *Partisan Review*, 24 (January-February, 1947), 73–80.

44. Staples provides this information in one of his valuable appendices.

45. Mazzaro has an enlightening discussion of the Cain motif in *Land of Unlikeness* and *Lord Weary's Castle* in his second and third chapters. Frank Parker's title-page drawing depicts Cain skulking away from the murder of his brother.

46. "Thomas, Bishop, and Williams," 501.

47. The root meaning of "Salem" is "peace."

48. The main source of this poem is Edwards's "Narrative of Surprising Conversions," cast in the form of a letter of 6 November 1736; see Staples, "Appendix I," for further information on the sources.

49. It is interesting to note that in "Jonathan Edwards in Western Massachusetts" in *For the Union Dead*, Lowell does not attempt to disguise an analogy between himself and Edwards, here the ego to his alter ego.

3: THE LOGIC OF CONTRADICTION

1. On these two interpretations, see Will C. Jumper, "Whom Seek Ye?: A Note on Robert Lowell's Poetry," *Hudson Review*, 9 (Spring 1956), 123.

2. The comments are reported in Stanley Kunitz, "Telling the Time," *Salmagundi*, 1, 4 (1966–67), 22.

3. See, e.g., Randall Jarrell, "Three Books," in *Poetry and the Age* (1953; rpt. New York: Random House, Vintage, 1959), pp. 230–236; and William Arrowsmith, "Five Poets," *Hudson Review*, 4 (Winter 1952), 624–627. Herbert Leibowitz, "Robert Lowell: Ancestral Voices" *Salmagundi*, 1, 4 (1966–67), 34–35, typifies readers' reluctance to write about this volume, as he dismisses it in a paragraph as "transitional." Phillip Cooper, *The Autobiographical Myth of Robert Lowell* (Chapel Hill: University of North Carolina Press, 1970), does not have one substantive comment on the volume. Marjorie Perloff, *The Poetic Art of Robert Lowell* (Ithaca, N.Y., and London: Cornell University

Press, 1973), p. 187, calls this volume and *Near the Ocean* "problematic transitional volumes" and says: "Accordingly, I cite examples from these texts only occasionally." As is frequently the case, Richard J. Fein, *Robert Lowell* (New York: Twayne, 1970), p. 41, makes the most judicious comment: "In the best sense of that much abused term, *The Mills of the Kavanaughs* is a transitional volume; it shows us the poet's development."

4. At 608 lines, the title poem is easily the longest poem (as distinct from a sequence) that Lowell has ever written. Only "The Fat Man in the Mirror" is under 60 lines.

5. Jerome Mazzaro, *The Poetic Themes of Robert Lowell* (Ann Arbor: University of Michigan Press, 1965), p. 78, notes that August 23 was the date of the execution of Sacco and Vanzetti, another pair whose culpability was open to question.

6. Lowell's lines—"O Brother, a New England town is *death* / And incest—I saw it whole"—seem to echo Arnold's famous description of "a Friend" as one "who saw *life* steadily and saw it whole." If there is an intention here, it is doubtless ironic.

7. The bird imagery is one of several things about this poem that recommend a comparison with Stevens's "Sunday Morning." Both poets adopt personae who dream their way into the past and both poems take the place of a sermon. With others of Lowell's poems, this one might also owe something to Tate's "Aeneas at Washington." In the relationship among its images, it recalls Dylan Thomas's "After the Funeral."

8. In the *Aeneid*, the passage in quotation marks is spoken by Jupiter, but the identity of the speaker at this point in Lowell's poem is not clear.

9. Mazzaro, *Poetic Themes*, p. 77, seems to think that "Vergil" is actually the *name* of the speaker. I see no reason to think so, even though this would establish the parallel between the persona and the Roman poet that I do think is implied here.

10. The idea that history is an endless succession of wars is a recurrent one in Lowell's work. Cf. "Beyond the Alps" *(Life Studies)* and "Waking Early Sunday Morning" *(Near the Ocean)*. One of the main motifs in Fein's book is the military motif in Lowell's work.

11. Jarrell, "Three Books," p. 233, speaks of the "sense of the terrible continuity of the world" with which this poem left him.

12. See John Holloway, "Robert Lowell and the Public Dimension," *Encounter*, 30 (April 1968), 73–80. Patrick Cosgrave, *The Public Poetry of Robert Lowell* (New York: Taplinger, 1972), p. 23, develops Holloway's point.

13. See Hugh B. Staples, *Robert Lowell: The First Twenty Years* (New York: Farrar, Straus, 1962), pp. 56–64. My interpretation of Anne is, I think, compatible with Staples's and owes something to him. He sees that Harry combines both connotations of "Plutonic" (i.e., "subterranean" and "opulent"), but he does not seem to regard him, as I do, as a symbol of a Janus-faced deity.

14. Arrowsmith, "Five Poets," 625.

15. Staples, *The First Twenty Years* pp. 54–55, briefly compares this version of "The Mills of the Kavanaughs" with the first published version, in which the images and allusions were decidedly more Christian. The first version was published in the *Kenyon Review,* 13 (Winter 1951), 1–19.

16. Jarrell, "Three Books," p. 235.

17. It should be noted that in the first version of the poem, the last stanza begins: "She banks her boat. Climbing toward the church, / She hears her

husband; when he nears the sluice / And burial ground above the burlap mill. . . . " The only vestige of this passage in the revised version is in stanza 37—" 'Now we near the sluice / And burial ground above the burlap mill' "—which might or might not indicate that Anne has reached shore. In the third stanza from the end of both versions, we are told that Anne's " 'reflection' " is in some sense " 'aground.' " The revised version informs us that the leaves on the water " 'reach / For my reflection, but it glides through shoal / Aground to where' " she and Harry once spent their days. Now, because there seems to be a pun on " 'reflection,' " it seems likely that the movement ashore is mental rather than physical, especially since it is *after* this section that the stanza beginning " 'I think we row together' " occurs. In the first version, because the corresponding lines are in the past tense (" 'And when we rowed together' "), the implication that she is ashore is not controverted. Here, however, if that implication is present, contradiction is evaded only if one supposes that Anne speaks just of a past experience in the present tense—which, in view of the change in tense, seems highly unlikely. But in any case, even if one imagines Anne ashore at the end of the poem, one must see her in the autumn, near the burial ground, asking herself rhetorically why we should mistrust ourselves with death. If the water is not the means of death, it is the sign of it, even as the Acheron is in "Death from Cancer" and the bay is in "Her Dead Brother." Either view throws a new light on Frank Parker's drawing on the title page, which is of a dying swan, afloat on the water, beak open in its fabled, final cry.

18. This interpretation of Persephone is not consistently adhered to in the poem (see the following discussion).

19. Staples, *The First Twenty Years*, p. 63, sums up many of the dualisms in the poem by noting that the throne is a grave, but the grave is a garden.

20. Golgotha is alluded to in "Skunk Hour" (*Life Studies*) in much the same way.

21. On the importance of the observation of detail to Lowell, see his brief comparison of himself to Roethke in "The Art of Poetry III: An Interview [with Frederick Seidel]," *The Paris Review*, no. 25 (Winter-Spring 1961), p. 87, and his poem "Hawthorne" in *For the Union Dead*. When he introduced Elizabeth Bishop at a reading at the Guggenheim Museum in May 1969, he made much of her "famous eye." Cf. also Lowell's remark, quoted in chapter one above, on Dylan Thomas's inability to keep his eye on the object.

22. It is obviously one thing to say that people and institutions are "self-contradictory" and another to say that truth itself is. I do not think that my discussion implies that either Lowell or I should argue for the second claim. Jarrell, in "Some Lines from Whitman," in *Poetry and the Age*, p. 116, puts the point to be made in this way: "When you organize one of the contradictory elements out of your work of art, you are getting rid not just of it, but of the contradiction of which it was a part; and it is the contradictions in works of art which make them able to represent to us—as logical and methodical generalizations cannot—our world and ourselves, which are also full of contradictions."

23. This strategy also lies at the heart of *The Old Glory*, Lowell's dramatic trilogy, based mostly on stories by Hawthorne and Melville, of more than a decade later. In the speech that climaxes *Endecott and the Red Cross*, the protagonist—a Puritan sensualist and God-fearing executioner—points out that in England's civil wars, another of which he feels obliged to begin, "the opposing captains were indistinguishable." Earlier, Morton, his enemy and

counterpart—a paganizing Anglican and gunrunning royalist—has maintained before the Anglican minister Blackstone (who, like *his* counterpart Palfrey, the Puritan minister, is truly a "lunatic of one idea") that "the world is changeable. It's like a playing card: / a king in all his theatrical pomp in front—/ and what's on the other side? Black and white squares." In the more complicated *Benito Cereno*, the third play in the trilogy and the one to which the expanded *Endecott* was to "give support," as Lowell says in his note to the revised edition of 1968, American captain and Castilian don, slave and king, rugged individualist and wan aristocrat are all gradually and inexorably equated.

24. It is interesting to note that the distinctive rhythms of John Berryman's *Homage to Mistress Bradstreet* sound a good deal like this section of Lowell's poem. The opening stanza of the *Homage*, where the "New World" is the subject, seems particularly close to Lowell's lines in cadence. There is a similar possible influence of the rhythms in parts of "Thanksgiving's Over" (especially the fifth stanza) upon Sylvia Plath's poetry in *Ariel*. M. L. Rosenthal, *The New Poets* (New York: Oxford University Press, Galaxy, 1967), p. 74, suggests that the language of this last poem might have been a source for Plath's "Daddy."

25. One source of this poem is Baudelaire's "La servante," and Lowell's translation of that poem's last line in *Imitations* is virtually identical with the last line of "Mother Marie Therese."

26. *Smith's Bible Dictionary*, ed. William Smith (New York: Pyramid, 1967), p. 350.

27. Cf. the comments on "In the Cage" in chapter two and those on the title sequence of *Near the Ocean* in chapter seven.

28. See the discussion in chapter five of "Eye and Tooth" and "Myopia: a Night."

29. See George Dekker, *Sailing after Knowledge: The Cantos of Ezra Pound* (London: Routledge & Kegan Paul, 1965), pp. 154–165 for a discussion of "Hugh Selwyn Mauberley" in this light.

30. In her reference to a "new earth" Michael's wife seems to be echoing Miranda's "brave new world" speech in *The Tempest*.

31. It is worth noting that *El* means "God" in Hebrew.

32. She further thinks of life as a cell and therefore coins the phrase " 'life's a sell.' " The pun here seems as meretricious as the recollection of "locks" in her reference to herself as " 'Goldielocks,' " which appellation, if juxtaposed with her " 'El Dorado,' " succinctly expresses her paranoia.

4: DIVORCE AND RECONCILIATION

1. "Introduction: Robert Lowell and the Uses of Modern Poetry in the University," in *Robert Lowell: A Collection of Critical Essays*, ed. Thomas Parkinson (Englewood Cliffs, N.J.: Prentice-Hall, 1968), p. 9.

2. "New Thresholds, New Anatomies," in *Form and Value in Modern Poetry* (New York: Doubleday Anchor, 1957), pp. 273–274.

3. "Several Kinds of Short Poem," in *Poets on Poetry*, ed. Howard Nemerov (New York: Basic Books, 1966), pp. 40–47.

4. Both of Lowell's comments may be found in "Thomas, Bishop, and Williams," *Sewanee Review*, 55 (Summer 1947), 500.

5. Jarrell's review is reprinted in *Poetry and the Age* (1953; rpt. New York: Random House, Vintage 1959), pp. 205–212. This comment is on pp. 205–206.

6. Ibid., p. 207. Richard J. Fein, *Robert Lowell* (New York: Twayne, 1970), p. 47, says that *"Life Studies* is the most structured book that Lowell has yet written," but he does not elaborate as much as one might wish. The superlative in his comment seems to me unwarranted, as the following chapters will suggest.

7. The musical analogy is an especially interesting one in the case of *Life Studies,* for the parallel between the structure of this book and that of a symphony could be drawn in some detail. The book has four "parts" which correspond to the four movements of a symphony and could conceivably be labeled allegro, adagio, scherzo, and adagio, respectively, on the grounds of style and pace. The first and third parts have four sections each, as does sonata form (exposition, development, recapitulation, coda), and that form is common in the first and third movements of a symphony. Moreover, the repetition of motifs throughout is itself characteristic of some "cyclical" symphonies.

8. M. L. Rosenthal in "Poetic Theory of Some Contemporary Poets," *Salmagundi,* 1, 4 (1966–67), 72, intimates that he "invented" the modern use of the term "confessional." Interestingly enough, Lowell himself had used the adjective casually in his review of Eliot's *Four Quartets, Sewanee Review,* 51 (Summer 1943), 432–433. A fine discussion of "the role convention plays" in Lowell's confessional poems is contained in Marjorie Perloff, *The Poetic Art of Robert Lowell* (Ithaca, N.Y., and London: Cornell University Press, 1973), chapter three.

9. See the discussion of Anne Kavanaugh in chapter three above and Hugh B. Staples's comments on her in *Robert Lowell: The First Twenty Years* (New York: Farrar, Straus, 1962), esp. p. 64.

10. The poem once comprised four sonnets; the fourth section was restored when "Beyond the Alps" was reprinted in *For the Union Dead.*

11. Jerome Mazzaro puts forward the cyclical view in *The Poetic Themes of Robert Lowell* (Ann Arbor: University of Michigan Press, 1965), pp. 91–92. Irvin Ehrenpreis, in "The Age of Lowell," in *American Poetry,* Stratford-on-Avon Series, 7, ed. Irvin Ehrenpreis (New York: St.Martin's Press, 1965), p. 87, regards Greece as an ideal culture rather than as a prototype; while Stephen Stepanchev, *American Poetry Since 1945: A Critical Survey* (New York: Harper and Row, 1965), pp. 20–31, seems to think that Lowell sees history as a process of cultural degradation. Glauco Cambon, "Dea Roma and Robert Lowell," *Accent,* 20 (Winter 1960), 51–61, suggests that this poem was written from a Catholic point of view; for the report of Lowell's correction, see Cambon, *The Inclusive Flame: Studies in American Literature* (Bloomington: University of Indiana Press, 1963), p. 245, n. 9.

12. Perhaps no two of these views are necessarily contradictory. But the realization that Lowell is not formulating any theory of history, including some compromise version, obviates the possibility of self-contradiction that arises when one tries both to derive such a theory from the poem and to discuss the poetry in any depth.

13. Mazzaro, *Poetic Themes,* p. 91, also notes this allusion. When he published this poem in *For the Union Dead,* Lowell prefaced it with a quote from Napoleon: "Au delà les Alpes est l'Italie."

14. The recognition of this disillusionment facilitates explanation of the obscure passage in the third section, for in addition to describing the train pulling out of the Alps onto the plains of France at dawn, this passage summarizes the speaker's rejection of all aspects of "Rome." He too had come down to earth, as it were, having grown weary of the querulous placation ("hush-hush") of the public by the Pope and assorted political leaders ("wheels"?); consequently, his discouraged self ("the blear-eyed ego") gave up the struggle to adopt the optimistic view and the new way of life offered by the Church ("kicking in my berth / lay still") and relapsed into a pessimistic quasi-pagan philosophy that could at least account for such a worldly phenomenon as Mussolini.

15. The antimelioristic strain in Lowell's poetry has been as constant as any other thematic factor over the years.

16. Staples, *The First Twenty Years*, p. 73. This poem is another descendant of "On the Eve of the Feast of the Immaculate Conception 1942."

17. Lowell's recollections of Ford are in "Visiting the Tates," *Sewanee Review*, 67 (Autumn 1959), 557–559; brief comments on Ford, Schwartz, and Crane can be found in *"The Art of Poetry III: An Interview* [with Frederick Seidel]," *The Paris Review*, no. 25 (Winter-Spring 1961), pp. 56–95, and in John McCormick, "Falling Asleep over Grillparzer: An Interview with Robert Lowell," *Poetry*, 81 (January 1953), 269–279. Lowell's foreword to Ford's *Buckshee (Last Poems)* (Cambridge, Mass.: Pym-Randall, 1966) is a sparkling piece of writing. Although Lowell has written nothing in prose on Santayana, one of his shorter pieces is relevant to the interpretation of "For George Santayana" that is offered here; see "A Note [on Gerard Manley Hopkins]," *Kenyon Review*, 6 (Autumn 1944), 583–586.

18. M. L. Rosenthal, *The New Poets* (New York: Oxford University Press, 1967), pp. 45–46, seems to credit the poem more than either Mazzaro, *Poetic Themes*, pp. 100–102, or Staples.

19. Wordsworth's lines are in stanza 7, following the tributes to Chatterton ("The sleepless Soul that perished in his pride") and Burns ("Him who walked in glory and in joy").

20. This is the implication, for example, of Herbert Leibowitz, "Robert Lowell: Ancestral Voices," *Salmagundi*, 1, 4 (1966–67), 37, when he says that Lowell, "without fussing to extract a pattern, leafs through the family annals" in this poem. (As well as distracting attention from the structure of the volume, the "Family Album" notion seems to hinder the investigation of the organization of individual poems).

21. Rosenthal, *The New Poets*, p. 65. Phillip Cooper, *The Autobiographical Myth of Robert Lowell* (Chapel Hill: University of North Carolina Press, 1970), p. 59, having quoted these lines, says, "The strength of this meterless poem is hard to describe."

22. *Annals*, xii-xiv, trans. J. Jackson (1937; rpt. London: William Heinemann, Loeb Library, 1951).

23. Louis Martz, "The Elegiac Mode," *Yale Review*, 54 (Winter 1965), 290.

24. Some lines toward the end of Lowell's poem—"Grandpa! Have me, hold me, cherish me! / Tears smut my fingers"—probably derive from Vaughan's last stanza:

> Either disperse these mists, which blot and fill
> My perspective (still) as they pass,
> Or else remove me hence unto that hill,
> Where I shall need no glass.

They also bear an ironic relationship to the lyrics of "Summer Time," the song referred to earlier in the poem. The first two verses of this song are as follows: "Summer time, / And the livin' is easy, / The corn is jumpin', / And the cotton is high. / Your daddy's rich, and your ma is good-lookin', / So hush, little baby, don't you cry. // One of these mornin's / You're gonna rise up singin', / You're gonna spread your wings, / And take to the sky. / Until that mornin', ain't nothin' gonna harm you, / With mommy and daddy standin' by." Lowell's grandfather, his "real father," is no longer standing by.

25. Stephen Spender, "Robert Lowell's Family Album," *New Republic*, 8 June 1959, p. 17; and Rosenthal, "Poetic Theory of Some Contemporary Poets," 71. Cf. Michael Fried, "The Achievement of Robert Lowell," *London Magazine*, 2 (October 1962), 54–64, who goes so far as to maintain that the alleged "confessional, even bathetic" tone of parts of *Life Studies* is a grave flaw because Lowell's strategy in this volume makes that tone necessary.

26. Spender, "Family Album," p. 17; and Mazzaro, *Poetic Themes*, p. 118, who quotes Spender approvingly.

27. Mazzaro, *Poetic Themes*, p. 112.

28. "Sacrificial"—which makes more sense than "sacrificed"—is the adjective in all but the Vintage edition of *Life Studies*.

29. The relationship between the Lowells and Hearn once worked the other way. Hugh Kenner, *The Pound Era* (Berkeley, Los Angeles, and London: University of California Press, 1971), p. 293, notes that it was a book by Percy Lowell, Amy's brother, "which lured Lafcadio Hearn to Nippon."

30. For a brief comparison of the two poems, see Cambon, *The Inclusive Flame*, pp. 248–249.

31. This poem was published in *Questions of Travel* (New York: Farrar, Straus, 1966), but it deals with visits made to Pound in 1951, and Lowell might well have seen it long before it was published.

32. See "The Art of Poetry III," 80. The title, however, is from Chaucer, "The Wife of Bath's Prologue," 1.3. Perhaps it is not impertinent to note that Lowell and his first wife, Jean Stafford, once lived in Bath, Maine.

33. When the first (Vintage) paperback edition of *Life Studies* appeared, the concluding poem, which had not been in the first edition, was "Colonel Shaw and the Massachusetts' 54th," which later became the title poem of *For the Union Dead*.

34. "On Robert Lowell's 'Skunk Hour,'" in *The Contemporary Poet as Artist and Critic*, ed. Anthony Ostroff (Boston and Toronto: Little, Brown, 1964), p. 109.

35. Ibid., pp. 82–110. The other contributors to this instructive symposium are Richard Wilbur, John Frederick Nims, and John Berryman.

36. Ibid., p. 108.

37. Ibid., pp. 103, 107.

38. Ibid., p. 107.

39. Ibid. See *Paradise Lost*, IV, 73 ff. for the pertinent speech by Satan and the chapter on "The Absurd Reasoning" in Camus's *Myth of Sisyphus* for a possible source of the passage on suicide. As some of his other sources for this poem, in addition to Bishop's "Armadillo," Lowell names Hölderlin's "Brot und Wein," Annette von Droste-Hülshoff's "Am letzten Tage des Jahres," and an ancedote about Walt Whitman in his old age. Speaking of Whitman, anyone who knows "Out of the Cradle Endlessly Rocking" will probably hear in the sixth stanza of "Skunk Hour" an echo of Whitman's

lone bird's song: "*O throat! O throbbing heart!*" That there are so many avowed and evident sources for this poem indicates the extent to which "imitation" is a natural and conscious mode of operation for Lowell. How much easier it is, then, to see in his echoes of his own poems a strategy facilitated by temperament.

5: MANY PERSONALITIES, ONE VOICE

1. "*Imitations:* Translation as Personal Mode," *Salmagundi*, 1, 4 (1966–67), 44–56.

2. See, e.g., John Simon, "Abuse of Privilege: Lowell as Translator," *Hudson Review*, 20 (Winter 1967–68), 543–562. There is a rather heated exchange between Lowell and Simon in the "Letters" section of the *Hudson Review*, 21 (Summer 1968), 248.

3. "Robert Lowell's *Near the Ocean:* The Greatness and Horror of Empire," *The Hollins Critic*, 4 (February 1967), 5, 4.

4. Richard J. Fein, *Robert Lowell* (New York: Twayne, 1970), pp. 72–92.

5. *Harvard Brief Dictionary of Music* (New York: Washington Square Press, 1965), p. 139. Cf. chapter four, n. 7, above. There are of course many other meanings of this much-bandied term that Lowell might have had in mind. To the Elizabethans, for example, *imitatio* meant the process of converting the substance of another poem to one's own use. In his preface to Ovid's *Epistles*, Dryden notes that "imitation" is not necessarily "translation." Lowell's comments clearly indicate that he sees his work in this tradition.

6. The drawing of Daphne's metamorphosis is by Frank Parker.

7. Ernst Robert Curtius, *European Literature and the Latin Middle Ages*, trans. Willard R. Trask (New York: Pantheon Books, 1953), pp. 128–129. Cf. Charles Feidelson, Jr., *Symbolism and American Literature* (Chicago and London: University of Chicago Press, Phoenix, 1953), the indexed references to "Voyage as Symbol." Fein, *Robert Lowell*, pp. 85–87, touches upon the voyage theme in connection with Lowell's Baudelaire.

8. Irvin Ehrenpreis, "The Age of Lowell," in *American Poetry*, Stratford-on-Avon Series, 7, ed. Irvin Ehrenpreis (New York: St. Martin's Press, 1965), p. 89.

9. The other, less striking deviations from the general chronological order are the advancement of Leopardi and the retardation of Annensky. Rimbaud is placed before Mallarmé, but this position is not necessarily anachronistic since the former died first. In any case, for the reasons suggested in this chapter, Lowell would certainly want Rimbaud to follow Baudelaire. Leopardi's poems, even after Lowell's accentuation of their darker sides, seem too restrained and objective to follow Hebel or Heine; similarly, Annensky's "Black Spring," with its suggestions of rebirth, would seem to come too soon if it succeeded Mallarmé.

10. The use of "hissed" in both cases is evidence of Lowell's characteristic touch. The comparable verb in "Au lecteur" is "berce," "lulls" (Lowell also changes the tense). Rimbaud refers only to "un sifflement," "a whistling."

11. As Lowell notes, two of his Sappho imitations are new poems based on the Greek. In the bilingual *Penguin Book of Greek Verse*, ed. Constantine A. Trypanis (Harmondsworth, England: Penguin, 1971), the three fragments are numbered 55, 64, and 62, respectively. Richard Lattimore has his versions of these poems in his *Greek Lyrics*, 2d rev. ed. (Chicago: University of Chicago Press, Phoenix, 1966), pp. 39–40. Allen Tate's translation of "Farewell to

Anactoria" can be found in *The Swimmers and Other Selected Poems* (New York: Charles Scribner's Sons, 1970).

12. See D. S. Carne-Ross, "The Two Voices of Translation," in *Robert Lowell: A Collection of Critical Essays*, ed. Thomas Parkinson (Englewood Cliffs, N.J.: Prentice-Hall, 1968), p. 160.

13. The poem that Lowell calls "The Great Testament" represents only a part of Villon's much longer work. Other parts appear under different titles immediately following this one.

14. The German is "diu sunne schein," "the sun shone."

15. This translation is that of Renato Poggioli, whom Lowell in his preface credits with correcting his Italian. See *The Poem Itself*, ed. Stanley Burnshaw (1960; rpt. New York: Schocken, 1967), pp. 276–277. My discussion draws upon Poggioli's commentary on "L'Infinito" in this book.

16. Lowell's last line's inflected verb ("find") is not in Baudelaire, who concludes with an incomplete sentence ("Au fond de l'Inconnu pour trouver du *nouveau*," "To the depths of the Unknown in order to find the *new*") that is in effect an object of the preceding construction ("Nous voulons . . . plonger," "We want . . . to dive"). Lowell's last line is thus somewhat less terrifying and correspondingly more positive than Baudelaire's. It is as though the upswing of the last half of the volume were being anticipated.

17. Rimbaud has only "Je ne puis plus," "I can no more. . . . " The only way in which one could reconcile Lowell's use of "wings" and "to swim" would be to invoke the image of a flying gurnard, the butterfly fish of the Atlantic.

18. The image, in a stanza original with Lowell, is a surprisingly accurate if accidental description of the famous Greek relief of the birth of Aphrodite in the Museo delle Terme, Rome. Cf. his probable use of the Nike of Samothrace in the last stanza of "Beyond the Alps."

19. Montale's lines are "ma una storia non dura che nelle cenere / e persistenza è solo l'estinzione," "but a story (history) endures in ashes alone / and persistence is only extinction." The rendering of "storia" by "autobiography"—like the seemingly superfluous phrase "An autobiographical poem" in the headnote to "Nostalgia" (after Rimbaud)—is one of the many little touches by means of which Lowell guides the narrative of the poet's life.

20. "The Expense of Greatness," in *The Lion and the Honeycomb* (New York: Harcourt Brace, Harvest, 1955), p. 95.

21. Lowell has persisted in writing of the inextricability of persistence and error. In "Lévi-Strauss in London" in *History*, he says: "Even the best writer in his best lines / is incurably imperfect."

22. Jerome Mazzaro, *The Poetic Themes of Robert Lowell* (Ann Arbor: University of Michigan Press, 1965), pp. 120–122.

23. Cf. the concluding lines of "To George Santayana" in *Life Studies* and the discussion of those lines in chapter four above. This image is also one of those that recalls the Achilles figure.

6: PARABOLIC STRUCTURES

1. Robert Bly, "The Dead World and the Live World," *The Sixties* (Spring 1966), p. 5.

2. "Poems that Deal a Jolt," *Chicago Tribune Books Today*, 15 November 1964, p. 11.

3. The tension in Lowell's poetry between the public and the historical, on the one hand, and the private and the lyrical, on the other, is one of the main subjects of Jerome Mazzaro's *The Poetic Themes of Robert Lowell* (Ann Arbor: University of Michigan Press, 1965) and of John Holloway's "Robert Lowell and the Public Dimension," *Encounter*, 30 (April 1968), 73–79. The "entry of the personality into the business of public judgement" in Lowell's work is a chief concern in Patrick Cosgrave's *The Public Poetry of Robert Lowell* (New York: Taplinger, 1970).

4. Mazzaro, *Poetic Themes*, p. 135. Although I disagree with Mazzaro frequently in this chapter, I am indebted to him for his provocative discussion.

5. This is the accusation leveled by Thomas Parkinson, "For the Union Dead," *Salmagundi*, 1, 4 (1966–67), 95. Parkinson refers in passing to the "general architecture" of the book, but he does not outline that architecture.

6. Mazzaro, *Poetic Themes*, p. 135. Surprisingly enough, *For the Union Dead* has also been called Lowell's "least uneven book." See Josephine Jacobsen, "Poet of the Particular," *Commonweal*, 4 December 1964, p. 351.

7. Herbert Leibowitz, "Robert Lowell: Ancestral Voices," *Salmagundi*, 1, 4 (1966–67), 141; Mazzaro, *Poetic Themes*, pp. 129, 133. Richard J. Fein, *Robert Lowell* (New York: Twayne, 1970), pp. 94–105, distinguishes several groups of poems—not very closely related to mine—but finds the organization of the volume "makeshift."

8. "On Political Poetry," *The Nation*, 24 April 1967, p. 522.

9. Wylie Sypher, *Loss of the Self in Modern Literature and Art* (New York: Random House, 1962), pp. 58–59.

10. Fein, *Robert Lowell*, p. 95; Mazzaro, *Poetic Themes*, p. 127.

11. Cf. Mazzaro, *Poetic Themes*, pp. 127–128, where he notes that along with other elements in this poem, the image of the "ghostly / imaginary lover" is drawn from Jean Stafford's "A Country Love Story" (collected in *The Interior Castle*) and infers that Lowell's figure is virtually identical with her "character." This inference, however, does not allow sufficiently for the poet's adaptation of his source material, and it is at least as likely that Lowell's figure is a projection of the poet-speaker.

12. Amy Lowell, a distant relative of Robert, has a three-line poem to which this one might owe something. This is the whole of her "Middle Age": "Like black ice / Scrolled over with unintelligible patterns by an ignorant skater / Is the dulled surface of my heart."

13. Elizabeth Bishop's story is the fulcrum of her *Questions of Travel* (New York: Farrar, Straus, 1966), which is otherwise a book of verse. It is interesting that Bishop's volume might in turn owe its format to Lowell's *Life Studies*.

14. Arthur Schopenhauer, *The World as Will and Idea*, trans. R. B. Haldane and J. Kemp (1883; rpt. Garden City, N.Y.: Dolphin, 1961), p. 323.

15. See "To Peter Taylor on the Feast of the Epiphany" in *Lord Weary's Castle*.

16. See Mazzaro, *Poetic Themes*, p. 122.

17. The source of the title is Exod. 21:24. Deut. 28:65 provides a good gloss on this poem and might well have been another source.

18. Mazzaro, *Poetic Themes*, p. 123.

19. The lines from Arnold, which are quoted by Sypher, *Loss of the Self*, p. 34, and sum up the concerns of much of this volume, are:

Hast thou then still the old unquiet breast,
Which neither deadens into rest,
Nor ever feels the fiery glow
That whirls the spirit from itself away,
But fluctuates to and fro,
Never by passion quite possessed
And never quite benumbed by the world's sway?

20. The sources of both the Hawthorne and the Edwards poems have been pointed out by Mazzaro, *Poetic Themes,* pp. 130–132.

21. This sentence seems to echo the conclusion of "Home After Three Months Away" in *Life Studies:* "Cured, I am frizzled, stale and small."

22. It is interesting to contrast Lowell's gloss on his poetry—if such it is—with Robert Frost's remark on the "figure that a poem makes." For Frost, this figure "begins in delight and ends in wisdom." He goes ahead in the preface to his *Complete Poems* (1949; rpt. New York: Holt, Rinehart and Winston, 1967) to say that a poem is a "clarification of life" and a "momentary stay against confusion."

23. See the Loeb Library edition of Suetonius's *Lives of the Caesars,* Vol. I, trans. J. C. Rolfe (1914; rpt. London: William Heinemann, 1951), for this and many other biographical details alluded to in this poem.

24. The only interesting discussion of this poem is in Fein, *Robert Lowell,* pp. 101–104.

25. In commenting explicitly on the earlier poems, Lowell has said that they had "a stiff, humorless and even impenetrable surface. . . . [They] seemed like prehistoric monsters dragged down into the bog and death by their ponderous armor." "On Robert Lowell's 'Skunk Hour,' " in *The Contemporary Poet as Artist and Critic,* ed. Anthony Ostroff (Boston and Toronto: Little, Brown, 1964), p. 108.

26. It might be frivolous to suggest that Lowell had W. D. Snodgrass in mind. Nevertheless, the type of poetry that is described and the images in which it is described recall *Heart's Needle* (1959). Moreover, although Snodgrass was Lowell's student, the older poet has made a point of implying that he might have been influenced by his pupil. See "The Art of Poetry III: An Interview [with Frederick Seidel]," *The Paris Review,* no. 25 (Winter-Spring 1961), pp. 69–70, where Lowell also speaks of Snodgrass's ability to write "on agonizing subjects," of his "pathos," and of his "fragility along the edges" with a "main artery of power going through the center." Another candidate, I should think, would be Allen Tate, whose poem called "The Maimed Man" (first published in 1952), also in *terza rima* and also involving a severed head, might have inspired Lowell's.

27. These now well-known terms, which are pretty much synonymous with "excessively emotional" and "excessively academic," were of course derived from Lévi-Strauss by Lowell. See Hugh B. Staples, *Robert Lowell: The First Twenty Years* (New York: Farrar, Straus, 1962), p. 13, for a longer quote from Lowell's speech in acceptance of the National Book Award in 1960.

28. It might be argued that "Alfred Corning Clark" is at least as objective as "Hawthorne," and that "Going to and fro" is as dramatically effective a subjective poem as "The Severed Head." Indeed, elements of such argu-

346 NOTES

ments have been incorporated in the discussions of these poems above. At the most, however, these poems seem to be exceptions to the general course of the volume, and it is as a generalization that admits of possible exceptions that this statement is intended.

29. Mazzaro, *Poetic Themes*, p. 122. The attitude most characteristic of the volume is better summarized by Louis Martz, "The Elegiac Mode," *Yale Review*, 54 (Winter 1965), 284, where he calls the best poems "thin-lipped, tense diminuendos with which the stoic mind reveals its clear acceptance of a sombre fate."

30. Mazzaro, *Poetic Themes*, p. 129.

31. See D. S. Carne-Ross's "Conversation [with Robert Lowell]," *Delos*, 1 (1968), 174.

32. The image here is curiously similar to one that Lowell used in accepting the National Book Award for *Life Studies*, when he said that he wasn't certain whether the question mark on which that book had left him hanging was a lifeline or a noose. There are a number of other instances in which Lowell seems to be echoing or anticipating his poetry. Thus, in his refusal of an invitation to the White House Festival of the Arts in June 1965, he said, in terms remarkably similar to those employed in several of the poems in this volume, that "we are in danger of imperceptibly becoming an explosive and suddenly chauvinistic nation, and we may even be drifting on our way to the last nuclear ruin." See Richard F. Shepard, "Robert Lowell Rebuffs Johnson as Protest over Foreign Policy," *New York Times*, 3 June 1965, 1, 2.

33. Five generations back, Colonel Shaw's sister, Josephine Shaw, married Colonel Charles Russell Lowell, Jr. (1835–1864). For an account of the marriage and the last months of the courageous Colonel Lowell, who is the subject of a poem in the *Notebook*s and *History*, see Ferris Greenslet, *The Lowells and Their Seven Worlds* (New York: Houghton Mifflin, 1946), pp. 288 ff. A sketch by Frank Parker of the Boston Monument by Augustus Saint-Gaudens to Shaw and his black regiment appears on the dust jacket and the title page of the first edition.

34. Snodgrass's lines are: "I have learned how often I / Can win, can love, but choose to die." Taken as a whole, Lowell's elegy might be fruitfully compared with John Berryman's "Boston Common," an earlier poem that involves the same monument (and, interestingly enough, adapts the phrase from Melville that Lowell quoted in "Christmas Eve Under Hooker's Statue"), and Melville's "The College Colonel," whose main figure bears some resemblance to Lowell's Colonel Shaw.

35. Parkinson, *"For the Union Dead,"* 95, has commented on Lowell's recognition of "the danger that lies in the American sensibility, and his own, in wanting total drastic solutions to the human condition."

36. The inscription on the monument is "Omnia relinquit servare rempublicam," "he leaves all behind to serve the state." As Fein notes in *Robert Lowell*, p. 106, Lowell's change to the third-person plural fittingly includes the black soldiers and perhaps "makes the statement ironically relevant to an urban renewal effort the poem describes."

7: DARK DESIGNS

1. "A Murderous Solvent," *The Nation*, 24 April 1967, p. 537.

2. "A Meaning of Robert Lowell," in *The American Literary Anthology 2*, ed. George Plimpton et al. (New York: Random House, 1969), pp. 74–75.

3. Ibid., p. 75.

4. What Murray Krieger calls a poem's "special temporality, the circularizing of its linear movement," is the subject of his essay on *"Ekphrasis and the Still Movement of Poetry; or, Laokoön* Revisited," in *Perspectives on Poetry,* ed. James L. Calderwood and Harold Toliver (New York: Oxford University Press, Galaxy, 1968), pp. 323–348.

5. "Fuel on the Fire," *Poetry,* 110 (September 1967), 414.

6. "Foreword," *Ariel* (New York: Harper and Row, 1966), p. x.

7. This is Zweig's phrase, but Carruth would agree. Howard, on the other hand, compliments "the organization of the imagery," and Patrick Cosgrave, *The Public Poetry of Robert Lowell* (New York: Taplinger, 1970), pp. 196 ff., finds the "argument" of this poem, which he thinks Lowell's finest, perfectly articulated.

8. The stanza was significantly different when it appeared in the *New York Review of Books,* 5 August 1965, p. 3:

> Time to grub up and junk the year's
> output, a dead wood of dry verse:
> dim confession, coy revelation,
> liftings, listless self-imitation,
> whole days when I could hardly speak,
> came pluming home unshaven, weak
> and willing to read anyone
> things done before and better done.

Phillip Cooper, *The Autobiographical Myth of Robert Lowell* (Chapel Hill: University of North Carolina Press, 1970), pp. 122–125, quotes this stanza and discusses the theme of poetry in this poem.

9. Ps. 107:23–24: "They that go down to the sea in ships, that do business in great waters; These see the works of the Lord, and his wonders in the deep."

10. Paul is also the poet's "example" because he too was "banished" and imprisoned. See Acts 20.

11. The lines on the doorknobs oddly recall Lowell's remarks on the composition of "Skunk Hour" in the symposium on that poem: "I began to feel that real poetry came, not from fierce confessions, but from something almost meaningless but imagined. I was haunted by an image of a blue china doorknob. I never used the doorknob, or knew what it meant. . . ." "On Robert Lowell's 'Skunk Hour,' " in *The Contemporary Poet as Artist and Critic,* ed. Anthony Ostroff (Boston and Toronto: Little, Brown, 1964), p. 110.

12. Ibid., p. 108.

13. The rhythms here, along with the reference to "the wordless sign" and the reflections upon history, suggest "Gerontion" in particular.

14. In fact, a comparison of "Falling Asleep over the Aeneid," "Beyond the Alps," and "Waking Early Sunday Morning" could disclose the contours of Lowell's career from 1951 through 1967. These poems have approximately the same scope and subject and almost constitute a genre of their own.

15. "Three Books," in *Poetry and the Age* (1953; rpt. New York: Random House, Vintage, 1959), p. 233.

16. Carruth, "A Meaning," pp. 72, 76.

17. Cf. "1930's 9" in *History,* where an artist's "brushwork wears; the hand decayed. A hand does— / we can have faith, at least, the hand decayed."

18. It will be noticed that Lowell has never tired of piling exactly this kind of thematic fuel on the fire of inspiration. In addition to the images in these poems in *Near the Ocean* and *For the Union Dead*, one thinks of those in "From Palestine" in *Land of Unlikeness* ("The *lignum Vitae* is your pyre"); in "At the Altar" in *Lord Weary's Castle* ("The bier and baby-carriage where I burn"); in "Little Testament" in *Imitations* ("an autobiography can only survive in ashes"); and in "To Summer, 2" in *Notebook 1967–68* ("Strange, a life is the fire and the fuel").

19. Cooper, *Autobiographical Myth*, pp. 88–89, notes that the garden party and firework images, along with other details in this poem, derive from Hugh Thomas, *The Spanish Civil War* (New York: Harper and Brothers, 1961).

20. The lines seem to parody Rilke's famous description of the task of the artist: "Yes, for it is our task to imprint this provisional, perishable earth so deeply, so patiently and passionately in ourselves that its reality shall arise in us again 'invisibly.' *We are the bees of the invisible. Nous butinons éperdument le miel du visible, pour l'accumuler dans la grande ruche d'or de l'Invisible.*" Letter to Witold von Hulewicz (1925), rpt. in *The Modern Tradition: Backgrounds of Modern Literature*, ed. Richard Ellmann and Charles Feidelson, Jr. (New York: Oxford University Press, 1965), p. 191.

21. This is a term used by Jerome Mazzaro, "Lowell After *For the Union Dead*," *Salmagundi*, 1, 4 (1966–67), 64–65, for the recurrent female figure in Lowell's poetry.

22. The Latin text and translations of Horace in this chapter are based on the *Odes and Epodes*, trans. C. E. Bennet (London: William Heinemann, Loeb Library, 1952).

23. Sidney Nolan's drawing on the title page and on the back of the dust jacket is of a Roman chariot and a charioteer who wears what seems to be a laurel garland, the symbol of poetic achievement.

8: IN THE ROUND

1. For the sake of simplicity, and because *Notebook*, although larger, is organized in the same way as its predecessor, I refer throughout this chapter, until its last pages, to *Notebook 1967–68*, the first edition. Everything said of this edition, however, is applicable also to the "revised and expanded" *Notebook*, itself revised in the form of *History*. In most cases, the passages quoted from *Notebook 1967–68* are virtually identical with the corresponding passages in *Notebook*. In the few cases where they are not, the differences are immaterial to the discussion or are noted.

2. The "Afterthought" is slightly altered in *Notebook*, and the last two italicized phrases have been omitted altogether.

3. The term "gigantism"—by which Lowell might mean either continual padding out of individual poems so that they reach fourteen lines or excessive growth of the series owing to facility acquired with the form—is only one of several vagaries in the "Afterthought." In view of the brilliant clarity of Lowell's prose in such pieces as "91 Revere Street," the obfuscations, equivocations, and redundancies that cloud this "Afterthought" would seem to be parts of a general strategy, the purpose of which would be to reveal the main features of the terrain that he has covered without supplying a detailed map of it.

4. William Meredith, in his review in the *New York Times Book Review*, 15 June 1969, pp. 1, 27, speaks of a "usual movement . . . between the reporter's view and the mystic's" in the *Notebook 1967–68*, but he offers little evidence and seems reluctant to define it precisely.

5. See "End of the Saga" for another example of Lowell's adaptation of the Shakespearean sonnet. "The Worst Sinner" is the best example of his adaptation of the Italian sonnet.

6. Like Mallarmé and other French symbolists and post-symbolists, Valéry himself produced comparatively little poetry. He once said that he was capable of working on a poem until it had recorded several stages of his life. Lowell's affinity with the symbolist tradition is perhaps indicated by his similar capacity, just as his divergence might be suggested by his insistence upon the importance of imperfection.

7. *Notebook* has: "A nihilist has to live in the world as is, / gazing the impossible summit to rubble." *History*, returning to a quibble, substitutes "impassable" for "impossible."

8. It is the appearance of these poems that this statement describes, not the actual manner of Lowell's creative process.

9. In *Notebook*, two poems interpose between "Grave Guild" and "Reading Myself." Both poems, "In the Back Stacks" and "Gap," also deal with the poet.

10. The very titles of several poems not dealt with in this chapter would suggest Lowell's obsession with the circle. See, e.g., "Roulette"; "Another Circle"; and the thirteen-poem sequence, "Circles," enlarged to twenty poems in *Notebook*.

11. The phrase is also reminiscent of the "Hope of the hopeless launched and cast adrift" in "The Flaw."

12. With the whole first sequence one might also compare "Robert Kennedy: 1925–1968." Several images from the earlier one—e.g., "The search," "The circle," the "flies"—recur here.

13. The poem from which this line comes is retitled "Fever" in *Notebook*. Cf. also "High Blood" ("On my great days of sickness, I was God; / and now I might be. I catpad on my blood, / and the universe moves beneath me when I move") and the last lines of "Nantucket: 1935," which apply nominally to Frank Parker's work but really to Lowell's as well.

14. Other pertinent uses of "the round" and associated images can be found in "Charles River, I, II," "Playing Ball with the Critic," and passim. Motifs that would be worth following through their metamorphoses if there were space enough and time include "green things," "roots," "swords," and "shells" and other carapaces.

15. Interestingly enough, Lowell's imagery derives from Jarrell's comments on the author of *The Mills of the Kavanaughs:* "He is a poet of both Will and Imagination, but his Will is always seizing his Imagination by the shoulders and saying to it in a grating voice: 'Don't sit there fooling around; *get to work!'*—and his poor Imagination gets tense all over and begins to revolve determinedly and familiarly, like a squirrel in a squirrel-cage." "Three Books," in *Poetry and the Age* (1953; rpt. New York: Random House, Vintage, 1959), p. 236.

16. See Herbert Marcuse, *Eros and Civilization* (New York: Random House, 1962), esp. pp. 177–178.

17. This poem is number 139 of a total of 279 poems. Lowell similarly entitles the twenty-ninth of fifty-eight sections "Midwinter." In *Notebook*

"The Golden Middle" occurs well before the halfway point; and "Midwint-er" is the thirty-seventh of seventy-seven sections.

18. In *Notebook* Lowell, perhaps wishing to avoid association with a "school," alters "surrealism" to "unrealism."

19. Hayden Carruth, "A Meaning of Robert Lowell," in *The American Literary Anthology 2,* ed. George Plimpton et al. (New York: Random House, 1969), pp. 73–74.

9: HISTORY REPEATING ITSELF

1. The figure is Lowell's in his note. I count fewer if I exclude poems revised from volumes earlier than *Notebook.* (See the Appendix.)

2. "From the Kingdom of Necessity," in *Poetry and the Age* (1953; rpt. New York: Random House, Vintage, 1959), p. 193.

3. See "The Added Artificer," in *On Translation,* ed. Reuben Brower (1959; rpt. New York: Oxford University Press, Galaxy, 1966), p. 142. In neither "Helen" nor "Achilles," it should be noted, is there any overt indica-tion that the work is even "imitative." As early as *Lord Weary's Castle,* of course, Lowell was insisting that an "imitation . . . should be read as though it were an original English poem"; and in the cases of two poems in *Notebook 1967–68* ("Die Gold-Orangen," after Goethe's "Mignon," and "Le Cygne," after Mallarmé's "Le vierge, le vivace, et le bel aujourd'hui"), he referred to his originals only by means of the foreign language titles. The virtual expung-ing of some of the sources in *History* seems to be the next step in the course of Lowell's dissolution of himself in others.

4. The original poem is in Heredia's *Les Trophées.* That Lowell's poem is a translation was pointed out to me by my colleague Charles Gullans.

5. Cf. "From Genesis to Robert Lowell," *Times Literary Supplement,* 10 August 1973, pp. 1–3. When he speaks of "the decisive alteration of structure which turned the circularity of *Notebook* into the linear stride of *History,*" the *TLS* reviewer indicates the extent of the revision but only half of the resulting configuration. In fact, *History,* like so many of the other works discussed above, from "Between the Porch and the Altar" to the *Notebooks,* has as one of its aims the circularizing of a linear arrangement.

6. "Kingdom of Necessity," p. 193.

7. The fact of the matter is that Lowell and Caroline are now married. For some reviewers, of course, it was not the laconic but the candid aspect of *The Dolphin* that was so annoying. An interesting rejoinder to those reviewers is Alan Williamson's " 'I Am That I Am': The Ethics and Aesthetics of Self-Revelation," *American Poetry Review,* 3 (January-February 1974), 37–39.

8. These lines used to open the third poem in the section in *Notebook* called "Lines from Israel." They are among the few lines in *The Dolphin* that Lowell has used before. Lest the opening lines of "Fishnet" be thought another example of carelessness or obliquity, it should be noted that in fact dolphins have been employed by fishermen in some cultures for centuries. Details of this practice, along with much else of interest to the delphinophile, can be found in Ashley Montagu, "The History of the Dolphin," in Ashley Montagu and John C. Lilly, *The Dolphin in History* (Los Angeles: William Andrews Clark Memorial Library and University of California, Los Angeles, 1963), pp. 3–30.

9. *Essays of Four Decades* (1968; rpt. New York: William Morrow, Apollo, 1970), p. 552.

The evanescent must, however, be considered essential.
—HEGEL, "Preface" to *The*
Phenomenology of the Spirit

Writers can be taught to return the ball
to the police, smile and even like it;
the critics like it, smile, kick back the ball.
Our hurt blue muscles work like testicles;
Low will we learn to duck and block the knock?
—"Playing Ball with the Critic"

SELECTED BIBLIOGRAPHY

I. BIBLIOGRAPHIES

Mazzaro, Jerome. "The Achievement of Robert Lowell: 1939–1959."
Fresco, 10 (Winter-Spring 1960), 51–77; expanded and rpt. as *The
Achievement of Robert Lowell: 1939–1959*. Detroit: University of De-
troit Press, 1960.
———. "A Checklist of Materials on Robert Lowell: 1939–1968."
Robert Lowell: A Portrait, ed. London and Boyers.
Staples, Hugh B. "Robert Lowell: Bibliography 1939–1959, with an
Illustrative Critique." *Harvard Library Bulletin*, 13 (1959), 292–318;
expanded and rpt. as "Appendix II" in Staples, *Robert Lowell: The
First Twenty Years*.

II. WORKS BY ROBERT LOWELL

1. POETRY
Land of Unlikeness. Cummington, Mass.: Cummington Press, 1944.
Lord Weary's Castle. New York: Harcourt Brace, 1946; rpt. with *The
Mills of the Kavanaughs*, New York: Meridian, 1961; rpt. New York:
Harvest, 1968.
Poems: 1938–1949. London: Faber & Faber, 1950, 1960.
The Mills of the Kavanaughs. New York: Harcourt Brace, 1951; rpt.
with *Lord Weary's Castle*, New York: Meridian, 1961; rpt. New
York: Harvest, 1968.
Life Studies. London: Faber & Faber and New York: Farrar, Straus,
1959; rpt. New York: Vintage, 1960; rpt. with *For the Union Dead*,
New York: Noonday, 1968.

Imitations. New York: Farrar, Straus, 1961..

For the Union Dead. New York: Farrar, Straus, 1964; rpt. with *Life Studies*, New York: Noonday, 1968.

Selected Poems. London: Faber & Faber, 1965.

Near the Ocean. New York: Farrar, Straus, 1967.

"The Voyage" and Other Versions of Poems by Baudelaire. New York: Farrar, Straus, 1968.

Notebook 1967–1968. New York: Farrar, Straus, 1969.

Notebook. Rev. ed., London: Faber & Faber, 1970; 3d ed., rev. and expanded, New York: Farrar, Straus, 1970.

The Dolphin. New York: Farrar, Straus, 1973.

For Lizzie and Harriet. New York: Farrar, Straus, 1973.

History. New York: Farrar, Straus, 1973.

2. DRAMA

Phaedra. With Jacques Barzun's translation of *Figaro*. New York: Farrar, Straus, 1961.

The Old Glory. New York: Farrar, Straus, 1964; rpt. New York: Noonday, 1966; rev. ed., 1968.

Prometheus Bound. New York: Farrar, Straus, 1969.

3. SELECTED CRITICAL ESSAYS

Review of T. S. Eliot, *Four Quartets*. *Sewanee Review*, 51 (Summer 1943), 432–435.

"A Note [on G. M. Hopkins]." *Kenyon Review*, 6 (Autumn 1944), 583–586.

"The Verses of Thomas Merton." *Commonweal*, 22 June 1945, pp. 240–242.

Review of Walter E. Houghton, *The Art of Newman's "Apologia."* *Kenyon Review*, 7 (Spring 1946), 340–341.

"Current Poetry." *Sewanee Review*, 54 (Winter 1946), 143–153.

"Imagination and Reality [review of Wallace Stevens, *Transport to Summer*]." *The Nation*, 5 April 1947, pp. 400–402.

"Thomas, Bishop, and Williams." *Sewanee Review*, 55 (Summer 1947), 493–503.

Review of William Carlos Williams, *Paterson: Book II*. *The Nation*, 19 June 1948, pp. 692–694.

Review of Randall Jarrell, *The Seven League Crutches*. *New York Times Book Review*, 7 October 1941, p. 7.

"Prose Genius in Verse [review of Robert Penn Warren, *Brother to Dragons*]." *Kenyon Review*, 15 (Autumn 1953), 619–625.

"The Muses Won't Help Twice [review of A. E. Watts, trans., Ovid's *Metamorphoses*]." *Kenyon Review*, 17 (Spring 1955), 317–324.

Review of I. A. Richards, *Goodbye Earth and Other Poems*. *Encounter*, 14 (February 1960), 77–78.

"Yvor Winters, A Tribute." *Poetry*, 98 (April 1961), 40–43.

"The Poetry of John Berryman." *New York Review of Books*, 28 May 1964, pp. 3–4.

"Foreword" to *Ariel*, by Sylvia Plath. New York: Harper and Row, 1966.

"Foreword" to *Buckshee (Last Poems)*, by Ford Madox Ford. Cambridge, Mass.: Pym-Randall Press, 1966.

4. AUTOBIOGRAPHY, INTERVIEWS, MISCELLANEOUS

"John Ransom's Conversation." *Sewanee Review*, 56 (Summer 1948), 374–377.

"Falling Asleep over Grillparzer: An Interview with Robert Lowell [by John McCormick]." *Poetry*, 81 (January 1953), 269–279.

"91 Revere Street." *Partisan Review*, 23 (Fall 1956), 445–447.

"Visiting the Tates." *Sewanee Review*, 17 (Autumn 1959), 557–559.

"The Art of Poetry III: An Interview [with Frederick Seidel]." *Paris Review*, no. 25 (Winter-Spring 1961),pp. 56–95; rpt. *Modern Poets on Modern Poetry*, ed. Scully; *Essays*, ed. Parkinson; and *Robert Lowell: A Portrait*, ed. London and Boyers.

"Robert Lowell in Conversation [with A. Alvarez]." *The Observer*, 21 July 1963; rpt. in part *The Review*, no. 8 (August 1963), pp. 36–40.

"A Talk with Robert Lowell [an interview with Stanley Kunitz]." *New York Times Book Review*, 4 October 1964, pp. 34–38.

"A Talk with Robert Lowell [an interview with A. Alvarez]." *Encounter*, 24 (February 1965), 39–43.

Shepard, Richard F. "Robert Lowell Rebuffs Johnson as Protest over Foreign Policy [with Lowell's letter to the President]." *New York Times*, 3 June 1965, pp. 1, 2.

"Conversation [with D. S. Carne-Ross]." *Delos*, 1 (April 1968), 165–175.

III. WORKS ON ROBERT LOWELL

1. BOOKS, PAMPHLETS, AND ANTHOLOGIES

Cooper, Philip. *The Autobiographical Myth of Robert Lowell*. Chapel Hill: University of North Carolina Press, 1970.

Cosgrave, Patrick. *The Public Poetry of Robert Lowell*. New York: Taplinger, 1970.

Fein, Richard J. *Robert Lowell*. New York: Twayne, 1970.

Harvard Advocate, 142 (November 1961). (A special Lowell issue.)

London, Michael and Robert Boyers, eds. *Robert Lowell: A Portrait of the Artist in His Time*. New York: David Lewis, 1970.

Martin, Jay. *Robert Lowell*. Minneapolis: University of Minnesota Press, 1970.

Mazzaro, Jerome. *The Poetic Themes of Robert Lowell*. Ann Arbor: University of Michigan Press, 1965.

Meiners, R. K. *Everything To Be Endured: An Essay on Robert Lowell and Modern Poetry*. Columbia: University of Missouri Press, 1970.

Parkinson, Thomas, ed., *Robert Lowell: A Collection of Critical Essays*. Englewood Cliffs, N.J.: Prentice-Hall, 1968.

Perloff, Marjorie. *The Poetic Art of Robert Lowell*. Ithaca, N. Y., and London: Cornell University Press, 1973.

Salmagundi, 1, 4 (1966–67). (A special Lowell issue.)

Staples, Hugh B. *Robert Lowell: The First Twenty Years*. New York: Farrar, Straus, 1962.

2. SELECTED ARTICLES AND BOOKS CONTAINING ESSAYS

Anon. "From Genesis to Robert Lowell." *Times Literary Supplement*, 10 August 1973, pp. 1–3.

Arrowsmith, William. "Five Poets." *Hudson Review*, 4 (Winter 1952), 619–627; rpt. *Essays*, ed. Parkinson, and *Robert Lowell: A Portrait*, ed. London and Boyers.

Bayley, John. "Robert Lowell: The Poetry of Cancellation." *London Magazine*, NS, 51 (June 1966), 76–85; rpt. *Robert Lowell: A Portrait*, ed. London and Boyers.

Bedient, Calvin. "Visions and Revisions." *The New York Times Book Review*, 29 July 1973, pp. 15–16.

Belitt, Ben. *"Imitations:* Translation as Personal Mode." *Salmagundi*, 1, 4 (1966–67), 45–56; rpt. *Robert Lowell: A Portrait*, ed. London and Boyers.

Berryman, John. "Lowell, Thomas & Co." *Partisan Review*, 14 (January-February 1947), 73–80.

Bewley, Marius. *The Complex Fate*. London: Chatto and Windus, 1952; rpt. *Robert Lowell: A Portrait*, ed. London and Boyers.

Blackmur, R. P. "Notes on Eleven Poets." *Kenyon Review*, 7 (Spring 1945), 339–352; rev. and rpt. as "Notes on Seven Poets," *Language as Gesture*. 1952; rpt. *Form and Value in Modern Poetry*, New York: Doubleday Anchor, 1957; rpt. *Essays*, ed. Parkinson, and *Robert Lowell: A Portrait*, ed. London and Boyers.

Bly, Robert. "The Dead World and the Live World." *The Sixties*, no. 8 (Spring 1966), pp. 2–7.

Bogan, Louise. Review of *The Mills of the Kavanaughs*. *New Yorker*, 9 June 1951, pp. 109–113.

Braybrook, Neville. "The Poetry of Robert Lowell." *Catholic World*, 198 (January 1964), 230–237.

Cambon, Glauco. "Dea Roma and Robert Lowell." *Accent*, 20 (Winter 1960), 51–61.

———. *The Inclusive Flame: Studies in American Poetry*. Bloomington: University of Indiana Press, 1963.

Carne-Ross, D. S. "The Two Voices of Translation." *Essays*, ed. Parkinson.

Carruth, Hayden. "Freedom and Style." *Poetry*, 107 (August 1965), 358–360.

———. "A Meaning of Robert Lowell." *Hudson Review*, 20 (Autumn 1967); rpt. *The American Literary Anthology 2*, ed. George Plimpton et al. New York: Random House, 1969, and *Robert Lowell: A Portrait*, ed. London and Boyers.

Cunningham, J. V. "Several Kinds of Short Poem." *Poets on Poetry,* ed. Howard Nemerov. New York: Basic Books, 1966.

Davison, Peter. "Difficulties of Being Major." *Poetry,* 91 (October 1967), 116–121.

Donoghue, Denis. *Connoisseurs of Chaos: Ideas of Order in Modern American Poetry.* New York: Macmillan, 1965.

Eberhart, Richard. "Four Poets." *Sewanee Review,* 55 (Spring 1947), 324–336.

———. "Five Poets." *Kenyon Review,* 14 (Winter 1952), 168–176; rpt. *Robert Lowell: A Portrait,* ed. London and Boyers.

Ehrenpreis, Irvin. "The Age of Lowell." *American Poetry,* Stratford-on-Avon Series, 7, ed. Irvin Ehrenpreis. New York: St. Martin's Press, 1965; rpt. *Essays,* ed. Parkinson, and *Robert Lowell: A Portrait,* ed. London and Boyers.

Fitts, Dudley. Review of *The Mills of the Kavanaughs. Furioso,* 6 (Fall 1951), 77.

Fried, Michael. "The Achievement of Robert Lowell." *London Magazine,* 2 (October 1962), 54–64.

Gray-Lewis, Stephen W. "Too Late for Eden—An Examination of Some Dualisms in *The Mills of the Kavanaughs.*" *Cithara,* 5 (May 1966), 41–51.

Gross, Harvey. *Sound and Form in Modern Poetry: A Study of Prosody from Thomas Hardy to Robert Lowell.* Ann Arbor: University of Michigan Press, 1964.

Gunn, Thom. "Excellence and Variety." *Yale Review,* 44 (Winter 1960), 295–305.

Hardison, O. B., Jr. "Robert Lowell: The Poet and the World's Body." *Shenandoah,* 140 (Winter 1963), 24–32.

Harrigan, Anthony. "American Formalists." *South Atlantic Quarterly,* 440 (July 1950), 483–489.

Hartmann, Geoffrey. "The Eye of the Storm." *Hudson Review,* 32 (Spring 1965), 277–280; rpt. *Robert Lowell: A Portrait,* ed. London and Boyers.

Hecht, Roger. "Rilke in Translation." *Sewanee Review,* 71 (Summer 1963), 513–522.

Hivnor, Mary Otis. "Adaptations and Adaptors." *Kenyon Review,* 30 (March, 1968), 265–273.

Hoffman, Daniel. "Robert Lowell's *Near the Ocean:* The Greatness and Horror of Empire." *The Hollins Critic,* 4 (February 1967), 1–16.

Holloway, John. "Robert Lowell and the Public Dimension." *Encounter,* 30 (April 1968), 73–80.

Howard, Richard. "Fuel on the Fire." *Poetry,* 110 (September 1967), 413–415.

Jacobsen, Josephine. "Poet of the Particular." *Commonweal,* 4 December 1964, pp. 349–352.

Jarrell, Randall. "A View of Three Poets." *Partisan Review,* 18

(November-December 1951), 691–700; rpt. as "Three Books," *Poetry and the Age*. 1953; rpt. New York: Random House, Vintage, 1959; rpt. *Essays*, ed. Parkinson, and *Robert Lowell: A Portrait*, ed. London and Boyers.

––––––. "From the Kingdom of Necessity." *The Nation*, 18 January 1947, pp. 74–75; rpt. *Poetry and the Age*; rpt. *Essays*, ed. Parkinson, and *Robert Lowell: A Portrait*, ed. London and Boyers.

––––––. "Poetry in War and Peace." *Partisan Review*, 12 (Winter 1945), 120–126.

Jones, A. R. "Necessity and Freedom: The Poetry of Robert Lowell, Sylvia Plath, and Anne Sexton." *Critical Quarterly*, 7 (Spring 1965), 11–30.

Jones, T. H. "The Poetry of Robert Lowell." *The Month*, NS, 9 (March 1953), 133–142.

Jumper, Will C. "Whom Seek Ye?: A Note on Robert Lowell's Poetry." *Hudson Review*, 9 (Spring 1956), 117–125; rpt. *Essays*, ed. Parkinson.

Kunitz, Stanley. "Telling the Time." *Salmagundi*, 1, 4 (1966–67), 22–24.

Leibowitz, Herbert. "Robert Lowell: Ancestral Voices." *Salmagundi*, 1, 4 (1966–67), 25–43; rpt. *Robert Lowell: A Portrait*, ed. London and Boyers.

Martz, Louis. "The Elegiac Mode." *Yale Review*, 54 (Winter 1965), 285–298.

Mazzaro, Jerome. "Lowell After *For the Union Dead*." *Salmagundi*, 1, 4 (1966–67), 57–68; rpt. *Robert Lowell: A Portrait*, ed. London and Boyers.

Meredith, William. Review of *Notebook 1967–68*. *New York Times Review of Books*, 15 June 1969, p. 1.

Mills, Ralph J. *Contemporary American Poetry*. New York: Random House, 1965.

Nims, John Frederick. "Two Catholic Poets." *Poetry*, 65 (February 1945), 264–268.

Ostroff, Anthony, ed. "The Poet and His Critics, III: A Symposium on Robert Lowell's 'Skunk Hour' [with contributions by John Berryman, John Frederick Nims, Richard Wilbur, and Lowell]." *New World Writing 21*. New York: Lippincott, 1963; rpt. *The Contemporary Poet as Artist and Critic*, ed. Ostroff. Boston and Toronto: Little, Brown, 1964. (Berryman's and Lowell's contributions are reprinted in *Essays*, ed. Parkinson.)

Parkinson, Thomas. "For the Union Dead." *Salmagundi*, 1, 4 (1966–67), 87–95; rpt. *Essays*, ed. Parkinson.

Pearson, Gabriel. "Robert Lowell." *The Review*, no. 20 (March 1969), pp. 3–36.

Phelps, Robert. "A Book of Revelations." *National Review*, 29 August 1959, pp. 207–208.

Ricks, Christopher. "Authority in Poems." *Southern Review*, NS, 2 (January 1969), 203–215.

Rosenthal, M. L. *The Modern Poets*. New York: Oxford University Press, Galaxy, 1960.

———. *The New Poets*. New York: Oxford University Press, 1967.

———. "Poetic Theory of Some Contemporary Poets." *Salmagundi*, 1, 4 (1966–67), 69–77.

Simon, John. "Abuse of Privilege: Lowell as Translator." *Hudson Review*, 20 (Winter 1967–68), 543–562.

Snodgrass, W. D. "In Praise of Robert Lowell." *The New York Review of Books*, 3 December 1964, pp. 8, 10.

Spender, Stephen. "Journal Extracts." *Art and Literature*, no. 9 (Summer 1966), pp. 198–215.

———. "Robert Lowell's Family Album." *New Republic*, 8 June 1959, p. 17; rpt. *Essays*, ed. Parkinson.

Stafford, William. "Poems that Deal a Jolt." *Chicago Tribune Books Today*, 15 November 1964, p. 11.

Stepanchev, Stephen. *American Poetry Since 1945: A Critical Survey*. New York: Harper and Row, 1965.

Tate, Allen. "Introduction" to *Land of Unlikeness*; rpt. *Essays*, ed. Parkinson, and *Robert Lowell: A Portrait*, ed. London and Boyers.

Wain, John. "The New Robert Lowell." *New Republic*, 17 October 1964, pp. 21–23; rpt. *Robert Lowell: A Portrait*, ed. London and Boyers.

Wiebe, Dallas E. "Mr. Lowell and Mr. Edwards." *Wisconsin Studies in Contemporary Literature*, 3 (Spring-Summer 1962), 21–31.

Williams, William Carlos. "In a Mood of Tragedy: *The Mills of the Kavanaughs*." *Selected Essays of William Carlos Williams* (New York: New Directions, 1951); rpt. *Essays*, ed. Parkinson, and *Robert Lowell: A Portrait*, ed. London and Boyers.

Williamson, Alan. " 'I Am That I Am': The Ethics and Aesthetics of Self-Revelation." *American Poetry Review*, 3 (January-February 1974), 337–339.

Yenser, Stephen. "Half Legible Bronze?" *Poetry*, 113 (February 1974), 304–309.

Zweig, Paul. "A Murderous Solvent." *The Nation*, 24 April 1967, pp. 537–539.

IV. OTHER SOURCES

Abrams, M. H. *The Mirror and the Lamp: Romantic Theory and the Critical Tradition*. New York: Oxford University Press, 1953.

Ammons, A. R. *Collected Poems: 1951–1971*. New York: Norton, 1972.

Auden, W. H. *The Dyer's Hand*. New York: Random House, 1962.

Berryman, John. *Homage to Mistress Bradstreet and Other Poems*. New York: Noonday, 1968.

Bishop, Elizabeth. *Questions of Travel*. New York: Farrar, Straus, 1966.

Blackmur, R. P. *The Lion and the Honeycomb*. New York: Harcourt Brace, Harvest, 1955.

Bodkin, Maude. *Archetypal Patterns in Poetry*. London: Oxford University Press, 1934.

Burnshaw, Stanley, ed. *The Poem Itself*. 1960; rpt. New York: Schocken Books, 1967.

Camus, Albert. *The Myth of Sisyphus*, trans. Justin O'Brien. New York: Random House, Vintage, 1955.

Conrad, Joseph. *Under Western Eyes*. 1911; rpt. New York: New Directions, 1951.

Crane, Hart. "From Mr. Crane to the Editor." *Modern Poets on Modern Poetry*, ed. Scully.

————. "General Aims and Theories." *Modern Poets on Modern Poetry*, ed. Scully.

Curtius, Ernst Robert. *European Literature and the Latin Middle Ages*, trans. Willard R. Trask. New York: Pantheon Books, 1953.

Day-Lewis, Cecil. *The Poetic Image*. London: Jonathan Cape, 1947.

Dekker, George. *Sailing after Knowledge: The Cantos of Ezra Pound*. London: Routledge & Kegan Paul, 1963.

Dembo, Lawrence S. *Conceptions of Reality in Modern Poetry*. Berkeley and Los Angeles: University of California Press, 1966.

Dewey, John. *Art as Experience*. New York: Minton, 1934.

Eliot, T. S. *On Poetry and Poets*. 1956; rpt. New York: Noonday, 1961.

————. *Selected Essays*. London: Faber & Faber, 1951.

Ellmann, Richard and Charles Feidelson, Jr., eds. *The Modern Tradition*. New York: Oxford University Press, 1965.

Empson, William. *Seven Types of Ambiguity*. Rev. ed., New York: Meridian, 1955.

Feidelson, Charles, Jr. *Symbolism and American Literature*. Chicago and London: University of Chicago Press, Phoenix, 1953.

Frost, Robert. *Complete Poems*. 1949; rpt. New York: Holt, Rinehart and Winston, 1956.

Frye, Northrop. *Anatomy of Criticism: Four Essays*. 1957; rpt. New York: Atheneum, 1966.

Greenslet, Ferris. *The Lowells and Their Seven Worlds*. New York: Houghton Mifflin, 1946.

Hegel, G. W. F. *Hegel: Texts and Commentary*, trans. and ed. Walter J. Kaufmann. 1965; rpt. New York: Doubleday Anchor, 1966.

Horace. *Odes and Epodes*, trans. C. E. Bennet. London: William Heinemann, Loeb Library, 1952.

James, Henry. *The Art of the Novel*. 1934; rpt. New York and London: Charles Scribner's Sons, 1962.

Kenner, Hugh. *The Pound Era*. Berkeley, Los Angeles, and London: University of California Press, 1971.

Krieger, Murray. "*Ekphrasis* and the Still Movement of Poetry; or, *Laokoön* Revisited." *Perspectives on Poetry*, ed. James L. Calderwood and Harold Toliver. New York: Oxford University Press, Galaxy, 1968.

Langer, Susanne K. *Feeling and Form.* New York: Charles Scribner's Sons, 1953.

———, ed. *Reflections on Art.* New York: Oxford University Press, Galaxy, 1961.

Lattimore, Richard. *Greek Lyrics.* Rev. ed., Chicago and London: University of Chicago Press, Phoenix, 1960.

Leibniz, Gottfried Wilhelm von. *First Truths, from Descartes to Leibniz,* trans. and ed. T. V. Smith and Marjorie Greene. 1940; rpt. Chicago and London: University of Chicago Press, Phoenix, 1966.

Marcuse, Herbert. *Eros and Civilization.* New York: Random House, 1962.

Montagu, Ashley. "The History of the Dolphin." In Ashley Montagu and John C. Lilly, *The Dolphin in History.* Los Angeles: William Andrews Clark Memorial Library and University of California, Los Angeles, 1963.

Poggioli, Renato. "The Added Artificer." *On Translation,* ed. Reuben A. Brower. 1959; rpt. New York: Oxford University Press, Galaxy, 1966.

Pound, Ezra. *Selected Poems.* New York: New Directions, 1962.

———. *The Cantos.* New York: New Directions, 1970.

Richards, I. A. "The Interactions of Words." *The Language of Poetry,* ed. Allen Tate. Princeton, N. J.: University of Princeton Press, 1942.

Schopenhauer, Arthur. *The World as Will and Idea,* trans. R. B. Haldane and J. Kemp. 1883; rpt. Garden City, N.Y.: Dolphin, 1961.

Scully, James, ed. *Modern Poets on Modern Poetry.* London and Glasgow: Collins, The Fontana Library, 1965; and as *Modern Poetics,* New York: McGraw-Hill, 1965.

Snodgrass, W. D. *Heart's Needle.* New York: Knopf, 1959.

Stafford, Jean. *The Interior Castle.* New York: Harcourt Brace, 1953.

Suetonius. *Lives of the Caesars,* I, trans. J. C. Rolfe. 1914; rpt. London: William Heinemann, Loeb Library, 1951.

Sypher, Wylie. *Loss of the Self in Modern Literature and Art.* New York: Random House, 1962.

Tacitus. *Annals,* xii-xiv, trans. J. Jackson. 1937; rpt. London: William Heinemann, Loeb Library, 1951.

Tate, Allen. *Essays of Four Decades.* New York: William Morrow, Apollo, 1970.

———. *The Swimmers and Other Selected Poems.* New York: Charles Scribner's Sons, 1970.

Treece, Henry. *Dylan Thomas: Dog Among the Fairies.* Rev. ed., London: E. Benn, 1957.

Trypanis, Constantine A., ed. *Penguin Book of Greek Verse.* Harmondsworth, England: Penguin, 1971.

Warren, Robert Penn. *Brother to Dragons*. New York: Random
    House, 1953.
Williams, William Carlos. *Paterson*. New York: New Directions,
    1963.
Winters, Ivor. *The Function of Criticism*. Denver: Alan Swallow, 1957.
Yeats, W. B. *A Vision*. Rev. ed., 1956; rpt. New York: Macmillan,
    1961.

INDEX